Towards a
Polemical Ethics

NEW HEIDEGGER RESEARCH

Series Editors:

Gregory Fried, Professor of Philosophy, Boston College, USA

Richard Polt, Professor of Philosophy, Xavier University, USA

The New Heidegger Research series promotes informed and critical dialogue that breaks new philosophical ground by taking into account the full range of Heidegger's thought, as well as the enduring questions raised by his work.

Titles in the Series:

Proto-Phenomenology and the Nature of Language
Lawrence J. Hatab

Heidegger in the Islamicate World
Edited by Kata Moser, Urs Gösken and Josh Michael Hayes

Time and Trauma: Thinking Through Heidegger in the Thirties
Richard Polt

Contexts of Suffering: A Heideggerian Approach to Psychopathology
Kevin Aho

Heidegger's Phenomenology of Perception: An Introduction, Volume I
David Kleinberg-Levin

Confronting Heidegger: A Critical Dialogue on Politics and Philosophy
Edited by Gregory Fried

Proto-Phenomenology, Language Acquisition, Orality and Literacy: Dwelling in Speech II
Lawrence J. Hatab

Transcending Reason: Heidegger's Transformation of Phenomenology
Edited by Matthew Burch and Irene McMullin

The Fate of Phenomenology: Heidegger's Legacy
William McNeill

Agency, Freedom, and Responsibility in the Early Heidegger
Hans Pedersen

Heidegger's Phenomenology of Perception: Learning to See and Hear Hermeneutically, Volume II
David Kleinberg-Levin

Towards a Polemical Ethics: Between Heidegger and Plato
Gregory Fried

Towards a Polemical Ethics

Between Heidegger and Plato

Gregory Fried

ROWMAN & LITTLEFIELD
Lanham • Boulder • New York • London

Published by Rowman & Littlefield
An imprint of The Rowman & Littlefield Publishing Group, Inc.
4501 Forbes Boulevard, Suite 200, Lanham, Maryland 20706
www.rowman.com

6 Tinworth Street, London SE11 5AL, United Kingdom

ISBN: HB 978-1-78661-000-3 | PBK 978-1-5381-7406-7

British Library Cataloguing in Publication Information Available

Library of Congress Cataloging-in-Publication Data

Names: Fried, Gregory, 1961– author.
Title: Towards a polemical ethics : between Heidegger and Plato / Gregory Fried.
Description: Lanham, Maryland : Rowman & Littlefield, [2021] | Series: New Heidegger research | Includes bibliographical references and index.
Identifiers: LCCN 2020057009 (print) | LCCN 2020057010 (ebook) | ISBN 9781786610003 (cloth) | ISBN 9781538174067 (pbk) ISBN 9781786610027 (epub)
Subjects: LCSH: Plato. | Ethics. | Heidegger, Martin, 1889-1976. | Political science—Philosophy.
Classification: LCC B395 .F74 2021 (print) | LCC B395 (ebook) | DDC 170—dc23
LC record available at https://lccn.loc.gov/2020057009
LC ebook record available at https://lccn.loc.gov/2020057010

♾️™ The paper used in this publication meets the minimum requirements of American National Standard for Information Sciences—Permanence of Paper for Printed Library Materials, ANSI/NISO Z39.48-1992.

For Richard Polt

Question:	Do you desire your sight more than anything else in the world?
Answer:	No! No! I would rather walk with a friend in the dark than walk alone in the light.

—Helen Keller, in Joseph P. Lash, *Helen and Teacher*, 498

COME said the Muse,
Sing me a song no poet yet has chanted,
Sing me the universal.

In this broad earth of ours,
Amid the measureless grossness and the slag,
Enclosed and safe within its central heart,
Nestles the seed perfection.

By every life a share or more or less,
None born but it is born, conceal'd or unconceal'd the seed is
    waiting.

—Walt Whitman, from "The Song of the Universal"

Contents

Illustrations

Acknowledgments

This book owes so much to so many that I will hardly be able to thank them properly. I have been teaching Plato's *Republic* for over twenty-five years, at least once a year on average, sometimes more, and so my first thanks must go to all the students with whom conversation about that book has taught me so much. I cannot name you all, but you know who you are.

Richard Polt, to whom this book is dedicated, has been my friend and companion in philosophy for over thirty years. He first led me to Heidegger, and he brought me through and beyond Heidegger. He also read this work in draft, and so it is not an exaggeration to say that dialogue with him has helped light every step of my way, although any stumbles are my own.

I owe a great intellectual debt to two other scholars and friends: Drew Hyland, whose *Finitude and Transcendence* was an inspiration to me in bringing Heidegger and Plato into conversation to recuperate Plato, and David Roochnik, whose book *Beautiful City* taught me to see the *Republic* as a dialogue between Plato and his readers in ways I had never considered, and whose various works on retrieving the ancients show a way grounded in the present to do phenomenology with those authors.

Others have read drafts and contributed to making the writing process a dialogue. My father, Charles Fried, with his astute eye helped me to clarify the arguments so that the nonspecialist in Heidegger studies might read without losing patience. Marina McCoy was exceedingly generous with her expertise in Plato in reading the book draft and providing suggestions. Research assistants Maxwell Wade and David Abergel made many thoughtful suggestions that would not have occurred to me otherwise. Research assistants over the years helped with various stages of the project: Brian Smith, Anton Janulis, Georgina Holmes, Mandeep Minhas, Molly Chandler, Jeremy O'Brien, Weitao Liu, and Zachary Willcutt. Colleagues Matthew Caswell,

Dermot Moran, and George Heffernan, as well as Boston College librarian Christopher Strauber, assisted with finding source materials when the university library was closed due to the Covid-19 pandemic. Alan Letarte kindly read my discussion of mathematics on the Divided Line. I thank an anonymous reviewer of the book proposal who encouraged me to do more of my own philosophical exploration. Faculty and students at St. Johns College, Annapolis, heard a lecture on an earlier interpretation of the crossroads of the cave and gave very valuable feedback.

I am extremely grateful to Lauren McGillicuddy, who served as an editor at the final stage of this work. A skilled editor is a fine thing, but to have one who has a keen eye, philosophical acumen, and patience for working though ideas is a true blessing.

In devising the four illustrations for this volume, Marc Ngui was remarkably focused and creative in reading the Allegory of Cave and my analysis, sketching detailed drafts, and patiently discussing multiple revisions with me.

Suffolk University, the Deutscher Akademischer Austauschdienst, and Boston College provided vital support for research and time to think.

My thanks also to *Continental Philosophy Review*, Springer Nature, and Indiana University Press for permission to adapt three essays for this book, as well as to Penguin Random House for permission to reproduce an illustration from *The Great Dialogues of Plato.*

Frankie Mace and Scarlet Furness, my editors at Rowman & Littlefield, were indefatigable in making sure this volume got to press, despite the considerable challenges of the pandemic.

Finally, to my family of cyclopes, Christina, Jonah, and Eliza, I give thanks for the gift that anyone attempting philosophy needs: to remember to laugh at myself whenever I trip on the way. Completing this work during the 2020 pandemic was no easy task, and for their patience and good humor I am deeply grateful.

Abbreviations and Translations

This volume follows the conventions used in volumes of the New Heidegger Research series by employing abbreviations for in-text citations for works by frequently cited authors.

For the meaning of Greek words, I rely upon the *Thesaurus Linguae Graecae*, also known as Liddell and Scott, the 2011 online edition. For etymologies, I rely upon Calvert Watkins, *Dictionary of Indo-European Roots*.

Wherever I amend a translator's rendering of a passage, I will note this in the cite as "tm" (translation modified).

WORKS BY PLATO

For Plato's *Republic*, I follow closely the translation by Allan Bloom, cited by Stephanus number. I have consulted other translations, especially the one by C. D. C. Reeve in *Plato, Complete Works*. For Plato's *Apology* and *Euthyphro*, I rely on *Four Texts on Socrates*, translated by Thomas West and Grace Starry West. Translations of other works of Plato are my own or acknowledged in a note.

WORKS BY MARTIN HEIDEGGER

Works listed here are not included in the Bibliography to this volume.

Being and Time

SZ = *Sein und Zeit*. Tübingen: Niemeyer, 1953. Later editions share the same pagination, which is also provided in the English translations and in the

Gesamtausgabe edition (GA 2). The first edition was published in 1927. For translation of *Being and* Time, I have consulted the ones by John Macquarrie and Edward Robinson (Harper & Row, 1962) and Joan Stambaugh, revised by Dennis J. Schmidt (State University of New York Press, 2010). Translations from SZ are my own, but I rely heavily on Macquarrie and Robinson.

GA = *Gesamtausgabe*

All volumes of Heidegger's *Gesamtausgabe*, his collected works, are published in Frankfurt am Main by Vittorio Klostermann (1975–). The date of publication, or dates if there is more than one edition, are followed in the listing below by the date of original composition in parentheses. All translations of Heidegger in this book are my own and all emphasis in quotations is original, unless otherwise noted. Published translations of corresponding volumes by Heidegger are listed below when available. Not all translations listed include the entire contents of the corresponding GA volumes. Recent translations generally include references to the pagination in the German collected works, so readers interested in considering the context of quotes should usually be able to find the relevant passages in these translations.

GA 1 = *Frühe Schriften.* Ed. Friedrich-Wilhelm von Herrmann, 1978 (1912–1916).

GA 4 = *Erläuterungen zu Hölderlins Dichtung.* Ed. Friedrich-Wilhelm von Herrmann, 1981, 2012 (1936–1968). / *Elucidations of Hölderlin's Poetry.* Tr. Keith Hoeller. Amherst, NY: Humanity Books, 2000.

GA 5 = *Holzwege.* Ed. Friedrich-Wilhelm von Hermann, 1977 (1935–1946). / *Off the Beaten Track.* Tr. Julian Young and Kenneth Haynes. Cambridge: Cambridge University Press, 2002.

GA 7 = *Vorträge und Aufsätze* (1936–1953). Ed. Friedrich-Wilhelm von Herrmann, 2000.

GA 8 = *Was Heißt Denken?* Ed. Paola-Ludovika Coriando, 2002 (1951–1952). / *What Is Called Thinking?* Tr. J. Glenn Gray. New York: Harper & Row, 1968.

GA 9 = *Wegmarken.* Ed. Friedrich-Wilhelm von Herrmann, 1976, 1996, 2004 (1919–1961). / *Pathmarks.* Ed. William McNeill. Cambridge: Cambridge University Press, 1998.

GA 16 = *Reden und andere Zeugnisse eines Lebensweges.* Ed. Hermann Heidegger, 2000 (1910–1976).

GA 18 = *Grundbegriffe der aristotelischen Philosophie.* Ed. Mark Michalski, 2002 (1924). / *Basic Concepts of Aristotelian Philosophy.* Tr. Robert D. Metcalf and Mark Basil Tanzer. Bloomington: Indiana University Press, 2009.

GA 19 = *Platon: Sophistes.* Ed. Ingeborg Schüßler, 1992 (1924–1925). / *Plato's "Sophist."* Tr. Richard Rojcewicz and André Schuwer. Bloomington: Indiana University Press, 1997.

GA 22 = *Die Grundbegriffe der antiken Philosophie.* Ed. Franz-Karl Blust, 1993, 2004 (1926). / *Basic Concepts of Ancient Philosophy.* Tr. Richard Rojcewicz. Bloomington: Indiana University Press, 1997.

GA 24 = *Die Grundprobleme der Phänomenologie.* Ed. Friedrich-Wilhelm von Herrmann, 1975, 1997 (1927). / *The Basic Problems of Phenomenology.* Translated by Albert Hofstadter. Bloomington: Indiana University Press, 1982.

GA 25 = *Phänomenologische Interpretation von Kants Kritik der reinen Vernunft* (1927–1928), Ed. Ingtraud Görland, 1977. / *Phenomenological Interpretation of Kant's "Critique of Pure Reason."* Tr. Parvis Emad and Kenneth Maly. Bloomington: Indiana University Press, 1997.

GA 29/30 = *Die Grundbegriffe der Metaphysik. Welt—Endlichkeit—Einsamkeit.* Ed. Friedrich-Wilhelm von Herrmann, 1983, 2004 (1929–1930). / *The Fundamental Concepts of Metaphysics: World, Finitude, Solitude.* Tr. William McNeill and Nicholas Walker. Bloomington: Indiana University Press, 1995.

GA 34 = *Vom Wesen der Wahrheit. Zu Platons Höhlengleichnis und Theätet.* Ed. Hermann Mörchen, 1988, 1997 (1931–1932). / *The Essence of Truth: On Plato's Cave Allegory and "Theaetetus."* Translated by Ted Sadler. London: Continuum, 2002.

GA 36/37 = *Sein und Wahrheit.* Ed. Hartmut Tietjen, 2001 (1933–1934). / *Being and Truth.* Translated by Gregory Fried and Richard Polt. Bloomington: Indiana University Press, 2010.

GA 40 = *Einführung in die Metaphysik.* Ed. Petra Jaeger, 1983 (1935). / *Introduction to Metaphysics.* Translated by Gregory Fried and Richard Polt. Revised and expanded edition. New Haven, CT: Yale University Press, 2014.

GA 53 = *Hölderlins Hymne "Der Ister."* Ed. Walter Biemel, 1984 (1942). / *Hölderlin's Hymn "The Ister."* Translated by William McNeill and Julia Davis. Bloomington: Indiana University Press, 1996.

GA 56/57 = *Zur Bestimmung der Philosophie.* Ed. Bernd Heimbüchel, 1987, 1999 (1919). / *Towards the Definition of Philosophy.* Tr. Ted Sadler. New York: Continuum, 2000.

GA 59 = *Phänomenologie der Anschauung und des Ausdrucks. Theorie der philosophischen Begriffsbildung.* Ed. Claudius Strube, 1993, 2007 (1920). / *Phenomenology of Intuition and Expression.* Tr. Tracy Colony. London: Continuum, 2010.

GA 64 = *Der Begriff der Zeit.* Ed. Friedrich-Wilhelm von Herrmann, 2004 (1924). / Partial translations: *The Concept of Time: The First Draft of "Being and Time."* Tr. Ingo Farin. London: Continuum, 2011. *The Concept of Time.* Bilingual edition. Tr. William McNeill. Oxford: Blackwell, 1992.

GA 65 = *Beiträge zur Philosophie (Vom Ereignis)*. Ed. Friedrich-Wilhelm von Herrmann, 1989, 1994, 2003 (1936–1938). / *Contributions to Philosophy (Of the Event)*. Tr. Richard Rojcewicz and Daniela Vallega-Neu. Bloomington: Indiana University Press, 2012.

GA 94 = *Überlegungen II–VI (Schwarze Hefte 1931–1938)*. Ed. Peter Trawny, 2014. / *Ponderings II–VI: Black Notebooks 1931–1938.* Tr. Richard Rojcewicz. Bloomington: Indiana University Press, 2016.

GA 95 = *Überlegungen VII–XI (Schwarze Hefte 1938–1939)*. Ed. Peter Trawny, 2014. / *Ponderings VII–XI: Black Notebooks 1938–1939.* Tr. Richard Rojcewicz. Bloomington: Indiana University Press, 2017.

GA 96 = *Überlegungen XII–XV (Schwarze Hefte 1939–1941)*. Ed. Peter Trawny, 2014. / *Ponderings XII–XV: Black Notebooks 1939–1941.* Tr. Richard Rojcewicz. Bloomington: Indiana University Press, 2017.

GA 97 = *Anmerkungen I–V (Schwarze Hefte 1942–1948)*. Ed. Peter Trawny, 2015.

Other Works by Heidegger

NGS = Martin Heidegger, "Über Wesen und Begriff von Natur, Geschichte und Staat," in *Heidegger-Jahrbuch 4—Heidegger und der Nazionalsozialismus I, Dokumente*. Ed. Alfred Denker and Holger Zaborowski (Freiburg in Bresigau: Verlag Karl Alber, 2009), 53–88 / "On the Essence and Concept of Nature, History, and State," in *Nature, History, State: 1933–1934*. Tr. Gregory Fried and Richard Polt (London: Bloomsbury, 2013).

Preface

Address to the Reader

Still when, to where thou wert, I came,
Some lovely glorious nothing I did see.

—John Donne, "Air and Angels"[1]

Dear Reader,

Forgive the anachronism of addressing you this way, but I am a Platonist, or more exactly, a Socratic, and dialogue is essential to how I think and to what I hope to accomplish with this book. While philosophy may begin in private reflection, it fulfills itself and lives in conversation with others before returning again to the internal forge of contemplation. In fact, before private reflection can encounter the questions that impel it, conversation in the larger sense must have brought reflection to where it no longer understands and from there to wonder, reflect further, and then again respond. That larger conversation is the ever-ongoing discourse of human community, across generations, that establishes a world of meaning for each of us. Meaning-making conversation extends from those we have known most intimately—family, friends, mentors—to those we hear from and hear about—the strangers and acquaintances we encounter in everyday life, anonymous bureaucrats, political leaders, entertainers, and storytellers of all kinds. It also includes those we imagine: ancestors, historical figures, characters in myth and story. Without this prior world, there could be no breakdown of that world to engender philosophical reflection.

In the *Phaedrus*, Plato has his Socrates argue that writing displaces and thereby corrupts the immediacy of speech, because the written word cannot speak, cannot answer the reader's questions and enter into conversion (274b–277a). In spoken dialogue, the conversation partner is directly present, engaging in the activity that makes the conversation a διάλογος: dia-logue, a talking-through of an issue in conversation with another. The written word, by contrast, is outside of time; it is locked down by its form and can no longer change and be changed by the reader. But Plato ironically undermines this argument by having Socrates make his statement in a written dialogue that imitates the form of spoken dialogue.[2] Plato's *form* of writing suggests that writing may also beckon us into the kind of conversation necessary for philosophical reflection.

If you are reading this book, I assume that you have read Plato and that you also have imagined yourself in conversation with Socrates while reading a work over two thousand years old. To refuse that invitation and nevertheless continue to read would be to treat the dialogues as mere artifacts, dead letters of intellectual history. My own first experience of accepting this invitation was in high school, where a history teacher, Paul Jefferson, had us read the *Crito* and then write our own dialogues between Socrates and ourselves—an assignment I now give to my own students. From Plato to pupil, we all make Socrates up, and each other as well, and even ourselves, through dialogue.

At stake in dialogue, and in polemical understanding more generally, is what I will term *ideation*, a respectable if clunky English word. Dictionaries define it as the formation of ideas or concepts as well as the ideas and concepts so formed. For example, ideation is both the power to form a mental image of a unicorn and the specific image itself. I will use the word to indicate more than the formation of ideas, especially if taken in the sense of deliberately formulating theories and producing precise definitions and rigorous arguments. That is an important aspect of the phenomenon, but I also want to employ 'ideation' as both the latent capacity and the engaged activity of the *imagination* to make present what is absent by giving it a form that makes it intelligible and distinct, whether or not this is done consciously and then deliberately thematized. In keeping with ordinary usage, in which ideation is both process and product, I will speak of ideation in both its verbal and its nominal sense, as both 'thinking up' something and the thing thought up.

Ideation suggests a resonance between *idea*, which Plato places at the pinnacle of knowledge, and *imagination*, which he seems to place at the bottom, but which is better understood as the foundation for understanding. For example, ideation is happening, right here, right now, as I write and as you read, each of us giving life to inanimate print on a page or pixels on a screen. While I may have written long ago and be long gone, ideation makes me present to you, just as it makes you present to me, whether you were my former teacher or student, or are a friend or colleague, or will be someone entirely unknown or unknowable to me, if I am lucky enough to have you as a reader far distant in place and time.

Of course, an ideation may be pure fantasy. Fantasy is certainly both a strength and a peril of imagination, depending on its use: a strength, because improbable but conceivable imaginings can free us from the given for the sake of the possible; a peril, because absurd but engrossing imaginings can unmoor us from what is possible and drive us into illusion and delusion. Nevertheless, even if it goes astray, my ideation of you as reader and yours of me as writer is a prime example of what I believe Plato recognized in the *Phaedrus*: that structurally, ideation is an *a priori* foundation to all communication, whether spoken or written.[3] We may well make each other up all the time. Even in direct conversation, where the other person is putatively entirely present, in fact their *personhood* is not directly accessible to us at all by the senses. I can see and touch and smell the body. I can hear the voice. But not the person. I can only impute personhood to the other, because it is insensible, invisible. But *impute* is probably too weak a word for how we attribute personhood to others, as if it were a merely intellectual exercise. Before the intellectual attribution of personhood is a deeper, *a priori* empathy, unconscious yet constant, for otherwise we would interact like sociopaths with animated manikins as our companions. Yes, I can logically deduce that other beings that look, sound, feel, smell, and act like me are probably persons, too, but I can have no direct experience of their personhood, only of the physical manifestation, the external, empirical shell. I can have direct access only to my own personhood—not in a comprehensive way, but in the simple sense that I can have access only to my own consciousness. Even if that self of mine can be fractured, uncertain, and fleeting, it is nonetheless individuated and my own—*jemeinig*, as Heidegger would say. I cannot experience the internality of any other person, although I can imagine it by analogy with my own.

And yet all dialogue and communication requires my ideation of your personhood. Even the most dogged empiricist pays indirect tribute to the invisible whenever entering into conversation. To make up the other is not to plaster over a merely brute physical presence with the cosmetic veneer of personhood as a metaphysical fantasy. Making up is how we reconcile the other to the invisibility of personhood. This ideation of the other as person is not delusional, it is an idea that we cannot do without if dialogue is to be possible at all. It is constitutive of discourse. All imagination is make-believe, but it is also true that the world makes-us-believe, for otherwise we would be petrified by incomprehension. There is no way around this belief, which Plato calls *pistis*, the constitutive trust endowing the world with provisional intelligibility. Dialogue is co-constitutive of the world, because without the imputation of the other as person, I would be thrown back upon a solipsism that the world itself belies, because the world constantly refutes my pretensions to treat myself as the origin of its meaning.

I am not the source of the intelligibility of the world. I am not alone in meaning-making. Dialogue has already made sense of the world for me, and I can only make better sense of the world in and through dialogue, because, as the Greek *dia-logos* suggests, dialogue is the through-way to meaning. The world as significant opens up only in communication with the things and persons that impinge upon us and to which we respond. Dialogue involves the ideation of the other-as-person in this ongoing meaning-construal. What Plato understood is that writing can also address us, and by addressing us, involve us in dialogue, and by so involving us, evoke the presence of the other as person. It is not just that writing should 'also' be granted the stature afforded to speech but that writing provides an *exemplar* of how the ideation of personhood underlies all discourse, something that speech can obscure because of the seeming immediacy of the other person.

In *Being and Time*, Heidegger says that "hearing constitutes the primary and authentic openness" of each of us "for our ownmost potentiality for being, as hearing the voice of the friend" that we each "carry along with ourselves" (SZ, 163). While I may disagree with Heidegger about many things, I agree emphatically about this. This "hearing" is not auditory in the physical sense of hearing sounds; it is the capacity for listening to the other, as another person, that transcends any particular sensory medium of communication. Who is this "friend" whose "voice" we each "carry along" with us in our "ownmost" existence? Is it the voice of a specific person, a best friend? Or different friends on different occasions? Or an anonymous voice of conscience? I would say any and all of these, for the definite article of "*the* friend" indicates a structural feature of our existence as human beings, a placeholder that can be and must at times be occupied by the voice of a friend known or unknown, specified or unspecified. Hearing this voice "constitutes" (*konstituiert*) our individual openness to a meaningful world, not in the bland sense of 'constitute' as being-the-equivalent-of, but rather as what con-stitutes our world: *brings together* its intelligible elements and *establishes* them as a meaningful whole that we can inhabit. More specifically, it is a world that *I* can inhabit, what I and I alone can experience as my possibilities. Why the friend? Because of the trust, the *pistis*, that necessarily underlies language, from womb to grave. The friend is whomever we trust enough to listen to in making sense of the world as a whole in the co-constituting work of hearing and dialogue.[4] That whole is always provisional. It can transform, fray, decay, or fall apart entirely at any time, and so the voice of the friend returns ever again, in forms as specific or as anonymous as the occasion demands.

If you are reading this in the spirit of my invitation, then you are enacting exactly this point through the ideation of me as your imagined conversation partner. In other contexts, 'I' might be the imagined voice of a long-passed grandparent, a childhood friend, a lover, a teacher, a colleague, an adversary. The friend might even be yourself; for some, it might be a divine presence, such as Socrates's *daimonion*. I trust that you know what I mean from personal experience. It is not simply that we make up or imagine this friend. The ideation of the friend is what makes *us* up, through a "voice" that arrives unbidden to help us make sense of the world and thereby to help us remain open to our possibilities. The voice of the friend both builds our world and returns to us in reconstituting a world whose meaning has frayed enough to break down.

Friendship therefore precedes any possibility of enmity, as truth precedes any possibility of lying. Levinas was right and Hobbes was wrong. Ethics is first philosophy because the trust entailed in dialogue is essential to the formation of a meaningful world.[5] Our natural condition is not a state of war but of friendship, because without the preliminary trust in some other as a person-like-us, we could not even begin to absorb the sense-making practices of language that articulate the world.[6] Like a wild-child raised by wolves, we might have some kind of world, but it would not be a human world. We all begin, quite literally *in utero*, taking in the meaning of the world through the *philia*, the friendship in this most broad sense, provided by the mother; research has shown that already in the third trimester, a fetus is taking in and responding to the particular linguistic rhythms of the mother's voice and social environment.[7]

I have noted that dialogue, from the Greek *dialegesthein*, means to talk (*-legesthein*) something through (*dia-*), to speak in alternation with someone, to converse with others. The *dia-*, the alternating and reciprocal talking-through of something with another or other persons, intimates the *temporal* nature of discursive understanding, language, and being human. A world of meaning cannot be constituted in one immediate and non-discursive cognition, and, because of our finitude, whatever provisional whole we do assemble will erode with time and must be reconstituted, in time, in dialogue. To deny the enduring necessity of dialogue is to deny our human finitude, to deny our need for the friend, and it implies a dictatorial will to impose a final answer on the meaning of the world. Only a tyrannical and cowardly violence can sustain such a dogmatic answer, because meaning does fray. We are not alone, as if each one of us were the creator-God of all meaning. The ideation of the other as a person, in the necessity of dialogue, is phenomenologically essential to our humanity.

I seek to enact this philosophical point by dialoguing with you, as reader, to make you the voice of the friend whom I will carry throughout. The ideation of personhood in dialogue is itself a prime example of what I want to defend in this book: the role of idea, image, and imagination as necessarily constitutive of our ethical life, united in ideation. I hope that you, too, will carry-through this dialogue, which certainly does not mean agreeing with me. I trust that you have experienced the phenomenon of ideation, that you experience it even now, in this moment, as you turn the inanimate letters into animate language, and that you will think-through all this with me in dialogue. Ideation of the other as a person in dialogue is emblematic, indeed constitutive, of other forms of ideation that are essential to ethical life.

Gregory Fried
Auburndale, Massachusetts
July 13, 2020

NOTES

1. Donne, *The Complete Poetry*, 19.

2. For *Plato's* irony as distinct from Socrates' irony, operating through the "dramatic irony" of the action of the dialogues themselves, which includes the speeches as well as the settings, characters, and events depicted, see Griswold, "Irony in the Platonic Dialogues." Griswold provides a concise yet compelling analysis of the essential hermeneutical principles for reading Plato; see also the essays collected in Griswold, *Platonic Writings/Platonic Readings*, especially Griswold's own on "Plato's Metaphilosophy: Why Plato Wrote Dialogues."

3. On the basis of Socrates's argument in the *Phaedrus*, Jacques Derrida accused Plato of "logocentrism," the notion that speech conveys pure presence and stands as the metaphysical paradigm for an absolute fullness of meaning requiring no further interpretation and serving as the basis of unquestionable authority. But the complex irony of the *Phaedrus*, where Plato *writes* about Socrates *saying* that writing is a degenerate form of communication, shows that Plato was well aware that both speaking and writing have the power, when done properly, to draw us into an ethical ideation of the other. See Jacques Derrida, "Plato's Pharmacy" in *Dissemination*.

4. Unlike Gadamer, who says that authority is based on "an act of acknowledgment . . . that the other is superior to oneself in judgment and insight and that for this reason his judgment takes precedence," albeit an authority that is not beyond question (*Truth and Method*, 291), I would amend Gadamer to say that authority, as a trust that structures access to meaning, is something we necessarily impute to the other as a precondition to dialogue. The trust bestowed upon the partner in dialogue as a *person* and *author* of meaning is an *a priori* constitutive existentiale of any meaningful exchange whatsoever and precedes the granting of authority in Gadamer's sense.

5. For Levinas on the relation of ethics as first philosophy to the meaningful construal of the world epistemologically, see Crowell, "Why Is Ethics First Philosophy?"

6. See Tomasello, *A Natural History of Human Morality*.

7. See Hatab, *Proto-Phenomenology, Language Acquisition, Orality, and Literacy*, 93–94.

Introduction

Towards a Polemical Ethics

Think not that I am come to send peace on earth. I came not to send peace, but a sword.

—Matthew, 10:34 (KJV)

But love cannot sleep, can never be peaceful or permanent.

—Emmanuel Levinas, "Ethics of the Infinite"[1]

The question of Being, as a question about how the world can be intelligible and meaningful to us, and so how things can be what they are to us, is an ancient one, not Heidegger's private preserve. An analysis of the existential-hermeneutical structures of our being-human, as Heidegger undertook in *Being and Time* as a way to unfold the question of Being, is both brilliant and not obviously political, even if Heidegger ultimately made it so. Heidegger's understanding of the historicity and temporality of being-human led him to a radically anti-universalist politics of human community. But the road to atavistic ethno-nationalism has and will continue to take forms well beyond Heidegger's own thought or National Socialism's specific history. We see this in our times because it is human to fall prey to an exclusivist belonging. In facing such questions, 'Heidegger' is not the historical person or even his particular texts. His thinking stands for both a danger and an opportunity we must face up to in responding to what it means to *be* as human-beings.[2]

A premise of this book is that in doing justice to Heidegger's thought, we must insist on the absolute freedom of philosophy, which means taking up a thinker's questions and the responses given to that question in our own way, so long as this does justice to what is at issue. At his best, Heidegger would have wanted this. He chose as motto for his collected works "*Wege, nicht*

1

Werke," loosely "Pathways, not treatises" (GA 1: 437). As Jürgen Habermas wrote in 1953, "It appears to be time to think with Heidegger against Heidegger."[3] We must stay open to a *constructive confrontation* with Heidegger, so that we may discern where we part company in responding to essential questions lying at the heart of ethics about what it means to be human. In this endeavor, I have made Plato my partner, in part because Heidegger makes him his principal adversary, in part because after teaching his *Republic* for twenty-five years, Plato's Socrates is the philosophical friend I carry ringing in my ear.

TOWARDS A POLEMICAL ETHICS

A joke explained is a joke ruined, but a title explained may assist in following the trajectory of this book's project and entering into dialogue with it. That title is *Towards a Polemical Ethics: Between Heidegger and Plato*.

Towards: This book will not provide a systemic or programmatic theory of ethics. It is a propaedeutic metaethics, a work that seeks to furnish the foundations for fuller treatment. As a movement towards a goal, the book invites you to participate in telling a philosophical story. It is a dialogue.

Polemical: The Greek word πόλεμος (*polemos*), is a central concept for Heidegger.[4] *Polemos* in Greek means war, but already in Fragment 53 of Heraclitus the word takes on a metaphorical, philosophical, or even cosmological meaning deeper and wider than war in the usual sense. Heidegger follows Heraclitus in making *polemos* a name for Being itself. The fragment reads as follows:

Πόλεμος πάντων μὲν πατήρ ἐστι πάντων δὲ βασιλεύς, καὶ τοὺς μὲν θεοὺς ἔδειξε τοὺς δὲ ἀνθρώπους, τοὺς μὲν δούλους ἐποίησε τοὺς δὲ ἐλευθέρους.

Polemos is father of all and king of all, and it reveals some as gods, others as human beings; it makes some slaves, others free.[5]

My use of 'polemical' and related words departs from ordinary usage, and in this I agree with Heidegger. It will *not* mean a relentlessly aggressive and disputatious attitude, intent on wounding or destroying, incapable of self-criticism and self-correction, although that certainly *can* be an effect of the *polemos* as I interpret it. *Polemos* is a constitutive feature of being a person, what Heidegger calls Dasein, but I will diverge from him significantly in what this entails. Heidegger says that "*polemos* and *logos* are the same" (GA 40: 66; cf. GA 97: 39), by which he does not mean that they are identical but rather facets of the same phenomenon. For Heidegger, drawing upon Heraclitus, *logos* does not simply mean word, account, speech, rational argument, or language. It means the *gathering* and *collectedness* of phenomena such that they are intelligible as distinctly meaningful things in an interrelated whole, as only then can we name them in language or debate them in speech or argue them in logic. This gathering allows things to *be* what they are, and it therefore also delineates what they are *not*. It separates, distinguishes, and demarcates things so that they may be distinct and not fall into a meaningless jumble. This is the *polemos*, what Heidegger sometimes translates as *Auseinandersetzung*, a setting-out-and-apart-from-one-another, a con-frontation in which things can fit together as what they are because they delimit themselves in their respective identity and difference.

To indicate my departure from Heidegger in my treatment of dialogue, I would say that *polemos* and *dialogos* are the same. We make sense of the world in dialogue with others and also through our experience of the world of things. As an anonymous commentator on Plato wrote in the sixth century CE, "the dialogue is a cosmos and the cosmos a dialogue."[6] Sense-making is at issue because we are temporal and finite: we cannot lock the cosmos into a fixed, absolute meaning without falsifying experience, which often does *not* make sense, if we pay attention. We are brought up short in confrontation with things that do not fit with the meaning established by prior dialogue in the larger, world-forming sense. We either enter this *polemos* by reengaging in dialogue or repress it to remain undisturbed in the unexamined life. This being-brought-up-short-by-the-world will be a recurring theme of this book. We must not hear this polemical aspect of the human condition as necessarily negative, violent, or adversarial, although it can degenerate into these. To be human is to be dialogically polemical as ever-ready to confront the world anew and reform it interpretively.

In reviewing a draft of this book, Plato scholar Marina McCoy asked, "Are all forms of dialogue polemical? Can some forms of dialogue be purely cooperative and not polemical? If dialogue and polemics are two sides of the same coin, what does each offer as a term that is lacking in the other term?" My answer is yes. All dialogue is polemical, because in the most cooperative, friendly, and even loving dialogue, one is still *working out* what the other *means* as well as the meaning of *what is at issue* in the dialogue.[7] That requires confronting this double-acting meaning, testing it, exploring it, and reconciling to it. This is why the *polemos* is always there in the *dia-logos*, the working-through of conversation, and I think this is why Levinas, for example, argues that ethics is first philosophy: because recognition of the Other by confronting the Other, face to face, is what jolts us from our solipsistic construal of the world, to make sense of its discontinuities and contradictions that is the heart of dialogues with others and the world itself. Otherwise, we would already be of one mind, with nothing more to say, the dialogue done. The opposite of *polemos* is not *logos* but silence: either the silence of indifference or the silence of a complete meeting of the minds. The latter is a *non-discursive logos.* Fully realized, it would have to be something like a *lingua mentis* shared with divinity as *unspoken*, because as discursive, *dia-logos* is the temporal formation of mutual understanding, but the fullness of a realized *logos* is eternal in its unspoken silence—but a silence that nevertheless 'speaks' volumes. Such fully realized *logos* is beyond our finite embodiment in this existence, as it would have to resolve all questions of meaning. What *polemos* offers discursive *logos* is the engagements with what is at-issue that keeps the *logos* going, unfolding as *dia-logos*; what *logos* offers *polemos* are the intimations of mutual understanding that give purpose and hope to dialogue. Otherwise, there would only be polemics in its ordinary sense.

Ethics: This is not primarily a work in normative ethics, although it touches on normative themes. I will use ethics in its Aristotelian sense of *ēthos*: a way of life, a mode of being, that informs our normative decisions and everyday morality. Such an ethics involves a conception of what it means to be human as confronted with the choices that living with others necessarily raises, and so it also entails politics. The project is *metaethical*, which includes the meta-political: establishing the grounds for the possibility of an ethical life, norms, and morality, as well as the customs, laws, and institutions needed to sustain such a life. For a brief period at the onset of the Third Reich, Heidegger also spoke of a metapolitics, for example: *"The end of 'philosophy:'"*—by which he means the supposedly dogmatic idea-ism of all Western thought since Plato—"We must bring it to an end and thereby prepare what is entirely Other: metapolitics" (GA 94: 115). It means, for him, a revolution in thinking as profound as the one in politics, one that would up-end the entire historical Being of a people (GA 94: 124), and thereby of the West, if not the globe, in a radically other inception to history.[8] This is why the *polemos* between Heidegger and Plato is so vital.

BETWEEN HEIDEGGER AND PLATO

This project moves between Heidegger and Plato in multiple senses. First, it brings Plato and Heidegger into confrontation with each other over the question of ethics. Second, while I aim to defend Plato against Heidegger, this defense is not a polemic that simply dismisses the latter without taking his critique seriously. I will respond to the question of ethics in a way that navigates between Plato and Heidegger by showing how the former provides resources to take up the substance of the latter's critique. Finally, Plato and Heidegger serve as points of punctuation to the history of Western thought so far. Sometimes I will delve into that history in order to draw forth what is at stake between them.

Plato: That Plato towers over the origin of Western philosophy is as self-evident as Whitehead's much-cited observation that "the safest general characterization of the European philosophical tradition is that it consists of a series of footnotes to Plato."[9] Heidegger holds that Western thought had its genuine but concealed and misunderstood inception with the so-called pre-Socratics, chiefly Anaximander, Heraclitus, and Parmenides, but that this inception failed to maintain its potential. For Heidegger, Western philosophy does indeed begin with Plato due to that initial failing. In particular, it is Plato's "doctrine" of the ideas that Heidegger identifies as the explicit or implicit driving force of all the subsequent history, even in those who think, like Nietzsche or Marx, that they are upending Plato or the tradition based upon him. Heidegger throws down a gauntlet before Plato, or what he takes as *Platonism*.[10] I will take up that gauntlet, in part because I agree that Plato undergirds the Western tradition in philosophy and that Plato's idea of the *ideas* is decisive for the political question facing us now. At stake is ideation itself as a defining feature of being human, and this, for me, makes Plato unavoidable for metaethics and metapolitics. Finally, Plato experts will note that I follow the so-called literary school of reading Plato, which holds that interpreting Plato's philosophical meaning requires taking into account characters in the dialogues, setting, dramatic action as well as the surface structure of the arguments presented by Socrates and other characters. This method also does not assume that Socrates is simply Plato's mouthpiece, as beloved as he may have been by Plato.[11]

Heidegger: Much of my previous work has focused on the connection between Heidegger's thought and his active participation in the Nazi movement. There is a huge literature on this topic, and I will not reproduce here in detail my participation in these discussions. In my "Letter to Emmanuel Faye," I explained that I began working on Heidegger more than thirty years ago because I wanted to find a thinker who could make the most trenchant critique of what I took to be the best aspects of the liberal-democratic tradition and the Enlightenment.[12]

By *liberalism* I mean neither contemporary neo-liberalism, as a political and economic program of global capitalism, nor contemporary liberalism as what happens to be considered left-of-center in American politics and cultural life—although aspects of both may be entailed by the liberalism I mean. A larger sense of liberalism holds that liberty, or freedom, is essential to what makes us human; that the individual person is worthy of a presumptive respect grounded in that freedom and for that reason is a bearer of rights; that these rights extend universally and equally to all persons, without regard to time, place, or other contingencies; that political power and social policy are legitimate only to the extent that they accord with these rights; and that we, as both individuals and societies, have the obligation to develop the personal relations and sociopolitical institutions that engender, sustain, and defend freedom. Vital to this conception of freedom is an understanding of equality before the law and as an economic principle: that all members of the body politic have the material opportunity to realize their freedom as well as the obligation to employ it responsibly to contribute to the common good. This is an affective equality of citizens' dispositions as members of the integral body politic, cultivated through education and participation in civic life as necessary to devotion to the commonweal and its legitimacy, and sustained by whatever political economy grants citizens this foundation. I will call freedom so conceived an *eleutheric freedom*, for reasons I will sketch in this volume and defend more fully in subsequent work.

All this may sound like a liberalism centered on the Kantian conception of the person or on the Lockean conception of legitimate government as grounded in consent. While such issues are important, my concerns here are metaethical, which as I understand it includes the metapolitical. I am interested in defending the justificatory grounds for believing in such a liberalism at all, not in spelling out a systematic normative ethical theory or a political philosophy of institutions. Furthermore, I believe this is important now, in our times, because liberalism in this larger sense is going through a period of profound stress, even crisis, as evidenced by the rise of Donald Trump in the United States and of a similar authoritarian ethno-nationalism in Europe and across the globe. The specter of fascism looms again. It cannot be countered effectively by a merely ideological polemic but only by a *polemos* that exposes, examines, critiques, and reassesses the justificatory grounds of liberalism, because historical liberalism certainly has its share of faults and failings. At stake is a *reconstruction* of liberalism through a polemical ethics in response to some of its most serious vulnerabilities. The goal is to provide the metaethical foundation for a reconstructive liberalism, what I hope to defend in subsequent volumes as an *eleutheric liberalism* that will engage polemically with the history of liberalism in this broader sense.

I take Heidegger seriously as a critic of liberalism's metaethical foundations, and so, I have not treated him merely as an ideological adversary to be refuted. To read an author philosophically does not require that you agree with his or her concepts, methodologies, arguments, or conclusions. It does, however, require that you believe there is something of philosophical merit, at least in questions opened up by that thinker and the way that thinker responds to them. Otherwise, the encounter, no matter how learned and scholarly, becomes merely an exercise in intellectual history or ideological polemic with no relevance to our lives together. I trust that you will read me in this spirit.

So, I seek a proper *polemos* with Heidegger, not a polemic against him. I consider that confrontation worthwhile, because while I may oppose his critique of the liberal Enlightenment and loathe his decision to join the Nazis, I do think he is right that at the heart of the matter lies the question of liberalism's universalism, and that this universalism has its deepest source in Plato's idea-ism as the most powerful current in Western philosophy. While this confrontation with Heidegger, in particular through an interpretation of Plato's Allegory of the Cave, will be supported through scholarship and analysis, the project itself is not a conventionally academic one but rather an occasion for a philosophical meditation on the polemical ethics of being human. As such, I have attempted to make it as accessible as possible to readers not expert in Heidegger or Plato.

Furthermore, as I have argued elsewhere, I disagree with critics such as Emmanuel Faye and Sidonie Kellerer, who believe that there is nothing of philosophical value in Heidegger.[13] They do not think this simply because they find his conceptual vocabulary and reasoning to be so nonsensical and specious as to fail to rise to the level of philosophical concepts or arguments, as have critics like Rudolf Carnap.[14] More to the point, they see Heidegger's work as so entirely devoted to promoting a worldview dedicated to Nazism that it does not deserve the designation of philosophy, because such a worldview, in its advocacy of anti-rationalism, violence, domination, extermination, and racism, *prima facie* cannot be reasonable or philosophical. For these critics, Heidegger merely lends a philosophical veneer to an incantatory jargon that seeks to disseminate Nazism.

I simply disagree. As terrible as this may be, a thinker may argue and even do evil but still be a philosopher. I think there is merit to many of Heidegger's concepts, methodologies, and analyses, even if I disagree emphatically with some of his conclusions, especially the political ones. Moreover, I think that conventional polemics against Heidegger miss a vital opportunity. The true threat we face is not Heidegger but the reemergence of fascism in new forms. There is something about the crisis of our late modernity that keeps churning fascism to the surface of history as a symptom of our era's form of nihilism, which I contend has to do with the collision of universalism and embedded, historical belonging. By confronting the weakness in liberalism that Heidegger exposes, we may reconstruct a politics that rises to this challenge. A concise way of saying this is that what is at issue in Heidegger's thinking does not lead inevitably to fascism, but it also did not lead him there simply by accident in his response to what human-being means. In the space opened up by this neither-nor is an opportunity to appropriate what is at stake philosophically on our own terms.

THE 'AND' BETWEEN HEIDEGGER AND PLATO: HERMENEUTICAL CONSIDERATIONS

The immediate scholarly dialogue I take up in this book is between Heidegger and Plato. The more fundamental dialogue that I seek is between you, as reader, and me, as writer, as well as with an audience open to reflecting upon the political crisis of our age, a crisis which makes more vivid what is at stake in being human and a life well lived. Heidegger *and* Plato serve as an *occasion* for this larger ethical inquiry. The 'and' is the site of the *polemos* at issue. Heidegger and Plato are conjoined here by more than a merely academic interest in a comparison of their positions on ontology, metaphysics, ethics, or politics, or even just because Heidegger takes aim at Plato as the motive force for the decline into nihilism. Taken together, Heidegger *and* Plato can provide the impetus into the questions that are most decisive for this inquiry.

Engaging in this *polemos* requires being explicit about its methodological principles. First is the role of scholarship. We presume that the more adequate one's interpretation of a great author, the closer we come to their philosophical insights. When done well, such interpretation can lead to greater clarity about a thinker's work, and it can advance an argument of its own. But the danger is that our sense of modesty before a great thinker's authority may make us lean so heavily into exposition that we never quite get to asking, or answering, the question at issue for ourselves. This is especially a risk with Heidegger, whose conceptual vocabulary, phenomenological analyses, and studies of authors and texts in the Western tradition are so rich (some would say obtuse) that interpretive struggle with them can devolve into endless exegesis, never quite getting to one's own point. To try and counteract this danger, I attempt to develop an English-language terminology as much as possible rather than relying too much on Heidegger's.

My goal is also not to provide a systematic or entirely 'correct' interpretation of Heidegger or Plato, but that certainly does *not* mean that I am simply indifferent to the task of 'getting right' what an author argues. I bring Heidegger and Plato into dialogue to bring myself into dialogue with them and with you, and most of all, with what is philosophically at issue. While careful attention to an author's concepts and arguments is vital out of respect and as a way to sharpen what is at stake philosophically, an obsession with getting an author right can derail reflection on *die Sache selbst*, the matter for thought within the inquiry that may transcend the interlocutor's initial understanding, as well as one's own. Dialogue must leave room for discovery and surprise, because we are bounded by our finitude and should not presume to have mastered an interpretation of the whole.

WONDER, QUESTION, AND RESPONSE

A second methodological consideration at issue in the 'and' between Heidegger and Plato has to do with the nature of philosophy itself as dialogue. It is a view at least as ancient as Socrates that philosophy is not confined to specific texts or arguments but is a way of life and that "a life unexamined is not worth living" (*Apology*, 38a). Philosophy is more a verb than a noun, a doing rather than a doctrine, a way of engaging with the world and with people more than a system of concepts, arguments, and positions, but not excluding these either.

What, then, *occasions* the activity of examination? What sets the heart of philosophy beating? This brings us directly into Plato's famous cave, where a prisoner "is released and suddenly compelled to stand up" and to turn to the light (515c). The passive construction in the Greek leaves unspoken *who* or *what* does the releasing and the compelling. The allegory is so powerful as a story that we may forget that the prisoners are "like us" (515a) *as* an allegory for the activity of philosophy. Again, who or what provokes the sudden compulsion into the examination that is philosophy? Is it an event that happens once, so that the scales fall from our eyes and we are ready to examine everything, or is it an ongoing, episodic occurrence that, once occasioned, can be sustained to punctuate life ever on?

While examination is not synonymous with skepticism, a *comprehensive* skepticism that doubts everything is self-refuting, not just logically but existentially. We cannot examine everything all at once. Even Descartes's radically comprehensive attempt to doubt everything cannot doubt its own understanding of *what* it is doubting. Wittgenstein and Heidegger share an insight that every act of doubting necessarily entails a prior understanding that makes the doubt intelligible. Wittgenstein called this the language game, Heidegger called it the unconcealment of a world of meaning.[15] The same is true of the examined life. Examination requires, as its scaffold, certain assumptions that may go unexamined for a time in order to make sense of a specific question. Thus philosophy is punctuated, piecemeal, and precarious. It is always embedded in an already-operative understanding, situated in a context that makes sense to examine, even when that examination 'compels' a departure from that rough-and-ready, everyday understanding. Chapter 4 will examine what shocks philosophy's heart into beating, but to address the 'and' between Heidegger and Plato, I will focus here on philosophy's cyclical motion.

The life of philosophy has three moments: it begins in wonder, proceeds into a question, and develops a response.[16] Both Plato (*Theaetetus*, 155d) and Aristotle (*Metaphysics*, 982b) attest to the first moment: that philosophy begins in wonder, *thaumazein*.[17] Something about the world brings us up short. We will address this *something* more thoroughly later as the *breakdown* of understanding, but whatever it is, it breaks in on us and compels our attention. It can be something as simple as a physical phenomenon that defies our expectations, such as a straight straw that appears broken in a glass of water. Or it can be something that throws our entire ethical life into unmeaning, such as the realization, for an American living in, say, 1852, that the fact of slavery completely negates the founding idea of the republic, as Frederick Douglass proclaimed in his great Fourth of July oration of that year: "America is false to the past, false to the present, and solemnly binds herself to be false to the future."[18] The polemical heart animating that declaration is not despair but an idea and ideal that allows Douglass to discern the contradiction between what is and what ought to be, thereby venturing a reconstruction of the world. The role of the idea in confronting the unmeaning of the world and then reconstituting it, as a defining feature of being-human, is what this project seeks to illuminate and defend.

Wonder expresses itself in moods ranging from joyful, quiet awe to awful, wrenching horror. As such, wonder is a response to what the Greeks called *to deinon*, the wondrously awe-full as a marvel or a terror or both. Heidegger was well aware of the inceptive role of wonder, both among the Greeks and in philosophy as such. It animates the question he asks in *Introduction to Metaphysics*: "Why are there beings at all rather than nothing?" (GA 40: 3). About *alētheia* (truth) in Heraclitus, he says, "Astonishment [*Erstaunen*] first *begins* with the question, what does this all mean and how could it have happened? . . . Thoughtful astonishment speaks in questioning" (GA 7: 267). This connects with his well-known declaration in "The Question Concerning Technology" that "questioning is the piety of thinking" (GA 7: 36).[19] The question of philosophical piety *as* questioning will both link Heidegger and Plato and illuminate where they part ways.

Some might claim, like Descartes in the opening and closing passages of his *Meteorology*, that the purpose of natural philosophy is to abolish the causes of a wonder that leads only to superstitious myth and illusion.[20] But while we can ignore the call of wonder or treat it as something to overcome, this repression always hobbles us, betraying what it means to live in polemical dialogue with our situated existence. The moment of wonder calls us to confront our finitude, the reality that our understanding and our knowledge are never absolute. Wonder is a defining feature of our *discursive* understanding: that our comprehension unfolds dialogically with the world; that this comprehension is never comprehensive and often needs revision; that it winds through time, rather than manifesting as the all-at-once of a non-discursive, eternal understanding. In wonder, a prior meaning breaks down into an unmeaning nevertheless ripe with the potential for meaning restored. Wonder is sublime because it exposes us to what overawes us and provokes us to pursue a deeper understanding. Pure wonder is at first inarticulate in these moments of awe, but that does not mean it does not share in the *logos*, that it is illogical; rather, it opens us to a dialogue with the world. Wonder is also more than idle curiosity, because it breaks down what our prior understanding can articulate, if we do not avoid it by repressing it. Nevertheless, to avoid breaking down entirely, we must permit our prior understanding to be challenged by what is wondrous, using our existing comprehension as best we can, if only to articulate the risks of breakdown in face of the wondrous.

This is how wonder passes over into the second moment of philosophy: *formulating a question.* Wonder defies understanding but nevertheless demands that we address what is at issue to drive the discursive dialogue beyond mute wonder into an attentive reconfiguration of an understanding of a phenomenon. This is part of why Heidegger sees questioning as the expression of the piety of thinking: it invokes a trust that questioning, as a response to wonder, is meaningful as such, even if thinking does not dispel the cause for wonder in some final answer but rather intensifies the wonder itself. A good philosophical question illuminates very precisely what is at stake, using what it does comprehend to clarify what defies comprehension, pointing the way to how understanding might reconstitute itself.

And that is how a question passes over to a response. Philosophical responses to well-articulated questions attempt to reconstruct what is not understood in terms of a new, but never entirely new, understanding. I say *response* rather than *answer* because philosophy is a necessarily ongoing dialogue with the world, encompassed by an understanding that is finite. This dialogue is provoked by wonder, articulated in questioning, and addressed in a response rather than by a final answer. Good philosophy seeks to remain open to wonder out of respect for its own finitude and for the ways the world can unexpectedly unsettle us. At its best, philosophy strives to unite all three moments as part of the same, simultaneous activity. That ideal is very hard to instantiate, but one we can attempt to approach.

Of the three moments, the third, response, is what many consider to be philosophy. "What's your philosophy of —?" Of politics. Of art. Of truth. Of business. Of sport. There's a problem, or set of problems, and a field of inquiry, and one expects anyone claiming to do philosophy to have a rigorous, comprehensive, systematic answer in the form of clear concepts, cogent arguments, and compelling conclusions. We expect a book on the shelf or an article in a journal, making its case in an integrated constellation of arguments, varying in form from the somewhat haphazard (Epictetus, Kierkegaard, Nietzsche) to the methodically systematic (Aristotle, Kant, Hegel). Rarer are the thinkers who make the questions, the second moment, their focus, but they do exist, such as the later Wittgenstein especially—"How small a thought it takes to fill a whole life!"[21] Rarer still are those who dwell on the first moment, wonder. Examples include Heraclitus, Lao Tzu, and Meister Eckhart. Academic philosophers tend to deny the name of philosophy to such thinkers' work, because it seems too close to mysticism and too far from rigorous argument. That is a mistake, because attentiveness to what awakens our wonder, and a body of work that seeks to emulate and incite that sense of wonder, is a vital facet of philosophy.

No thinker fits neatly into one single mode of philosophizing. Some fit one more than others, of course, and some straddle the distinctions—Wittgenstein, for example, from the systematicity of the *Tractatus* to the exploration of the *Investigations*, the third and second modes, respectively. Rarest of all are thinkers who endeavor to work in all three modes at once. I believe Plato falls into this category, and also Heidegger. To address what is at issue for us now, what should evoke our wonder and what we need to articulate as a question, is something that we can elicit in the *polemos* between Plato and Heidegger. To enter into the triad of wonder-question-response, especially in reading an author with whom one seriously disagrees, means to return to the wonder that animates a question to be able better to formulate that question, to sharpen what is at stake, so that one may respond yet more fully.

AT ISSUE: THE PARTICULAR AND
THE UNIVERSAL IN BEING-HUMAN

In *Heidegger's Polemos*, I claimed that what is at issue in Heidegger is the Being of our politics.[22] By that I meant not only a specific set of historical crises facing us, a planetary humanity at the close of modernity, but also the broader question of what it means to be political. I presented this in terms of a conflict between universalism and particularism, with Heidegger supporting the latter by joining with National Socialism. Since writing that book, some of the most important texts exposing more fully Heidegger's political thinking have been published. These include his lectures of 1933–1934, at the height of his involvement in the Nazi revolution, in the volume *Being and*

Truth. In those lectures is a passage that provides the most distilled version of the connection between Heidegger's ontology and his politics:

> If one interprets [Plato's] ideas as representations and thoughts that contain a value, a norm, a law, a rule, such that ideas then become conceived of as norms, then the one subject to these norms is the human being–not the historical human being, but rather the human being in general, the human being in itself, or humanity. Here [that is, in Platonism in all its forms—which includes almost everything from Christianity to Hegel to Marx, for Heidegger], the conception of the human being is one of a *rational being in general.* In the Enlightenment and in liberalism, this conception achieves a definite form. Here all of the powers against which we [that is, Germany under the National Socialist regime] must struggle today have their root. Opposed to this conception are the *finitude, temporality,* and *historicity* of human beings. (GA 36/37: 166)

In *Introduction to Metaphysics,* Heidegger writes, "the word *idea, eidos,* 'idea,' comes to the fore as the definitive and prevailing word for Being (*phusis*). Since then, the interpretation of Being as idea rules over all Western thinking, throughout the history of its changes up to today" (GA 40: 189). The Platonic ideas are supposed to offer us the truth by *transcending* the particular givens of the world, by climbing up and out from the transient realm of the cave and into the light of eternal realities. Again, *Introduction to Metaphysics*: "[Plato's] *idea* constitutes the Being of beings. But here, *idea* and *eidos* are used in an extended sense, meaning not only what we can see with our physical eyes, but everything that can be apprehended" (GA 40: 190).

The ideas supposedly give us access to meaning, what it means for any particular thing *to be*, by comprehending that thing "in general," in terms of its abstract, universal features that constitute its form, its idea, as an eternal reality "apprehended" with the mind's eye. In the human domain, "not the historical human being, but rather the human being in general" becomes the object of inquiry. This is the human being as subject to timeless, universal laws, such as those familiar to us in the liberal notion of human rights, which supposedly apply to all humanity, irrespective of time and place—that is, how we are situated and embodied as finite, temporal Dasein.

"Here," says Heidegger, "all of the powers against which we must struggle today have their root." In Plato's idea-ism, his moral and epistemological idealism, Heidegger finds the universalizing roots of the liberal Enlightenment. Against "the powers," both ideological and political, which represent that liberalism writ large, "we must struggle today." The "we" here is his audience of young German students, in the fall of 1933, in an introductory lecture course at Freiburg University, at the dawn of the National Socialist revolution. Heidegger says that "Opposed to this conception" of the human in Platonic-Enlightenment liberalism "are the *finitude, temporality*, and *historicity* of human beings." Why?

For Heidegger, Plato's ideas offer up a notion of truth that is not *finite* but rather *infinite*, transcending all flux and limitation; not *temporal* but rather eternal; not *historical* but rather universal and trans-temporal. If philosophy means escaping the cave to emerge into a realm of timeless, eternal ideas that fix the meaning of reality forever, then Heidegger wants to upend philosophy altogether. For Heidegger, there is no "rough, steep upward" pathway out of the cave (*Republic*, 515e). The cave is all there is, even if we can be yanked out of the shackles of everydayness and faced with some liberating power that turns out to be a recognition of the power of history itself, and not an escape beyond the cave.

This does not mean that the world we inhabit is meaningless. Far from it, for Heidegger, who seeks an alternative to nihilism. That there *is* meaning is a phenomenological given. The shadows manifestly *do mean something* to us. But it is a *historical us* for whom they have meaning, a *bounded* us, a community of shared traditions and understandings that are largely unspoken, serving as the background to our everyday lives, and which therefore cannot be universalized because such understanding is unaccountable. These background practices and understandings are unaccountable because to give them a *logos*, in the sense of a rational account, would be precisely to dissolve them as that background to our existence, as if one were to shine a light on a shadow to see it better. At its most pernicious, for Heidegger, Platonism devolves into nihilistic moralism by opposing Being as what actually is to what ought to be: "As Being itself becomes fixed in its character as idea, it also tends to make up for the ensuing degradation of Being. But by now, this can occur only by setting something *above* Being that Being never yet is, but always *ought* to be" (GA 40: 206).[23]

To be properly human, for Heidegger, means to be Da-Sein: *Being-here, situated* in a historical reality that always-already is, bounded by a constellation of meaning that we did not make up and which we have been given as a kind of fate that we share with a community and a tradition. There is no absolute transcendence for Heidegger, no way out of the cave, in the sense of arriving at a timeless realm of ultimate truth; the truth is always given as a time-bound, particular openness to a world of meaning that has a necessary limit, a definite finitude. Historical meaning will shift, drift, and ultimately pass away into the nothing that time brings to all finite things. All the more reason to embrace the cave, for it is all we will ever have. For Heidegger, nihilism consists precisely in denying the finite given in the name of a reality that supposedly transcends it, but really only negates it.

As Alexander Duff has properly seen, the rejection of universalism constitutes Heidegger's "*particularist* revolution."[24] It does not merely reject the progressive's ameliorating idealism that repudiates the putatively confining bonds of tradition to sacrifice the *was* and the *is* on the altar of the *ought*; his ontological metapolitics also opposes, with a steely hardness, the conservative's resentful obsession to make the present and future replicate the past. This is Heidegger's radical historicism as a radical *situatedness* that takes on the *polemos* with its own historicity but without relying upon pre-given standards, whether aspirational or traditional. Heidegger presents his political stance through a conception of human-being arising directly from key concepts in his phenomenological analysis of human existence: "*finitude, temporality,* and *historicity.*"

Against these, Heidegger opposes Platonism in its millennia-long domination of the West: the *ideas,* and the corresponding understanding that what is most essential to human beings is *not* their finite belonging to a specific world, *not* their dynamic unfolding in time, *not* their embeddedness in a history that provides their world with meaning, but rather "the human being in general." For Heidegger, this involves what can be abstracted from all such specificity in order to provide timeless ethical and political principles, accessible to a timeless rationality—what we today might call 'human rights'— that apply infinitely, as it were, to all persons and peoples, in whatever time and however placed in historical context. Heidegger gives this opponent, against which Germany must "struggle" in *polemos,* a name: Liberalism. While Heidegger also does mean what we would conventionally call the liberalism of the modern era in this concept, with its emphasis on personal rights and liberties, limited government, equality of persons, and so on, it is crucial for this project to underline that what he has in mind with Liberalism (capitalized to distinguish it) has a much broader scope, reaching back to the dawn of the West with Plato. What defines that scope is the *universalism* of the Platonic ideas, how they apply to particulars, regardless of time or place. Such a Liberalism encompasses conservatism, not just progressivism, as grounded in standards that transcend human historicity. *Particularism* is what he opposes to this Platonic, universalist Liberalism. It is a politics grounded in a metapolitics, itself grounded in an ontology.

These ontological issues might seem distant from concrete ethical and political concerns. They are not as distant as they might seem, though, because the nature of *what is* and *how* it is relates inescapably to what and who *we are,* both you and I, reading and writing in our dialogical individuality, and us, as communities of lesser and greater and overlapping scopes. For the Socrates of Plato's *Republic,* knowledge of the transcendent, everlasting ideas, and of the idea of the good that exceeds all other ideas, is what would make effective rule possible at all, assuming such knowledge is attainable. The presumptive philosopher-kings and queens of his imagined polity would have to know the forms of justice, courage, and all the other virtues, as well as the nature of the good itself, in order to make out how these apply to the shadows and contingencies of the changeable world: "Once they see the good itself, they must be compelled, each in his turn, to use it as a pattern for ordering city, private men, and themselves for the rest of their lives" (540b). Only then can they educate and lead their fellow citizens.

So began the reign of "idealism" through many avatars in Western thought, the notion that life must be guided by ideas, which are more than concepts because they establish the ideals by which to measure our shared world as ethical and political beings, and hence to improve or repair it when it does not measure up (progressivism) or to protect and preserve it when it threatens to decay (conservatism), according to these standards. I will put aside for now the vexed question of what distinguishes between ideas and concepts, and between first- and second-order concepts, and rely at first on our ordinary sense of the word *idea*, especially in its connotation of an illumination that beckons and guides us. By calling generalizations from particulars 'ideas,' Plato makes the problem of abstraction from experience as difficult as possible, and properly so, because the ontological status of such purely intelligible constructs should remain in question, not harden into dogmatic theory.[25] So, just as you must have the idea of the triangle 'in mind' when drawing some particular triangle when teaching a class on geometry, so too must the educators and leaders of a community have an idea as ideal for what makes good citizens and good institutions when raising them up in actuality. This only makes sense if the projection of these ideals, and our ability to enact them, even if incompletely, is not *a priori* delusional. It means that what is most real and enduring about who we are is something universal, transcending our radically singular particularity as persons of this or that ethnicity or nationality, male or female, rich or poor, and so on, just as the idea of the triangle abstracts from any particular type of triangle, be it a scalene, isosceles, right, or obtuse.

If that priority is reversed in favor of finitude and situated particularity, other ways of understanding what and who we are come into view. One does not have to go to the extreme of believing that there is no such thing as natural kinds, independent of human cognition (such as trees or atoms or even numbers and physical laws), to think that human cultural constructs, such as understanding something to sit on as a throne rather than as a chair, and evaluative concepts, such as justice, are in fact subject to the trajectory of history by coming into being, lingering for a while, then falling into decay and finally into the nothing of unmeaning. Such human constructs of meaning would be like living creatures, or even entire species and ecosystems, which emerge in geological time and then fade away. Finitude would trump transcendence, at least in the domain of what actual, historical human beings consider their meaningful anchors to life. That there be no permanence to the things that matter to us on the human scale need not lead to nihilism. Rather, it might open us up to an insight that connects us more meaningfully and more intimately to what life truly is, while we have it in our embodiment here and now, enmeshed in the meaning we manifestly do inhabit. Between origin and demise, between birth and death, time whiles away at us, but in that temporal whiling-away we do have *our while*. Like a revolving kaleidoscope, in which patterns emerge, remain a while, and then collapse, the flux of human existence is not sheer chaos.

The ethics and politics of human-being as a temporal being-here-and-now, where the now is constituted by an interpretive, existential spanning of past to future, is not obvious. It does seem to suggest, though, that a meaningful life cannot be guided by eternal ideas and universal abstractions, for these uproot life in favor of an inhuman other-world. It might then mean, as Nietzsche writes, that "Whatever is done for love always occurs beyond good and evil."[26] Ethics, as an embedded, situated way of life that has been owned up to, could not be predetermined by some abstract ethical calculus such as we find in the familiar works of moral philosophy, as in Kant or Mill, or as the result of figuring out the Trolley Problem thought experiment.[27] Political life would not take its bearings from universal principles of the natural law or human rights, but rather from the attachments that give meaning to the historical community, in its particular shared purposes, conflicts, and struggles, that we simply always already *are*.

While this might not obviously or necessarily lead to chauvinism or ethnic nationalism, we can certainly see how it could. There is a parallel though not identical danger in ethical and political universalism, cited on the Right by figures such as Carl Schmitt and on the Left by decolonial thinkers such as Enrique Dussel, that the logic of universalism leads to an imperial imposition of norms on peoples and nations who do not live up to a Eurocentric liberalism's interpretation of those ideals.[28]

At issue is whether we should be guided by ideals that transcend us or by attachments that embed us. The *polemos* between Plato and Heidegger is timely because these poles of universalism and particularism are now colliding on a global scale. At the end of modernity, we have reached a decisive and unprecedented moment. This crisis is not what a Heideggerian might call a merely ontic issue, a merely 'factical' circumstance of our contingency. It pierces the heart of who we are as human beings and whether that 'we' encompasses us all in an understanding of the political stakes of the dawning future, or whether the 'we' has an operative scope that can *properly* reach only as far as distinct and incommensurably bounded human communities.

This is a crisis in the Greek sense: a turning point, inescapable not only because of modernity's interlacing of planetary humanity through commerce and communication technologies. There is also the blunt fact of a planetary ecological crisis that threatens humanity on a global scale, which only a humanity cooperating globally can address, not to mention the Covid-19 pandemic surging across the world at the time of this writing. The global aspect of such crises forces the question of universalism, not just for action on the climate crisis, but also in the concomitant political crisis of our age: whether who we most properly *are* as human beings is members of distinct and ultimately incompatible, but not necessarily hostile communities, or whether our particularity has its dignity only because we can rise above our historical contingency to what universally unites us. History itself seems to have brought us to the outermost edge of this *polemos* between Being and Becoming, universalism and particularism, cosmopolitanism and rootedness, the One and the Many, affirmation and negation.

The thesis I explore in this book is that the metaethics of universal and particular, of transcendent and situated, is not an either/or but rather a both/and. It is not 'Plato' *or* 'Heidegger,' universal *or* particular, transcendent *or* situated, affirmation *or* negation, unity *or* diversity, but rather a reconciliation of these poles. If this is a reconciliation in favor of Plato, of universalism and transcendence, it does not set aside the other pole of finitude and contingency but subsumes it and accounts for it, just as the idea does with the particular, by acknowledging that we can only start within the concrete.

Great philosophers, such as Aquinas and Hegel, have attempted such a reconciliation with far great systematicity and fullness than I can hope to emulate. My goal is far humbler: to demonstrate that Plato's work contains resources to anticipate Heidegger's critique by showing how the life examined requires an ongoing polemical integration of the temporal situatedness of human existence with what transcends that embedded understanding. Rather than Da-sein as a fundamentally finite being-here, I will argue that being-human is a *situated transcendence*. At the heart of this reconciliation is the insight that our temporal existence is most meaningful in a life worth living if challenged by ideas that we project beyond the limits of that existence. Reciprocally, this means that such ideas, as ethical and political ideals, can only be properly understood and enacted if brought into a discerning dialogue with the radical contingencies of temporal life through practical wisdom, *phronēsis*. That reconciliation, in short, is a *polemos* between the poles of our paradoxical nature as situated-transcendence.

HEIDEGGER AND *POLEMOS*

The synopsis that follows is adapted from my book, *Heidegger's Polemos*, which the reader may consult for fuller exposition of these themes. For Heidegger, to *be* is to be in confrontation, to be in *polemos*. This struggle to interpret our Being is the most basic meaning of *polemos*. *Polemos* is a name for Being itself, because it is *how* a field of meaning deploys for historical understanding. The following points orient the subsequent chapters, and we will return to some of these themes in greater depth:

1. *Polemos* is a keyword in Heidegger's confrontation with Platonism. In his masterwork, *Being and Time*, Heidegger says that the "question of the meaning of Being" (SZ, 1) has receded and must now be asked again. This means going to war against the over two-millennia reign of Platonism, which locates Being in a static, timeless, otherworldly realm of ideas and forms. For Heidegger, *polemos*, as a temporal unfolding of meaning displaces *idea*, as eternal and static, in accounting for the intelligibility of things and the world.

2. *Polemos* describes the way that Being happens and how it concerns us. It also describes our relation to Being as what Heidegger calls Dasein, the site, the There, in which Being manifests itself as a domain of meaning that forms a navigable world. Being-human is itself polemical.

3. *Truth* is both a part of and a possible outcome of *polemos*. For Heidegger, truth is the opening up of a world, the making-manifest of beings for Dasein's understanding of Being. But along with this revealing of truth is the struggle to bring forth from concealedness. The struggle to reveal is met by the struggle to conceal. Truth stands up to and depends upon *polemos*.

4. Time also is a feature of *polemos*, because, Heidegger tells us, beings and Being are always rooted in a specific time. We can only interpret what it means to be, for things and ourselves, as enmeshed in time as our time. We move both with and away from the past into a future as we engage in the *polemos* of interpretation in order to make sense of the present.

5. *Polemos* with the past also may be understood as a method, or even an ethic, for the interpretation of texts, authors, and works of art. To so engage with a work is to cast it in its most powerful light, so that both it and one's own position are most radically exposed to examination.

6. History is polemical as both the full sweep of history and the history of individuals, but it is never simply ours. We do not create history or control its direction. Heidegger speaks of a "confrontation between the first and an other inception to history" (not simply *another* inception) that will overturn the reign of Platonism.

7. In this *polemos* of construction and destruction with history, Dasein engages with its authentic task *as a community*, because the past it inherits is never simply a solipsistic individual's own.

8. Heidegger understands the proper relation of historical peoples as distinct communities as a *polemos*. True respect among peoples, as among individuals, demands that each be allowed to come into its own while insisting on a conversation that puts everything into question, in the face of history's challenges.

9. The *polemos* with Being must take place within the compass of a finite world of a historical community, a *Volk*, a collection of people with their shared inherited past, place, and language. By confronting the trajectory of the givenness of its own history, a people simultaneously preserves its particularity and renews its history, while making possible a transformative conversation, a *polemos*, with other peoples.

10. It was with this idea of creative *polemos* among the nations of the world that Heidegger supported Hitler's National Socialism. Each national community would remain free for the self-assertion of its historical uniqueness, its identity and its difference. At the extreme, *polemos* may entail the impossibility of sharing a common community with some peoples or nations, because no dialogue with them could result in the shared understanding necessary for a unitary body politic.

11. Heidegger counters the perpetual peace envisioned by Kant with perpetual *polemos*. In confrontation with themselves and with each other, in setting themselves out and apart from one another, peoples might retain the singularity of their own historical destinies.

12. Heidegger was a Nazi for philosophical reasons that are still in *polemos* with other ideas, most particularly what I want to defend: a *reconstructive* liberalism, with 'liberalism' understood in the broadest scope of the *eleutheria* of liberation in Plato's Allegory of the Cave.

To understand the link between Heidegger's thinking and his politics, we must come to grips with the matter for thought announced by fascism as a challenge to freedom that makes its own claim on what true freedom is. We cannot think of Heidegger's fascism as an error of an otherwise great thinker, a merely personal fact to be ignored when considering his work. Likewise, we cannot understand and respond to new manifestations of such politics if we think of fascism as a past mistake that has been corrected and can be forgotten or suppressed. Beyond Heidegger's personal history or his thinking we must think through what is at stake in fascism then, now, and in the future. This is what can make Heidegger an *occasion* for thought, not just a controversial figure in the history of thought. Such an encounter must itself be a *polemos.*

GLOSSARY OF KEY TERMS

Philosophy sometimes demands that we push language to its limits to express explicitly what strikes us as meaningful in some previously unarticulated way, given the ordinary bounds of language. If ordinary language were enough to resolve our genuine wonder and perplexity, we would not need the poetical-conceptual departures of philosophy in the first place. Such moments call for *meta-translation*, often even within a language. The difference between translation in the ordinary sense and meta-translation is that the latter runs the risk of expressing something in a way that seeks to convey what is at-issue but that cannot be communicated simply through a rendering familiar to ordinary language or by conventional, literal translation. An example on the grand scale would be Alain Badiou's "hypertranslation" of Plato's *Republic*.[29]

The following terms express concepts discussed in this book that depart from ordinary usage. Terms borrowed from Heidegger are noted as such.

at-issue This adverbial term designates what animates a particular line of philosophical inquiry. It is what we stumble up against in wonder, what we try to articulate in formulating a question, and what we attempt to address in composing a philosophical response. Identifying what is at-issue is a matter of discernment closely related to *phronēsis*, practical wisdom. Discerning what is at-issue is always embedded in a particular hermeneutical situation that is not up to us and that cannot be scripted. I will sometimes hyphenate this term to emphasize its adverbial sense.

always-already This Heideggerian term describes the way that we exist in a world that is given to us in a web of connections in which beings are interpreted as meaningful to us in advance. This meaning may be provisional or incomplete, but it necessarily precedes us as the background to all inquiry and understanding. As individuals and as communities, we are thrown into this always-already world.

Being Translators of Heidegger render the German *Sein* as either 'being' or 'Being,' but I will generally use the latter to prevent confusion with *beings*, specific things as we understand them to be. *Sein* is the infinitive of the verb 'to be' made into a verbal noun, which German and other languages can do (as *l'être*,

in French). It is important not to read this big-B Being as a substantive, some sort of super-thing that
serves as the metaphysical foundation for all other
things.[30] For Heidegger, *Sein* is not a *Seiendes*, a
particular being or entity that is, or even the whole
of what is. The *to-be*, Being, is not a being, a thing
among other things. The question of the meaning of
Being is the question of what it means for anything,
ourselves included, to be, to show up phenomenologically as meaning this, not that, and as having
distinct possibilities grounded in its finite, contingent historicity.

being-human and
human-being

These are my meta-translations for the word that
Heidegger uses for the kind of being that we are:
Dasein. In Heidegger, 'Dasein' is already a special
term, because in ordinary German it means simply
existence. Heidegger adopts it for the kind of being
that is a 'who,' not a 'what,' and *for whom* its own
being, what it is to be, is always (potentially) open to
question. For Heidegger, the combination, Da-Sein,
as a name for who we are, points to the necessarily
situated aspect of human-being. To be, for us, means
always-already to understand a particular world of
meaning. I will often render *Dasein* as either the hy-
phenated being-human or human-being, depending
on the context.

breakdown

A term inspired by *lusis tōn desmōn*, the breaking of
the prisoner's bonds in Plato's Allegory of the Cave.
A breakdown is a moment of both crisis and opportunity, terror and wonder, that overwhelms the way
we have previously understood something about
the world or the world as such. Breakdown has two
aspects. One is the passive and negative confusion
or even despair in face of a rupture in meaning and
collapse into unmeaning; the other is the active and
positive breakdown, or analysis, of what has taken
place in the rupture, with the implicit or explicit
prospect of a reconstruction of meaning.

echonicism

From the Greek *echein*, to have, hold, possess: a conception of philosophy that expects or claims to find

the final, ultimate answers to its questions. The philosopher queens and kings who rule the ideal city in Plato's *Republic* supposedly achieve this possession of the truth (q.v. *zeteticism*).

ideation The process through which imagination and idea-formation interact; more specifically, the process through which we imagine things that exist in the mind's eye, such as when we form a 'mental image' of a person, place, or thing; but also entities that may have no perceptible physical existence, such as concepts or the insights of mathematics. Although usually based in metaphors of sight, it need not be confined to these. Ideation is essential to our existence as beings who interpret the world for ourselves and for each other, for if we could not form and share ideas about things that are not directly perceptible to us, we could not communicate at all across the gaps of our individuated embodiment, nor reflect for ourselves on an existence that might be other than it is. In ideation, idea (the most exalted level of understanding) and imagination (the most uncertain level, yet also the most creative) meet up. Ideation is what allows us to pluck meaning from unmeaning.

intimation In standard English, an intimation is a hint, a suggestion, an inkling, of something hovering on the edge of perception and meaning. It is glimpsed, as it were, from the corner of the eye because peripheral to our direct and directed vision, our ordinary, everyday understanding. Here, I use it to mean the sense that occasionally steals upon us of some meaning beyond or behind what we ordinarily perceive or understand. Sometimes, these are abstract virtues, such as justice, without which we could not recognize anything as fair or unfair *in general* because we would be unable to see beyond or behind our always-already historical, situated context. In another sense, these abstractions are always-already here, woven into the world as it is, and intimations of them inform our daily lives, but in an unexamined, unreflective manner. Intimations are *intimate* in the sense that they are closely tied to our personal situatedness and how we make sense of it to ourselves and to others. Intimations are fleeting and fragile, setting our being-human on edge, because they suggest that our ordinary way of seeing, of understanding, may be inadequate, that it frays, that there are liminal things whispering or clamoring to be understood that do not yet fit into our current construals of meaning. *Ideation* (q.v.) is closely connected to intimation, because it is how we endeavor to understand and integrate the intimations that break into, disrupt, and even break down our field of vision. Intimations are both a threat and an invitation. An intimation may turn out to be nothing at all, but that is because this 'nothing' is the background to all meaning, not as a collection of no-things, but as the domain of *unmeaning* (q.v.) from which the not-yet-fully-meaningful (as intimated) arises and into which the no-longer-meaningful (as when a language or a practice dies) returns.

meaning   The phenomenological given that things (entities of all kinds) and practices are always already provisionally intelligible to us, that they are intelligible as part of a larger whole, not just as isolated units, and that they are significant to us, that they matter to us as being-human. Meaning is not first and foremost a grand purpose or design, although it is the ontological precondition for such projects. As used here, *meaning* shares aspects of both *Bedeutung* (how individual entities and practices are understood and interpreted; 'meaning' in the narrow sense) and *Sinn* (structure of an entire domain of intelligibility; *sense*, as the overarching orientation to meanings as a whole) in Heidegger.[31]

ontic and   Heidegger famously articulated "the ontological differ-
ontological   ence" between beings (*Seiendes*) and Being (*Sein*). I follow his usage in using *ontic* to refer to what has to do with beings or entities as we understand them and *ontological* to refer to how we understand what it means to be as such. Ontic questions assume a meaning that we already ascribe to beings; ontological

questions address the ascription of meaning itself and is therefore tied to hermeneutics.

polemos, polemics, and the polemical

The Greek word *polemos* means 'war,' but ever since Heraclitus it has taken on a very wide range of meanings. In this book, 'polemical' usually does not have its everyday meaning of bitterly or intransigently belligerent. Instead, it describes a fundamental feature of what it means to be human as the beings who must ever confront the meaning of their world in interpretation and reinterpretation. That confrontation arises from the specificity of our particular, embedded embodiment in a historical context as what is significantly at-issue in that given hermeneutical situation.

preconstruction

When meaning ruptures, as it may during a personal, physical, or political cataclysm, we must reassemble a meaningful world in order to function. Generally, this is described as a two-phase process of de- and reconstruction, but I posit an intermediate phase, preconstruction, to describe the process by which we imagine a better possible world between that which has broken down and that which emerges as the new reality. As such, preconstruction is the moment of ideation where the imagination first en-visions an as-yet unrealized possibility and endeavors to work it out conceptually.

situated transcendence

A description of what it means to be human, embedded in a finite, historical understanding and also projected into what exceeds that understanding. As another way of defining human-being, or Dasein, situated transcendence is an adverbial, existential characterization of *how* we are *who* we are ontologically, rather than *what* we are ontically as mere things (e.g., as *homo sapiens*; complex organic compounds; neural networks; atoms in space; etc.).

unmeaning

The counterpart, not the opposite, of meaning (q.v.). This term is a meta-translation of what Heidegger calls *das Nichts*, the Nothing, which is not an ontically impossible domain of no-things but rather the ontological precondition for the *polemos* of meaning. All perplexity, all wonder, all breakdown, all

questioning begins in a confrontation with unmeaning, the way that some thing, some practice, some
context either fails to be meaningful or threatens
to cease to be meaningful to us, and yet still com-
mands our attention. What *is*—as intelligible, as
meaningful—both emerges from unmeaning and
recedes into it, much in the sense that Heidegger
identifies truth as *a-lētheia*, un-concealment.

zeteticism   From the Greek *zetein*, to seek, search, inquire: a
skeptical but not cynical conception of philosophy
as using dialogue and questioning to make better
sense of the world and being-human in light of both
our finite historicity and our intimations of transcendence. Zeteticism may be called a *skeptical idealism*
because it finds meaning in the search for truth but
insists upon its own refutability (q.v. *echonicism*).

NOTES

1. Levinas, "Ethics of the Infinite," 81.

2. Here I agree with Reiner Schürmann, who writes that in thinking with Heidegger, one must not take "the name 'Heidegger'" as referring to the man, but to the
questions at issue in the work, and that 'Heidegger' "will not be the proper name,
which refers to the man from Messkirch, deceased in 1976"; *Heidegger on Being
and Acting*, 3.

3. Jürgen Habermas, "On the Publication of the Lectures of 1935," 197.

4. Excepting long passages, Greek words will usually be transliterated.

5. See Kirk, Raven, and Schofield, *The Presocratic Philosophers*, 189; the translation is my own, but close to theirs.

6. See Proclus, *Proclus' Commentary on Plato's* Parmenides, 3.

7. For an instructive discussion of a more expansive conception of dialogue and
dialectic in Plato, see Roochnik, *Beautiful City*, 140–49.

8. For further discussion, see Love and Meng, "Heidegger's Metapolitics."

9. Whitehead, *Process and Reality*, 39. Less often cited are his next two sen-
tences: "I do not mean the systematic scheme of thought which scholars have doubt-
fully extracted from his writings. I allude to the wealth of general ideas scattered
through them."

10. Jussi Backman has convincingly argued in "All of a Sudden: Heidegger and
Plato's *Parmenides*" that Heidegger's 1930–1931 seminar on that dialogue, in addition to his 1924–1925 *Sophist* lecture course, shows that he was aware of the radical
potential in Plato's later work for countering what later became entrenched as metaphysical Platonism and the ideal of a perfect, atemporal beingness. My claim is that,

even if so, Heidegger never lingered on this potential, instead eliding the ambiguity between Plato and Platonism, and he certainly failed to discern the complex dialectic between historicity and transcendence in the *Republic*.

11. For a manifesto for this approach, see the essays by various authors collected and edited by Charles Griswold in *Platonic Writings/Platonic Readings*, especially Griswold's Preface for a succinct presentation of the issues involved. For an example of taking Plato as speaking through Socrates by a preeminent scholar, see Julia Annas, *An Introduction to Plato's Republic*, 9.

12. See Fried, "A Letter to Emmanuel Faye," in *Confronting Heidegger*, 4–9.

13. See the contributions by Faye and Kellerer in Fried, *Confronting Heidegger*.

14. See Carnap, "The Elimination of Metaphysics through the Logical Analysis of Language"; for the surprising complexity of the relationship between Heidegger's and Carnap's thought, see Friedman, *A Parting of the Ways*.

15. For an exhaustive comparison of these two thinkers, see Lee Braver, *Groundless Grounds*, especially chapter 5.

16. For the triad, see Fried, "A Letter to Emmanuel Faye," 33–36.

17. For a contrast between Plato as conserving wonder and Aristotle as seeking to end it, see Andrea Nightingale, *Spectacles of Truth in Classical Greek Philosophy*, 253–68.

18. Douglass, "What to the Slave Is the Fourth of July?" *Portable Frederick Douglass*, 205.

19. For a helpful treatment of wonder in Heidegger, see Braver, *Groundless Grounds*, 46–52; for a provocative study of wonder from Plato to Heidegger and beyond, see Mary-Jane Rubenstein, *Strange Wonder*.

20. Cf. Renée Descartes, "Meteorology," in *Discourse on Method*, 263 and 361.

21. Ludwig Wittgenstein, *Culture and Value*, 57e.

22. Fried, *Heidegger's Polemos*, 3.

23. On moralism, see Fried, "Whitewashed," in *Heidegger and Jewish Thought*, 55–74.

24. See Alexander Duff, *Heidegger and Politics*, 186–91.

25. For example, Kant, drawing from Plato, holds that "Just as the understanding unifies the manifold [of sensory experience] in the object by means of concepts, so reason unifies the manifold of concepts by means of ideas, positing a certain collective unity as the goal of the activities of the understanding"; *Critique of Pure Reason*, B672.

26. Nietzsche, *Beyond Good and Evil*, 90 (§153).

27. For the Trolley Problem, see Section I of Frances M. Kamm, *Intricate Ethics*.

28. For example, Carl Schmitt, *The Concept of the Political*, 54, and Enrique Dussel, *Ethics of Liberation*, 51–52.

29. See Badiou, *Plato's 'Republic,'* xxiv. See also Polt, "*Plato's Republic*, by Alain Badiou," in *Teaching Philosophy* 37, no. 1 (2014): 122–26.

30. On big-B Being, see Thomas Sheehan, "A Paradigm Shift in Heidegger Research," in *Continental Philosophy Review*.

31. On this point, I follow Thomas Sheehan in *Making Sense of Heidegger*, xvii–xix.

Chapter One

Between Earth and Sky

The Polemics of Finitude and Transcendence

I believe Icarus was not failing as he fell,
but just coming to the end of his triumph.

—Jack Gilbert, from "Failing and Flying"[1]

In the *Theogony*, Hesiod tells us that, "Surely first Chaos was born, but then / Broad-bosomed Earth, firm seat forever for all / Immortals" (119–21), and then that "Earth gave birth to star-studded Sky / As equal to herself so that he would cover her over all around / So that she would be a firm seat forever for the blessed gods" (125–27).[2]

If you step outside or look up from your reading through a window, especially on a starry night, you can experience what Hesiod meant. Enveloped by the sheer wonder of "Why this?" we stand upon the earth, the goddess Gaia, and we stand beneath the sky or heavens, the god Ouranos. Modern science, abstracting from where we stand as mere mortal humans, tells us that the earth is round, that there is no absolute up and down or over and under to its spherical gravity, that the sky does not cover the earth like a barrier dome but rather extends so far in spacetime that to the feeble human imagination it might as well be infinite. Yet scientism taken to an extreme belies what it means to live, embodied, on the human scale. In *The Human Condition*, Hannah Arendt, drawing upon the sensibility evoked by the invention of the microscope and telescope, says that "we look and live in this society as if we were as far from our human existence as we are from the infinitely small and immensely large, which, even if they could be perceived by the finest instruments, are too far away from us to be experienced."[3] David Roochnik quotes from Donne's "An Anatomy of the World"[4] that this

new philosophy calls all in doubt,
The element of fire is quite put out;
The sun is lost, and th' earth, and no man's wit
Can well direct him where to look for it.
And freely men confess that this world's spent,
When in the Planets, and the Firmament
They seek so many new; then see that this
Is crumbled out again to his Atomies.
'Tis all in pieces, all coherence gone,
All just supply, and all relation

Roochnik puts it this way: "Whether we care to admit it or not, at the end of the day, when we leave our laboratories and turn off the computers and then finally go home we are *anthropoi*"—human, earth-bound beings, who live amidst the concerns and relations that give life a meaning that we must inhabit, or else dissolve into the despair and unmeaning of Donne's "all in pieces, all coherence gone."[5]

One might object that this is just naïve anthropocentrism, but the audacious claim must be that *any* being, even if quite alien to *homo sapiens*, but like ourselves in being able to wonder at and reflect upon the world and itself, is also *human* in the sense of being earthly: grounded and rooted in a particular existence that is mortal and finite, suffused with the gravitational force of involvements that bring it into the meaningful orbit of its affective cares. In *The Crisis of European Sciences and Transcendental Philosophy*, written in 1935, soon after the rise to power of the National Socialists, Edmund Husserl writes that "Galileo *abstracts* from the subjects as a person leading a personal life; he abstracts from all that is in any way spiritual, from all cultural properties which are attached to things in human praxis." In his Vienna lecture of the same year, Husserl proclaims that "I am certain that the European crisis has its roots in a misguided rationalism" that had its beginnings in the telescope of Galileo, luring humankind from the earth to the heavens and to a thinking that led to modern mathematical physics as the understanding of nature:

> Einstein's revolutionary innovations concern the formulae through which the idealized and naively objective *phusis* is dealt with. But how formulae in general, how mathematical objectification in general, receive meaning on the foundation of life and the intuitively given surrounding world—of this we learn nothing; and thus Einstein does not reform the space and time in which our vital life runs its course.[6]

What Husserl here calls "our vital life" is what I am calling existence on *the human scale*. To *be* human, as the root of the word implies, is to be *earthly*; phenomenologically, human life as lived is necessarily geocentric. To inhabit the world is to stand upon the earth as a given, encompassed on all sides by the finite horizon rimming the border between earth and the sky-dome of the heavens. We inhabit the Between *between* earth and sky, the out-in-the-open within which a meaningful world spreads out and greets us as provisionally coherent and navigable as a delimited, bounded cosmos. In one of his earlier readings of the Cave Analogy, Heidegger puts it this way: "Human Dasein, living upon the earth as upon a disk domed over by the heavens, is like living in the cave" (GA 24: 403). Ontologically, we seem imprisoned by a cosmos that confines us to a world of established meaning that we cannot escape.

Yet humans have always desired to break the bonds of earth and to pierce the bounds of sky and leave behind all the stifling contingency of our situated earthliness. As Arendt says about the invention of the airplane, "It is in the nature of the human surveying capacity that it can function only if man disentangles himself from all involvement in and concern with the close at hand and withdraws himself to a distance from everything near him. The greater the distance between himself and his surroundings, world or earth, the more he will be able to survey and to measure and the less will worldly, earth-bound space be left to him."[7] The flight of the bird is an image for freedom. That longing for flight has been fulfilled in the last centuries, first with balloons, then with aircraft that provide genuine aerial mobility. More recently still, rare human beings, astronauts, have indeed broken past the bonds of earthly gravity in space flight. They have seen the earth not as a ground bounded by the horizon of sky but as a sphere suspended in a void, an experience we can share vicariously in photographs taken from outer space. For several generations now, the lure of this final frontier has seized the imagination of many ambitious and gifted writers, scientists, and astronauts, as well as funding from governments eager for prestige. But this aspiration has its disquieting side. In his 1966 *Spiegel* interview, Heidegger brings up the image of Earth taken by an orbiting spacecraft, probably NASA's Lunar Orbiter 1, a month before: "I do not know whether you were terrified, but I certainly was terrified when recently I saw the pictures of the earth taken from the moon. We do not need atomic bombs: the uprooting of human beings is already here" (GA 16: 670; cf. GA 16: 559). We will return to the question of "uprooting" (*Entwurtzelung*) later.[8]

The longing for flight into and even beyond the sky, away from the contingencies and limitations that ground us, embodies what is most ambitious about human-being, what Sophocles called our *tolma*, the daring that wagers all risks, pushing at all boundaries, limited only by death.[9] That longing for the literal abstraction of flight can also lead us into what is most inhuman, into a *hubris* of dislocation and disregard that is out-of-bounds. As the philosopher-soldier J. Glenn Gray reminds us, the most cruel, indifferent, and relentless destruction of the wars of the last century arrived long-distance, carried by air, in the form of artillery, carpet bombing, and atomic weapons. Gray calls such weaponry an aspect of the godlessness of modernity, "that remoteness from reality in warfare that I called abstraction," a "forgetfulness of the encompassing world to which we are so totally bound."[10] Each one of these weapons, as well as other technologies of mass extermination, was first animated by advances in mathematics, chemistry, and the grandest, most cosmically soaring abstractions of theoretical particle physics.[11] At the same time, the longing for flight, to disconnect and see the world 'in theory' from far above, is an existential feature of what it means to be human. By a strange ambiguity of the word *bound*, which means both attached or constrained and underway or destined, we are at once positively and negatively earth-bound, tied to but also grounded by our situated particularity and horizons. We are also sky-bound in the calling to transcendence and to freeing ourselves from our earthly roots. If we forget that we inhabit the Between, nihilism beckons at the extremes of earth and sky: in the narcissistic atavism of the particular or the uprooting abstraction of the universal, the former forgetting our finitude by burrowing into it without reflection, the latter by a heedless negation of our contingency.

1.1 PHILOSOPHY AS ABSOLUTE FREEDOM

Philosophy is absolute freedom.[12] Philosophy necessarily begins in freedom, because the movement from wonder to question to response and back again requires that we give heed to what calls us in our astonishment, departing from the received opinions, expectations, and certainties in which we find ourselves embedded. The freedom of philosophy, as a yearning of flight from our earth-bound contingency, is therefore potentially ridiculous or dangerous or both.

Ridiculous, because, like the Socrates of Aristophanes's *Clouds*, who swings around hoisted in a basket to better observe the heavens at a remove from the earth, philosophy risks such a precipitous rupture from the common sense of everyday understanding that it may stumble into absurdities. Like the tale told by Socrates about Thales falling into a well while on a walk to contemplate the stars (*Theaetetus*, 174a–b), philosophy's starry-eyed ramblings lead to pitfalls and pratfalls.[13] Aristophanes depicts the filthy, impoverished students in Socrates's "Thinkery" (his putative school of instruction) as prostrate, with their faces jammed into the ground, observing the goings-on beneath the Earth, their buttocks raised simultaneously to scan the Heavens, all in the pursuit of a natural science that discards all the received wisdom of myth and tradition.

Dangerous, because the rupture with and departure from received wisdom is not always merely laughable. It may well entail a direct threat to the articles of faith, religious or secular, that bind a community together in a common understanding of the norms by which its members may live a good, or at least a decent, life together.

Aristophanes's parody of the philosophic life astutely portrays the extremes of this project. Socrates's students seek to explain Heaven and Earth, the cosmic whole, with methods that lampoon the incipient natural sciences of the period. Conventional Greeks both mocked and feared these natural philosophers, whose scientific accounts demythologized and desacralized the traditional religious narratives of nature in favor of impersonal, scientific ones. By investigating the sacred beings of Sky and Earth, Ouranos and Gaia, the natural philosophers assume that human reason can make rational sense of the entire universe. In *The Clouds,* the comic arrogance of the students' absurd posture, noses to the ground, bums to the air, masks a tragic threat. Such hubristic probing might unhinge a people entirely from the inherited narratives that make human communities coherent, as we live together in the present and gaze backward and forward to our ancestors and descendants. The myths and stories deserve respect, because the Earth is the inexhaustible repository of hidden wealth on whose mere surface we plant ourselves and cultivate our historical world. Heaven as sky is what rises far above us, yet beckons us to transcendence, a transcendence that both frees us from narrow everydayness and sanctifies it. For Aristophanes, a tragi-comic conservative himself, philosophy's extremism threatens the only coherence in life we can hope for, the living traditions of the stories we tell about ourselves.

The Athenians may well have laughed at the Socrates of Aristophanes's play or at the buffoonish self-importance of Euthyphro, a citizen who claimed such profound insight into things divine that he could prophesize the future (*Euthyphro*, 3b–c). Nevertheless, the Socrates of *The Clouds* ends up burned out of his Thinkery and ejected from the city. Athens put the historical Socrates to death after his conviction on charges of impiety and corrupting the youth. Philosophy, viewed as the freedom to break away from our finite understanding in an attempt to reconstrue it, is a tragi-comedy.

At the end of the *Symposium* (223c–d), Plato has Socrates argue that the greatest poet must be able to compose both tragedies and comedies in order fully to capture the human condition, but the dialogue only tells us *that* Socrates made this argument, not *what* he argued and *how* he argued it. Perhaps that is because to be human means having the freedom to take the risk of this rupture with our finite understanding, but that there is no formula, no argument, to show us the way forward, to navigate between absurdity and hubris, once we have broken with the familiar. But the burden of philosophy is that such a risky freedom is inevitable in the examined life, the life worth living. The task of this book is to argue that such a difficult freedom is equally inescapable whenever we take seriously the *polemos* of our ethical and political lives.

1.2 THE STRIFE BETWEEN EARTH AND WORLD

Heidegger addresses human beings as residing between earth and sky, but much more famous is his discussion of earth and world, especially as a feature of the work of art. For Heidegger, earth and world are in strife (*Streit*) with one another, which Heidegger explicitly, if subtly, connects with the *polemos* of Heraclitus. I do not here provide a comprehensive treatment of these concepts in Heidegger, but rather set forth how they allow us to say what is at stake in the question of situatedness and transcendence. That will lead us to what is at issue in the polemical ethics of being-human.

In his elucidation of Hölderlin's poem "As When on a Holiday," in which the poet speaks of a holy Chaos, Heidegger refers back to Hesiod's divine Chaos, first of the gods.[14] Heidegger insists that this Chaos is not a meaningless jumbling together of things as we think it in modernity. Instead, we must understand Chaos according to its Greek root, which means to yawn open, to gape, to form a chasm. So, writes Heidegger:

> This χάος means above all the yawning, the gaping cleft, the primally self-opening Open, wherein all is swallowed. The cleft denies every support for the distinct and the grounded. And therefore, for all experience that knows only what is derivative, chaos seems to be the undifferentiated, and thus mere disturbance. Nevertheless, the 'chaotic' in this sense is only the degraded and contrary essence of what 'chaos' means. Thinking it in accord with 'nature' (φύσις), chaos remains that gaping apart out of which the Open opens itself and by which this Open grants truth [*gewähre*] to each differentiated thing in a bounded presencing. (GA 4: 62–64)

For Heidegger, *chaos* is therefore akin to *chora*, space in the sense of this Open.[15] It is also etymologically related to *chasma*, a chasm or gulf. It might seem strange and contradictory that *chaos* would be both an abyss that "denies every support for the distinct and the grounded" and the source for the Open of a meaningful world in which "each differentiated thing" whiles away for a time as a "bounded" presence to our historical understanding. Also problematic is imagery of the metaphor: When a chasm opens up, or a mouth or abyss yawns open, does this not depend first on there being sides to the space opened up, just as the Between of the world depends first on there being

Earth and Sky? How can the space come before the contours that define its bounds, like the edge of a precipice or the rim of a horizon? How, in short, can *chaos*, in the sense of this ungrounded space, come *first*?

We must understand this *chaos* ontologically. It is like Lao Tzu's emptiness (無, *wu*), that makes a jug a jug, the emptiness of a wheel's hub that makes it a wheel. Ontically, of course, the potter must form the bounding sides of the pot, the wheelwright must craft the rim, spokes and hub of the wheel, and then the emptiness within each takes shape. Ontologically, however, the jug can only be a jug, the wheel a wheel, because the emptiness at their center gives them the meaning of what they are to be. The bounding walls that contain this emptiness—the ceramic sides of the jug, the wooden or metal hub of the wheel—each only take shape as guided in advance by the emptiness, the potential, that they will contain. In Aristotelean terms, their emptiness is the formal cause that precedes their material production. Just as unmeaning is the latent ground of meaning, emptiness is filled with potential. *Chaos* is first-born because *all* meaning deploys from a ground that is ungrounded, a formless form, that is simply a given: we are always already thrown into a world of meaning as given. That is why, borrowing from Heidegger, we might say that Earth is next-born: there is always already a world of meaning into which we are thrown and on which we must take our situated stand. This is the ontological meaning of the temporal *ekstasis* of the past. Only on its basis, *as* a basis, can the space beneath the heavens open up to us and provide a horizon to our meaningful, future-oriented action in a determinate world.

Starting in the mid-1930s, most famously in "The Origin of the Work of Art" lecture and continuing in his lectures and then-unpublished manuscripts, Heidegger discusses earth and *world*, *Erde* and *Welt*. Less often, but still importantly, Heidegger addresses earth and *sky*, *Erde* and *Himmel*—and in what follows we must understand the German *Himmel*, like the Greek *ouranos*, means at once sky, the heavens, and the heavenly.[16] For example, in a 1955 talk, Heidegger discusses a phrase of the poet Johann Peter Hebel, who wrote that "We are plants, who—we may admit it or not—must arise with their roots from the earth in order to bloom in the aether and to be able to bear fruit." For Heidegger, this means that "Wherever a truly joyful and healthful human work should flourish, there must the human being be able to arise from the depth of the homeland's soil into the heights of the aether. Here, 'aether' means the free air of the high heavens, the open expanse of the spirit" (GA 16: 530).

Let us set aside for a moment the worrying echoes of *Heimat* (homeland) and *Blut und Boden* ("blood and soil") from the Nazi era. Heidegger reads Hebel as speaking "neither just about the earth, nor just about the heavens. He seeks to intimate something else, namely, the region *between* earth and heavens that human beings creatively and patiently inhabit"—and, Heidegger insists, "This Between is the dimension of the human sojourn upon the earth. This open expanse *between* earth and heaven, in which human beings stand and move, is nevertheless not an empty space" but rather a domain of human dwelling (GA 16: 530). Understood ontologically, the Between is not simply a physical space 'under' the sky and 'on' the earth but rather the abode of meaning within which historical human beings inhabit their world. An abode, a dwelling place, is one that finds Hesiod's "firm seat" upon the earth where life can take a stand, inhabiting an intelligible and bounded horizon.

So why does Heidegger speak of earth and *world* as well as earth and *sky*? In these concepts, Heidegger provides us with a compelling foil for a polemical ethics. Heidegger addresses earth and sky through his engagement with Hölderlin, starting in 1934. Through Hölderlin, at the onset of the National Socialist regime, Heidegger seeks to forge a new philosophical language to address and propel what he began then to call "the other inception" to history, an inception in thought to match the revolutionary departure in politics that he at one time believed would serve as a countermovement to the nihilism of the West.[17] "World" is a term Heidegger had deployed since the 1920s as an ontological category of Dasein's existentiality, and he never abandoned it. *World* is not a totality of things; it is the domain of intelligibility that we can inhabit as historical beings and in which things find their place as meaningful to us. To *be* at all, for us, is to *have* a world, to be-in-a-world.

"Earth" as a term of art does not originate in Heidegger's earlier fundamental ontology of Dasein. It derives instead from his efforts at "poetizing-thinking" in conversation with Hölderlin to craft a post-metaphysical language that might take philosophy beyond the supposed limitations of its previous nihilistic metaphysics. At issue in Heidegger's fundamental ontology with the world is how Dasein always operates 'in' an understanding of things and involvement, and in being-human, we do not have to ask why this world of understanding that we inhabit *is* so for it to *be* so. If we do ask, we run up against the sheer thrownness, the brute givenness, of the world we occupy. In *Being and Time*, Heidegger calls this the *nullity* of our thrown existence (SZ, §58). The question is not who or what created the ontic world of things, but rather why ontologically this world has the meaning it does, and has it for me rather than someone else or even no one else. To push behind this ontological question is to stare nullity in the face, to glimpse the hint of the *chaos* that opens the world in the first place as its groundless ground.[18]

In "The Origin of the Work of Art," Heidegger introduces earth as a counter-concept to world. He speaks there of the "strife of world and earth" (*Streit von Welt und Erde*). As Michel Henry says, things in opposition are not absolute contraries, or simply indifferent to one another ("A whale is not opposed to an equation"), because "opposition in general presupposes a bond."[19] Earth and world belong to each other in their strife, a strife that Heidegger explicitly links to Heraclitus's *polemos* fragment (GA 4: 29). He uses a Greek temple as his example of a work that gives a world its comprehensive meaning to a historical people: "The temple, in its standing there, first gives things their look and to human beings their outlook on themselves" (GA 4: 29). It is not that distinct, brute stuff is not 'there' already, but to be a world, things must have a "look" that unites them in a meaningful way to human understanding and activity in their "outlook" upon themselves. Referencing again the *polemos* fragment, Heidegger says that the historical world of a people depends on the struggle (*Kampf*) that distinguishes "what is holy and what unholy, what is great and what petty, what is brave and what cowardly, what is noble and what fickle, what is master and what slave" (GA 4: 29). None of these is a 'natural kind,' if such kinds exist at all, but takes on its meaning as a result of a historical, situated interpretive struggle in language, art, and deed that defines a world of human habitation.

So, world is not simply the same as sky, although more than twenty years later, Heidegger brings the *polemos* fragment to bear on his analysis of "*Hölderlins Erde und Himmel*," where, he says, "The earth is only earth as the earth of heaven, heaven only the heaven insofar as it works its way down and across the earth" (GA 4: 160–61). World, like the heavens, does define the scope of the horizons of meaning that we inhabit, in the sense of living *in* a world of habituation to practices and understandings that encompass our possibilities. We are existentially and temporally a thrown-projection: given over, as thrown, into a world of meaning we did not produce, as having-a-past, but also cast forward by the trajectory of this throw into having-a-future within a horizon of possibilities that are finite but also determinate and intelligible because thus delimited.

But how does earth enter into this temporal dynamic, and—contentiously, polemically—into a struggle with world? Heidegger says that earth is not physical mass or the dirt under our feet or the planet Earth in the solar system (GA 4: 28). He connects earth with *phusis*, what emerges unbidden into meaningful presence to the understanding. Furthermore, Heidegger relates both earth and world to a polemical truth as he understands it ontologically, as *a-lētheia*, *Unverborgenheit*, un-concealment, which is to say, to what makes it possible for us to be who we are, and things what they are, and accessible to understanding in a meaningful world: "The essence of truth is in itself the primal strife [*Urstreit*] in which that open center [*offene Mitte*] is struggled forth [*erstritten*] and into which beings stand forth and from which they set themselves back" (GA 5: 42). This "center" (*Mitte*), which in later texts he calls the Between, the *Zwischen*, Heidegger describes here as the open region, the clearing or illumined realm, *Lichtung*, in which intelligibility as such becomes manifest and a world of beings can come to presence for us. As this Between, it is akin to the *chaos* that first allows earth and sky to take shape, support, and encompass us, but just as readily threatens to swallow us whole—about which more in a moment. Crucial is what Heidegger says next: "To this open region belongs a world and the earth. But the world is not simply the open region [*das Offene*], which corresponds to the clearing, and the earth is not the closed region [*das Verschlossene*], which corresponds to concealment" (GA 5: 42).

This is, admittedly, rather obscure to anyone not well versed in Heidegger's idiolect, but it helps to bear in mind what is at-issue, namely, what makes possible that we understand meaning at all, that a world be *open* to us, not as a pile of inert if distinct things but as beings that matter to us integrally as the situated, historical beings we are. Concealment and refusal are bound up with this openness because *a* world of meaning is not *the* world in the sense of a final, absolute world about which everything has been revealed and in which there are no further possibilities of meaning. Concealed in each world and from each world are other possible worlds, not in the sense of the multiverse of theoretical physics, but in the sense of worlds of meaning that might involve all the same 'stuff' we now have an outlook upon, but assembling its meaning in a profoundly other interpretation, as if in the turn of the kaleidoscope. We cannot *be* in all such worlds at once, given our finitude.

So, Heidegger says that "World and earth are constantly, inherently, and according to their essence in strife, by nature strife-torn. Only as such do they step forth into the strife of clearing and concealing" (GA 5: 42). Why? One way to think of this is to remember what the Greeks certainly knew from long experience: that the temple Heidegger describes is vulnerable to *earthquake*, the prerogative of Poseidon, the earth-shaker (*Poseidōn ennosigaios* or *enosikhthōn*). The ground can shift beneath our feet, the world of a given historical understanding can suddenly (*exaiphnēs*) shudder, shake, and collapse, the horizon can shift, and the sky can, figuratively, fall by bringing our world crashing down around us. The clearing that once opened up the world for us may swallow that world whole, and us with it in the sense of being deprived off a nexus of meaning that makes sense and that matters to us. This is why Heidegger, in a later note to the passage quoted above, wrote that the *Urstreit*, the primal strife, the *polemos*, is the *Ereignis*, the event that inaugurates and appropriates a new world of truth for historical understanding (GA 5: 42fnA).

Furthermore, to explain this bond in strife between earth and world, Heidegger says, "Earth can do no else but jut up through the world, and world grounds itself only upon the earth, so long as truth happens as the primal strife between clearing and concealing" (GA 5: 42)—the *a-* against *-lēthē*, the *Un-* against *verbogenheit*, and the *un-* against *concealment*. No world of meaning is ever simply static; the horizon is always *pro-visional*, the sense that things make is never totally complete, and what we do not yet understand may reveal itself more fully—or it may undo us with unmeaning. Our world of meaning is grounded on the earth in the sense that our having-a-past, our thrownness into a prevailing world of meaning, is given in a way we can never get behind to make, as it were, our birth our own decision, creating *ex nihilo* the entire world of meaning for ourselves. The earth juts up into the world wherever we can be compelled into confrontation with whatever we do not fully understand. This is the heart of our *polemical* situatedness as historical beings: that the world as it makes sense to us also drives us to confront interpretively what does not, yet, make sense—and the resolution of this 'yet' is forever postponed in the primal strife. As worldly, we seek ever to broaden the scope of the clearing; as earthly, we must be at once grateful to and at the mercy of the sheer question-worthiness and obscurity of what is and of what we are, an interrogation that threatens ever and suddenly to throw our world off balance. The primal strife, the *polemos*, of being-human is the ever-again of interpretation and reinterpretation, facing down and facing up to the destruction of earthquakes in meaning and the reconstruction that must follow if we are still to have an abode in a historical world, lest the earth open up and swallow us whole, as it did Oedipus.

1.3 THE FLIGHT OF ICARUS

In Ovid's *Metamorphoses*, just before embarking on their escape from the prison of King Minos, the legendary inventor and artist Daedalus warns his son Icarus to fly a middle path between sea and sky, *inter utrumque vola*, to avoid the damp of the waves and the heat of the sun on the wings he had devised from wood and wax and feathers. But in their flight, Icarus becomes enraptured and leaves his father's side:

> *Cum puer audaci coepit gaudere volatu*
> *Deseruitque ducem caelique cupidine tractus*
> *Altius egit iter.*

> When the boy began to rejoice in his daring flight
> And deserted his leader, drawn by a longing for the sky,
> He beat a higher path.[20]

The myth of Icarus is an ancient one, from at least the sixth century BCE.[21] King Minos of Crete had employed Daedalus, the legendary inventor, technician, sculptor, and engineer, to design and oversee the building of the Labyrinth, where the king hid the Minotaur. In most versions of the myth, Minos later imprisoned Daedalus and his son Icarus for assisting Theseus of Athens to kill the Minotaur and escape the Labyrinth, because Minos's daughter Ariadne had fallen in love with Theseus. That phrase of Ovid's, *caelique cupidine tractus*—drawn by a longing for the sky, points to what has always been so arresting about the myth: that longing for an ever-upward flight as an escape into a kind of absolute freedom, to soar with all the grace of a bird above the earth, almost as if unbound by natural laws. Of course, for Icarus, the unchecked longing for a freedom that transcends all earthly attachments and worries leads to disaster, for the sun melts his wings and he falls to his death in the sea.

The flight of Icarus is potent as myth because it captures the miraculous 'between' of the human condition, the *inter* of Ovid's *inter utrumque vola*, the flight *between* earth and sky. Being-human is a miraculous flight, because being-here has no *verifiable* explanation, no way for any of us to account empirically for why I am someone rather than no one or for why there is something rather than nothing. That the world be a meaningful one to us, and not just what William James called a "blooming, buzzing confusion" or Nietzsche "the chaos of sensations," may seem a given in the ordinariness of our everyday doings, but we cannot confirm what or who gives the given.[22] We simply leap off into the *trust* that our given understanding of things as what they are will hold us aloft after we jump into our daily routines. Like Icarus, we may well fall by suffering some breakdown, and few, if any, may notice. Haunting our being-human is the possibility of what the poets W. H. Auden and William Carlos Williams called, respectively, the "forsaken cry" and the "splash quite unnoticed" of Icarus's fall and the lonely meaningless-ness of it beyond one's own suffering.[23] In Heidegger, it is the angst in the face of the groundless ground of our own unaccountable thrownness into the happenstance of a particular historical world of meaning.

The "longing for the sky" that draws, or drags, Icarus upwards towards the sun, the *caelique cupidine tractus*, is the human lure of transcendence. In Latin, *cupido* is a desire, an eagerness, a passion, a longing for some-thing; it is inspired by the god Cupid, the counterpart to the Greek Eros. The overwhelming longing of love is the one thing that Socrates says he does know (*Symposium*, 177d), because love is a lack, and he knows what he lacks and what it means to lack, to yearn, and to seek—*zetein*. We make our compromises and settle into an understanding of the world, as Daedalus did at Knossos after building the Labyrinth for King Minos. But even so, some intimation of freedom, like Theseus arriving in secret to slay the monster Minotaur, may break in upon us. We can ignore that break-in of something unaccountable that threatens a breakdown of our dependable understanding of the world; or, like Daedalus, we can heed it and dare an escape from a world that has become a Labyrinth, a maze that amazes us with its sudden confusion and the stifling sense that there is no way out, an *aporia*. To-be-human, an earthling, is to have some *inkling* that there might be some Other, some new and as-yet inconceivable understanding of a meaning still beyond us, if we break away to transcend the bonds of received opinion and routine. We can fail to notice, turn away, ignore, or repress this inkling, but that is to belie the human condition by living a life *unexamined*, fearful of the irruption of the ontologically miraculous that breaks us down and bodes something Other.

In confrontation with Heidegger, we must use the word *transcendence* cautiously. Heidegger insists in many places that the problem of transcendence is about how it is possible that we be open to and out in a world of meaning. For example: "Being-in-the-world belongs to the fundamental constitution of that being that is in each instance my own, that in each instance I *my-self* am. Self and world belong together, they belong to the unity of the constitution of Dasein and define equiprimordially the 'subject.' In other words, the being that we in each instance ourselves are, Dasein, is the *transcendent*" (GA 24: 423). Heidegger seeks to dissolve the Cartesian conundrum of how we, as subjects, can have knowledge of a world 'out there' by stepping across, transcending, from the internality of the self to be 'in' an external world. Inspired by Kant's transcendental philosophy (GA 24: 423), which seeks the conditions for any possible experience, Heidegger says that we, Dasein, *are* the *transcendent* as such, because as Dasein, as being (*-sein*) here (*Da-*), we are always already 'out' and 'in' the world, stepping (*-scending*) beyond (*trans-*) ourselves in a historical context of meaning that we have been thrown into and that already makes a provisional sense. The burden of Heidegger's existential analytic of Dasein is to show how what he calls the *existentiales*, as features of the hermeneutical understanding, serve to embed us in the always-already of a world of meaning. Transcendence for Heidegger is therefore *not* what he comes to oppose as *metaphysics*: an account of a reality that subsists beyond (*meta-*) worldly beings (*ta phusika*). This metaphysics he dismisses: "The transcendent, according to the popular philosophical meaning of the word, is otherworldly beings" (GA 24: 424). Such an account of a transcendent reality would be a form of Platonism, where the truth of things resides not in our immediate experience of an ever-changing world, but rather rises beyond it, trans-ascends it, in some heavenly realm of supra-sensory forms and ideas and the good that exists eternally, outside of time, and which we can only apprehend with the mind's eye.

At-issue in the confrontation between Plato and Heidegger is transcendence and whether the notion of a meaning that transcends our finite, historical situatedness makes any sense at all, or if it is a nihilistic delusion that slanders the only world we will ever have, as messy and inconstant as it may be. In this confrontation, my conception of situated transcendence, as a theme immersed in the Platonic dialogues, is deeply indebted to Drew Hyland's reading of a "finite transcendence" in Plato as a strategy,

> that does not pretend that our finitude can be comprehensively overcome, yet does not on the other hand possibly capitulate to it. This is to acknowledge and understand the finitude as what it is, to recognize it in its depth and complexity, but to respond to that limiting condition by transforming it into possibility, to engage in what we may call 'finite transcendence.'[24]

It is not that Heidegger denies an otherness to Being. Quite the contrary, he commits much attention to the Greek *deinon*, the awesomely terrible and astonishing, to the overpowering sway of *phusis*, nature, and to our *Unheimlichkeit*, our uncanniness, our homelessness even in the midst of our being-situated in a given world of familiar meaning, our habitation. Heidegger traces these disorienting features of Dasein's hermeneutical existentiality back to the nullity, the *Nichtigkeit*, of our existence, the usually only dim awareness that our very being-here, and all the meaning and attachments to the ground we stand on, is grounded on nothing, that we cannot get behind the throw of our being thrown into *this* place, *this* time, *this* body, *this* historical concatenation of language, tradition, and relationships. For Heidegger, our finitude necessarily means the fraying at the edges of our understanding, the impossibility of keeping meaning together as a whole. We may bump up against this uncanniness of an angst in the face of the Nothing in either the most trivial or most momentous of events.

What such an experience emphatically does not do is grant us access to a Beyond, something that transcends us as an otherworld. All is immanence for Heidegger, not as an inward subjectivity that we must overcome to 'be' in the world (GA 24: 424–26), because there is no eternal, stable, otherworldly realm that we can ascend into that explains the meaningfulness of a world that we always already *are* in. Nevertheless, Heidegger says that "*Being is the* transendens *pure and simple*. The transcendence of the Being of Dasein is distinct in that this transcendence involves the possibility and necessity of the most radical *individuation*" (SZ, 38). Without transcendence in this sense of already being out into a world of meaning that makes a world of sense to us, there would be no world for us to be 'in' at all. *But this is the specific world of an individuated historical meaning for specific human-being.* The finitude that characterizes our being-human defines us as worldly beings, as both having and being in a world *immanently*. This is not transcendence to an absolute or radically other plane. We always-already transcend to a finite situated Here of meaningful existence that can be challenged, broken down, enlarged, and so on in hermeneutical confrontation, but never becomes infinite so long as we are human-being. Therefore, authenticity in the examined life can only result in a deeper sense of our own historicity through a *polemos* with the given, and through that, an insight into possibilities handed down but overlooked by our given past and that we can appropriate in projecting a meaningful future as our own, rather than as something by which we are merely swept along.

At stake in the relationship between finitude and transcendence is freedom and its role in ethics and politics, as well as in philosophy itself. What I want to argue as the distinctive feature of ethical life, and to show phenomenologically through a reading of the *Republic*, is that we can and do have intimations of other possible meanings that transcend the constellation of opinions and practices that for the most part so absorb us, and that we can and do have access to such meaning beyond the given that we might bring back to transform the world as we have known it. At issue is not an ontic otherworld of things truer than those of this world, but rather an ontological other-world of transformed meaning. We can affirm in faith, deny, or remain agnostic about whether there is an 'otherworld' somehow 'beyond' this one. I will not take a position on that question, only that we are driven by a longing to transcend the given. Heidegger might say the same, given his analysis of uncanniness that we will examine in chapter 8, but at-issue is the ethical status of the *idea*. If not Plato's idea then something like it is essential to the phenomenological encounter with a transformative otherness and to the ethical beings that we are. Philosophy entails the possibility that we can break free of the bonds of opinion and attain truth. We understand our freedom phenomenologically in terms of this possibility to rise, like Icarus, beyond the bonds that hold us down. The question to address is how we can avoid the fate of Icarus in flying too close to the sun and, instead, fly like Daedalus between earth and sky.

1.4 SUN AND SOIL

As earth and sky serve as concrete images for the phenomenon of the interrelated polemics of situatedness and transcendence in being-human, there are two subsidiary images that have their place in each domain: sun and soil. These two elements play key roles in the confrontation between the two protagonists of this study: soil for Heidegger and sun for Plato.

As an image for situatedness, soil is particularly fitting. Soil is the face of the earth, that part of the earth with which human beings have the most contact under the dome of sky and as what most immediately supports life. As an image for the thrownness of our historical existence, earth corresponds to what Heidegger calls the nullity of this thrownness. The sheer fact that the givenness of your situatedness, in this body, at this place and time, is ultimately inexplicable as yours and not someone else's, even if we could trace the physical chain of causes from parents to Big Bang. This is like the earth: No matter how deeply I dig the ground or how minutely I split a stone, I cannot expose everything concealed within the earth to light, because it would then be annihilated as earth. Earth is inherently self-concealing, where we bury our secrets and our dead, expecting them never to be revealed. As earth's outer face, though, soil beckons and flatters us with the illusion of taking possession of the earth, even if such possession is ultimately impossible. Soil is how the withdrawn and boundless earth presents a fertile, life-giving face to ordinary human existence.

Because we live so enmeshed with the soil, we take it for granted, just as we generally take the inexplicable contingency of existence for granted, sometimes to the extreme of forgetting our dependency upon it by ravaging and polluting the earth. Soil sustains us in life, quite literally as the earth beneath our feet, and also as the ground in which we grow crops, plant our gardens, build foundations for our homes, and bury our dead. If earth is a basis in the sense of the inexplicable thrownness of historical meaning that we can never fully expose, that may break open our meaningful world in earthquakes we cannot control, then soil is the surface of things that makes everyday life accessible. To be human also means to stand *here*, upon some particular, situated soil in a specific place and time that has its own concrete and personal meaning for us as the landscape of our involvements and memories. When we speak of settling down somewhere, truly inhabiting it and making it a home, we say we are *putting down roots*. Whether for good or ill, soil defines the embeddedness of situated human-being, the sheer givenness of what is one's own, even if we resist exploring beneath this surface.

Unlike the soil, which is the earth under *my* feet, the sun shines down universally upon us all, a role acknowledged at least as early as the Sun-god Aten in the monotheistic religion of the pharaoh Akhenaten (reigned c. 1353–1336 BCE): "Whenever you are risen upon the eastern horizon / you fill every land with your perfection. . . . Although you are far away, your rays are upon the land."[25] When risen, the sun's light and warmth coax life from the soil everywhere. Both distant in form and close in effect, the sun belongs to everyone and to no one. We feel it but cannot touch it. We see it but cannot look at it, at least not safely or for long. So, despite its detachment from us, we nevertheless apprehend it and recognize we could not live without it. This is the sun that Socrates describes in the Allegory of the Cave, which the escaped prisoner comes to realize "is in a certain way the cause of those things he and his companions had been seeing" (516c) back in the cave, as well as of all that exists in the outside world; its light makes the world comprehensible in both the distinction among things and the interrelation of things. The sun, then, is an image for the transcendence of being-human that we feel but do not fully know in our longing for something that simultaneously illuminates and lifts us out of our contingency and attachments, while uniting us in what is universal to human-being and even with the cosmos as a whole, as when an astronomer contemplates the vastness of the heavens and gratefully, or at least without regret, forgets her own miniscule rootedness in an earthly contingency. This is the liberating, sky-bound rapture of a contemplation that even in otherwise miserable circumstances can lift us out of ourselves in the study of a microbe or a distant galaxy or a poem or a mathematical theorem or a philosophical question or text.

We will discuss the Plato's sun later, so now a word about soil and Heidegger. In a critical dialogue with Emmanuel Faye, I argued that the confrontation with Heidegger points us to something important about being-human that we must take seriously, even if he distorted it and even if we must rethink it for ourselves: *rootedness*. Faye took exception to this claim, because the whole language of *uprootedness* (*Entwurzelung*) and *soil* (*Boden*) played a key role in what Werner Klemperer has called the *Lingua Tertii Imperii*, the language of the Third Reich in Germany under National Socialism, especially in the slogan *Blut und Boden* (Blood and Soil).[26] The organic metaphor of that slogan served to combine the notions of a *people*, a *Volk*, united by blood and racial identity, and of a *homeland* (*Heimat*), as rooted to a particular soil, a fertile territory bonded to the blood of the people by its history and traditions. For the Nazis, both blood and soil were threatened with contamination and *uprooting* by the cosmopolitanism, the commercialism, and the superficiality of modern life, represented in persons by the Jews and in places by the cities, with their soil paved over by concrete.

Faye is certainly right that when Heidegger waxed most enthusiastic about the National Socialist revolution, he also spoke the language of blood and soil. In one seminar, for example, he talked of "Semitic nomads"—a thinly veiled reference to Jews—who would never have a connection to "the nature of our German space" (NGS, 82).[27] In the Black Notebooks of the early 1930s, around the start of the Third Reich, Heidegger explores how enrootedness might be restored to the people, how Germany might achieve its *Boden-ständigkeit*, its standing firmly rooted in the soil (GA 94: 38–40). In another entry, Heidegger writes: "The projection of Being as time overcomes

everything prior in Being and in thinking; not idea, but rather task; not release, but rather binding. The projection does not dissolve itself into pure
Spirit, but rather first opens and binds blood and soil to readiness for action
and to the *capacity* for effectiveness and *work*" (GA 94: 127; but cf. 181).
This is revealing, because unlike in Plato, where the ideas draws us to transcendence as a liberating "release" from the cave's bonds, Heidegger focuses
on "task" as what constitutes a "binding" (*Bindung*) to the intense blood and
soil particularity of a people's historical cave. For Heidegger, freedom is
release *for* the authentic realization of one's boundedness.

Such evidence is important for understanding Heidegger's support for
National Socialism as a countermovement to a putatively nihilistic liberal
universalism overrunning the planet. But what is important for this inquiry
is not Heidegger the man and how his thought is entangled with his politics;
rather, it is to expose, through a confrontation with that thought, what is at-
issue for our own thinking. As I wrote in my response to Faye, the metaphor
of rootedness in the earth is not the private property of Heidegger or the
National Socialists, nor does it lead inexorably to fascism. I cited a passage
in *The Need for Roots*, written in 1943 by Simone Weil, the philosopher and
anti-fascist, when she was working for the Free French cause and envisioning
the reconstruction of her country after victory:

> To be rooted is perhaps the most important and least recognized need of the hu-
> man soul. It is one of the hardest to define. A human being has roots by virtue
> of his real, active, and natural participation in the life of a community which pre-
> serves in living shape certain particular treasures of the past and certain particu-
> lar expectations for the future. This participation is a natural one, in the sense
> that it is automatically brought about by the place, conditions of birth, profes-
> sions and social surroundings. Every human being needs to have multiple roots.
> It is necessary for him to draw well-nigh the whole of his moral, intellectual
> and spiritual life by way of the environment of which he forms a natural part.[28]

The metaphor of soil and roots is "a natural one" because the temporality
of being-human involves *phusis* in the sense of a spontaneous upsurge and
growth, as a plant emerges from the soil. To be human at all means having
a past that *in-forms* us, that serves as the nourishing soil in which a properly
constructive understanding of the world may be embedded and rooted. This
is not craven submission to the past and to tradition, because the future demands drawing upon this past as a "treasure" in the sense of a resource both
cherished and expended in *living*—that is, in confronting new circumstances
and thereby adapting those traditions interpretively to preserve and transform
them, even in modest everyday practices. Roots are how we draw upon the
soil of the past to emerge into the open, into the light of day—but it is the

sunlight that draws us forth. This is why Weil says that participation in the community is "wellnigh" (*presque*, nearly) all we draw upon for our "moral, intellectual, and spiritual life," because we must also transcend the intimate particularity of our roots to engage in the polemical and reconstructive reappropriation of the past for the sake of the future.

The contemporary feminist thinker, bell hooks, puts it this way in a chapter on "Touching the Earth" in her book *Belonging: A Culture of Place*:

> When we love the earth, we are able to love ourselves fully. I believe this. The ancestors taught it was so. As a child I loved playing in dirt, in that rich Kentucky soil, that was a source of life. Before I understood anything about the pain and exploitation of the southern system of sharecropping, I understood that grown-up black folks loved the land. I could stand with my grandfather Daddy Jerry and look out at fields of growing vegetables, tomatoes, corn, collards, and know that this was his handiwork. I could see the look of pride on his face as I expressed wonder and awe at the magic of growing things.[29]

For hooks, a passion for justice is rooted in the life-giving love of place and belonging in a "soil" that both nourishes community and provides a context for understanding what exploits and degrades it. Her own struggles for racial justice emerge from these roots in a profoundly embedded situatedness. Having what Weil calls "multiple roots" is also why we are always *polemically* disposed, never *simply* rooted. We are always *exposed* to entanglement and conflicts among these roots of our identities, having to engage in ongoing interpretive disentanglement, healing, and repair. Weil envisions a freedom that knits together both the obligations of interdependency rooted in circumstance and the rights pertaining to us as persons who transcend the accidents of our particular situatedness. The sun, as an image for the call of transcendence, is what energizes the resources we draw upon from the soil of the past. Just as a plant cannot exist without its soil, being-human cannot exist without an organic past that meaningfully informs a situated understanding. But to grow and adapt to circumstances, we must reach for the light that allows us to gain perspective and then reflect upon and transform meaning through confrontation. This is our human photosynthesis.

The danger, as with Icarus, lies in a nihilism at the extremes. The cry of "Blood and soil!" reemerged in the United States at the "Unite the Right" rally in Charlottesville in 2017, where Nazis, neo-Confederates, and alt-right allies marched with flaming torches. When soil and blood are united in a conception of community as an atavistic belonging to an exclusive, embodied race, entrenched in a closed tradition, then fascism is at the door. This form of chthonic nihilism denies the light of the sun as a call to transcendence that can illuminate all human-being as sharing in a universal, yet properly polemical, dialogue about meaning, life, and justice, rather than an exclusive bond to an equally exclusive slice of soil as a homeland. The sun that shines on all intimates that in transcendence, human communities need not be utterly incommensurate, that there is hope for constructive dialogue across the borders of rootedness in tradition, because each tradition also must confront itself as temporal and finite, and therefore ever in need of reconstruction.

At the other extreme, a fixation on the sun, a yearning for a detached and distant perspective that rises above the messy contingency of historical existence, presents another form of nihilism. In recoiling from embedded contingency out of impatience, embarrassment, or revulsion, this solar nihilism denies the earth-bound aspect of being-human by finding solace only in abstraction from a rooted existence. It imagines it can be entirely liberated from the organic human need for roots, from the particularity of historical belonging and tradition that informs our everyday, embodied existence. At its most extreme, this nihilism denies any meaning whatsoever to being-human: radical trans-humanists refuse to be bound to the accidents of embodiment as *homo sapiens*, envisioning instead a post-human future where sentient entities would be entirely free to design their own incarnation, tearing humanity up by the roots. What such hubris ignores is that no inner-worldly being can be the Creator-God of the totality of its own existence, a master over contingency, immune to the fatal accidents and fateful attachments of finitude.[30] Any living being, of whatever species, that would be *like us* (*Republic*, 515a)—in a capacity to respond to wonder, to reflect interpretively upon itself and its world, and to *articulate* its reflections with others in dialogue—would be 'human' in this larger sense of rising to its reflection only out of an organic, earthly contingency of embodiment that it could never get fully behind and control. Transcendence, to arise at all, is dependent upon a situatedness that it dynamically and dialogically confronts.

While it may seem strange to say, the human-being, like Heidegger's Dasein, is not limited to *homo sapiens* as a biological species. This is not a concession to trans-humanism as a frontal assault on our contingency as such, only an admission that there may be others like us, in forms we have not yet met or recognized, because all life must be both bound and enlivened by the specificity of its finite material embodiment. The nihilism of solar abstraction converts Weil's "treasure" into a fool's good, either to be dissolved as an obstruction to the distance required for a detached perspective or, at its worst, to be used as a mere resource, stripped of all affective significance and concern, of all love and loyalty, to be disposed in the manipulation of all resources, humans included. The polemical challenge of being-human, as a situated transcendence, is to navigate a course between sun and soil, recognizing both as essential to but neither as exhaustive of what we and the world are, and

using practical wisdom to strike the right balance in each interpretive, reconstructive encounter with the situation one inhabits. How this may properly be
accomplished is the theme of subsequent volumes in this project.

1.5 CONSTRUALS OF MEANING

Before proceeding to a confrontation between Plato and Heidegger on the
meaning of the Allegory of the Cave, it is worth elaborating on why being-
human is constitutively confrontational in how we interpret and navigate our
historical world of meaning. The Allegory is about how interpretation itself is
inherently confrontational, or polemical, and how this relates to ethics, politics, truth, and Being. A pivotal text is a section in Heidegger's 1927 lecture
course, *The Fundamental Problems of Phenomenology*: "The Methodological
Character of Ontology: The Three Fundamental Elements of the Phenomenological Method." Here he explains his famous starting point: that the study of
Being must begin with the analysis of the being *who* has an understanding of
Being—namely, ourselves, Dasein. Heidegger names the three components of
the analysis of Dasein, as the path to addressing the question of Being, *reduction, construction*, and *destruction*. While his discussion ostensibly deals with
the methodology of phenomenology as a properly scientific discipline of the
study of Being, this method is not simply an academic one for application in
a subfield of philosophy. It is also a description of our way of being-human.

    Reduction is a term that Heidegger takes from Husserl. He deliberately ap-
propriates this term, rather than simply borrowing it, because in this lecture
course of 1927, the same year as the publication of *Being and Time*, Heidegger wants to demonstrate both his continuity with the phenomenology of
his erstwhile mentor and to clarify his own decisive departure: "With this [i.e.,
phenomenological reduction], we are adopting the wording of a central term
in Husserl's phenomenology, but not its content" (GA 24: 29).[31] For Husserl,
as Heidegger says in the lecture course, phenomenological reduction is "the
method of taking phenomenological vision and leading it from the natural attitude of human beings, living amidst the world of things and persons, back to
the transcendental life of consciousness and its noetic-noematic experiences
[that is, the confirmation in experience of a conception of an object as projected by consciousness] in which objects constitute themselves as correlates
of consciousness" (GA 24: 29). Emphasizing the Latin root of re-duction as a
leading-back, Heidegger distinguishes his phenomenological reduction from
Husserl's. He is endeavoring to make sense of the meaning of Being, but "Being is in each case the Being of beings, and therefore it becomes accessible at
first only by way of starting with some being" (GA 24: 29).

The analytic of Dasein, the kind of being that we are, therefore, is not done simply for its own sake but as a way to lead to an understanding of Being as such. *"For us,"* says Heidegger, contrasting his approach to Husserl's, "phenomenological reduction means leading the phenomenological vision from the comprehension of a being, in whatever form it takes, back to the understanding of Being (as projected upon the manner of its unconcealment) of this being" (GA 24: 29). Husserl wanted to derive knowledge of pure eidetic forms of entities through his reduction, a knowledge that would transcend the vagaries of the natural consciousness in its absorption with everyday things. Heidegger seeks to understand Being precisely *as it is manifested in the understanding* that interprets its everyday world, the understanding that is ours as being-human. This *manifestation* of meaning connects Heidegger's reduction to his conception of truth as *unconcealment*, the opening up of a historical domain of sense and meaning, that is itself in turn a manifestation of the way we *are* in the everyday world that we always already provisionally understand. Heidegger does not want to leave the "natural attitude" behind but dig deeper into it in order to see what is presupposed and unspoken in it. For example, a particular object might register to us as an armchair rather than as a throne, but what is it about the historicity of the understanding that makes it meaningfully revealed to us this way? There is nothing to the brute object that necessitates this interpretation.

This leads Heidegger to phenomenological *construction*. Re-duction, leading-back from beings to Being, as the domain of meaning formation, is not yet a positive accomplishment, because "Being does not become accessible in the way a being does; we do not simply discover it lying at hand, but rather it must, as will be shown, be brought into view in a free projection. We designate this projection of a being, which is already given, upon its Being and the structures of its Being as *phenomenological construction*" (GA 24: 29–30). In this rather dense passage, Heidegger indicates what he will go on to accomplish in his existential analytic of Dasein in this lecture course and then more fully in *Being and Time*: the elaboration of the existential categories of a being such as ourselves in order to illuminate how Being informs our being-human. We understand what it means to be as *Being-in-the-world* in terms of care, temporality, historicity, which Heidegger holds are among the existential structure by which Being construes a meaningful world for us.

The positive *construction* as an exposition of these existential structures will not be possible without a *destruction*, however, because the whole history of philosophy inhibits a clear phenomenological insight into the question of Being: "The reservoir of fundamental philosophical concepts from the philosophical tradition is still today so influential that the repercussions of this tradition can hardly be exaggerated" (GA 24: 31). Words that now have become commonplace to us once had a beginning as jarring concepts in their day, ripped from everyday usage and given a distinct philosophical meaning. For example, one of the most important is the word *idea*, which Socrates and Plato took from everyday language—something that has been seen—and elevated to a metaphysical, epistemological, and ethical keyword; there is also *ousia* in Plato and in Aristotle, which in ordinary Greek means one's resources, both in character and wealth, in the sense that we might describe someone as "a person of substance," but which became a philosophical term meaning *substance* in the sense of a thing's essence as what defines its being, usually in terms of an *eternal* essence, such as the Platonic idea. But the everydayness of such words obscures how profoundly the historical force of the tradition may inhibit a new departure in responding to the question of what it means *to be*: "This is why there necessarily belongs to the conceptual interpretation of Being and its structures, that is, to a reductive construction [*zur reduktiven Konstruktion*] of Being, a *destruction* [*Destruktion*], that is, a critical dismantling [*Abbau*] of the inherited concepts—which at first must be employed—down to the sources from which they have been drawn" (GA 24: 31).

Although such inherited concepts can inhibit us, there is no escaping history: they "at first must be employed" because they are the way we have habitually addressed the questions that hit us. There is no alternative to employing them provisionally until we have analyzed those concepts by breaking them down in the Greek sense of *ana-lusis*, dis-assembling something into its component parts in order better to understand how they work together to make it what it is. Only after this dismantling might we be free to reassemble the components and forge a new meaning for a philosophical vocabulary. This reformation of conceptual apparatus is precisely what Heidegger attempts throughout his career in order to open up new avenues for philosophy. We see this in the terminology of the *Being and Time* period that is initially so jarring, with terms like *Being-in-the-world* as an alternative to consciousness or *unconcealment* for truth or *Wesung* (essencing) as an ontological alternative to metaphysical essence (*ousia, Wesen*)—and then even more radically in his middle and later periods, where he uses terms like *Ereignis* (event) or the *Ge-stell* (the en-framing) to describe aspects of Being's self-presentation in history that he thinks have never been adequately addressed in philosophy.

Heidegger insists that there is not only a unity to the "reductive construction" of the question, but that:

These three fundamental elements of the phenomenological method—reduction, construction, destruction—belong together inherently and must be grounded in their inherent relation. Construction in philosophy is necessarily destruction, that is, a dismantling of what has been handed down, carried out through a historical return back [*Rückgang*] to the tradition; this means neither a negation of the tradition nor a condemnation of it as rubbish [*Verurteiling . . . zur Nichtigkeit*: damning it to oblivion], but to the contrary a positive appropriation of it. (GA 24: 31)

While Heidegger addresses this triad in the context of his specific ontological task of addressing the question of Being, he also asserts that it applies to all "philosophical insight" as intertwined with historical insight (GA 24: 31). The "history of philosophy" is not merely a matter of information about the concepts, arguments, and treatises of the tradition as "some expedient and easy subject to prepare for exams" (GA 24: 31–32), because that history is not a sideshow of idle curiosity to philosophy, as the history of alchemy might be to the modern science of chemistry. The history determines the horizon of how the fundamental questions matter to us at all: how they strike us through wonder in the first place; how we then pose them and compose ourselves to respond to them; and finally how we *do* answer them and then seek to reintegrate those answers into a larger comprehension of the world, which in turn may lead to more questions, pathways of inquiry, results or dead ends— because only a moribund conception of philosophy endeavors to conclude the helicoidal cycle of its questioning once and for all.

While he does not make this so apparent in the *Fundamental Questions* lecture course, which aspires to a more detached and scientific cast of doing phenomenology, we must recall that for the Heidegger of the 1920s, the question of the meaning of Being is intimately bound up with the question of "my 'I am.'"[32] This is not solely about Heidegger's initial, intense rejection of the prevailing academic philosophy of the time, which he deemed to have lost contact with the meaningfulness of life as it is lived. Also at stake in the question of the meaning of Being is the question of what it means *to be* for the being that asks that question, the being he calls Dasein—or simply *us*: I writing this, you reading it, as somehow present to each other, through but beyond ink on page or pixels on screen. It is not just the academic-philosophical question of Being that 'is' historical, it is we, too, who are. Being-human, as Dasein, is defined by the triad of reduction, construction, and destruction.

These three words rhyme, both in English and in German, which emphasizes their interrelation as moments of the intertwining interpretative response to anything facing us. While these 'structure'-words all derive from the Latin compounds *struere* and prefixes, what unites these meanings may usefully be referred back to the older Indo-European root: *ster-*, meaning *to spread*. That root has cognates in English words such as *strew* and *street*, and in related words in other languages such as *Streusel* in German, *perestroika* in Russian, and *stratos* (multitude, army, expedition) in Greek, from which English has *strategy*. The thread connecting these words is the connotation of distribution in space in some greater or lesser order, which clearly underlies words such as *structure, construction,* and, as their negation, *destruction*. This spatial meta-phoric also informs how this word-family describes cognition, just as a spatial metaphoric informs *under-stand*; for example, consciousness has a *structure* that explains the relations and hierarchies of self-aware cognition: a *con-struct* is a representation that brings together related features of a phenomenon into an orderly whole that allow us to make better sense of diverse instances of a thing and experiences with it. When we *construe*, we always construe something *as* something in an interpretation that articulates its meaning within a larger structural whole that makes sense to us. Construal is the meaning-making process by which we fit things and actions into the larger architectonic of our historical inhabitation of a world that has significance for us.

All understanding, and not just the specialized understanding of the question of the meaning of Being, is structural in this extended sense. To engage the world, we *con-strue* meaning. From the diverse aspects of some experience or phenomenon, which would otherwise be an unintelligible jumble of impressions, we bring together (*con-*) these elements by interpreting them *as* some unitary, distinct thing; we build up these distinct entities as parts of an articulate whole, a *structure*, that allows us to navigate our world, not in a literally spatial way (although that also may be true), but as a realm of understanding that allows us to make sense of our situation.

Construal and construction, as modes of understanding and interpreting the world, fit with ontological making-room, the opening of a hermeneutically habitable world. that Heidegger calls *Auseinandersetzung*, his preferred word for translating *polemos*. It means discussion or confrontation in German, but Heidegger sometimes breaks the word apart into its component roots as *Aus-einander-setzung*, the setting-out-and-apart-from-one-another, the distinguishing and gathering, that establishes the intelligibility of a meaningful world. We can get this sense in the English 'con-frontation': a world, meaningfully articulated in all its inner relations, is only possible if all things can uphold their 'fronts' in identity with themselves and in distinction from others. Without this, there is only *Durcheinandersetzung*, a confused interspersion of things in a muddled heap, a *sarma* (Heraclitus, fragment 124), James's "blooming, buzzing confusion," rather than a structured whole. As such, a construction is also an aspect of the *logos,* the gathering that assembles a world of meaning that can be articulated in language. This brings us back to the earlier point, that *polemos* and *logos* are the same, although not identical (GA 40: 66; GA 97: 39): meaningful structure and an engaged construal of things within it depend for their intelligibility on a simultaneous unity and separation, identity and difference, of distinct elements articulated together within a world of meaning. Without fronts, there are no borders, no shape to things, and so no structure to a world that can be inhabited in everyday life.

But this account risks a misunderstanding if construal is taken as simply up to us, subjectively, as either individuals or collectives. Our finitude and our historicity mean that the structure of an intelligible world is always-already there for us, in some provisional way. At the same time, the meaning of the world and things within it is not fixed. To use Heidegger's concepts from *Being and Time*, the *understanding* grasps the world in a fore-structure of meaning that *has-been* articulated for us in advance, and interpretation assigns things and actions their place in an as-structure within the fore-structure (SZ, §32). I can interpret a chair *as* an armchair and not as a throne because a range of possible meanings is already there *be-fore* me, as it were. A provisional structure of meaning for what things can *be* is already accessible, in the *fore* of lived existence, given by a particular historicity that in-forms my world: it *forms* the intelligible structure of the world so that I may exist in understanding *in* it. For Heidegger, the metaphorics of structure serves also to overcome the dualism of thinking subject as separated from world as thought-about. The structures of Dasein's Being, as understandingly in-the-world, mean that we exist as the world so structured. Ontologically, we *are* this Being-in-the-world.

This is where the triad of reduction, construction, and destruction come into view in a larger context. In section 5 of the *Fundamental Problems* course, Heidegger pivots from the Latinate *Destruktion* to the German word *Abbau*. Above, I rendered this word as "dismantling," which is certainly correct linguistically, but not the only way. Albert Hofstadter, in his translation of the lecture course, renders it as "de-constructing" (GA 24: 31), which more literally conveys the German: *Ab-bau*, a negation (*Ab-*) of building or constructing (*-bau*), which itself fits with the metaphorics structure as an abode of meaningful inhabitation. Heidegger makes this shift from Latin to German in part to make as clear as possible that the moment of interpretive de-struction is not mindless destructiveness and that he is using the Latinate word in a very specific way as a philosophical term of art. Within this clarifying move, though, is hidden the need to give a name to a critical feature of our interpretive existence; although we ourselves do not create the always-already of a world that provides our provisionally meaningful context, we are not simply its passive recipients. *Wonder* allows us to catch glimpses of that very contingency of the given world-structure. To be alive to the experience of wonder is to be open to those moments in personal and communal history when the need for *reinterpretation* becomes, or at least can become, both overwhelmingly urgent and enticingly possible.

Deconstruction, then, is not a nihilistic, ontological vandalism against the structural meaning of a world; it is a responsiveness to the possibility of new, regenerative interpretations, grounded in the meaningful structures already given, but also departing from them in new constellations of the elements of those structures. Deconstruction is intimately connected to freedom, therefore, both in the negative sense of throwing off the absolute hold of the past, and in the positive sense of opening up new horizons of meaning for inhabiting a meaningful world. Deconstruction is the call of the future, in confrontation with the past. This is why Derrida would say that "Deconstruction is justice," because if being-human means that we inhabit a world as *finite* beings, then to do justice to ourselves and to meaning itself we must remain ever-alive to how meaning frays and reconstitutes itself ever-anew, as well as being ever-vigilant against totalizing, absolutist, and tyrannizing claims to have brought the necessity of reinterpretation to an end.[33]

Heidegger does not say all this in that passage in the 1927 lecture course. The triad of reduction, construction, and destruction there seem mainly (but not only) directed to the question of Being as specific to ontology as a discipline in philosophy. Reduction is supposed to lead us from the analysis of being-human, Dasein, to Being as such; construction is supposed to enable us to provide a coherent, positive account of the structures of Being; destruction, or deconstruction, is supposed to free us from the stifling hold of long-unexamined philosophical concepts so that we can accomplish both the reduction and the construction in as unencumbered a manner as possible. Deconstruction grants us new insight into what has been overlooked but remains at-issue in those concepts, and to appropriate them, once deconstructed, for new purposes.

Thus, *construction* is *futural*: it is what we are always already doing as the world-interpreting beings that we are, both as being given over in advance (fore-) to the structures of intelligibility and as forging new domains of meaning with the elements we have; that *destruction* is how we genuinely *are* our past: not simply being borne along passively by it, nor obliterating it, but confronting it and reconstruing it. *Reduction* is how we exist as present: not as a fixed now-point, but as making sense of our situatedness, here and now, by leading back an understanding of what it means to be human from a futural horizon of possibility newly illumined by a deconstructed past.

These moments are not sequential, because our temporality is not ticks on a timeline. Instead, they intersect each other at all times, informing each other's activity, as what Heidegger called the *ek-stases*, the standing-outside-of-oneself of temporality, acknowledging that we exist not at now-points in time but as stretched back and forth as the thrown-projection of a meaningful world. In that world, the future is the most defining *ekstasis*, because the horizon of our Being, what it means for us to be, is worked out, polemically, in terms of futural possibilities, in-formed by the past, and instantiated in the situatedness of the present. The future is where freedom articulates itself, in dialogue with the past, for the sake of the present.

My claim is that this temporality, as elastically stretched through past-present-future, is itself motivated and defined by the *polemos*, the confrontational dialogue of meaning between past and future that illuminates the present. In my reading of the Allegory of the Cave, I will develop these three elements of our interpretive being-human, using an expanded language to describe the de-, pre-, and reconstruction of our historically interpreted world. I make these terminological distinctions because I hope to show how each plays a distinct but interlacing role in the polemical cycle of thought. This triad of meaning-formation, deterioration, and reformation, as a constitutive feature of human-being as polemical hermeneutics, is guided by the triad of wonder, question, and response. I will endeavor to show that Plato, far from neglecting what is at stake for being-human in this confrontation with meaning, displays it in greater depth than Heidegger, and that by doing so, provides a fuller account of our ethical freedom, personal and political.

NOTES

1. In Gilbert, *Collected Poems*, 228.

2. *Works and Days*; *Theogony*; *Testimonia*, trans. Glenn Most (Cambridge, MA: Loeb Classical Library, 2018).

3. Arendt, *The Human Condition*, 323; see also 248.

4. Donne, "The Anatomy of the World," *The Complete Poetry*, 198–99, lines 203–14.

5. Roochnik, *Retrieving Aristotle in an Age of Crisis*, 3, 13.

6. Husserl, *The Crisis of European Sciences and Transcendental Philosophy*, 60, 290, 295.

7. Arendt, *The Human Condition*, 251.

8. For a sympathetic critique of Heidegger, Husserl, and Arendt on human "earthliness," see Kelly Oliver, "Phenomenology and an Ethico-Politics of Earthbound Limits," in Pfeifer and Gurley, *Phenomenology and the Political*.

9. On *tolma*, daring, see Fried, "How Dare We Read Heidegger?"

10. See Gray, *The Warriors: Reflections on Men in Battle*, xvii–xviii and 238.

11. See Fried, "Odysseus on the Beach."

12. See Fried, "A Letter to Emmanuel Faye," 32, and Fried, "Peter Trawny: *Freedom to Fail.*"

13. For a treatment of the tale of Thales and woman by the well, the nature of theory, absentmindedness, and the role of ridicule, as well as its significance for Heidegger and philosophy, see Blumenberg's *The Laughter of the Thracian Woman*.

14. See Fried, *Heidegger's Polemos*, 148–50, where I discuss this text in detail.

15. For the most fruitful examinations of the *chora* in the phenomenology of space, especially in Plato and Heidegger, see Sallis, *The Verge of Philosophy* and *Chorology*.

16. Although, consider a passage such as this one from "*Gelassenheit*," whose language, in 1955, is disturbingly close to the *Blutt und Boden* rhetoric of the previous decades: "Is there anymore such quiet dwelling of human beings between earth and sky? Does the contemplative spirit still hold sway over the land? Is there yet a home-land strong in its roots, in whose soil the human being can take a standing stance, that is, standing constant in the soil?" (GA 16: 521).

17. For a fuller discussion, see Fried, *Heidegger's Polemos*, chapter 4.

18. For an excellent discussion of this theme, see Braver, *Groundless Ground*, chapter 5.

19. Michel Henry, *The Essence of Manifestation*, 444 (III.51).

20. Ovid, *Metamorphoses*, trans. A. D. Melville (Oxford: Oxford University Press, 1986), 8.223–25.

21. See Hornblower and Sparforth, *Oxford Classical Dictionary*, 409.

22. James, *The Principles of Psychology*, vol. 1, 488; Nietzsche, *The Will to Power*, §569.

23. See Auden's "Musée des Beaux Arts," *Collected Poems*, 179, and Williams, "Landscape with the Fall of Icarus," *Selected Poems*, 238; both are responses to the painting by Peter Bruegel at the museum in Brussels.

24. Hyland, *Finitude and Transcendence*, 29; cf. 32; also *Questioning Platonism*, 4, 9.

25. The Great Hymn to Aten in Simpson, *The Literature of Ancient Egypt*, 279. See also Hoffmeier, *Akhenaten and the Origins of Monotheism*, chapters 7 and 8.

26. In Fried, *Confronting Heidegger*, see Fried, 39–42, 230–31; Faye, 66, 252–53; and Kellerer, 182–86. Also Klemperer, *The Language of the Third Reich*, 197, 246–48, 263.

27. For a critical discussion of Jews and nomadology, see Gordon, "Heidegger in Purgatory," in Heidegger, *Nature, History, State*. On related themes, see the essays collected in Lapidot and Brumlik, *Heidegger and Jewish Thought*.

28. Weil, *The Need for Roots*, 41.

29. hooks, *Belonging*, 34.

30. For my critique of trans-humanism, see Fried, "Odysseus on the Beach."

31. For an overview of Heidegger's departure from Husserl, see Dermot Moran, *Introduction to Phenomenology*, 226–33.

32. Heidegger, "Drei Briefe Martin Heideggers an Karl Löwith," 29; also GA 61: 172–74.

33. Derrida, "Force of Law," 7; see also Fried, *Heidegger's Polemos*, chapter 5.

Chapter Two

Back to the Cave

From Heidegger to Plato

Even such a Shell the Universe itself
Is to the ear of Faith; and there are times,
I doubt not, when to You it doth impart
Authentic tidings of invisible things

—Wordsworth, from "The Excursion"[1]

If you are like most students of Western philosophy, Plato's Allegory of the Cave may have been one of your first encounters with philosophy's claim upon us.[2] Plato's Cave is perhaps the single most important depiction in Western philosophy of human freedom in all its dimensions, from the metaphysical, through the ontological and epistemological, to the ethical and political. The Allegory also provides the best opportunity to conduct the *polemos* between Plato and Heidegger, because Heidegger seizes upon the Cave to identify where Platonism decisively signals the onset of nihilism in the West, a nihilism that now, in the modern era, encompasses the globe. Furthermore, Socrates characterizes the story he tells as one of prisoners being released and making their escape from the bonds of their subterranean prison into the open light of the world. It is a story of freedom, and of philosophy as the engine of that freedom.

The basic details of the parable are well known: A society of prisoners resides in a cavern, chained up so that they cannot look around or see each other; above them burns a fire that projects shadows upon the cave wall that they face, shadows they take to be reality. Somehow, some of the prisoners get free of their chains, turn around, see the fire, and then make a long, arduous journey up and out of the cave into the light of day; having seen what the real world is, they are compelled to return to the cave, risking disorientation and persecution, to provide a leadership informed by the truth and undeceived by the shadows. (See Figure 1, The Cave.)

As a description of the human condition, Socrates declares outright that the prisoners of the cave are "like us" (*homoious hēmin*, 515a), *all* of us. The Greek *homoious* makes this sound as if he were declaring an analogy. *Homoios* not only means "like" in the sense of *resembling*, but also *akin to*, *equal to*, or even *same as*, in the sense of the expression "like for like." So, it is not just that we resemble the prisoners, we are *just like* them in a decisive way concerning our freedom.

As I have suggested, freedom is the point of inflection to distinguish a polemical ethics inspired by Plato in contrast to Heidegger's *polemos*, while also accounting for Heidegger's critique of Plato. The confrontation between these two conceptions of freedom turns on how we are free as finite beings inhabiting our world through an interpretive confrontation with that world as defined by our temporality and historicity. While I agree with Heidegger that confrontation, as *polemos*, is a constitutive feature of our existential-hermeneutical structure, my claim is that Plato also shows how and why this must be so, and in a way that leads to very different ethical-political implications. The guiding thought is that our finitude means we can never have an absolute and final interpretation of the meaning of things. This is not simply a lack of ability on our part, it is a matter of time: how meaning frays and needs reconstituting. The incompleteness of our understanding entails that the given meanings of the historical world will repeatedly present us with unexpected puzzles, contradictions, and outright crises. Confrontation, *polemos*, is how the world, as interpreted, faces us, and how we must face up to it if we take the examined life seriously as our ethical burden. The Allegory of the Cave presents a powerful portrait for why this must be so.

2.1 HEIDEGGER'S CAVE: FREEDOM UNDER FIRE

As explained in the introduction, I do not intend to provide a comprehensive interpretation of Heidegger's readings of Plato. Other scholars have done this well already, most notably Francisco Gonzalez.[3] Instead, my goal is an interpretation that exposes what is at issue for us in the confrontation between Plato and Heidegger, for which an overview of Heidegger's interpretation of the Allegory of the Cave will suffice. Heidegger's reading of the Allegory goes to the heart of his critique of Plato, and that critique grounds his understanding of the full sweep of the history of philosophy in the West as "metaphysics." That conception of the onset of metaphysics with Plato in turn informs Heidegger's conception of the history of the West as a long slide into an increasingly virulent nihilism.

A caveat: Heidegger at times insists, even in his readings of specific Plato texts, that he is confronting not Plato but *Platonism*: "We say 'Platonism' and not 'Plato,' because here we do not examine the conception of knowledge that pertains to that title [i.e., Platonism] through an original and exhaustive treatment of Plato's works, but rather only through drawing out in rough outline here one particular strand" (GA 43: 184).[4] I ask the reader for a similar latitude to address Heideggerianism if not Heidegger.

Heidegger offers three major treatments of the Allegory of the Cave and multiple shorter discussions.[5] I will not address all of these systematically, but it is worth noting the history of the major ones. The first is in his lecture course of Winter Semester (WS) 1931–1932, *On the Essence of Truth* (in GA 34). The second is his lecture course of WS 1933–1934, of the same title (GA 36/37). This course follows the structure of the previous one, and often repeats it, but is not identical. It includes Heidegger's most developed interpretation of *polemos* in Heraclitus's Fragment 53 as a prologue to the Cave interpretation, as well as political discussions and asides relevant to the historical events of the time.[6] The third is the essay "Plato's Doctrine of the Truth," which is based on the first lecture course, although also not identical to it, and the only one he published in his lifetime, first in 1942 and then 1947.[7]

Scholars have debated the significance of the differences among Heidegger's major treatments of the Allegory of the Cave. Gonzalez cogently argues that Heidegger's published essay is much more dogmatic about the *transformation* through Plato of truth as unconcealment in favor of truth as correctness, whereas the earlier lecture courses leave room in the Cave Analogy for correctness as "derivative of truth as unconcealment," even if Plato himself failed to understand this relationship originally enough because he did not grasp the significance of concealment in truth as unconcealment.[8] Even so, on Gonzalez's nuanced reading of Heidegger's interpretation of the Cave Analogy, Heidegger's essential thesis is still that through Plato a decisive turn in Western thought occurs that obscures the question of Being and the meaning of truth in a way that has decisive consequences, not just for philosophy but for the history of the West, which, for Heidegger, becomes the history of the planet in global modernity.

Each of Heidegger's major readings of the Allegory does three key things. First, each treats the Allegory as revealing Plato's *doctrine* of truth (and the ideas), a doctrine that affects the whole subsequent history of philosophy as metaphysics, that is, as forgetting the question of Being as a question about how meaning as such is possible and focusing instead on what constitutes the ultimate beingness of beings, whether that is the idea (which is the progenitor of all the others, for Heidegger), God, substance, mathematical physics, or the will to power, to name only some contenders.[9] While only the 1942 essay speaks explicitly of Plato's "doctrine of truth," the earlier ones are just as emphatic about the doctrine of the ideas as the foundation for the conceptions of what most properly 'is' throughout Western history. For example, in one passage Heidegger attributes to Plato's *Ideenlehre* a progeny that includes the Christian concept of God and all created beings, the modern notion of reason in the Enlightenment and the elevation of rationalism to a cult, the Marxist concept of ideology, and finally Nietzsche's misfired but still prophetic countermovement to Platonism's degraded forms in humanism, Christianity, and the Enlightenment (GA 34: 324–25).

Second, each major reading locates in the Allegory a fundamental transition in the meaning of truth, from what Heidegger holds to be the primordial meaning of truth as *alētheia*, *Unverborgenheit*, unconcealment, to truth as *homoiosis*, correctness.

Third, each considers the Allegory an account of liberation as moving through four stages (*Stufen*) in relation to truth, itself an uncontroversial reading, but which, when combined with the other two, has important implications for an understanding of freedom in thinking, ethics, and politics.

I will focus here on Heidegger's best-known treatment of the Cave Allegory, "Plato's Doctrine of Truth" (1942), in part because it is the version he chose to publish in his lifetime. Also, "Plato's Doctrine of Truth" is the version that most effectively establishes the domain of confrontation between them as a locus for addressing our own historical situation and the meaning of a polemical ethics. The German word translated as "doctrine" is *Lehre*. Because *Lehre* can mean "teaching," rendering it as "doctrine" might seem prejudicial, as if Heidegger were unfairly assigning a dogmatism to Plato. Heidegger writes that "The '*Lehre*' of a thinker is what is unsaid in what he says and is that to which human beings are exposed so that they might devote themselves to it" (GA 9: 203). What I have rendered as "devote themselves" is *sich verschwende*, which has a range of meanings from "lavish" to "expend" to "waste" oneself upon something. That range captures the ambiguity of *Lehre* as the "unsaid" of a thinker's thought. The unsaid can be a treasure for subsequent readers to unearth, or it might conceal what needs to be thought and lead readers to squander their energies upon something superficial. *In neither case would Lehre be an explicit and dogmatic doctrine.* Nevertheless, Heidegger writes that "What remains unsaid [in Plato] is a shift [*Wendung*] in the determination of the essence of truth" (GA 9: 203). That "shift" comes to define subsequent thought in a manner concealed from that thought, and so while it is not an explicit dogma, it serves as a doctrine all the more effectively precisely because unsaid and therefore not confronted.

So, the doctrinal nature of Plato's teaching connects directly with the second theme: truth. The said and the unsaid correspond to Heidegger's conception of truth as *alētheia*, unconcealment, because in everything said openly something essential remains concealed. The unsaid can therefore be understood as the positive content of unmeaning: a meaning as yet unarticulated but nevertheless intimated and, as such, what impels philosophical searching and questioning. I claim, against Heidegger, that the process of Platonic ideation is necessary to engage and elicit the unsaid in the triads of wonder, question, response and of de-, pre-, reconstruction.

Thought and speech can never exhaust meaning. Heidegger acknowledges that on the surface the text of the Allegory is about the education and thus the liberation of the philosopher-rulers, but its *implicit* and unsaid content is this shift in truth (GA 9, 218). Truth, on the surface of the argument, is what entitles the philosopher-rulers to rule, and so their education corresponds to "stages" (*Stufen*) in their ascent within, out of, and back to the cave. Heidegger discerns four such stages to the prisoner's progress, each a different "dwelling-place" (*Aufenthalt*) in the truth (GA 9: 219).

The first is the lowest cave floor, where the prisoners are enchained and "caught up in what most proximately engages them" such that the prisoners (in my translation of Heidegger's translation of the Greek) "'would consider as unhidden'"—*alethes*, what Heidegger renders as *unverborgen*, conventional translations as "true"—"'nothing other than the shadows of those artifacts'" (GA 9: 219) being carried along the lateral path above the cave floor (*Republic*, 514b–c). The second stage is the initial release from bondage, but it is hardly an improvement, because the prisoners, unaccustomed to the light of the fire, cannot discern the things that cast the shadows, even if those things are now "*alēthestera*, 'more unhidden [conventionally: *truer*]'" (GA 9: 220). As Heidegger rightly says about the cave floor, "Removing the chains does indeed bring a release. But liberation is not yet real freedom" (GA 9: 220–21).

Real freedom comes only at the third stage, when the unchained prisoner emerges "outside the cave and is transposed into *das Freie*"—the free, the open (GA 9: 221). Here, "The look of what the things themselves are, the *eidē* (ideas), constitutes the essence in whose light each individual being shows itself as this or that, and in this self-showing what shines forth in appearance first becomes unconcealed and accessible" (GA 9: 221). Heidegger says that according to Plato's Allegory things are now not just *alēthestera*, more unconcealed, but *alēthestaton*, most unconcealed—conventionally, most true.

The fourth stage is the "descent back down into the cave and the struggle [*Kampf*] inside the cave between the liberator and the imprisoned who resist all liberation" (GA 9: 223). This stage might at first seem contradictory. Glaucon initially calls it "an injustice" (519d) that the philosophers be made to return. If the third stage is the most truly unconcealed, then no further progress in liberation seems needed. A return down back into the cave seems to be a regression, not a further stage in the progress of freedom and truth. In the Allegory's narrative, going back to the cave, both to rule it and to free others capable of liberation, is precisely what the philosopher-rulers must do as their duty to the city that first put them on the path of genuine education (*Republic*, 520a–d). But why is this particular narrative not simply arbitrary?

Heidegger accounts for this *explicit* fourth-stage role of education in the Allegory by relating the surface narrative to what he claims is the unsaid yet most enduring content: the fate of truth as *alētheia* in Western thought. He focuses on "the alpha-privative (*a-lētheia*)" by insisting that "Truth inceptively means what has been wrested from a concealment" (GA 9: 223). Here, Heidegger calls truth a "wresting forth" as the "revealing" (*Entbergung*) of unconcealment from its many forms of concealment—"closing-off, safekeeping, veiling, masking, disguising, feigning" (GA 9: 223)—just as elsewhere he calls it a *Raub*, a robbery:

> In the truth, beings are torn from concealment. Truth is understood by the Greeks as a robbery, a deprivation that must be torn from concealment in an *Auseinandersetzung* in which *phusis* [nature in the sense of what surges or grows into meaningful appearance without our agency] strives to conceal itself. Truth is the innermost confrontation [*Auseinandersetzung*, i.e., *polemos*] of the essence of the human with beings as a whole. (GA 29/30: 43–44)

The fourth stage, the return to the cave, is an existential necessity of being-human because 'The Truth' is never fully and finally revealed.

According to Heidegger, Western thought since Plato has understood truth as somehow located in statements, such as "The sky is blue this afternoon." Such statements are true if they correctly correspond to the way the world is or if they cohere together in a way that makes pragmatic sense of the world. Heidegger does not reject this conventional conception of truth, but he does consider it derivative. The sheer givenness of a meaningful world is what makes individual things intelligible to us in such a way that we can make statements about them at all. This givenness of a meaningful access to things and a world as intelligible, for Heidegger, is a deeper dimension of truth.

Here I draw inspiration from Thomas Sheehan's typology of three layers of truth in Heidegger, which Sheehan designates as *alētheia*-3, *alētheia*-2, and *alētheia*-1 (or *alētheia*-prime): the propositional truth of statements as corresponding to a state of affairs; the pre-propositional disclosedness of a thing or state of affairs *as* meaningful and therefore *about which* one can make statements; finally, truth as the clearing, the space, the world in which meaningfulness as such is possible and so also the possibility of making correct and incorrect statements.[10]

Our being open to the possibility of the truth of statements, truth in its most conventional sense, is the most derivative layer, what Sheehan calls *alētheia*-3. We might also call this ontic truth, as it has to do with making correct statements about beings as already meaningful, whereas the other layers involve ontological truth, how meaning as such is possible. For it to be possible to make statements in the first place, the things of the world, including general states of affairs and actions, must already be meaningful to us. This openness to meaning, *alētheia*-2, precedes us in such a way that it is more accurate to say that we are *opened to* the meanings of things rather than open to them as if it were our choice. For Sheehan, the world itself, as an integrated whole of meaning as at least provisionally opened up to us (not by us), is *alētheia*-prime: the world opened up as an interlacing web of meanings and thereby things within it disclosed as meaningful. This disclosure of things as having-meaning (*alētheia*-2), grants the ontological possibility of making statements about them (*alētheia*-3). This unconcealment is not discovery in the sense of uncovering new truths about the physical or cultural world, as explorers or scientists or historians might accomplish; such discoveries remain at the level of ontic, propositional truth. Heidegger takes his inspiration for this layer of truth from the Greek word *alētheia*, whose etymological roots, *a-* and *lēthē*, mean the negation of concealment or forgetting. Every such world of meaning as unconcealed to us is a *historical* world, where meaning is subject to emergences, shifts, and dissolutions.

Sheehan's *alētheia*-prime describes the ontological given that the meaning of things is opened to us in an *a priori* way. Here I depart from Sheehan. We may grant that a historical world opens us up to meaning, but what performs the opening? Why *this* world of meaning rather than another? This layer is the most difficult to describe because so far removed from the ordinary language used to express the conventional understanding of truth as the claim-making of propositions. Let's call it *alētheia*-0, because it describes the way that the meaning and unmeaning of worlds transpires as an ontological something rather than nothing. Over his career, Heidegger experiments with a variety of words to express this irruptive truth, such as the *Es gibt*, the "it gives" of the phenomenological given that "there is" always-already a meaningful world for us (GA 14: 9ff); *Ereignis*, the event of appropriation that assigns a particular world of meaning to a historical community (GA 65); and *polemos* as *Auseinandersetzung*, the confrontation that divides a world up into meaningful distinctions and identities among things, including us. He even equates *polemos* and *Ereignis* (GA 94: 217).

Polemos best describes the involvement of human-being at all four layers of truth. At the level of *alētheia*-3, propositional truth, *polemos* involves our disputes about what is and is not the case; at *alētheia*-2, the givenness of meaning, *polemos* involves our hermeneutical confrontation about what words and things mean; at *alētheia*-1, the clearing or openness of a world as such, *polemos* in turn opens us to wonder and so to questioning; at *alētheia*-0, the event of opening itself as disruptive or irruptive truth, *polemos* implicates us in the dissolution and emergence of worlds of meaning. The unsaid that hovers between meaning and unmeaning may bring down or raise up a world in disruptive-irruptive truth. Emmanuel Levinas, who confronts Heidegger's failure to address the ethical, expresses succinctly what is at stake here in the unsaid:

> Now, what I am interested in is precisely this ability of philosophy to think, to question itself, and ultimately to unsay itself. And I wonder if this capacity for interrogation and for unsaying (*dédire*) is not itself derived from the preontological inter-human relationship with the other. The fact that philosophy cannot fully totalize the alterity of meaning in some final presence or simultaneity is not for me a deficiency or fault. Or to put it in another way, the best thing about philosophy is that it fails. It is better that philosophy fail to totalize meaning—even though as ontology [for Levinas, the endeavor to systematize meaning], it has attempted just this—for it thereby remains open to the irreducible otherness of transcendence.[11]

As Levinas says, *unsaying* is what happens, especially in ethical life, if we allow what transcends established systematization of meaning to irrupt as an unmeaning that must be confronted because it interrupts our settled understanding of the truth. We can take on or shirk the responsibility of participation in the *polemos* at each layer of truth. Primordial truth as *a-lētheia*, unconcealment, is defined by human-being's finitude. Truth is not the sum total of ontic facts waiting out there to be unconcealed in the sense of the discovery of new natural laws, or gold mines, or planets, and then making factually correct assertions about them. We live in truth only by engaging and re-engaging in the *polemos* that itself is truth, because truth is what first makes possible a context of meaning in which discoveries of specific beings (laws, objects, concepts, and so on) can make sense in the first place.

Heidegger says that we live in untruth as well as in truth (SZ, §44), because our idle chatter, even or especially about things we pretend are most profound, tends to turn revealing moments into 'correct' assertions that are merely repeated without insight. It is not that living in untruth means we are constantly making empirically false statements, but that a resistance to engaging in the *polemos* with meaning is endemic to being-human. Because we always-already depend upon a given meaningfulness of the world as a whole, we cannot question everything, all the time, for the sake of constantly fresh insight. But an openness to a kind of hermeneutical *phronēsis*, a practical wisdom about where and how meaning has broken down or should be broken down, is possible if ethical life is properly mindful of what matters in our situated being-human.

In making sense of the world, we must endure the anxiety that things have failed or will fail to make sense. The world may break down into non-sense. Anxiety about unmeaning is Janus-faced. We either face up to this unmeaning as an opportunity to re-imagine, reconstruct, and make sense of the world anew, or we face away from this *polemos* and repress unmeaning with dogma. The sense-making aspect of ontological rather than ontic truth always takes place as a struggle because the whole of possible meaning is never available to us in a total enlightenment. Heidegger's analyses and style might give the impression that only a constant state of morbidly vigilant angst is authentic and that there is no place for everyday experiences of joy and serenity. To respond generously, the point is that no experience of being utterly absorbed in joy is constant, let alone eternal, for human finitude, but that same transience is potentially true for experiences of crushing despair and alienation, too. Meaning is temporally dynamic, which means that we must be ready for and open to ontological tectonic shifts in our meaningful world. Such change *happens*, ready or not. A familiar meaning may break apart, at least in part, as it develops and reconstitutes dynamically. *This* is the play of unmeaning in meaning. Our situated rootedness will always be subject, eventually, to disruptive uprootings of meaning that displace us into unmeaning—sometimes for the better, because in contexts of great injustice, the prevailing world of meaning may well need deconstructing, even if a new meaning cannot yet be envisioned, let alone enacted in a reconstructed world.

To be mindful of our being-human is to be ready, when it properly matters, for a polemical ethics that negotiates the dissolution and reconstruction of meaning. Refusing this readiness for the cycle of thoughtful reconstruction is to insist upon a constancy that human finitude cannot bear and to repress any challenge to familiar meanings. Such constancy, however, will not stand, and insisting upon it leads to a violent intransigence that can only end in tragedy or farce in the return of the repressed. This is why the third stage of the Allegory, emergence into the abode outside the cave, is not the final one. Historical human-being must always confront an understanding that is partial, that must learn to see anew, and that *may* and probably *will* resist this reinterpretation of its world, just as the cave-dwellers may well resist, perhaps violently, a returning former prisoner who tries to liberate others as their mentor. Truth as *a-lētheia* is an existential aspect of who we are as human-being, *as* thrown into a confrontation with the meaning of the world as always-already-interpreted but also as polemically open to reinterpretation.

Heidegger discerns this ontological *polemos* of truth as a feature of the unsaid in Plato's narrative of the Allegory. It is important to distinguish among: (1) what Heidegger thinks the historical Plato meant by the Allegory, which does not especially interest him; (2) what happens as the unsaid in thought *through* Plato, without Plato's thinking it explicitly; and (3) what happens to the history of thought as Platonism, the "doctrine" of truth that hardens after Plato, making the unsaid all the less accessible. A thinker's biography matters little to Heidegger: "Concerning the personal history of a philosopher, only this is of interest: he was born in this or that place, he worked, and he died" (GA 18: 5). This is an odd view to profess for someone who lends so much importance to our situated existence and "my 'I am,'" but Heidegger is not yet a thinker of embodiment such as Maurice Merleau-Ponty or, in a more political orientation, Iris Marion Young.[12] What matters is what can be thought as unsaid through these thinkers and how this unsaid then influences subsequent historical horizons of thought. This is why Heidegger can discern an *echo* of primordial *a-lētheia* in the Cave Allegory without ascribing it to Plato's own intention. But that echo remains unsaid by Plato, according to Heidegger, and so the Allegory buries this ontological truth as unconcealment in favor of a new form of truth compatible with the task of the philosopher-ruler: truth as *homoiōsis*, correctness of representation.

This new form of truth is a direct result, according to Heidegger, of the philosopher-rulers' mandate for rule, legitimated by their education through the stages of the cave. It is further explained by the Divided Line in Book 6 where the ideas or forms (*ideai* and *eidē*) correspond to the liberated prisoner's vision outside the cave of what most properly *is in being*. (See Figure 2, The Divided Line.) The Allegory does not *ostensibly* address the meaning of truth as such, Heidegger concedes. "And nevertheless the point stands: This 'allegory' contains Plato's 'doctrine' of truth, for that allegory is grounded upon the unsaid process of the *idea* becoming master over *alētheia*" (GA 9: 230). Not *a-lētheia*, as ontological unconcealment, but the *idea*, as metaphysical principle, comes to determine what truth is, and indeed what Being itself is, because the ideas are what all beings themselves most truly *are*.

This shift, this turn-about (*Wendung*) in the meaning of truth occurs because, "If everywhere in every case our comportment to beings depends upon the *idein* [act of seeing] of the *idea*, upon catching sight of 'the look,' then all effort must first arrange itself according to the enabling of such a seeing" (GA 9: 230). Instead of truth as the ongoing hermeneutical-polemical encounter between finite understanding and an inexhaustible domain of concealed meaning, "Everything depends upon the *orthotēs*, the correctness of sight"

(GA 9: 230). That correctness of sight after an arduous education legitimizing the rule of the philosophers, is clear enough from the surface of Plato's text. Unsaid, for Heidegger, is the shift to the ideas as the marker of truth and of Being and the forgetting of ontological unconcealment (GA 9: 230–31). This is the *doctrine* that becomes the Platonism of Western thought for Heidegger, whatever Plato himself intended: "And for a long time in Western thought, 'truth' has meant the agreement of representation in thought with the fact of the matter [*Sache*]: *adaequatio intellectus et rei* [correspondence of the intellect and the thing]" (GA 9: 218). We should remember that Heidegger does not mean simply to dismiss truth as correctness of representation. His point is that the correctness and coherence of statements ("The sky is blue") depends on a prior *Auseinandersetzung*, a truth as unconcealment that grants a meaning to the terms of a statement ("the sky"; "blue"; even the "is" itself) as individually intelligible (set out and apart from one another as identifiably distinct), as intelligible as a unitary statement, and as part of an intelligible world about which statements can be made. This is the difference between *alētheia*-3, ontic truth, and the layers of ontological truth, *alētheia*-2, 1, and 0, that ground it.

This brings us to the third theme of Heidegger's reading of the Allegory, freedom, although it has shadowed the discussion all along. The Allegory, on its surface, is about *paideia*, education, as the path of liberation from the chains of the cave. It consists in a "turning around" (*periagōgē*, 518d) of vision from the shadows into the light and upon "things themselves" (516a), that progresses through the stages Heidegger has described. So, he writes:

> Liberation is not achieved right away by the release from the chains and does not consist in lack of restraint, but rather first begins as the constant becoming-accustomed to fastening vision upon the firm boundaries of things as standing fast in their look. Authentic liberation is the constancy of the turning-around towards that which shines forth in its apparent look and, in this shining-forth, is most unconcealed. Freedom consists only in a turning-around constituted in this way. (GA 9: 222)

For Heidegger, there would be no distortion of truth as unconcealment if the *idea* or the *eidos*, as the visible *or intelligible* form that gives each thing its discernable, clearly bordered self-identity (*logos*) and differentiation from other things (*polemos*), were simply to *announce* the unconcealment of things as part of a meaningful world *given to* us. Then *idea* would support unconcealment by "serving the unconcealed by bringing it forth, shining, into appearance" (GA 9: 234). The seer would not become the staging-ground or worse, the source of truth, but rather a witness to truth as an event that gives forth a world of beings in their historical meaning. But the opposite is the case. In Plato, "The *idea* is not a foreground that announces *alētheia* but rather the ground that makes *alētheia* possible" (GA 9: 234).

Vision as the metaphor for truth tends to locate truth in the subjectivity of the one seeing, in a correct turning-around-to-see and perspectival standpoint: "In this change in the essence of truth there transpires an exchange in the site of truth. As unconcealment, truth is still a fundamental feature of beings as such. But as correctness of 'vision,' truth becomes a distinction of the human relation to beings" (GA 9: 231). Once the site of truth shifts its location from the givenness of the phenomenal world in its unconcealed appearing to the way we see things out there in the world, it becomes increasingly incumbent upon us, as the seeing subject, to secure the meaning of the world by correctly representing it. Freedom becomes a matter of the correct education for this unfailing seeing, and what confirms such freedom becomes the power of the seeing-knowing subject to hold sway over all objects in its range of vision, a range extended, in principle, to complete enlightenment, extinguishing all concealment. "Ever since [this shift in the meaning of truth] there has been a striving for the 'truth' in the sense of correctness of seeing and of the point of view. Ever since, securing the correct view of the ideas has been decisive for all fundamental orientations to beings" (GA 9: 234).

While this may seem an innocuous feature of philosophical epistemology, it is why, for Heidegger, Platonism's doctrine of truth signals the onset of metaphysics in the West, where the *idea*, parsed as correctness of vision and of statement as features of a human knowing, determines all that is: "Through Plato, this word [*philosophia*] is first taken for use as the name for that knowing-one's-way-around [*sich Auskennen*] beings that at the same time determines the Being of beings as idea" (GA 9: 235). Nihilism, as the consequence of this metaphysics, consists in forgetting the truth of Being as *alētheia*, as the reciprocal relationship, in the *polemos*, of the bestowal of meaning upon us in a way we cannot give to ourselves, and of our ongoing confrontation with and reconstruction of that meaning in history. Nihilism, as the forgetting of a polemical truth that we are given over to and must take responsibility for, is the ground for what Heidegger came to call the essence of technology that seeks to bring all beings under the sway of a machinational will to power. This will to power reduces all beings, human and natural, to resources in a lust for mastery over all we survey.[13] In Heidegger's account, freedom, as this power of vision, turns on us in our pretension to mastery. It makes us the servants of an increasingly synoptic pursuit of control in which the only things that count as being are those that can be assessed and deployed as resources and quanta of power.

Heidegger's core charge against Platonism is that the doctrine of the ideas falsifies Being by obscuring truth as a temporal and polemical unveiling. By locating Being in an eternal, other-worldly domain of supra-sensuous forms, and by making truth the conformity of our assertions with these forms, Plato has succeeded in transforming Being, from the unfolding of the field of meaning as it is given historically, into a trans-temporal domain of eternally static absolutes (GA 40: 235–37). Truth as *alētheia* is no longer the free opening of a world of meaning to us; truth is now the marker of our correct apprehension of a permanent, transcendent reality. Philosophy begins its confusion of Being and beings and therefore its nihilistic decline into a forgetting of Being as the unfolding bestowal of meaning. Philosophy degenerates into a search for the key for the humanistic mastery of Being itself: "The onset of metaphysics in Plato's thinking is at the same time the onset of 'humanism'" (GA 9: 236). Truth, as the criterion of philosophical and, later, scientific rigor, becomes located in statements, or assertions, that correspond to a fixed reality. It is only a matter of time before the connection is made between *assertions about* reality and assertions that both reflect reality *and* permit us to *assert ourselves upon* reality as our dominion and so as the fullest expression of our freedom, as Descartes puts it in *The Discourse on Method*, to "render ourselves, as it were, masters and possessors of nature."[14]

2.2 TRUTH AND FREEDOM

Because the Allegory of the Cave intrinsically connects truth with freedom by depicting an apprehension of reality with a liberation through education, we need a sense of Heidegger's broader treatment of truth and freedom so that we can understand how these emerge in his critique of Plato. As many critics of classical liberalism have done, Heidegger decries liberal freedom as a fundamentally empty *negative* freedom, a freedom-*from* rather than a robust freedom-*for*. The clearest statement of Heidegger's condemnation of a merely negative freedom can be found in his Rectoral Address, a speech given to his assembled university as its head on May 17, 1933, as a committed party member in the National Socialist regime. In that speech he proclaims what constitutes the "highest freedom," in contrast to what it was under the Weimar Republic: "The much-vaunted 'academic freedom'"— that is, freedom *from* interference in one's research—"will be expelled from the German university, because this freedom was ungenuine because merely negative. It meant heedlessness, arbitrariness of intentions and inclinations, and lack of constraint in its conduct" (GA 16: 113). The force of this traditional critique focuses on the liberty-as-license conception of liberalism. Such a liberalism understands freedom only as the liberation of unattached individuals *from* coercive restraint to do as they please, to survive and to enjoy "the pursuit of happiness" as they see fit, so long as no one else is harmed.[15]

On such a view, the natural rights that the liberal state is supposed to preserve, though tricked out as something ennobling, are in fact nothing more than the demands of small-minded, self-involved, and timorous individuals when they gather as a populace, not a people, to form the social contract, fearful for their personal safety and greedy for their private satisfactions. The contract itself can produce only an association, not a genuine community where individuals may become properly free from their pinched and self-serving pettiness and thereby free for the ennobling purposes that can only be fulfilled by recognizing one's belonging to a historical community and by participating in the burden of its historical tasks. In his Rectoral Address, Heidegger calls on his students freely to take up their duties to the university as members of the German nation: "The first bond is the one to the *Volksgemeinschaft*." *Volksgemeinschaft*, "community of the people," is a Nazi term meaning the German people as nation, rather than a mere society composed of indifferent individuals lumped together by the social contract. "This bond commits [student-citizens] to involving themselves in the concerns, endeavors, and expertise of all classes and components of the *Volk*" (GA 16: 113).

For Heidegger, the "highest freedom" demands the utmost attentiveness to the struggles and challenges that history has bestowed upon the community that is truly one's own. The meaning of this freedom-for is not to dissolve individuals in a collective but rather to fulfill them in what is most ennobling in life, an active commitment to the community to which they belong. This cannot happen if they treat society as an arena for the pursuit of narrow self-interest, jealously protected by a merely negative freedom.

To be fair to the conception of positive freedom and the critique of classical liberalism, the dedication to the German *Volk* that Heidegger calls for is an extreme expression of positive freedom and should not blind us to its appeal in less pernicious forms. We will return to this in what follows, but we also should not ignore the danger that more moderate forms of dedication to one's own people may degenerate into virulent nationalism. This attraction of an exclusive and absorbing belonging is part of the challenge a reconstructed liberalism must address in the next stage of this project, enacting a polemical ethics.

Furthermore, Heidegger's conception of freedom has a much deeper dimension than its adherence to the traditional critique of a negative freedom that leaves individuals free only for their private interests. Freedom conventionally understood involves the ability to choose among available options, to act in the physical world, and to consent to social arrangements, all without constraint—at least without illegitimate, human-imposed constraint by accounting for the natural constraints that restrict our choices through physical limits to our actions. Heidegger certainly does not exclude the existential fact that human beings must make decisions. After all, his analysis of our temporality demonstrates that Dasein's having-a-future, as a feature of our temporal Being, involves a horizon of possibilities and that we *are* in part the decisions we make on that horizon.

But this is freedom in what Heidegger would call its ontic or "existentiell" sense, that is, the ability to choose among specific possibilities available to a specific person or community in a specific historical situation. Having a choice available requires that one already inhabit a world where those choices and their context are meaningful, and we never choose this always-already of being thrown into a world of meaning. The best metaphor for this situated freedom is language: without language we could not begin to think, let alone endeavor to think beyond the bounds of our present conceptual vocabulary. Without a meaningful world, ontic freedom would not be possible, and so the question of the meaning of *ontological* freedom is bound up with the question of the meaning of Being as what it means for anything to be meaningful *and so to matter* to us. Ontic freedom depends upon and derives from ontological freedom.

We can understand this problem in light of Heidegger's conception of truth, as discussed previously.[16] Briefly, Heidegger offers an assessment of truth that takes us from statements of fact ("The sky is blue today") to the web of *a priori* meanings that make factual statements meaningful to us (How do we know what 'blue' means?), to how a nexus of such meanings can form a world as a whole for us to inhabit hermeneutically, to how it is that, for us, anything has *this* meaning at all, instead of some other meaning. In tandem with this fourfold conception of truth, we can understand what freedom is for Heidegger. At the most derivative, but nonetheless existentially vital level, call it *eleutheria*-3, freedom is the capacity for choice and decision without which we could not navigate among the possibilities that define our future-oriented Being-in-the-world; Heidegger calls this *existentiell* choice (SZ, 12–13). The next level describes how this ontic freedom is available in the first place. Because the meaning of those choices is already open to us, we are freed *for* them in a particular historical world. Call this the first of the ontological layers of freedom, *eleutheria*-2. The next layer, *eleutheria*-1, what Heidegger calls *das Freie* (e.g., GA 9: 229), the free-and-open, is what grants us an interwoven con-text of meaningful action in world that preliminarily has made sense to us. Here, we can see how ontological truth and ontological freedom merge: the unconcealment of a world of meaning frees us up to engage in all our activity within that world, including our decisions. Finally, at the most primordial level, *eleutheria*-0, freedom describes the unaccountable spontaneity of a world opening up at all (GA 65: 5–9). By engaging in our polemical interpretation of a given world, we also engage with this dimension of freedom. We may even become the occasion for the *Ereignis*, the event of disruptive-irruptive truth in which a new historical world opens up from the old one, but we cannot make this event happen or control it when it does. The event is unaccountably free in its eventuation. At most, we can prepare for its arrival through interpretive *polemos* with the given.

Now we must understand how this multilayered conception of freedom connects to Heidegger's critique of a big-L Liberalism reaching all the way back to the purported onset of nihilism with Plato. As with truth, Heidegger does not want to deny freedom in its most derivative sense as the capacity for choice and decision; however, his treatment of the ontological dimension of freedom, as our opened-up-ness to a meaningful world, emphasizes the historicity and finitude of ontic freedom. We are free *to* choose in ways that are free *from* constraints only because we have already been made free *for* a world to which we belong in a meaningful way. Although Heidegger does not put it this way, conventional liberalism's obsession with individual freedom *for* choice and freedom *from* all illegitimate constraints necessarily plays into the hands of what he calls metaphysical nihilism. It does so because, by fixating on this ontic level of freedom, it promotes the individual subject as the arbiter, and even the author, of the meaning of its world. My meaning, my choice—and no interference from you, unless my choices illegitimately impinge upon your autonomy and rights.

The burden of Heidegger's critique of liberal modernity is that this hubristic subjectivism and its related nihilistic will to power reaches all the way back to the Platonic elevation of the idea as the key to Being because it establishes a tradition that locates the human subject as the arbiter of meaning and so of what simply *is*. Even if Platonism itself does not itself make this case, it launches the trajectory of this history that culminates in the crisis of modernity. Obsessive self-regard as the expression of freedom ignores that we are not the makers of our own worlds, and it cannot appreciate that our being-freed-for involvement in a meaningful world necessarily precedes our individual freedom of choice. It is a refusal to give thanks for the gift of givenness. Givenness is a gift because we ourselves are not the source of a meaningful world, and being thankful is a way of acknowledging this finitude and the simple wonder of having a world at all. Failing to appreciate our debt for our being-freed-to-a-world obscures the historicity of our world as a shared world of traditions, practices, language, and sociality that makes our freedom meaningful to us in the first place.

Embracing our freedom-for, therefore, brings us more fully into connection with our finite, situated historical existence. It would involve a thinking-as-thanking for and about the finitude that frees us for a world that matters and means to us (cf. GA 9: 310–12; GA 8: 149ff). Thankful thinking contemplates the primordial wonder that a world is given at all. It recognizes that there is no way to get behind the giving as such, but also that receiving this gift appreciatively makes us free to enter into the ontological polemics of the truth by ever-again reinterpreting the world as the work of zetetic philosophy. Appreciating this paradoxical freedom in finitude can make us more alive to our belonging in community that does not curtail our freedom but rather enhances and fulfills it. That embrace of a situated belonging allows us more fully to engage in a confrontation with the historical meaning of our world, which in turn frees up possibilities for our Being that would otherwise remain obscure. At the most primordial level, the level of the freedom of the eventuation of a historical world to us in the first place (*eleutheria*-0), Heidegger's critique of Liberalism suggests that the obsession with the free and autonomous self as author of meaning renders us ungrateful for the gift of meaning itself, a thanklessness that is the epitome of a thoughtless and hubristic nihilism. It deprives us of the opportunity for *properly* free participation in the confrontation with that givenness and so in participating in the epoch-making events that may engender new currents in history.

2.3 THE CHARGE OF NIHILISM

But why should big-L Liberalism lead to the denial of our place and our task in a historical community? The most significant accusation that Heidegger brings against Platonism is that the insistence on absolute *ideas*, unmoored from historical, situated existence, leads to a nihilism that ultimately, in the crisis of modernity, sets the human subject up as the master-surveyor of Being, rather than grounding being-human as entering into a reciprocal, interpretive *polemos* with Being as the temporally unfolding field of meaning given to us. We have now come to the heart of Heidegger's accusation and turn to nihilism itself in order to understand how it afflicts human-being as presented in the Allegory of the Cave.

Heidegger took up the problem of nihilism from Nietzsche, who proclaimed: "What does nihilism mean? *That the highest values devaluate themselves.* The aim is lacking; 'why?' finds no answer" (*The Will to Power*, §2).[17] For Nietzsche, this nihilism as meaninglessness and purposelessness sets in with the death of God, which is not merely a theological claim. It is an attack on Plato, because for Nietzsche, Christianity is merely Platonism for the masses. At stake is what Nietzsche calls "the true world," the world of eternal, undying truth, the genuinely real world that is our proper home, but temporarily separate from us and therefore other-worldly. That other-world had supplied the Platonic ideas and ideals that once guided us and supplied the answer to the "Why?" of life and action. Meaning, in the sense of the intelligibility and significance of all the things and customs once dear to us, begins to decay when meaning in the sense of an all-encompassing, other-worldly purpose dies.

When that transcendent otherworld dies, nihilism, "the uncanniest of guests" (*The Will to Power*, §1), arrives at the door. For Nietzsche, the healthiest response to this guest is to recognize that existence is not defined by Being as a permanent, otherworldly reality, but rather by the ever-churning Becoming of *this* world, here and now, as the life to be lived. His advice: "To stamp Becoming with the character of Being—that is the supreme will to power" (*The Will to Power*, §617). To stamp chaos with order is the act of the supreme artist and the supreme expression of life, for it creates temporary meaning amidst the flux; but in the eye of the will to power, this Being is only a semblance, a fleeting pause in the current of Becoming.

With Nietzsche in his sights, Heidegger asks in *Introduction to Metaphysics*:

> But where is the real nihilism at work? Where one clings to current beings and believes it is enough to take beings, as before, just as the beings that they are. But with this, one rejects the question of Being and treats Being as a nothing (*nihil*), which in a certain way it even 'is,' insofar as it essentially unfolds. Merely to chase after beings in the midst of the oblivion of Being—that is nihilism. Nihilism thus understood is the *ground* for the nihilism that Nietzsche exposed in the first book of *The Will to Power*. (GA 40: 212)

Heidegger's response to Nietzsche is that Nietzsche has also misunderstood the question of Being, merely standing Plato on his head by replacing Being with Becoming. Therefore Nietzsche only (albeit with great insight) grasped the epiphenomena of the ground of nihilism. The question of Being is "the question of the *meaning* of Being" (SZ, 1; italics modified). To ask this question is to ask how anything 'is' for us, *as meaningful*; whether it be a unicorn, a table, a number, or a concept, it *is* first and foremost meaningfully intelligible—its reality bracketed as a secondary matter. The question of Being is a question about how meaning, how intelligibility per se, is possible and happens phenomenologically for us.[18]

To put this in a way that Heidegger does not, the question of meaning "of" Being is not simply about how to define the word "Being"; rather, the "of" suggests that meaning *belongs* to Being, that the question is about how Being 'is' the unfolding of meaning in an intelligible world to us, for we manifestly cannot and do not live in a world of unmeaning, as if the things, sensations, language, and all that makes up our lived existence were just a muddled chaos of insignificance. As a *phenomenon* on the human scale, the world does *mean* to us, and Being's meaning confronts us as more than a world of brute sensation. The answer to the question, "Why is there Being rather than Nothing?" would be that meaning simply *is*, as a given, always already separated from unmeaning in the form of a world, beings, and practices that make sense to us—provisionally, because such meaning can degrade and slip into unmeaning. For Heidegger, the meaning of Being is always only accessible to us, as temporal beings, on the horizon of time; hence the book *Being and Time*. Also, because Being is what makes intelligibility and meaning possible, it itself cannot 'be' a 'being,' a thing, an entity among others, not even as a Supreme Being. It is much more like no-thing, because it is a non-entity. But this claim is not itself nihilistic for Heidegger, who holds that "real nihilism" is refusing to engage in such talk about "the Nothing," as he notoriously does, but rather to fail to distinguish between Being and beings, to chase as slaves to the will to power after dominion over beings, and to allow the question of Being to fall into oblivion. The impetus for that oblivion Heidegger lays at the feet of Plato, who supposedly taught that real Being, the fulness and origin of meaning, lies in a supra-sensory other-world of eternal ideas and forms.

2.4 SOCRATIC ZETETICISM

With this accusation in place, we turn to Plato and Plato's Socrates for a rejoinder. Socrates identifies himself in Book One of the *Republic* as one *who does not know*. After his long struggle against Thrasymachus's teaching that a life of injustice is best and that the life of the tyrant is the fullest expression of injustice, Socrates admits that "as a result of the discussion I know nothing [*mēden eidenai*]" (354b–c). He had begun the discussion in the same way, protesting that he is one who "does not know and does not profess to know" (337e). This looks like a version of the proverbial expression of Socratic ignorance in the *Apology*: that human wisdom consists in grasping that one "is worth nothing with respect to wisdom" (23b). Of course, Socratic irony is as famous as this quip about wisdom, and Thrasymachus is astute enough to call Socrates out for his "habitual irony" (337a). We must give Thrasymachus his due. If ironizing is a kind of lying, then Socrates does indeed seem to know more than he says. This is unmistakable to even the casual reader of the dialogues, and even more so in a dialogue as long and complex as the *Republic*: Socrates has thought through the issues and arguments before, and he often sets up his opponents many moves ahead. But this is not due to some crafty strategy to win prestige in the arena of elenchus—and thereby fees for teaching—in the style of the sophists, as Thrasymachus maliciously insinuates. If Socrates hesitates to speak entirely forthrightly about the nature of his wisdom in a particular conversation with a specific audience, this might be because that wisdom is complex and potentially disconcerting to precisely those about whom he is most concerned in his conversation with Thrasymachus: the young men gathered at the home of Cephalus who are on the cusp of making life-defining decisions about the nature of justice. Socrates, and by extension Plato, recognizes that the argument about justice and tyranny is not merely academic. It implicates the future aspirations of the most promising of the rising generation, and therefore it threatens the freedom of the polity.[19]

Thrasymachus does have a point: Socrates really does seem to understand more than he admits and his professed naiveté is partly an act. In Book 6, Socrates says, while discussing "what the good itself is," that "it looks to me as though it's out of the range of our present thrust to attain the opinions I now hold about it" (506e). Socrates clearly has an agenda, although it is not the vulgar one that Thrasymachus imputes, but the nobler one of turning a group of promising young men away from the allures of a life of injustice. In the context of an Athens that faced actual tyranny through the course of the Peloponnesian War, such a life is not merely hypothetical for these youths, and Thrasymachus has made a compelling case to them for the natural goodness of a life of tyranny. In fact, some of the youth present for this long, late-night conversation end up directly involved in resistance to the reign of the Thirty Tyrants who briefly ruled Athens after the war: Polemarchus, the son of the host to the gathering, was summarily executed by the Thirty for opposing them; his brother Lysias became an orator who sought justice against the Thirty in the courts. Glaucon and Adeimantus, Plato's brothers and Socrates's main interlocutors for most of the dialogue, begin by making forceful arguments for injustice and tyranny.[20] With their wealth and connections as aristocrats from an ancient Athenian family, they could have acted on these views. But Socrates wins them over to justice, and history does not record them living otherwise. So, although Socrates knows "nothing," he clearly does know enough to say that it would be "impious" (*mē . . . hosion*, 368b–c) to cede the field to injustice. How can this be, if he means what he says about his "human wisdom"? Even in Book 6, when Glaucon presses him in the name of justice to give his views of the good, the highest aim of knowing and action, Socrates demurs by asking if "it's just to speak about what one doesn't know as though one knew?" (506c).

Socratic denials of wisdom do not amount to a nihilistic skepticism. The nihilistically skeptical Socrates is the portrait one often gets from enthusiastic but hasty first readers of the dialogues, usually when they are just entering into philosophy. This is the wise-guy Socrates who wants to deflate anyone and everyone, who is so brilliant in the game of elenchus that he *can* beat anyone out of any opinion—which, of course, he sometimes fails to do, perhaps most famously with Parmenides in the eponymous dialogue. Glaucon and Adeimantus represent a developmental moment in the philosophical life, one especially attractive to the young, when the eristic techniques of philosophical interrogation first come to hand in a blaze of destructive glory. Aristophanes's *Clouds* supplies a satiric version of this youthful nihilism in the person of Pheidipides, who returns from his lessons in eristic at Socrates' Thinkery able to convince his own father that he should be able to beat him, as his father had done with him as a child.

Socrates himself hints at this moment in the *Apology*, when he suggests that one reason the Athenians might be angry with him is because young Athenians, who watch him use his method to break down the pompous and self-important, then use the same methods on their families. The nihilist skeptic embodies the purely deconstructive moment of philosophical analysis, gleefully annihilating any and all otherwise respectable claims to knowledge in order to build a reputation for a kind of negative wisdom and to promote an anarchic freedom from authority.[21] But Socrates does not beat just anyone and everyone out of any and every opinion. As Socrates responds to Callicles's accusations against him in the *Gorgias*, when he is destructive in discussion, this is not merely from spite or chagrin because he is at a loss for constructive arguments. Rather, says Socrates, it is because "I believe that I am one of a few Athenians . . . to take up the true political craft and practice the true politics. This is because the speeches I make on each occasion do not aim at gratification but at what's best" (521d). As Richard McKim puts it, Socrates's "professions are never merely ironical, they never preclude positive moral convictions."[22] The young Glaucon and Adeimantus *say* they want to believe in justice yet confess that they are almost won over by Thrasymachus. They want their wavering faith in justice restored by Socrates (358c–d). Does he give that faith its final push? He does the opposite. Why?

Because Socrates is a *zetetic* skeptic.[23] The term derives from the Greek *zētein*, meaning to search, to seek.[24] Philosophy for Socrates is a searching, a seeking, a yearning—an *eros*—for wisdom that entails that the search itself be meaningful (*Symposium*, 203b–204c). In his debate with Kojève about whether philosophy must always be sectarian because of its putative "subjective certainty" that divides thinking into antagonistic dogmas, Leo Strauss also has characterized Socrates as a zetetic. Strauss discerns an alternative to sectarian philosophy, if we recall that "philosophy in the original meaning of the term is nothing but knowledge of one's ignorance," that "philosophy is not wisdom but quest for wisdom" and "as such is neither dogmatic nor skeptic, and still less 'decisionist,' but zetetic (or skeptic in the in original sense of the term)."[25] Strauss recognizes that zetetic skepticism differs from nihilistic skepticism, because the zetetic search presumes a meaning, or a goal, or what I call an *intimation*, the provisional intuition of a truth not yet articulated and conceptualized. Nihilistic skepticism attacks both dogmatism *and the meaningfulness of the search for truth*. At issue is the status of the intimation underlying the search, but Strauss is oddly silent on this topic. Perhaps, for him, the politically relevant point is that the meaningfulness of the search *be posited*, not that it be detailed in any way, nor defended for its own sake. But an unspoken and undefended posit is hardly adequate to fend off a sophisticated and aggressive nihilistic skepticism, and so we need a more robust, positive defense of what I will call a Socratic *skeptical idealism*.

The famous term that Socrates employs in this context is *anamnēsis* (*Meno*, 81c–82a), usually translated as *recollection*.[26] I use the word *intimation*, provisionally, to describe an awareness that comes to us before we reach *anamnēsis*, before we recollect. In the *Meno*, Socrates explicitly presents the notion of *anamnēsis* as a matter of religious piety, a kind of myth, that he must "trust" as true in his zetetic pursuit of truth (81e: *hōi egō pisteuōn alēthei einai ethelō meta sou zētein aretē hoti estin*); he does not claim to know it, and certainly not as a doctrine. Rather, it is a heuristic device, a hypothesis, that he offers to make sense of a phenomenological datum: that we must have some pre-theoretical understanding of what it is we are seeking in any inquiry, or the search could not even begin. That we already have some access to what we do not yet know is a genuinely and profoundly puzzling matter, but without his version of philosophical piety, Socrates warns, we would fall prey to a sophist's trick, and "it would make us idle, and fainthearted men like to hear [this trick], whereas my argument makes them energetic and keen on the search [*ergatikous te kai zētētikous*]" (81d–e). Of course, there is a distinction between seeking as such and the intimation of what is sought. The example of the *Meno*, where Socrates elicits mathematical understanding from a slave boy, could suggest a fundamental gap between the two, because until you really do find the answer, you might not trust that you will ever be on track to solve the problem. But the lesson of the *Meno* is that without some intimation of what an answer might look like, you could not even get started on a path to it, much less recognize that you have arrived at an answer if you do.

This is the zetetic philosopher's manifesto against nihilistic skepticism. It foreshadows Heidegger's assertion in *Being and Time* that "Every questioning is a seeking. Every seeking takes its direction in advance from what is sought" (SZ, 5). In the prior phenomenological given, we simply do have such a pre-reflective understanding of what we seek, for without it, the seeking would not only be pointless, it would be senseless—as in not having any meaning at all. But that is manifestly not the case, because the intimation guides us and brings the questioning into a meaningful trajectory. It is the status and the meaning of these intimations that is philosophically problematic, and it is only as a heuristic and stopgap solution that Socrates offers up *anamnēsis* as a resolution in order to proceed in his conversation with Meno. The problem of *intimation* is phenomenologically prior to the Socratic myth (not the dogmatic theory!) of recollection, and Socrates himself understands this. To put it another way, *intimation* describes the phenomenon as a problem, and *recollection* offers a provisional explanation of how intimation is possible so that all subsequent philosophical inquiry does not become pointless. Otherwise, Meno would lose faith in learning about virtue and become "idle," or, in the terms of this project, he would give up on the polemical effort of philosophical dialectic. In this sense, the "doctrine" of recollection is a pedagogical and ethical second-best, made necessary by an ethical urgency in the absence of absolute knowledge.

Every hunt, as Socrates suggests in the *Meno* (80d–e), must begin with the scent of the quarry. We must have some intimation of what we are seeking, or the search quickly becomes pointless and philosophy gives way to nihilistic destruction of any and all belief. Surely this is why Socrates says that failing to defend justice would be impious. Socrates is not lying about the kind of wisdom he possesses, but he *is* dissembling, in the sense that he does not immediately explain what he is attempting to achieve in a given conversation. This is because an *intimation* of the good—or of anything decisive to the way we should live—is naturally elusive and hard to communicate, and hence vulnerable to the acid of a nihilistic skepticism. Socrates is willing to state his pious *conviction* that justice, virtue, wisdom, and the like all exist. He hesitates to state his opinion—or even that he has an opinion—as to what these *are*, because to describe and defend an intimation concerning the most decisive guides in life is to risk dispersing it altogether and thereby losing those listeners whose own convictions are at their most delicate. He says this explicitly: "[T]o present arguments [*logous poiesthai*] at a time when one is in doubt and seeking [*apsistounta de kai zētounta*]—which is just what I am doing—is a thing both frightening and slippery. . . . I'm afraid that in slipping from the truth where one least ought to slip, I'll not only fall myself but also drag my friends down with me" (450d–451a). Socrates is no absolute seer. *Logos* and dialogue do not lead invariably to insight, and he fears that conversation now may unhinge vital ethical beliefs.

Nevertheless, Socrates understands that there are times when one must run this risk. One cannot leave the young, who are the future of the polity, at the mercy of a mentor like Thrasymachus. This is why zetetic philosophy is not mysticism. While it adheres to a certain kind of faith in the meaningfulness of phenomena, it remains open to questioning and to reappraising all articulated

intuitions about that meaning and the theoretical elaborations of these intimations. Eventually, Socrates does offer an *argument*, a *logos*, rather than insisting on some privileged, gnostic insight. Mystical claims to gnostic insight
will not win over a Glaucon or an Adeimantus. Socrates is prepared to defend
and criticize his own intimations *rationally*, as need be, which distinguishes
his reliance on them from rank intuitionism.[27]

2.5 SOCRATIC PIETY, SOCRATIC TRUST, SOCRATIC PHENOMENOLOGY

The nature of the piety claimed by Socrates demands further investigation.
The passage of the *Republic* where he falls back on this piety comes in response to the vigorous arguments made by Glaucon and Adeimantus in favor
of injustice and tyranny as the best way to live, although they have left open
the possibility of being persuaded otherwise. Socrates replies to them by remembering their courage in the battle at Megara, and then says this:

> For something quite divine must certainly have happened to you, if you are
> remaining unpersuaded that injustice is better than justice when you are able
> to speak that way on its behalf. Now you truly don't seem to me to be being
> persuaded [by the argument for injustice]. I infer this from the rest of your
> character, since, on the basis of the arguments themselves, I would distrust
> [*ēpistoun*] you. And the more I trust [*pisteuō*] you, the more I'm at a loss as to
> what I should do. On the one hand, I can't help out. For in my opinion I'm not
> capable of it; my proof is that when I thought I showed in what I said to Thra-
> symachus that justice is better than injustice, you didn't accept it from me. On
> the other hand, I can't not help. For I'm afraid it might be impious to be here
> when justice is being spoken badly of and give up and not bring help while I
> am still breathing and able to make a sound. So the best thing is to succor her
> as I am able. (368a–c)

It is worth noting that Socrates refers to his duty to piety in the context of
the brothers' courage in battle in the service of Athens. Socrates adopts a language of courage, too, in his obligation to come to the aid of justice: "while I
am still breathing." Resisting impiety requires moral courage commensurate
to the physical courage displayed in battle for the sake of one's community.[28]
What connects them is trust, *pistis*: the morale of soldiers will break if they
cannot trust their companions to stand with them in face of death, and the
bonds of community will break if citizens cannot trust each other to be just.
Trust in the physical and moral courage of its members is necessary for the
polity to survive, and its members support each other reciprocally. Not giving up in battle implies a deep trust in shared convictions and the character

of one's friends, and trust in character and conviction lend spirit to physical courage when it is needed most.

In the image of the Divided Line described by Socrates in Book 6 of the *Republic*, trust belongs to the second of four divisions of the faculties of cognition, above imagination (*eikasia*), but below thought (*dianoia*) and intellection (*noēsis*). Trust and imagination apply to the changeable, sensible, visible realm of things, whereas thought and intellection, which cognize mathematical truths and the ideas respectively, belong to the eternal, supra-sensible, purely intelligible realm. Even if trust involves opinion rather than knowledge, a provisional trust in things and in people is indispensable for life. Trust is the mode of understanding that allows us to function in our everyday world of people and things, because life would be impossible if we had to confirm with apodictic certainty everything and everyone before engaging with them. It is the background of all our practices, weaving the fabric of sense and meaning and establishing the givens of what Heidegger would call our Being-in-the-world. Trust has a *dignity* for Socrates. It is not simply a debased version of comprehension, beneath the thought that grants understanding of mathematics or the intellection that grants insight into the ideas. Trust is a necessarily constitutive feature of our existence as knowers in the broad sense. That does not mean that trust is indefeasible, only that it is mostly inescapable for being-human and therefore must be respected in its proper place.

While Socrates does not mention his famous *daimonion*, the divine voice that would sometimes come to him, in his declaration of piety, it is worth noticing that his decision to argue in defense of justice fits his description in the *Apology* of his experience with his *daimonion*: "This is something which began for me in childhood: a sort of voice comes, and whenever it comes, it always turns me away from whatever I am about to do, but never turns me forward [*protrepei de oupote*]" (31d). Socrates was tried and executed on the twin charges of impiety and corrupting the youth. They go together because, as someone whom his accusers perceive as a sophist or some sort of teacher, Socrates's purported impiety threatens to spread to the young, undermining the shared convictions that sustain civic trust. Miletus had cited Socrates's *daimonion*, which must have been well-known to Athenians, as a mark of his impiety as not believing in the gods of the city. Socrates cites his *daimonion* precisely to prove his piety to the divine and to his city. For an example of the latter, he reminds the jury of an episode during one of the few times he had served in public office, as one of the prytaneis, an executive officer of the Athenian council:

> And it happened that our tribe, Antiochis, held the prytany when you [that is, the Athenian democracy] wished to judge the ten generals (the ones who did not

pick up the men from the naval battle) as a group—unlawfully, as it seemed to all of you in the time afterwards. I alone of the prytaneis opposed your doing anything against the laws then, and I voted against it. And although the orators were ready to indict me and arrest me, and you were ordering and shouting, I supposed that I should run the risk with the law and the just rather than side with you because of fear of prison or death when you were counseling unjust things. (32b–c)[29]

This illustrates what Socrates means by the moral courage necessary for political piety to face actual persecution rather than merely fractious insults. It also clarifies what Socrates means by saying that his *daimonion* "always turns me away [*apotrepei*] from whatever I am about to do, but never turns me forward [*protrepei de oupote*]." In the case of the generals, Socrates obviously did more than just turn away from an action, because he deliberately voted against charging the generals. That the voice "never turns me forward" is puzzling, because it seems that commanding an action is exactly what it did in this case. But while the voice did command him to act *against* (*apo-*) the motion for trial, it did not indicate what should be done with the generals going *forward* (*pro-*).

This form of deflective action to prevent an injustice explains how, in the *Republic*, Socrates feels an obligation to defend justice while also hesitating to come "forward" with some positive claim to knowledge. Glaucon, Adeimantus, and the other young men apply intense pressure on him to provide a positive teaching about the life of justice, rather than just a refutation of Thrasymachus. Furthermore, the dramatic context of the dialogue indicates that Socrates understands this might be a decisive moment for whether they actually become corrupted by the lure of injustice. Other young associates of Socrates, such as Critias, Alcibiades, and Charmides, were seduced by tyrannical ambitions later in life, and Athens surely had them in mind when bringing the charge of corrupting the youth against Socrates. In the *Republic*, which others have properly seen as constituting a second apology for Socrates against the city's charges, Socrates's piety wins out over his humility because the trust essential for the city as a unified body politic, not to mention for the well-being of the souls of the young men individually, is at stake.[30] Socrates cannot let that pass. While he does not say so, the daemonic voice seems to have commanded him to act. His offer to provide the young men his opinion about justice and the good is then a second best to a claim to unfailing knowledge, compelled by his piety to the trust necessary to sustain human community.

Socrates' autobiographical account in the *Phaedo* of his "second sailing" (99d) in philosophy sheds further light on the epistemic-ethical responsibility of the zetetic philosopher, which I am calling *Socratic piety*. Socrates describes his first foray into philosophy as follows: "When I was a young man I was wonderfully keen on that wisdom which they call natural science, for I thought it splendid to know the causes of everything, why it comes to be, why it perishes and why it exists" (96a–b).[31] Here, Socrates seeks a final knowledge of the cause of the Being of all things: why and how each and all come to be (*gignetai*), pass from being (*apollutai*), and simply *are* (*esti*). This was his first way of asking the question of the meaning of Being, which he recognizes as this temporal emergence, existing, and passing-away of things as meaningfully what they are. He begins by considering answers that we now would recognize as ones offered by natural science, though primitive by modern standards. These attempt to explain all phenomena, as well as our cognitive apparatus for knowing them, purely in terms of physical causes and processes, arising from some fundamental element or other (water or air or fire) and some process (combination or putrefaction).

After many false starts, the young Socrates came to realize that chasing these scientific explanations had "made me quite blind even to those things which I and others [*emautō kai tois allois*] thought that I clearly knew before, so that I unlearned what I thought I knew before, about many other things" (96c). What was it that he "knew" (*ēpistamēn*) before, and in what sense of knowing? Because clearly he neither knew it then nor knows it now, in the strict sense of an apodictic, fully justified certainty, because he was neither satisfied then nor now with the status of his knowing. He mentions both his own prior confidence and that of "others": the navigable meaning of the world was and is a shared meaning, dependent upon a provisionally convincing understanding among a historically situated community. At stake is a phenomenological knowing, one that allows discourse and action to make sense in a shared hermeneutical context. This is the context for what we will call a Socratic phenomenology, and his pursuit of the forms is a way of illuminating the sense-making meanings that fellow human beings bring to the *logos* of even everyday life.

As a prosaic example, he describes how while once he thought, as it seemed "obvious to anyone" (96c, *pro tou panti dēloun*), that people grow by eating and drinking, his scientific inquiries convinced him that no such commonsensical answer would be adequate, because our natural, everyday understanding of phenomena is superficial and naive. In modern terms, explaining the causes for why and how we grow requires knowing everything about ingestion and digestion, the genetics of how DNA instructs proteins for cell development and decay, the biology of how this transpires for a specific organism, the chemistry of how this happens at the molecular level, and probably also the particle physics that underlies the chemical reactions. Socrates's point is that chasing after such explanations detached him from the everyday understanding of something as straightforward as eating and growth that was already accessible to him and other human beings in life as it is lived *on the human scale*. This is the mode of life that ordinarily matters to us, that involves the human beings that we are, embedded in communities and located in place and time with all the cares, concerns, struggles, and attachments this entails. There is always-already an implicit ontological knowing of the meaning of things and how they matter within such a context, which is not the same as an ontic knowledge of the facts of the matter. Life on this human scale constitutes what is at-issue ethically for each of us in the life examined. Its meaning is accessible through a phenomenological attention to what people say about what and how things in fact do mean something to them, even if only provisionally and subject to revision through the *polemos* of *dialogos*. The ideas, as a heuristic, allow Socrates to focus on this phenomenological seeing.

Socrates has insisted that "I do not speak disrespectfully of such knowledge" (*Apology*, 19c) in natural science, only that he had "no aptitude at all for that kind of investigation" (*Phaedo*, 96c). More worrisome to him, though, is that such investigations made him "quite blind" to how it was that such simple things were somehow already meaningful, taken at that purely human scale of everyday life. His second sailing therefore begins with the realization that this human-scale understanding also deserves his attention, because establishing what enables that more directly accessible understanding would not only prevent the blindness that natural science threatened but also make such human-scale meaningfulness more secure. So, rather than look directly at the sun as careless people do during an eclipse, which risks blindness (99d)—that is, rather than seek causes so far removed from the lived human experience that this very endeavor risks eclipsing—he will seek an indirect way to do what Aristotle would later call "preserving the phenomena" (*Nicomachean Ethics*, 1145b2–7), much as the philosopher in his Cave Allegory does by returning back down after escaping. He will do this simply by dialoguing with people, asking their opinions at the human scale of understanding.

The more personal and political example that Socrates mentions next involves how one should explain the cause or reason (*aitia*) for why he was sitting there in the Athenian prison, waiting for the hemlock to be administered for his execution, and which he himself will later freely choose to drink without complaint or hesitation (117c). A reductive scientism would say "that the reason that I am sitting here is because my body consists of bones and sinews" and that the respective relaxation and tension of flesh, bone, and sinew is "the cause of my sitting here with my limbs bent" (98c–d). Such an account fails to save the phenomena, because it leaves out precisely what is most humanly relevant as the "true causes" (*alēthōs aitias*) for why he happens to be sitting there in that prison: "that, after the Athenians decided it was better to condemn me, for this reason it seems best to me to sit here and more right to remain and endure whatever penalty they ordered" (98e–99a). Of the merely physical aspects of why he is there, Socrates says, "To call those things causes is too absurd [*lian atopon*]. If someone said that without bones and sinews and all such things, I should not be able to do what I decided, he would be right, but surely to say that they are the cause of what I do, and that I have chosen the best course [*tou beltistou hairesei*], even though I act with my mind [*nōi prattōn*], is to speak very lazily and carelessly" (99a–b). In the context of what is humanly important, explaining Socrates's free choice (*hairesis*) to do what to his mind (*nous*) seemed best in purely physicalist terms—to stay and endure rather than to flee the city's punishment—would utterly lose touch with what is at-issue on the human scale. Physiology could not explain the relation of his freedom to his responsibility to the city, to his friends there with him, and to philosophy itself as the life worth living. Nor could it explain his specific free decisions in private and political life.

It is in the context of his blindness and perplexity about finding meaning on the human scale of existence that Socrates offers to explain "his second sailing [*deuteron ploun*] into the search [*zētēsin*] for the cause" of things (99d, tm). *Deuteros ploos* is a Greek expression meaning a second best, a backup plan, a new departure after the failure of a first attempt. The younger Socrates concluded that he "must take refuge in *logous* [words, discussions, arguments] and, through them, examine the truth of what is [*tōn ontōn*]" (99e). By this, Socrates says he means "nothing new" (100d), but rather what his companions would recognize as what he has been doing for many years now: dialoguing with them and others to make the best sense he can of things as what they appear to be, in terms of the forms, *eidē* (102b). There is a fundamental ethical component to this phenomenology of the *logos* and *dialogos*: that access to the meaning of things, the world, and even meaning as such comes from taking seriously what others say *as* a manifestation of what they mean, what matters to them, and what guides their lives. Even if what they themselves can identify as their intended meaning falls short of full consistency upon examination, the respect granted to their meaning-intending is a recognition of their personhood that cannot be reified.

This reversion to what people say is what I call a *Socratic phenomenology*. What Socrates has come to realize is that however naïve these might seem, people's words and talk, especially in the kind of conversations he conducts, do in fact contain a meaning. This meaning lies both on the surface—after all, language serves for everyday communication—and in a shared pathway through dialogue to a deeper understanding of the *context* for meaningful communication not yet understood by either the speaker or the philosophical inquirer. The simple, brute fact that some provisional meaning exists to sustain a background intelligibility for the world is given by everyday experience on the human scale. For Socrates, the best way available to tease out the cause of that meaning is through eliciting a deeper understanding of the forms, or ideas. This, he says, "is the safest answer I can give myself or anyone else" (100d–e). The most telling testimony for this Socratic phenomenology comes from Socrates himself, in his depiction of the Cave Allegory, after he has described its relation to the Divided Line and the released prisoner-philosopher's ascent from and return to the prison-house of the cave: "A god doubtless knows if it happens to be true. At all events, *this is the way the phenomena look to me* [*emoi phainomena houtō phainetai*]" (517b; my emphasis).[32] (See Figures 1 and 2.)

Socrates also says that "I by no means concede that whoever investigates what is [*ta onta*] by way of words and discourses [*tois logois*] is dealing in images [*eikosi*] any more than someone investigating it by way of the workings of things [*tois ergois*]" (100a). The Greek here is parsimonious, but Socrates is distinguishing *words*, language, and dialogue (*logoi*) from *deeds*, the workings of the world (*ergoi*), or perhaps what we would call facts or data, and claiming that *both* words and the facts are in a certain sense *images*, because neither is itself directly the *cause* of the meaning of what is. Otherwise we would not need to seek an explanation beyond direct experience, either through a scientific examination of beings or through dialogue with what people say about them. Beings, both people and things, always already have some provisional meaning to us that we understand; otherwise, we could neither function in the world nor share language. But we can talk with people in a way we cannot with things. What they say reflects, if only in part, the meaning already inherent to our shared experience of the world.

This is the heart of phenomenology as Socrates practices it: that what people *say* reflects the meaning that is in some way already there for them, even if that "look" of things as they appear, *phainetai*, to each person individually, is a finite, situated perspective. The reflection of the *logos*, then, is an image of a meaning we might be able to grasp more fully through dialogue, the communication (*logos*) and conflict (*polemos*) of perspectives. Here in the *Phaedo* and then in the *Republic*, Socrates calls the forms and ideas his *hypothesis*, a Greek word for something set down in advance that can underlie and hold up whatever is subsequently built upon it. The Latinate correlate would be *supposition*, the placing of a substrate to hold up a construction build upon it, as axioms or postulates do in geometry and mathematics. The forms and ideas are not a theory or doctrine; they are a hypothesis employed to explore the sense-making of our understanding. The world as it matters to us already has its rough-and-ready intelligibility. Its meaning is simply a given, but never without puzzles and contradictions through which meaning can be investigated, clarified, and revised. More emphatically, meaning can escape us into unmeaning in ways we cannot predict or prevent. We will see this in more detail as we proceed.

Socrates says that his second sailing is a *search*, a *zētēsis*, for the cause of the world's intelligibility. As such, it is an ongoing confrontation, a *polemos*, with the given meaning of things, one that Socrates conducts through his characteristic dialogues. But what keeps this ongoing dialogue going?

This returns us to the topic of Socratic piety. One might expect Socrates to have a dim view of piety, given how completely he demolishes the definitions of it offered by Euthyphro, the ludicrously self-important, self-appointed seer of the will of the gods. The *Euthyphro* dialogue ends in *aporia*, a failure to arrive at a definition of piety. Nevertheless, the narrative structure of the dialogue and Socrates's intense demolitions of Euthyphro's definitions suggest that genuine piety requires a sense of shame and modesty, which the dogmatic Euthyphro lacks. In the *Republic*, by contrast, Socrates is unusually forthright in advancing his own idea of justice, which he defines as each minding her or his own proper role in the community. Both dialogues lie in the shadow of Socrates' trial and execution for impiety.

The *Euthyphro* takes place on the steps of the courthouse where Socrates is about to be tried (2a). When Euthyphro tells Socrates that he is so wise that he "knows precisely" (*akribōs eideiēn*, 5a) the things divine, Socrates leaps at the opportunity to have him define piety. Socrates does so ostensibly to gain insight from Euthyphro for the upcoming trial, which pleases Euthyphro's vanity, but Socrates's numerous ironic, even bitingly sarcastic references to Euthyphro's pretensions suggest otherwise (4a–b, 6a–b). Socrates is shocked by Euthyphro's arrogance in violating filial piety by presuming to prosecute his own father, years after the fact, for what seems the father's justifiable or at least excusable homicide to defend others (9a–b). The narrative of the dialogue suggests that Socrates sought to undermine Euthyphro's confidence in pursuing the prosecution. In a sense, Socrates' *daimonion* was serving as a proxy in an attempt to prevent Euthyphro from perpetrating a gravely impious act. A negative *aporia* for Euthyphro would be an appropriate conclusion.

2.6 ZETETIC PIETY IN THE *REPUBLIC*: PLEDGING TROTH TO THE IDEA

The situation in the *Republic* is very different. In that gathering, Socrates cannot escape the positive task of defining justice and convincing some of the most promising youth of Athens that the life of injustice is not worth attempting. This is no merely academic question. When Socrates says it would be impious if he did not make the effort to defend justice, a Greek audience for *Plato's* dialogue would understand the context: that Socrates's piety reinforced the virtues of the men who would later resist a tyranny for the sake of Athenian democracy. Again, Plato offers an indirect defense of Socrates against the charges of impiety and corrupting the youth. Even more to the purpose here is the question of the phenomenological meaning of his Socratic piety and what gives it force. How does an "examined" life occasion this ethical piety, and what guides it?

My claim is that an engaged ethical confrontation with the circumstances of one's life, philosophy as a polemical ethics, demands piety in the following sense. One must assume and sustain the hypothesis that an ethical life does have a meaning, even if that meaning has not yet been worked out thematically and justified fully, as we would find in a treatise by an Aristotle, a Mill, or a Kant. The zeteticism of the life examined as the mode of philosophy requires that the search not be nonsensical or it will collapse into nihilism. The heart of Socrates's second sailing in the *Phaedo* is not merely an epistemological or metaphysical claim (although it is these as well), but rather an ethical one that allows him to sustain a meaningful life with others. Furthermore, if not the forms or ideas, then something *like* them is necessary as a hypothesis for any *specific* ethical engagement, in deed or discussion, with both persons and problems about justice, courage, piety, or any other ethical virtue or political principle. Without expansive concepts like 'justice' or 'fairness,' ethical engagement devolves into conventional polemics or outright violence over ever-changing rules with no real ethical substance. We would not be able to listen to one another, which requires harkening generously to both the meaning as intended in what others say and to what also exceeds their intended meaning as unsaid but as potentially the ground for discovery and reconciliation in confrontation.[33] There might be another, perhaps better, metaphor for what can guide a meaningful inquiry than the visual one of what-has-been-sighted-in-advance, the ordinary-language meaning of the Greek *idea* and *eidos*. Nevertheless, without something like the idea, projected in any discussion of what is at-issue ethically as the form of the matter in question, ethical life would not be possible.

That is the phenomenological claim. It is corroborated by an extraordinary passage in the *Republic*, in Book 7, after the Allegory of the Cave and during the discussion of the education of the philosopher-rulers in dialectic—extraordinary, because it is one of the rare places where Socrates seems to be speaking unironically and forthrightly about his most important beliefs. Instead of drawing opinions from his partners in dialogue, Socrates here declares a belief as his own. Glaucon asks Socrates to show him all the forms and stages of dialectic, "For these, as it seems, would lead at last toward that place which for the one who reaches it a rest from the road, as it were, and an end of his journey" (532e; tm). Glaucon refers to that upward path from the cave that finally *ends* the journey in the light of day; instead of *aporia*, no way out, he wants a *telos tēs poreias*, an end to the journey, a putting-aside of philosophy once it reaches its goal. This is an echonic conception of philosophy as completed in absolute knowing. But Socrates demurs:

> You would no longer be able to follow, my dear Glaucon, although there wouldn't be any lack of eagerness on my part. But you would no longer be seeing an image of what we are saying but rather the truth itself, *at least as it appears to me.* Whether it really is so or not can no longer be properly insisted on. *But that there is some such something to see must be insisted on.* Isn't it so? (533a, tm; my emphasis)

By an image (*eikōn*) in this context, Socrates means both the Divided Line and, as an image of that image, the Allegory of the Cave. These are only icons of the truth, not the truth itself, which may be seen directly (as Plato says in the Seventh Letter), but cannot be shared directly and discursively by image or argument, only prepared by these. The truth is *alogon*, what Mark Ralkowski has called *ontologically ineffable*, not because it is irrational but because there is no way to *compel* someone to apprehend it by argument or indication.[34] This is why Socrates famously describes philosophical education as a *turning around* (*periagōgē*, 518c–d) of the whole soul, because while one can move someone to look, one cannot force them to see. Socrates cannot *insist*, even if he can argue, that what truth is as it *appears to him* (*moi phainetai*) is what the truth *really is* (*ontōs*—"beingly is"), or not. Against Glaucon's absolutist expectation, Socrates reasserts his zetetic modesty. At the same time, he does not give up on his skeptical idealism, because he does say that, phenomenologically, there must be *some such something to see* that "must be insisted on." Otherwise, there simply could be no navigable, meaningful world, even in its ruptures and finitude, that could be engaged in the work of a polemically reconstructive life of philosophy.

The Greek here for "must be insisted on" is *ischuristeon*, from *ischurizomai*, to maintain something stoutly, to stand firm on something, to trust in something. That last meaning, to *trust*, is attested by the Indo-European root of *ischurizomai*, which is *deru-* or *dreu-*, which is the root for the English *tree*, *trust*, and *truth*, as well as more archaic words such as *troth*: when I pledge my troth, I pledge to stand firm, to stand true, like a tree deeply rooted, standing against adversity—as Socrates does when he affirms that it would be impious of him not to fight for justice when it is attacked.[35] So, while the

Greek for 'trust' is *pistis*, and for 'truth' is *alētheia*, the English word family of tree-trust-truth-troth, even more properly than the Greek, unites Socrates's meaning here: that whatever the truth is, we cannot *not* trust in some such something (*toiouton ti*) as what gives meaning to an intelligible world in which we can, provisionally, function. Socratic piety is pledging this troth to truth so that there be some ground to stand on as rooted in the world. But because human understanding is finite, the skeptical idealist's trust in truth is not a dogmatic insistence on any *existing* interpretations of the world. Rather, it is a trust that the polemical confrontation with meaning, through dialectical philosophy, is capable of ever-reconstructing meaning when it breaks down in deconstruction. Glaucon understands this when he says to Socrates, in this same passage, "it's not only now that these things must be heard [that is, concerning the Divided Line, the Cave, dialectic, and so on], but they must all be returned to many times in the future" (532d). Skeptical idealism, as polemical, as zetetic, is necessarily reiterative in its turning and returning.

2.7 THE POLEMIC BETWEEN ZETETIC AND ECHONIC PHILOSOPHY

This portrait of a piously zetetic Socrates is utterly at odds with the portrait that Socrates himself draws of the philosopher-kings—and queens, we must not forget—of Kallipolis, the supposedly ideal city, built through speech and imagination in the *Republic*.[36] Socrates and his interlocutors give these philosophers the right and the duty to rule because they are *knowers*: "Since philosophers are those who are able to grasp [*echontos dunamenoi ephaptes-thai*] what is always the same in all respects, while those who are not able to do so but wander among what is many and varies in all ways are not philosophers, which should be the leaders of a city?" (484b). We know the answer: the philosophers should rule! These are *echonic* philosophers, from the Greek *echein*, to have, to hold. They *possess* the truth; they *grasp* what is "always the same" and, presumably, can wield it ruling the polity: in establishing institutions, laying down laws, educating the young in civic and personal virtue, and cultivating the next generation of philosopher-rulers. Theirs are not mere intimations at the outset of a search into what the truth might be. They "come to the end" of their study (504c–d). They arrive at what Drew Hyland calls "absolute transcendence."[37] They *know* the forms of justice and virtue. They have *seen* the good in its full glory and can understand and apply it without mediating metaphors such as Socrates's sun or the Divided Line.

To know such things is to understand fully what is best for human beings, just as to know how the body works is to understand what diet is most healthy or when to perform an operation. Just as we want doctors who are knowers to tend the body, we need philosophers who are knowers to tend the city. They *have* what it takes. This version of the philosopher as absolute knower who has arrived at complete understanding at the end of the path of questioning approximates the humanistic model that Heidegger rejects. The path of the philosopher-rulers seems to result in a Platonic metaphysics, founded on an epistemology that locates the truth in a transcendent, eternal realm. This culminates in a nihilistic modernity making this truth the foundation for a machinational will to power, reducing the human and natural worlds to resources mastered by the application of ready-made formulae.

Remarkably, Socrates does *not* present *himself* as an echonic philosopher. This is pivotal in the confrontation between Plato and Heidegger, because *Plato* does not represent Socrates as the type of philosopher that the internal argument of the *Republic* establishes as paradigmatic of philosophy and of the right to rule in the supposedly ideal polity. This is no small irony. In the most famous philosophical work that makes the most famously exalted claims about philosophers, the famous philosopher making such claims does not pretend to be such a philosopher himself!

Is this just Plato's little joke? Hardly. Plato may be ironizing about the pretentions of philosophy, but the point is deadly serious. If *Socrates* is not a philosopher, who can hope to be? Or is Socrates *in fact* an echonic philosopher whose own dissembling irony is so profound that we cannot see that he has just stepped into the cave after a long sojourn in the light of the Good that is even beyond Being (509b: *epekeina tēs ousias*)? No. Plato is not playing the buffoon with Socrates, who may know more than he usually lets on, if there is a zetetic way of knowing that doesn't indulge in the absolutes of echonicism, but he has no pretensions of being a philosopher-king.

The implicit but unmistakable distinction between zetetic and echonic philosophy in the *Republic* affects the whole metaphysical-ontological-political-ethical-pedagogical teaching of Books 6 and 7, comprising the sun as an image of the good, the Divided Line as an image for the articulation of Being in the meaning of the world, and the allegory of the cave. That teaching takes on a very different aspect depending on which account of philosophy you think is the right one. Heidegger and his descendants have accepted the traditional view that Socrates and Plato cleave to the dogmatically echonic model of philosophy: Platonism is a *theory*, a *doctrine*, decisive for the West, about how philosophy may possess the truth. After all, 'everyone' from St. Augustine to Nietzsche says this is what Plato is about; so it must be so.[38]

For example, perhaps the most conventional and paradigmatic modern exposition of Plato as echonic philosopher adhering to a *doctrine* of the forms can be found in Russell's essay, "Plato's Theory of Ideas." It never crosses

Russell's mind that Plato might not identify totally with Socrates, much less that Socrates himself is at all tentative about his *hypothesis* concerning the ideas. At the other pole, in a postmodernist reflection of the echonic Plato, Reiner Schürmann asks, "Quite as happiness for Plato is the *possession* of the subsisting Good, [so does not nihilism] consist in the full *possession* of presencing, in a total presence that stills all desire and all absence?"[39] On such readings, Plato's Divided Line shows how reality, or Being, is divided into separate realms, one earthly and illusory, one heavenly and pure. This bifurcation of existence into the corruption of this world and the exaltation of another one must mean, as Henry Mendell has put it in a commentary on the *Phaedo*, that "The only good philosopher is a dead philosopher."[40] The cave allegory describes how one may ascend the Divided Line by correct representations of reality. This is Plato's conception of truth on such readings.

The echonic philosopher's vision of the good, the sun that sheds light on all reality and serves as the foundation of Being, renders all knowledge cohesive and secure. According to Heidegger, the good in Plato is the idea of the *enabling*, what allows things to *fit in*, to *serve their teleological purpose* (*das Tauglichmachende*, GA 9: 133–34). It is what makes possible the essence of everything in terms of each thing's specific *idea*, and thereby enables "all forms of foresighted insight into practical action" (GA 9: 135). Through the idea of the good, "*alētheia* comes under the yoke of the *idea*" (GA 9:136). To *know* the good, to possess the ideas, is to understand how to make *use* of everything that is, which is what Heidegger feared from an instrumental, machinational reason in service to the will to power. As discussed in the introduction, Heidegger locates in Plato the onset of nihilism: the will to subject Being to a representational system of ontic truth that can be placed at the service of the subjugation of nature, a project that forgets that ontological truth as unconcealment is not subject to the human will.

But the story of the cave reads differently depending on whether one accepts the echonic or the zetetic model of philosophy. The immediate narrative context of the dialogue in the *Republic* itself, of course, would suggest applying the echonic model of philosophy. The Allegory arises in discussing how to educate those worthy of rule, the philosopher kings and queens. Whatever we might say about their education, its culmination, on the narrative's surface, must be a vision of the final and absolute source, the cause and reason (*aitia*) for all that is. Even more than this, that vision of the ultimate source provides the now-qualified ruler with an understanding of how reality is articulated through all the ins and outs of a particular historical world. This articulation of the truth through all aspects of knowing that Socrates addresses in his image of the Divided Line, addressed in chapter 3, means that when the former seeker finds completion as a possessor of an inerrant truth, grounded in a transcendent reality, it becomes applicable, by those properly enlightened, to the shifting shadows of the temporal present. The philosopher-ruler can see the reality latent in all phenomena, even in the shadows of the cave, which correspond to the specific opinions and traditions of a particular historical community. This ability to grasp the real in all its refracted articulations is what both enables and entitles the echonic philosopher to rule, just as the proper understanding of chemistry, biology, and anatomy does for a doctor to practice medicine.

How would the zetetic model map onto the Allegory? The beginning of the story might be the same. The person enchained by the dominant opinions of historical circumstances might, under the influence of some accidental experience or the deliberate questioning of the right kind of teacher, break the bonds of the given. The unbound prisoner, no longer a prisoner but not yet enlightened, might then ascend a difficult path of education. But towards what? According to the Allegory, perhaps towards the light at the end of the tunnel along the "rough, steep, upward way" (515e) out of the cave into the light of day. But if philosophy as zetetic means a seeking rather than a coming to the end of inquiry in final possession of the truth, this process of striving can last only as long as ascending the tunnel out from the underground realm. To emerge into the light means to search no longer, to reach the absolute truth, to possess it, and so to be able to return into the cave with that truth as the power and the authority to rule.

Someone like Socrates seems condemned always to ascend through the upward path but never to emerge into the light. And yet Socrates clearly *does* see light at the end of the tunnel in two senses. First, he has his intimations of the truth. While these are not full possession of the truth, they are hopeful glimmerings that lead him onward and give the search meaning. Furthermore, he can *imagine* what the echonic experience of emerging into the full light of the sun *might* be like. This is precisely what Socrates is doing in recounting the parable of the cave, for he himself does not claim to have made it out.

To merge Heideggerian and Platonic idioms: the world is the realm of the cave—its historical setting, its beliefs, its customs, its social and political arrangements. To stand up, to throw off the chains, is to deconstruct: to take notice of hitherto unnoticed structures that bind our thinking and to break their hold. Many postmodernists remain fixated at this level: they become intoxicated with the initial thrill of liberation from the bonds of traditional structures, convinced that any new imposition of structure is simply a new style of ideological enchainment. Yet they secretly long for the would-be tyrant to make his attempt at subjugation because they are addicted to fighting all positing of structure, without realizing that there can be no intelligibility without some structure. To the postmodern anarchist, this is freedom—a purely negative dialectic that ever and again *requires* that unjust authorities arise so that freedom can manifest itself again through the deconstruction of their doctrines and regimes. Liberation becomes a perpetual adolescence.

Heidegger, of course, was not the anarchist that some of his postmodernist readers, such as Reiner Schürmann, have become. He did believe, at least in his middle period, that great creators could serve as a conduit for a new dispensation of Being, a new arrangement of the intelligible world, as result of the deconstruction of the past. Construction might follow deconstruction, but because Heidegger did not believe in a final vision of Being, there could be no standard for what new construction would be best. I suspect that this faith in unhinged creativity is one reason for Heidegger's complete lack of practical wisdom in siding with the National Socialists.[41] We will return to the question of what guides practical wisdom in chapter 7.

The Socratic or zetetic model of philosophy does allow for guidance to action. The *intimation* of a transcendent truth gives us something to go on, but it demands precisely the modesty that would counter the hubris that Heidegger at his best detects in the modern project. An intimation is not yet possession of the absolute. It is not yet a *doctrine*, if by doctrine we mean a *theory* that an author defends in the form of an orthodox *system*. Plato nowhere presents a theory of forms or ideas, only various hypotheses offered by Socrates that serve as tentative responses to an array of inescapable problems.[42] To use the term from chapter 1, in zetetic philosophy deconstruction is followed by *preconstruction*, the provisional construction of the outlines of an integrated account of something in the light of a truth only partially glimpsed. Such preconstruction must leave itself open to revision or even to complete rejection, but in the realm of praxis it can provide principled standards of action that are precisely *not* doctrinaire but rather address the specificity of our situatedness and remain open to correction as context changes.

Zetetic philosophy, as skeptical idealism, is bold enough to depart from the given but modest enough to return to it without laying claim to the final story. It straddles hubris and humility, tragedy and comedy. That is why it can also be *reconstructive* as well as preconstructive. It does not remain fixated on casting off the chains of the given past. It understands that attempts at an integrated understanding of the world, whether philosophical or traditional, *logos* or *mythos*, must fail to attain the absolute. In preconstructing a better arrangement in the light of the best account we can give so far, we necessarily draw upon the intimations of truth latent in the tradition to which we belong, because we always-already exist in the shadows of that understanding. Socrates clearly attends to this reconstructive ethos in the new departure he describes in the *Phaedo*, namely, to listen to what people say about what matters (*Phaedo*, 99d–100a). Surely this is what is going on in Socrates's enthusiasm for Cephalus's belief that justice exists, even as Socrates demolishes Cephalus's specific account of justice. Surely reconstruction is also at work in Socrates's pious defense of the young against Thrasymachus's incitement to tyranny. So, we have three moments to the zetetic journey: the liberation from the bonds (deconstruction), the ascent upwards (preconstruction), and the return to the cave (reconstruction). All three moments are necessary for the full expression of human freedom.

But then why does *Plato* give us this double model of Socrates as a zetetic philosopher and of the echonic philosopher as the ideal Socrates proposes? Because of the need for preconstruction, the *hypothesis* (cf. 533b–d). Without setting up (-*thesis*) something beneath (*hypo-*) the given as its support, however temporary a scaffold this may be, the search will lapse into despondency, hopelessness, and nihilism. If the given is unsatisfactory and we seek to make it better, then we need some intimation of the good to indicate that our striving is not meaningless. The intimation need not be, indeed should not be, final and absolute, but it can call us to construing (preconstructing, envisioning) alternatives to what presently is and to defend those alternatives with what we ordinarily recognize as philosophical arguments, all as part of the process of responding to the questions evoked by wonder about the breakdowns in ethical life that bring us up short. This cycle of philosophy as de-, pre-, and reconstruction is what distinguishes zeteticism from either intuitionism or doctrinaire absolutism.

Through the portrait of Socrates as a midwife of ideas (*Theaetetus*, 148e), Plato deliberately establishes a tension between the echonic and zetetic models of philosophy, because philosophy, especially for the young, might never get beyond the vague promise of an answer and abandon its search, but it may also misstep as philosophy if it believes that it has already arrived at its destination. Plato presents this tension and does not resolve it for us, because mature philosophizing requires that we resolve it for ourselves in a resolution that is precisely *not* completed but always under way. This always-under-way of philosophy is the *polemos* between the echonic and zetetic modes of philosophizing.[43]

So, Plato has even Kallipolis, the best city, decompose in Book 8 of the *Republic*, because the philosopher-rulers cannot maintain absolute command of the "nuptial number," a comically complex mathematical formula for the eugenics of procreation needed in the city to maintain the right proportions of the various kinds of citizens suited to the various necessary occupations. While the echonic wisdom of the rulers provides them with timeless truths, the finitude of the temporal world, which requires the constant biological reproduction of the social structures of the polity over the generations, prevents the formula from inerrant application. The equilibrium of the society eventually falters and the polity decays, because it fails to ensure that the right kinds of people serve in their proper roles, and so faction breaks up the body politic. The absurdity of the nuptial number is a deliberate joke on Plato's part, but a serious one that suggests the limits of hubris in pretending to a technocratic mastery of the world through echonic truth. Absolute possession of the truth cannot be maintained absolutely, if at all.

In the cosmic parable of the Myth of Er (614b–621b) at the close of the *Republic*, Socrates leaves the young men with a vision of the whole that is a *mythos*, not a full and thorough rational account, a *logos*. As a myth, it is a substitute for the complete, echonic *logos* of the truth that Socrates cannot provide. As *mythos*, Er's tale serves positively the goals of *logos*: as a modest confidence in reason. It reinforces the intimation that the world does make sense as a cosmos, and therefore that rational inquiry also makes sense—not by *making sense* of the whole as such, completely and absolutely, but as guided by the glimmering light at the end of the tunnel.

Plato presents the two models of philosophy, the echonic and the zetetic, simultaneously in the *Republic*, in the figure of the philosopher-ruler on the one hand and Socrates on the other. He does so because the zetetic journey (*poreia*, 621d) needs, as its fuel, the echonic preconstructions of the truth about the whole. Without thinking up in imagination alternative visions of the world and thinking through in argument why they might or might not be true, we could not make even the preliminary claims to knowledge that subsequent inquiry would analyze, criticize, debate, or defend in the living work of zetetic philosophy. The zetetic analysis of echonic claims is like digestion: by deconstructing them into their more elemental components, it can then reconstruct them in new configurations that serve the ongoing inquiry. Plato invites us to enter the *polemos* of the dialectic between these two models by enabling us to question the written but still living dialogue that is the *Republic*, through its apparent lapses and problematic arguments, deliberately providing us with a jump-start to philosophical dialogue. The *Republic* itself, after all, is a narrative, a myth, a conversation that can remain in motion. Plato presents such preconstructions as myths (the Er story) or as unrealized ideals (Kallipolis and the philosopher-rulers). And what is an unrealized ideal but a myth? But if, in our finitude, we can only make sense of our world through ideation and a narrative construal of the meaning of our situatedness, then myth is a positive feature of our sense-making, rather than a failure or just a second-best. So long as we do not reify the myth as ontic truth, myth provides the narrative context for the de-, pre-, and reconstructions of the historical world we inhabit. Such tales are *only* intimations, and as such, they must be constructively deconstructed to serve as the fuel for spurring on zetetic philosophy's search.

Philosophy, then, is a journey of reconstructions that ends only with death, as Plato and Socrates tell us in so many ways. Of the three moments of construing the world, deconstruction, preconstruction, and reconstruction, the last takes precedence, Although preconstruction envisions and formulates an alternative to a world that has broken down, reconstruction most properly engages with our future in the world by negotiating the situated transcendence of our existence. Far from setting up the goal of an absolute knowledge to which we may aspire as the tool of domination over the whole, Plato's reconstructive vision of philosophy establishes grounds for modesty even as we dare to re-collect the pieces of the whole, ever again. Platonic freedom is found neither in anarchistic deconstruction nor in the systematic imposition of a final theory, but rather in the outrageously everyday dance between myth and reason.

2.8 BACK TO THE CAVE

In his 1931–32 lecture course, *On the Essence of Truth*, in a discussion of the escape and subsequent return to the cave, Heidegger writes that "truth is no static possession by dint of whose enjoyment we can set ourselves up comfortably in some standpoint or other so that from there we can lecture everyone else; rather, unconcealment *happens* only in the *history* of ongoing liberation" (GA 34: 91). Heidegger's claim here may seem compatible with the zetetic interpretation, but we should note several things. One is that Heidegger's writings are equivocal about whether nihilism begins with Plato or with Platonism. Another is that, even assuming the latter, Heidegger fails adequately to rescue Plato, in the kind of sustained recuperation he bestows upon a Heraclitus, from the nihilism he ascribes to Platonism. Finally, to make sense of what we don't *possess* of the truth, much depends here on what Heidegger means by the historicity of the liberator's return to the cave and the truth achieved there.

Heidegger describes the escaped prisoner who returns to the cave as confronting a history that "is always a unique task, fate in a determinate situation for practical action, not some free-floating discussion in itself. The one who has become free should be there in the cave and assert his opinion about what, for those there, beings and the unconcealed are" (GA 34: 91). He says that "The climb down into the cave is no fun-filled afterthought," taken up in idle curiosity, "but rather is the properly authentic *fulfillment* of becoming free" (GA 34: 91). We know from *Being and Time* that fate as *Schicksal* is not crude, mystic predetermination of events but rather the ontological given that one's own possibilities of meaning are bound up in the structures of meaning carried forward by one's community in its history. Here we can agree with Heidegger. We cannot do otherwise but address our concerns in terms that make sense to the finite world in which we find ourselves. But Heidegger goes on to argue that the truth to be won here, in going back to the cave, is the truth of *alētheia* as the alpha-privative, as *Auseinander-setzung*, that is, as confrontation, as a setting-apart.

This is Heidegger's ontology of the *polemos*, according to which unhiddenness is torn from concealment by a "*primordial* struggle (not mere polemics), which means the struggle that first *creates* for itself its enemy and opponent and helps that one up to the *highest opposition*" (GA 34: 92). Because for Heidegger this *polemos* at the heart of truth is always historical and only historical, "we come to suspect that in Plato it is not yet, or no longer, grasped *primordially,*" and that "in Plato the fundamental experience from which the word *a-lētheia* emerged is already disappearing" (GA 34: 93). For Heidegger, then, Plato's truth as genuine transcendence, an exit from the cave, is a falling-away from the conflictual heart of truth as unconcealment. We cannot *possess* the latter truth because we do not own or master history or fate, although we confront them continually. And yet, without the touchstone of truth in Plato's sense, as an ideal to strive for, can there properly be an escape, a return, and a redemption (however partial) for the prisoner or the cave? Heidegger's polemical truth binds us just as firmly to the cave wall as the shadows do, for historicity has no exit. Plato's zetetic truth has a trajectory and a destination, even as it strives and struggles polemically with the given.

Another objection (connected to the first) is that the zetetic model of philosophy, while not absolutist in its own particular claims, still makes the absolute, or the transcendent, its ideal, even if never attained. As such, it is only a debased version of the same old otherworldly Platonism that Nietzsche derided and Heidegger deconstructed. There is some truth to this charge, though much of its weight depends on how much of a threat one takes transcendent ideals to be and whether they are in fact otherworldly in a pejorative sense that prevents them from having significance for a this-worldly endeavor to perfect the understanding and community as fully as possible.[44] Without any *intimation* of such ideals, ethical and political standards, together with all criteria for action, become indefensible as matters of rational discourse. Surely this also is a serious threat. Heidegger and postmodernists may be right to emphasize our finitude and our temporality, but the result of their deconstruction of the Western tradition is a lapse into an extreme relativism and historicism from which no appeal to transcendent principles is possible without hypocrisy. As I will argue in chapters 5 and 6, by contrast, Socratic zetetic philosophy begins in and returns to our finitude, just as the prisoner begins in and returns to the cave, bringing finitude and transcendence into a dialectic. Plato's lesson is that this dialectic can be taken up responsibly but never resolved, and that any attempt to resolve it will result in philosophical and political disaster. Plato's bold modesty, a dynamic between *tolma* and *sōphrosunē*, is what saves him from the worst excesses of scientistic modernism or its mirror image, dogmatic fundamentalism.

This leads to a third objection.[45] The passage up from the fire in the cave to the sun outside it, Plato says, is a "rough, steep, upward way" (516e). Would not many give it up in despair if it never reaches an end? If we postulate a transcendent truth but never reach it, won't those who follow this path finally become disillusioned and turn to either nihilism or dogmatism for comfort? This is indeed a danger, but it is one that freedom must risk. Surely it is the existential, epistemological justice that democracy must embrace, at some level, or else the deliberative electoral process becomes a sham, to be replaced by a leadership that claims total knowledge and prohibits the search for wisdom altogether in favor of dogmatic traditionalism. Here I agree with Stanley Rosen that nihilism is endemic to the human condition, so any attempt to eradicate it will only aggravate the problem.[46] Freedom must always include the freedom to deny meaning and standards, and the defense of these against nihilism must remain alive to there being no final solution to the predicament. Again, this means that in every generation we must do what Socrates does in the *Republic*: defend the rational faith in justice. And recall that zetetic philosophy is not nihilistic skepticism, debunking just *any* claim to wisdom. Robust liberal education and strong civic institutions must prepare and preserve a prudent freedom. There is no formula for this. It is a matter of a society's cultivation of the appropriate civic virtues and practical wisdom as a feature of an eleutheric liberalism.

Everything hinges, then, on the intimations of transcendence, for these are what provide hope on the upward path as well as on that same path *downward*, when the reformer descends to reconstruct the world in the light of an intimated ideal. Good education and institutions nurture and sustain the citizen's personal and civic dialogue with these intimations, just as they sustain us, each in our individuated situatedness and as members of a historical community. An intimation arises when, through reflection, discussion, or attentive observation, we recognize the limitation of an accepted opinion, grasp a new, potential truth, and return to our old opinion to find it and all its filiations more fully illuminated in their historical context. An intimation gathers to it all three moments of the zetetic journey: the wonder or shock at an irruption of unmeaning; the attempt to formulate a question to address that breakdown; and the response to the question as an attempt at reconstruction. Anyone who has thought critically about a matter of practical urgency that grips them personally—not just theoretically—in ethical or political life has had such an experience. Heidegger himself argues that intelligibility is not possible without some fore-structures of meaning that we posit, or, more properly, within which we find ourselves always already *positioned*, or in the terminology I am using, *situated*. These intimations of meaning allow us to make a fuller sense of our circumstances whenever we engage in an act of interpretation—which is always, because we *are* hermeneutical beings. It is our calling to enter into a polemical encounter with the structures of meaning within which we find ourselves.

To be sure, for Heidegger, the fore-structure is always the finite product of specific historical Dasein, not an intimation of the transcendent, but I would argue that without intimations in Plato's sense, the experience of engaging in philosophy, of entering into a discussion of a topic across the boundaries of culture and history, would be impossible. Our intimations of justice or virtue or wisdom may all begin within the finite bounds of our own historical situations, but they point to a realm that transcends them without utterly obliterating our finite habitations. We are contingently, not absolutely, free, but this contingency intimates the absolute. Hence the necessity of reconstruction after the liberation of deconstruction. Because total transcendence is beyond us, we should not despise, forget or annihilate the cave within which all meaningful inquiry begins and to which it must go back, if we follow the allegory—which we must, for human existence begins and ends enclosed by finitude, although it is punctuated by transcendence. To accept the burden of philosophy as zetetic and polemical in the larger sense is to recognize it as a lifelong, ongoing task, one that, properly understood, far from causing despair, opens up the richness of the human condition—suspended, as we are, between finitude and transcendence, between earth and sky.

NOTES

1. Wordsworth, "The Excursion," in *The Collected Poems*, 971, lines 1141–44.

2. In what follows, I will capitalize "Cave" and "Allegory" when referring to these as names for a feature of Plato's philosophy, and I will refer to the "cave" in lowercase when discussing its details as a narrative element in Socrates's argument.

3. Gonzalez's analysis in *Plato and Heidegger* is thorough and trenchant, although in my view it does not draw out the political meaning of Heidegger's interpretations sufficiently, especially in *Being and Truth* (GA 36/37). In addition, see his articles "Dialectic as 'Philosophical Embarrassment'" and "Confronting Heidegger on Logos and Being in Plato's *Sophist*."

4. Also, GA 43: 254: "In Plato's work there is as yet no Platonism. The 'true world' [a supersensible world as ultimate reality] is not yet the object of a doctrine."

5. Less comprehensive treatments include a short passage in Heidegger's 1926 lecture course on the history of ancient philosophy (GA 22: 102–107); another in the 1927 lecture course, *Basic Problems of Phenomenology* (GA 24: 403–405); a very short discussion in the 1927–1928 *Phenomenological Interpretation of Kant's Critique of Pure Reason* (GA 25: 398), where he gives a neo-Kantian reading of Plato's ideas as a precursor to Kant's transcendental analytic of the understanding. These do not develop the elaborate interpretation of the four stages of liberation found in the later readings.

6. E.g., GA 36/37: 119, 147–48, 178, 210–13, 225.

7. For the text history, see the editor's afterword by Hermann Mörchen to the 1931–32 course, GA 34: 333.

8. Gonzalez, *Plato and Heidegger*, 112–13. For other interpretations of Plato and Heidegger on truth and on the Cave Allegory, see the chapters by Michael Inwood, Enrico Berti, Maria del Carmen Paredes, Joseph Margolis, Stanley Rosen, Johannes Fritsche, and Tom Rockmore in *Heidegger and Plato: Toward Dialogue*, edited by Catalin Partenie and Tom Rockmore. Another helpful overview is James McGuirk, "*Alētheia* and Heidegger's Transitional Readings of Plato's Cave Allegories." For a reading that carefully situates Heidegger's interpretation of Plato in the context of neo-Kantianism dominant in Heidegger's early career, see Robert Dostal, "Beyond Being: Heidegger's Plato."

9. Cf. GA 36/37: 146–50, and especially 165–66 and following, where Heidegger describes Plato's "doctrine of the ideas" as linked to the failure to understand truth as *alētheia* adequately, which ultimately results in modern liberal universalism as a late degenerate form of Platonism.

10. See Sheehan, *Making Sense of Heidegger*, 71–78.

11. Levinas, "Ethics of the Infinite," 73–74.

12. See Merleau-Ponty, *The Phenomenology of Perception*, Part 1, "The Body," and Young, *Justice and the Politics of Difference*, chapter 5, "The Scaling of Bodies and the Politics of Difference."

13. The most comprehensive treatment of this theme in Heidegger is his "Question Concerning Technology" in GA 9.

14. René Descartes, *Discourse on Method*, 50.

15. Consider J. S. Mill's famous "harm principle" in *On Liberty*, in *The Basic Writings*, 86.

16. The best discussion of both the strengths and the critiques of Heidegger on truth is Daniel Dahlstrom's *Heidegger's Concept of Truth*. Especially helpful are Dahlstrom's explication of existential truth in chapter 4 and, in chapter 5.1–5.2, his careful exposition of and response to Ernst Tugendhat's important attack on Heidegger's ontological conception of truth as disclosedness as effectively rendering the operative meaning of truth void.

17. Here and following, I refer by section to Kaufmann and Hollingdales's translation.

18. Thomas Sheehan makes this point with admirable clarity in *Making Sense of Heidegger: A Paradigm Shift*.

19. For a discussion of the young men present and their future significance, see Bloom, *The Republic of Plato*, 440fn3.

20. For details about the lives of the historical figures in Plato's dialogues, see Debra Nails, *The People of Plato*.

21. For example, see the "Praise of Helen," a defense speech written by Gorgias for a woman more traditionally deemed guilty for plunging the Greeks and Trojans into war, or his deliberately outrageous proof that "nothing exists," in Curd, *A Presocratics Reader*, 148–53.

22. McKim, "Shame and Truth in Plato's *Gorgias*," in Griswold, *Platonic Writing/Platonic Readings*, 36.

23. For an account of philosophical knowing and practice compatible with the recognition of finitude in zeteticism, see Jean-Luc Marion, *Negative Certainties*.

24. The Pyrrhonist skeptics were the first to describe themselves explicitly as "zetetic," but Socrates was not a skeptic in their sense. Socrates expresses to Meno his wish *skepsasthai kai suzētēsai* ("to examine and to seek together") what virtue is (80d). See the rest of this passage for further uses of *zētein*. For zetetic Pyrrhonism, see Sextus Empiricus, *Outlines of Pyrrhonism*, Book 1, 2–3, 156–88, 162–63 (I.1.2, I.2.11, I.2.19). At issue between Pyrrhonist and Socratic zeteticism is whether the search alone has merit or if it requires, in order to avoid nihilism, what I call below a preconstruction of the aim of the search. Zeteticism calls for the latter; Pyrrhonism abstains from such suppositions.

25. See Strauss, *On Tyranny*, 208–10.

26. I rely here on Grube's translation of the *Meno* in Plato, *Complete Works*. Cf. Jacob Klein, *A Commentary on Plato's Meno* 94–99 and chapter 5.

27. Compare the discussion of "reflective equilibrium" in John Rawls, *A Theory of Justice*, 20–22, 48–51.

28. For Socrates' use of military language for the courage of philosophy, see Marina McCoy, *Plato on the Rhetoric of Sophists and Philosophers*, 30–31.

29. All quotations of the *Apology* are from the translation by T. G. West and G. S. West, *Four Texts on Socrates*.

30. Cf. Bloom, who calls the *Republic* "the true apology" for Socrates in his "Interpretive Essay" in *The Republic of Plato*, 307–10.

31. For the *Phaedo*, I rely on the Grube translation in Plato, *Collected Works.*

32. For a perceptive account of Socratic phenomenology for politics in the absence of decisive knowledge of the good, see Trott, "Saving the Appearances of Plato's Cave." I agree with Trott about the centrality of dialogue for healthy, anti-tyrannical politics on the Platonic account, but I would emphasize more than she the role of the ideas as the motivating intimations for the ameliorative work of a polemical ethics in political life.

33. This is the domain of respect for others in *meaning-intending* as a phenomenological-hermeneutical correlate to the Kantian respect for persons that I hope to address in subsequent work on enacting polemical ethics.

34. See Mark Ralkowski, *Heidegger's Platonism*, chapters 1 and 2.

35. See Julius Pokorny, *Indogermanisches Etymologisches Wörterbuch*, 215–16, and Calvert Watkins, *Dictionary of Indo-European Roots*, 17.

36. Here I follow David Roochnik in employing the name Socrates himself gives to the city constructed in speech: Kallipolis, "the beautiful city" (572c). See David Roochnik, *Beautiful City*, 8.

37. Hyland, *Finitude and Transcendence*, 57.

38. For a brief and compelling history of Platonism that supports my reading, see Ralkowski, *Heidegger's Platonism*, chapter 1.

39. Russell, "Plato's Theory of Ideas" in *A History of Philosophy*; Schürmann, *Heidegger on Being and Acting*, 215.

40. Henry Mendell, in an unpublished paper of this name, provided privately.

41. See Fried, *Heidegger's Polemos*, 251–25.

42. I am indebted here to the work of Drew Hyland and Stanley Rosen and to conversations with David Roochnik. See Hyland, *Finitude and Transcendence*, especially chapter 7, and Rosen, *Nihilism*, and Roochnik, *Beautiful City*.

43. As Francisco Gonzalez points out, it is puzzling that Heidegger, who insists that Dasein is *unterwegs*, cannot see this *unterwegs* at the heart of Plato's dialectic, a dialectic essentially different from the Hegelian one. See Gonzalez, *"Dialectic as 'Philosophical Embarrassment,'"* 374. My sense is that Heidegger cannot imagine a thinking that is both *under way* and not also utterly bounded by historical finitude. Apart from rare moments, Heidegger seems unable to read Plato as anything but the writer of treatises. The Platonic *dialogue*, as such, as an instantiation of the *dialectic* between finitude and transcendence, is quite simply invisible to him. Cf. Hyland, *Questioning Platonism*, 35.

44. On this issue, consider the powerful point made by Charles Griswold in "Longing for the Best: Plato on Reconciliation with Imperfection," 121: "A very different possibility is conspicuous by its absence from these seminal passages [in the *Symposium* and *Phaedrus*], namely that the uniqueness, passingness, and mixedness of an individual are the necessary conditions of his or her being lovable, indeed, lovable just as this imperfect, complex, particular being. This is a failure common to the *Republic* and the dialogues on love. That thought cannot be coherently pursued, I think, within a Platonic framework." This passage encapsulates what I am treating as Heidegger's claims about the failure of Platonist idealism to account for the belonging and meaningfulness of finite human existence. What I argue for is a reading of the Cave that allows us to reconcile the beloved imperfections of our specific and embedded historicity with a zetetic perfectionism, as always incomplete, that emerges from, returns to, reconstitutes, and defends a reconstruction of that finitude. For Griswold, "the Platonic view is an invitation to a dangerous reification of persons, and thus a negation of their moral status qua individuals" (129). My claim is that the work of situated transcendence we may glean from Plato both constitutes and reconstitutes the moral status of persons by taking their imperfection as an invitation to a dialogical and reiterative cycle of engaged polemical amelioration rather than passive acceptance or indifference.

45. I am grateful to Alan Rosenberg for suggesting this objection.

46. See Rosen, *Nihilism*, especially chapter 6.

Chapter Three

Seeing Sun and Shadow

The Metaphorics of Vision in the Cave

The name 'human' [*anthrōpos*] signifies that the other beasts neither scrutinize nor reflect upon what they see, nor do they look into it closely, whereas the human, once having seen—that is, '*opōpe*'—both looks closely into it and reasons upon what has been seen. Thus, the human, alone among the beasts, is correctly called '*anthrōpos*,' because the human looks closely into [*anathrōn*] what has been seen [*opōpe*].

—Socrates, in Plato, *Cratylus*, 399c

In chapter 2, I argued that we must go back to the cave in order to respond to Heidegger's charge that Platonism, especially Plato's idea-ism, represents the descent into the nihilistic degradation of ontological truth as *alētheia*. At stake in the return to the cave is not simply what we are but who we are as human beings, and how freedom and truth are integral to human-being. This lies at the heart of the metaethics of the human condition. My claim, against Heidegger, is that a certain kind of Socratic piety, or trust in the ideas, rather than being a foundation for a dogmatic metaphysics, is a constitutive feature of being-human, one that Socrates makes the core of his own phenomenology of ethical life. Now I must begin to defend the cave as the operative metaphor for the metaethics of knowing, understanding, and interpreting. The first step is to address the metaphorics of vision, light, and shadow as the epistemological and ontological context for the *idea*, the what-has-been-seen. For that, we need to understand why this metaphorics of vision is not merely arbitrary.

3.1 VISIONARY KNOWING

Plato's core metaphysical or epistemological concepts, *eidos* and *idea*, are grounded in vision. They mean what has a visible form (*eidos*) and what has been seen (*idea*), both having an etymological connection to modern English words such as *vision* and *video*. In *Republic* Book 6, Socrates's exalted explanation of the knowledge required by the philosopher-rulers of the ideal city takes the sun and vision as the way to make sense of truth and understanding. The sun, in his telling, is akin to the most exalted idea of all, the idea of the good (*idea tou agathou*), which bestows intelligibility upon all other ideas, and indeed upon all reality across what has been called the Divided Line. This line divides the world into things perceived by the mind and by the senses, most especially the sense of sight, and therefore into genuine knowledge and insecure opinion.

Sense-perception as metaphor for purely mental cognition is so natural because it shares with the problem of knowledge and meaning the experience of taking something in and appropriating it into a larger context of response to the world. Vision has been the dominant metaphor for knowledge in Western philosophy. As a metaphor for knowledge, vision has its strengths. Vision, like the understanding, can take in a wide nexus of things all at once, discerning their differences and relative positions to one another, as well as how they integrate as a whole. It also has its weaknesses, such as how vision can erect a distance between seer and seen, knower and known, which can become a pathology of disinterested *theoria*, of contemplation without engagement or concern, purely for one's own edification, risking an Icarean detachment from the involvements of human life that can culminate in nihilism.[1] It has other limitations, as critics of ocularcentrism have pointed out, as in the feminist critique of the male gaze as the aggressive assumption of ownership or the decolonial critique of theory as the way the West imposes its worldview on others.[2]

Nevertheless, all metaphor slips and fails to express adequately the phenomenal experience of the world because language is always at work renegotiating meaning. That is why at both the grand scale and in everyday speech language must remain poetic to go on living. The sheer pervasiveness of vision as metaphor for understanding makes it inevitable as a linguistic touchstone in discussions of epistemology and metaphysics. Even Heidegger is a Platonist in that his most prevalent metaphors for the understanding and for what makes understanding possible are also grounded in vision and light. There is the *Vorsicht* of Dasein's understanding that grants a provisional intelligibility to the world; there is the *Umsicht*, the circumspection of Dasein's engaged situatedness that 'sees around' in a context and allows Dasein to make sense of all the filiations of meanings among things; there is the *Lich-tung* that allows a world of meaning to light up as intelligible and to open up for the understanding to inhabit. What Heidegger wants to deny is that *phenomenological* seeing and illumination have anything to do with conventional ethics or with a capacity for transcendence beyond world as historical. Vision is where the *polemos* with Heidegger takes the field.

3.2 THE SUN AND THE DIVIDED LINE AS IMAGES FOR KNOWLEDGE

Interpretations of the sun and the Divided line in Book 6 of the *Republic* are legion for good reason. This is where Socrates gives one of the most detailed and metaphorically gripping presentations of his understanding of the ideas, knowledge and understanding, truth, and Being. In what follows, I do not survey in detail the many competing interpretations of the role of the sun, the idea of the good, and the Divided Line in Platonic metaphysics, epistemology, and political philosophy, as that would be a major study of its own. My goal is to provide a plausible reading of these elements, both to carry out the *polemos* between Plato and Heidegger and to set the foundation for my own interpretation of the Cave Allegory.

Socrates presents his position in Book 6 as his actual view. In so many other circumstances he pleads ignorance, perhaps because Socrates believes it is philosophically, pedagogically, and even politically more prudent to ironize about his own degree of understanding about a *ti esti*, a particular "What is it?" question that he has asked, such as the one about justice. This is precisely what Thrasymachus both misunderstands and berates him for in Book 1, calling him a "sycophant in arguments" (340d) and calling him out on his "habitual irony" (*eiōthuia eirōneia*), predicting that "you [Socrates] wouldn't be willing to answer [the question about what justice is], that you would be ironic and do anything rather than answer if someone asked you something" (337a). The word *eiōthuia*, habitual, is related the verb *ethein* and the noun *ēthos*, ethics in the sense of the way of life that one routinely in-habits. While we have had over two thousand years of admiration for and discussion of Socrates's famous irony, *eirōneia* was not obviously a compliment in Greek, as it meant a dissimulation, a phoniness, a self-disguising.[3]

All language, all conceptuality as such, is ironic, because language simultaneously illumines and obscures. Like Heraclitus's *polemos*, it allows things to 'show up' as what they are, but it also obscures their resistant earthiness, the 'fact' that no words and no metaphors can entirely capture the *onton sauthon*, that there will always be slippage in meaning, as (to use Heidegger's language about it) the earthiness of language consistently thrusts up into the world, destabilizing it. This *polemos* of earth and world is embodied in historical language, and it is an aspect of why *logos* and *polemos* are "the same" (GA 40: 66). Plato is ironic because Socrates is ironic because language is ironic.[4] As Plato says in the Seventh Letter, "because of the weakness of words" (*dia to tōn logōn asthenes*), no human language can totally and finally fulfill the *logos*. Because human reason and speech are discursive and finite, they cannot account all at once and eternally for the whole of all possible meaning. And yet for *dialogos* to be possible at all, we must make the attempt, absent this full presence of meaning, by confronting the given meaning of things and zetetically seeking to reconstitute the whole. We see this in both our grand and petty struggles and play with language, from the lowly pun that twists our expectations of words without transforming them, to poetry that coaxes new meaning from words, to the coining of philosophical terminology that endeavors to anchor insights in conceptual form.

The inevitable irony of genuine philosophizing fits with Thrasymachus castigating Socrates as a *sycophant* in arguments. Thrasymachus interprets Socrates's zetetic modesty as weakness and the inability to make echonic claims to wisdom. In Greek, the meaning of *sukophantēs* is not primarily an obsequious person who tries to garner favor with those of higher status, but a kind of a con-man, someone who earns a living through blackmail, slander, and denouncing fellow citizens to the courts. As Allan Bloom explains in his note on the text, sycophants "distorted the meaning of men's acts and statements, and Socrates, accused of making the worse argument appear the better, could be compared. He was trying to make trouble and make his interlocutors look bad before the public."[5] In this case, the "public" are the wealthy and high-status young men at Cephalus's house. Thrasymachus probably perceives himself in competition with Socrates to make them his paying pupils, at least at first, before his defeat by Socrates. He sees Socrates's ironizing as a feeble gimmick for deflating competitors, and certainly not as a mark of his bold yet modest ambition for what constitutes a philosophical life. Thrasymachus therefore assumes that for philosophy to be possible at all, it must achieve echonic wisdom, and that means Socrates is a failure and a fraud. But this echonic conception of the role of the ideas robs them of their positively aporetic role in opening our eyes to the contradictions in things, not for the sake of eristic refutation and victory in argument, as a sophist would have it, but for driving zetetic wisdom onward towards truth.

Socrates must have *looked* like a sophistical con-man to many Athenians, given the depiction of him in Aristophanes's *Clouds* and the fact of his indictment for impiety and corrupting the youth. This makes it especially significant that in Book 6 he does assert, seemingly unequivocally, that he has an *opinion* about what the good (*to agathon*) is. The young men have practically begged Socrates to tell them what that is, because they have just determined in the dialogue that the philosopher-rulers must know the good as the final seal of their knowledge and the legitimacy of their rule (505a), and they may also justifiably think that knowledge of the good would be indispensable for living a *good life*. In keeping with his refusal to identify with the echonic philosophers of Kallipolis, who have "come to the end" (504d) of their studies and possess the entire and absolute truth, Socrates, the zetetic philosopher, denies any such knowledge. He tells them, "Let's leave aside for the time being what the good itself is—for it looks to me as though it's out of the range of our present thrust to attain the opinions I now hold about it. But I'm willing to tell what looks like a child of the good and most similar to it" (506e).

Socrates's zeteticism is on full view here. While echonic philosophy must be static, having attained an eternal knowledge that will not alter, zeteticism means that Socrates must speak in terms of "the time being" (*to nun*), "our present thrust" (*parousan hormēn*), and "the opinions I now hold" (*dokountos emoi ta nun*) of the good (506e). Because of human finitude, zetetic philosophy is *temporal*, and so Socrates's opinions are always potentially *temporary* and, according to the metaphor he will now use, subject to re-vision. The "child of the good" is the sun, the first image he employs. The second is the Divided Line. These serve to illuminate on a topic apparently so difficult and abstract that Socrates himself does not claim to understand it fully and that is virtually impossible to describe directly: the good and the idea of the good. So, the first thing to note is that Socrates acknowledges, quite explicitly, that what he will be presenting is not, to borrow from Kant, the thing in itself, but rather an image of it: the sun as image (*eikōn*, 509a) of the good.

On the Divided Line (as illustrated in Figure 2), images are the lowest level of being, the furthest removed (apart from what simply *is not*) from what truly is. Crucially, Socrates will use an image, what is lowest, and call upon the imaginations of his companions in dialogue, as Plato calls on ours, to address what is the highest, the idea of the good. Although described as a *line* (*grammē*, 509d), the Divided Line bends back upon itself, as a kind of ontological moebius strip. The highest meets up with the lowest, idea with imagination, as evidenced that we can and must actively enact in understanding what Socrates is explaining. This is inherent to the dialectic between imagination and idea in ideation.

An important clue to how this works is that unlike the other faculties of mind, which only apprehend their objects, imagination is capable of *producing* its object as well (*poiēsis*). Imagination is therefore *like* or *akin to* the idea of the good. Socrates must *produce* an image of the good and invite his interlocutors to participate in this act of imagination, to discuss what is beyond (*epekeina*) image. The idea of the good is therefore like Heidegger's *Ereignis* in being beyond being in the usual sense. Both are what make meaning as such possible in the first place. The key difference is that the idea of the good has an ethical teleology to it. Consider also that the whole *Republic*, though portraying a dialogue, is in fact entirely narrated to a silent companion who, like us (*homoious hemin!*), must imagine it to understand it.

Socrates begins his analogy by reminding his companions that "for all the things that we then set down as many"—for example, I can draw "many" different particular triangles and different kinds of triangle on a blackboard— "we refer them to one *idea* of each as though the *idea* were one, and we address it as that which really *is* [*ho estin*]" (507b)—in my example, the idea of the triangle. He adds that "the former [that is, the many instances of a thing, such as triangles] are seen but not intellected, while the *ideas* are intellected but not seen" (507b). This makes sense if we consider that while someone might see the figures of triangles on a blackboard, they might not 'get' that these are all triangles, and that someone might see what 'triangle' is with the mind's eye without seeing a visible one.

Next, Socrates employs the sun as an offspring (508b) and image (509a) of the good as *analogon*, analogously proportionate to good (508b): "as the good is in the intelligible region with respect to intelligence and what is intellected [*noun te kai nooumena*], so the sun is in the visible region with respect to sight and what is seen" (508b–c). In this analogy, just as the sun provides the light that illumines things and allows our eyes to see them—that is, to discern them in their individual distinctiveness and their collective relations to one another so that we might navigate an environment—so, when the soul "fixes itself on that which is illumined by truth and that which *is*, it intellects, knows, and appears to possess intelligence" (508d). Bloom translates *nous* as "intelligence" in this passage, which is helpful in relating it to the cognate forms *noētos*, intelligible region, and *nooumena*, the things intellected. But it is important not to hear 'intelligence' in our ordinary sense of brainpower but rather as *intellection*, the capacity for taking things in through insight or rational intuition. For this reason, Socrates says that "what provides the truth to the things known and gives the power to the one who knows, is the *idea* of the good" (508e).

We can make some brief points about this famous assertion. One is that the truth here, *alētheia*, can be understood as close to Heidegger's sense of truth as *a-lētheia*, unconcealment. It is not the truth of propositions but rather the truth of an opening-up, an access to understanding, to intellection or insight. This is mysterious because one might think that the idea alone, such as the idea of the triangle, would be enough to explain that a variety of shapes, which have some but not all features in common, are all instances of the single abstraction 'triangle.' Why is the idea *of the good*, which seems to be an idea above and apart from the rest of the class of ideas, needed in addition to serve as the "sun" of the mind's eye? Only an *integrative* interpretation of the images of the sun and Divided Line can resolve this.

Socrates makes the idea of the good even more problematic when he tells Glaucon that not only is there this separate idea of the good, and not only that this idea is more beautiful than knowledge and truth, but that "not only being known is present in the things known as a consequence of the good, but also existence and being are in them besides as a result of it, although the good isn't being but is still beyond being, exceeding it in dignity and power" (509b). At these exalted heights of metaphysics, Socrates says that "Glaucon, quite ridiculously, said, 'Apollo, what a daimonic excess'" (509c). The Greek here rendered as "daimonic excess" is *daimonias huperbolēs*, and one might think that Glaucon is referring to what in English we call *hyperbole*: that the assertion about the good as beyond truth, existence, and being itself is an absurdly overwrought and portentous claim. In Greek, *huperbolē* is literally a throwing-beyond, but more figuratively *any* kind of superiority, excess, or preeminence. This can include hyperbole in our sense, but not as its primary meaning. By saying that Socrates has spoken *daimonias huperbolēs*, Glaucon is both punning on and echoing what Socrates has just said: that compared to being, the good is *dunamei huperechontos*. It exceeds being in power, as well as in dignity. So, while Glaucon might be poking playful fun at Socrates's lofty notion of the good, it is not obvious that he is contemptuously saying that Socrates is speaking pretentiously and hyperbolically. Rather, he is affirming that the superiority of the good, in exceeding *and* comprising truth, knowledge, beauty, and being, is a *daimonias huperbolēs*, a *divinely* overarching supremacy, above and beyond and yet still responsible for all other things.

Some have argued that when Socrates says that Glaucon made this outburst "ridiculously"—*gelaiōn*: laughably, absurdly—this is Plato's hint to the careful reader that what Socrates is saying here truly is laughably ridiculous, that this whole headlong flight of an Icarean metaphysics is seriously comic: *comic*, because an absurd extravagance of high-flying, cloud-cuckoo-land philosophy; *seriously*, because some people, like Glaucon, seem to need this kind of thing to keep them on the straight-and-narrow belief that truth, beauty, and the good all form a whole that supports the edifice of justice and virtue.[6] That is certainly the Nietzschean reading of Platonic metaphysics as the supremely creative but ultimately farcical and slanderous lie that strives to hold the chaos and the horror of the world at bay.[7]

But Socrates responds by soberly saying, "You are responsible for compelling me to tell my opinions about it" (509c), that is, about the good, and Glaucon bids him, "Don't under any conditions stop" and "don't leave even the slightest thing out" (509c). Plato has introduced an ambiguity here befitting the audacity of philosophy: that its aspirations for transcendent knowledge may be at once as laughable as Thales falling into the well *and* as divinely magnificent as the heavens he was contemplating as he journeyed. Skeptical idealism endeavors to achieve and maintain a balance within this ambiguity, within the compass of human finitude. That Glaucon is "compelling" (*anangkazon*) Socrates to give what he, Socrates, emphatically calls his opinions (*ta emoi dokounta*) on several occasions suggests that Socrates fully grasps as tragi-comedy the ambiguous situation of philosophy as the conscious and self-reflective activity of the situated transcendence of the human condition.[8] It also reverberates with two themes in the *Republic*. One is the necessity or compulsion imposed on the philosophers. The other is the opinions, rather than the knowledge, that the zetetic Socrates claims to hold about these most difficult conceptions of the nature of all being. Socrates underlines the temporality, and so the potential temporariness, of his understanding of these things by using the nominalized participle *dokounta* instead of the noun *doxa*: his *opinings* rather than more static *opinions*. This calls for an integrative interpretation that makes plausible Socrates's account of the sun, the good, and the Divided Line that is comically serious, rather than seriously comic: It is *comical*, because, like Thales falling down the well—a "going-down" underground that could well serve as a lampoon of the philosopher-rulers who must go down, *katabateon* (520c, *homoious hemin*), back into the cave—zetetic philosophy must remain open to the possibility of a pratfall (or worse), and therefore to re-vision. It is *serious*, because an integrated account of the good is needed to make a life of justice plausible, at least to intelligent and promising young people like those assembled at the home of Cephalus.

Next, Socrates introduces his second *analogon*, the image of Divided Line, followed by a third, the Allegory of the Cave. That in the development of the narrative, Socrates introduces images, which are at the lowest level of understanding and reality according to the Divided Line, to make sense of intelligibility as such should alert us to the integrated nature of the Line itself, despite its traditional name as the *Divided* Line—a name Socrates does not use. Rather, after reminding Glaucon of the distinction between the visible and the intelligible realms, Socrates introduces this image by saying, "Then, take a line cut in two segments, one for the class that is seen, the other for the class that is intellected—and go on and cut each segment in the same ratio" (509d).

An analogy, like all words and language, can never exactly match its subject. There is always slippage, things that don't match up. But this is not a bug. It is a positive feature of language as such, which must always return to the interpretive *polemos* with the given and thereby *think* anew. This is evident in the lack of explanation for some of the Line's details. It has been cut into four segments, where the two segments each in the visible and in the intelligible regions are of unequal length, but the ratio between their lengths is the same from region to region. If the ratio of segment a to b is proportional to the ratio of segments c to d, then mathematically, a:b::c:d means that segments b and c are equal in size. But that does not tell us what the other proportions are.[9] Socrates populates the four segments as follows (see Figure 2) in the visible regions, corresponding to opinion (510a), are images, including shadows, reflections, and the like (509e–510a), then things as we encounter them in the world (510a); then, in the intelligible region, corresponding to knowledge, are first the mathematical representation of things (510b–511b), then the ideas, or forms (511b–d). He completes the description by saying that intellection pertains to the intelligible realm, thought (*dianoia*, thinking-through) to the mathematicals, trust (*pistis*, which could also be rendered *belief*) to things, and imagination to the images (511d–e). What Socrates does not say is how the proportional segments of the line should be ordered, whether the smallest proportionately is at the top, for the forms or ideas, or at the bottom, for the images.[10] Such slippages should provoke grappling with what is at-issue in the image, such as the relation between the various domains of beings and understanding.

Another thing that Socrates does not tell us about the orientation of the line is whether it should be horizontal or vertical, and if the latter, with the ideas at the top and images at the bottom or vice versa. In this case, the sun, the Allegory of the Cave, and other textual evidence suggest a vertical orientation with the ideas at the top. The sun, first of all, appears above us in the sky as "one of the gods in heaven" (508a). Even if modern science tells us that the sun is neither up nor down from us in the solar system, phenomenologically, the sun is always experienced as 'up there.' Only astronauts actually experience it otherwise, and that experience is a radical departure from our human way of being, both literally and figuratively broken away from the gravitational pull of the earth. In the cave, which is itself an image of the image of the Divided Line, the released prisoner always progresses upward in understanding: the initial release requires the prisoner to "stand up" and to "look up" (515c), and then ascend an "upward way" (515e) on "the soul's journey up to the intelligible place" (517b)—and that the fully realized philosophers "must go back down" (520c) into the cave to rule. For these reasons, I represent the Line vertically, the smallest section for the ideas on top, because they are models of multiple instances, and images are in the largest section at the bottom, because images can present multiple representations of things (see Figure 2). The upward path of the philosophical journey mirrors the flight from the bondedness of finitude and situatedness among transitory things to the putative liberation of transcendence among the forms. We as readers must gather, imagine, and interpret all this by participating in dialogue with the imagery and argument of the text, which therefore implicates us in the integrative nature of the Line.

The productive slippage in the image of the Divided Line is particularly evident in Socrates's explanation of thought as the thinking-through (*dia-noia*) of the understanding of mathematicals. Thought is lower than intellection (*noēsis*), because it is discursive; it unfolds over time rather than in an atemporal insight. He says that geometers "use visible forms besides [hypotheses] and make their arguments about them, not thinking about them but about those that they are like" (510d). In thinking through a theorem in geometry discursively, I might draw an image of a triangle on a blackboard or craft a triangle from wood. I am not thinking about the drawings or objects as such, but rather what 'is' behind them, or above them, and that "are like" (*eoike*) them—such as the triangle I see with the mind's eye. So: "They [the geometers] make the arguments for the sake of the square itself and the diagonal itself"—that is, for the intelligible, mathematical conception of these—"not for the sake of the diagonal they draw" (510d–e). Even more pointed is what he says next: "These things that they mold and draw"—presumably, physical models as well as drawings, as represented in Figure 2 by the triangle on a sheet of paper and the pyramid—"of which there are shadows and images in water"—presumably, shadows of the physical models and reflected images in water of drawings—"they now use as images, seeking to see those things themselves [*auta eikeina*] that one can see in no other way than in thought" (510e–511a).

There is a strange slippage here, too, because Socrates treats reflections as images of images, but this is consistent with something he says earlier: "I mean by images first shadows, then appearances produced in all close-grained, smooth, bright things [like mirrors], and everything of the sort" (509e–510a). This suggests that even within the realm of images, there are some 'images' at a further remove from things than others. Shadows, reflections, and drawings have differing implications, as images, for the understanding. The crucial point is that I can use a drawing of a triangle to think about a physical triangle I have constructed. Furthermore, I can use *both* the drawn *and* the constructed triangle *as* images for thinking-through the square, diagonal, triangle as mathematical objects. In this way, the image straddles and transcends from the sensible, visible realm to the intelligible, serving as a ladder's rung to make the ascent in thought. In thinking the mathematical object, Socrates says, "this is the form I said was intelligible" (511a). Here, he means by intelligible form (*eidos*) the triangle, square, or diagonal as the "things themselves" (*auta eikeina*, 510d–511a) of pure mathematics, as illustrated in Figure 2 by the Pythagorean right triangle as understood by the mind's eye, not the drawings or physical modellings of them.

Nevertheless, these 'forms' are still only *mathematical forms*, not forms or ideas in the strict sense of the uppermost division of the line. On this point, I differ from readers, such as Gerasimos Santas, who equate mathematical definitions with the forms: "the form cube . . . is completely or perfectly a cube in that it has all the essential features captured by the definition of a cube."[11] This obscures the question of the difference between the mathematicals and the ideas, thought and intellection, what defines a cube and what allows us to 'see' that the definition makes sense. The mathematical 'form' is itself only an image, within the two-part intelligible realm, for the true idea or form of the triangle. What *that* would be is hard to grasp, but let's try.[12]

Socrates says that, unlike mathematical forms that depend upon hypotheses—presumably the axioms and the like that must be "set down" (*hypotithenai*) in mathematics to construct proofs—intellection, *noēsis*, of the actual forms requires dispensing with assumed premises such as axioms and the like. Intellection instead uses the "power of dialectic, making hypotheses not beginnings"—that is, unexamined premises and suppositions—"but really hypotheses—that is, steppingstones and springboards—in order to reach what is free from hypothesis at the beginning of the whole" (511b).[13] Such dialectical argumentation in intellection makes "no use of anything sensed in any way, but using forms themselves, going through forms to forms, it ends in forms too" (511c).

Unsurprisingly, Glaucon responds, "I understand, although not adequately—for in my opinion it's an enormous task you speak of" (511c). We readers are in the same position, and that is the point: to enter the dialectic ourselves. If we read the Divided Line as not rigidly but only heuristically divided, and therefore *integrated* in its divisions so that different sectors can each play a role in the understanding of others, then Socrates's very obscure claim that dialectical intellection makes use only of forms can start to make sense. The clue lies in what he has just said about mathematical objects, such as the triangle we can only 'see' with the mind, as being forms in a figurative sense but not forms in the fullest sense of the level of intellection of forms that lies above both thought and the mathematical objects. Form, *eidos*, is itself, after all, a *metaphor*, an *image* based on imagery itself. It is the distinctive shape of a thing seen, as contained within a delineation of itself, such that one can take it in as identical to itself and not confused with some other thing in the field of vision. Image therefore permeates the entire Line. Mathematical objects are forms in the *allegorical* sense of being things that can only be intellected, seen in their defining delineations by the mind's eye. Dialectic uses such 'forms' as mathematics uses images and models to think-through to the *pure* forms at the highest level.

Still, Glaucon is right. This is very hard to understand "adequately" (*hikanōs*). But that difficulty is entirely fitting to philosophy's zetetic journey. What Socrates says about the intellection (*noēsis*) of forms as higher than the thinking (*dianoia*) of mathematical objects—that *noēsis* would use forms alone, not unproven hypotheses, to perceive other forms—is something that seems available only to the fully realized echonic philosophers who have complete access to the ideas and to the good itself. Alternatively, it would be available only to gods who, akin to the perfected echonic philosophers, would have no need of the mediation of the body to possess cognition and knowledge. On our interpretation, echonic philosophers are themselves only hypotheses of the imagination, a heuristic devise for the sake of the argument about the nature of justice and of philosophy itself. In our embodiment, we rely on the metaphors of sense-perception to make sense of non-sensory ways of knowing and can only *imagine* what it would be like to think solely with a *lingua mentis*, a language of pure mind unmediated by the earthly meta-phorics of human language. Zetetic philosophy, by contrast, would always need to do precisely what Socrates is doing in conversation with the young men, what Plato is doing with us in the dialogue, and I with you reading this: using the integrated elements of the Divided Line, especially imagination twinned in ideation with intellection, to enable philosophical vision in the dialectic between situatedness and transcendence.

Consider the triangle. Say I am teaching a class in geometry. At the level of images, I can draw all sorts of triangles of many different types on the board—big and small ones, scalene and equilateral, and so on. They might be very badly drawn, with curvy lines that don't connect at the points, but still do their job illustrating triangles by somehow conveying the *idea* that is at issue—and note that this understanding, this grasping of triangle-ness, *precedes* a geometrical definition of triangles, even for the beginning student. It is *a priori*. At the level of things, I can fold or cut a piece of paper into a triangle, or bring a triangular piece of wood to class, very much trusting that these will serve as triangles for the purpose of instruction, even if none of these triangles perceived with the senses has absolutely straight lines or perfectly correct angles. At the level of thought, it gets more difficult. What is "the mathematical" of a triangle? In geometry, one *might* venture to say something like: a three-sided polygon that Euclidean geometry can prove to have angles adding to 180 degrees.

But then what is the *idea* or *form* of a triangle that differs from such a mathematical (in the broad sense) definition? Somehow, it involves our in-sight into what a triangle is that goes beyond its mathematical definition. This is true for all the ideas: they are not equivalent to definition; an idea exceeds the definition and animates it. An idea or form guides us in understanding ('intellecting') what even very poor drawings of triangles mean in terms of the mathematical properties of triangles that we can only think rather than the ones we can draw or touch, which are always imprecise *qua* triangles. To push this example further, one could say that the geometrical definition I just gave for a triangle at the level of thought and "the mathematicals" is true, but only in Euclidean geometry. If I draw a triangle on the surface of a ball, its lines will be straight in one sense, curved in another, and its angles will not add up to 180 degrees. This spherical triangle will violate several of Euclid's postulates (the "hypotheses" that Socrates says are the limitation of mathematical thought)—and yet, it will still be a triangle, because I have the *idea* of a triangle whose "form" can guide me in making sense of what triangles are in non-Euclidean geometry—a geometry that can get very complex, with insights that depart very far from our ordinary conception of "triangleness"![14]

This illustrates that the Divided Line is *necessarily integrative*, which is to say that the divisions are conceptual, heuristic, and porous, rather than defined by hard borders that exclude one another. At each level, other levels obtrude: possibly as helpful, such as using images of triangles to get students to 'see' the geometric principles; possibly as misleading, as when the shadow cast by a physical triangle might distort my sensory perception of it at the level of trust. This obtrusive integration of the Line's divisions serves as the basis for what I have been calling ideation, the way the Line loops back upon itself in the construal of meaning, especially from imagination to idea. The most dramatic example of this integration internal to Plato's *Republic*, and therefore something we might plausibly impute to Plato's intent, is a triple one that invites dialogue between reader and author. Just as I have just used the example of the triangle *as an image* for the meaning of the Divided Line, so has Socrates used the Divided Line as an image for the meaning of intelligibility, and so has *Plato* used the whole of the dialogue named *Republic*, in all its narrative and dialectical drama, as an image for what constitutes philosophy.

This underlines a striking feature of the Line's integrative structure. Unlike the other three faculties of the mind or understanding (trust, thought, intellection), which only *apprehend* or become *affected by* their objects (*pathēmata en tēi psuchēi*, 511d), imagination is also capable of *producing* its objects. Events or narrations may spur my imagination of things, just as the sting of a bee spurs my sensation of pain, but I can also choose to imagine things on my own, just as you and I may choose to imagine the dialogue in the home of Cephalus, or I with you or you with me. I cannot do the same with a sense-perception. I cannot feel a pain and thereby have a bee sting me. In this way, imagination resembles the idea of the good itself, which Socrates says is responsible for all that is because it exceeds even being. This is compelling evidence that the Divided Line doubles back on itself in its integration. What it doubles back *through*, we leave to later.

To reinforce this point about the Line's integration, and using the same example: at the level of images, I can draw a triangle. The reflection of that triangle in water or in a mirror might be more confusing than the drawing, but these still exist on the level of images on the Line. I can also build a triangular object from wood or paper or stone; this is at the level of things, which I can trust to be what they are (although I may be deceived). Such things cast triangular shadows, and so they cross the border, as it were, into the division of the Line for images. Next, I can use either the drawing *or* the crafted triangle *as* an image to assist in understanding what a triangle is in geometry, at the level of a mathematical object in the realm of intellection rather than sense-perception. And at all three levels, the *idea* of the triangle is present as the usually unacknowledged polestar of my orientation to the meaning of all these other modes of understanding triangles.

For another example of the integration of the Divided Line, let's consider a different kind of thing: social or political justice. We can have images of justice in a variety of ways, such as a statuary version of Lady Justice, who stands blindfolded to represent impartiality, holding a sword to represent the force of law, and lifting up scales to represent the deliberative process of weighing facts and arguments for guilt or innocence. At the level of things, we can find examples of just acts, just institutions, or just social arrangements. As an everyday example of the latter, consider a living space where roommates share payment, maintenance, and cleaning in a fair way. The level of the mathematicals might seem more difficult to conceive, but philosophers have done so, from Aristotle, in his mathematical distinction between restorative and distributive justice, to Rawls, whose "difference principle" establishes the fairest outcome as the one where the least well off are still better off than they would be in any other conceivable scenario.[15] When we speak of equality, inequality, distribution, proportionality, and the like for justice, we are already using the language of mathematics, and it is not obvious when we are doing so literally or imagistically.

Finally, the *idea* of justice will be hardest of all, but presumably it is always-already there, even if we have not grasped it thematically and explicitly, just as the idea of the triangle is there, in advance, when we draw or build triangles, both to teach and to learn about what triangles *are*. The idea, however imprecisely grasped, guides the hand of the painter, the agreement of the roommates, or the mathematizations of the political theorist. Note that this does not make them *correct* in how they have depicted justice, or performed just acts, or come up with a mathematical schema for justice. The idea only makes it minimally intelligible that they are seeking to understand and to do justice. It is the province of the fully realized, echonic philosopher-rulers to have completely integrated all portions of the divided line with a total and self-aware knowledge of the ideas and the idea of the good.

Finally, consider the example of ideation with which I began this book: the person. I can depict persons in artworks such as drawing, poetry, film, and story, and I can certainly imagine persons, such as you as reader, and you can do the same with me as writer. I can encounter persons as things, as objects of sense perception. You and I might meet 'in person.' At the level of mathematization, we can understand and quantify persons in the various aspects of *homo sapiens*: the chemical formulae of DNA; the electrical impulses of the nervous system; the neural networks of the brain that are the correlate to consciousness, and so on. Each of these modes of understanding may illuminate aspects of being-human, in terms of the specificity of our thrownness into the brute facticity of given physical and historical embodiment, by telling us about *what* we are and *how* we appear and in what *ways* these affect our being-human. Nevertheless, none of these modes of understanding gives us access to *who* other people are, unless we define the Who in terms of the materiality of the What. But this reductionism—the reducing of personhood to some lower level of being—would violate the very phenomenon at issue. For Heidegger, as for Kant, to be a person is to be a Who, not merely a What, a thing. To be a person entails what Heidegger calls *Jemeinigkeit*, the always-my-ownness of individuated embodiment as person. That ownness of your personhood is nothing I could ever experience directly, even if we were to meet in person: I can only impute it to you circumstantially, and you to me, because to experience that personhood directly, you would have to be me, or I you. Nevertheless, unless one suffers from a profound psychological disability, we must and do impute personhood as an idea to other persons *as* Other, simply as a way of being-human.

Ideation gathers all these elements together. Because persons matter to me *qua* persons, I may depict them in art or imagination. I may long for them or avoid them as things in the world. I may study them in genetics, or biochemistry, or neurology. Ideation serves to bring these partial aspects of personhood together in the light of the idea of the person. That idea of the person, in our finite understanding as human-beings, never gets finally and thoroughly grasped in an echonic vision so that no further inquiry is ever needed. It is an intimation of a truth phenomenologically confirmed as meaningful rather than illusory because it is hermeneutically indispensable to our everyday living-with-Others, at the levels of imagination, trust, and thought, and so as the metaethical grounding for an ethics. It also is essential to our reconstruction of what it means to be a person whenever that everyday understanding breaks down, as it must for finite beings such as ourselves, especially in the domain of ethical and political life. Ideation, as the active integration of the Line in the understanding of our finite existence, is how polemical, zetetic philosophy reconstructs, repairs, and heals its understanding of being-human when faced with contradictions in the phenomena that throw the meaningful world out of joint. This is where the idea of the good enters the picture.

3.3 THE IDEA OF THE GOOD

Now we return to the idea of the good, the *idea tou agathou*, to understand why it would be the final thing the almost-completed echonic philosopher would have to see in the realm of the intelligible to integrate fully all four regions of the Divided Line. The idea of the good is one of the most contentious features of the Platonic corpus, and I will not attempt to provide a comprehensive scholarly interpretation here. My goal is to offer a plausible alternative to Heidegger's rejection of Platonism and to show how the idea of the good might fit within what I am calling Plato's skeptical and zetetic idealism as a metaethical grounding for ethical life.

If the Line is integrated, and if, as Socrates says, the idea of the good is responsible for all that is, then the understanding of even those people who are furthest from being philosophers, who are firmly or even willingly bound in the bonds of the lower cave, is in some way made possible by the idea of the good, even if they are unaware of this grounding. The good filters through ideas to mathematical representations to physical objects to the even most tenuous shadows. A clue to the nature of the good lies in its ethical and political role as something the philosopher-rulers must know in order to rule with wisdom and authority. This is so even if the good applies to more than matters of justice and ethics, because the conversation in the *Republic* is rooted implicitly in what a good life would be (344e) and explicitly, as Glaucon requests, in whether justice is a virtue that is good for the soul and that makes a good life (357a–358d).

Knowledge of the idea of the good, says Socrates, is necessary for the "just thing and the rest"—that is, for all the virtues, as well as institutions for a just society—to "become useful and beneficial" (505a). This is why echonic philosophers must come to possess this idea in order to enact justice "and the rest." While Socrates never lays claim to the echonic vision himself, that does not mean that the idea of the good plays no role in the zetetic philosophical life or in ethics. The ubiquity of the good, its presence in even the most mundane ways in everyday life, is captured by ordinary expressions in English. We might say that a hammer is no good for setting a screw into place, but that a screwdriver is. My ticket on the subway is good for a few hours. Someone I work with might be a good-for-nothing. This *good-for* indicates a purposeful-ness, a teleology, of a thing within a much larger context of making sense of purposes, practices, and actions that defines an understanding of a world and how we interpret beings within it, what we take them *as* and what we take them *for* in being what they *are* in that context of meaning. To understand this conceptually is to "save the phenomena" (*sōzein ta phainomena*) in the most ancient sense of phenomenology. Any proper account of something must be able to explain how it appears and makes sense at the human scale.[16] The Be-ing of anything, its "is-ness," is already there for us, accessible in what it is as itself, as what it means for it *to be* in that context.[17]

This is not the Kantian "thing in itself" that lies behind phenomenal ap-pearances, to which our sensory and conceptual filters never have direct access. However, and this is pivotal to the polemical nature of understand-ing and interpretation, apprehension of what a being 'is' is not static: the earthiness of meaning resists the absolute view from know-where of the sky-bound understanding that tries to make final and total sense of the world as opened up within the horizons of an historical situatedness. What things *are*, as always-already interpreted, is ever-again open to breakdown, reinterpreta-tion, reconstruction, and reintegration in a re-envisioned world of sense. The thing-in-itself does not like a gremlin constantly overturn the tables of the understanding until we get 'things' right, except in the sense that what beings are "in themselves"—the *hōsautōs onta*, as Socrates puts it (479e)—is always subject to the polemical cycle of breakdown and reconstruction of meaning because of the finite, mortal, and temporal nature of human-being's under-standing. If there 'is' a thing-in-itself for Socrates and Plato, what anything 'really' is apart from what it appears to be to us, it is an idea of reason. We posit it as a heuristic, like the echonic philosopher as an idea of reason, to guide and motivate the self-moving polemical existence of being-human as ever-again interpreting its world.

The decisive question is what makes the knowledge of the echonic phi-losophers viable as the legitimate basis for their rule. The comic example of Thales falling into a well while contemplating the heavens is shorthand for conveying the distinction between *sophia*, theoretical wisdom, and *phronēsis*, practical wisdom. We can certainly imagine that a thinker might have astonishing insights into physical nature or the human condition but be incapable of conveying these insights intelligibly to others, and even more importantly in this context, incapable of engaging the world in any effective way to implement these insights in a way that would do any good. That last point is why the *idea* of the good would be so vital to the philosopher-ruler. One might have all sorts of knowledge and insight without knowing what these are *good for*. A geometer might know all about planar triangles and spherical triangles as mathematical objects but still not know that, as a *thing*, a triangle is *good for* building strong structures, such as load-bearing girders on a bridge, or that, as an *image*, triangles are *good for* lessons in geometry, or as illustrations for epistemological arguments in philosophy. If these seem like trivial examples, consider scientific breakthroughs that have led to epochal transformations in technology. Revolutionary discoveries in genetic engineering, such as gene-editing technology, promise previously unavailable therapies and cures for terrible diseases, but they could also produce population-obliterating diseases. Their beneficial application—their use for *the good*—depends both on knowing what the good would be as a goal, a *telos*, of action in a particular context, and on *phronēsis*, wisdom enacted in practice, to see one's way to attaining that good in the contingent, historically situated circumstances.

In ethical and political life, consider the virtue of courage. An artist or writer might do very well at depicting courage in a painting or a story, and we might recognize courageous deeds, and even understand why the neurophysiology of the brain can render someone so anxious that it derails the confidence needed for a normal life. But without knowing what courage is *good for*, an educator and leader would be working in the dark with this virtue, both for inculcating courage in a new generation and for making a place for courage in personal, civic, and institutional life. Above, we used the example of justice in art, in action, and in its mathematical considerations, but without knowing what justice is good for, one can imagine someone understanding justice conceptually, but not how to implement it in society or in her own conduct. This is not simply a question of 'applying' a philosophical idea. As Glaucon's initial demand of Socrates makes clear, the question at issue is what justice is good for, whether justice is vital for living well. Socrates insists that justice is intrinsically good, as well as instrumentally good (358a), and so the good is not merely a matter of consequences. An understanding of the good is constitutive of a good life, not just in its achievements but in itself.

One might argue that knowing what a virtue is good *for* is implicit to knowing what the virtue *is*, a position close to the Socratic claim that virtue is knowledge. But this assumes an echonic version of philosophical knowledge that possesses a complete and apodictically certain understanding of things, a version that is at best an idea of reason and that would not apply to what the zetetic Socrates emphatically describes as his opinions about such things. As Aristotle argues in the *Nicomachean Ethics*, equating knowing what virtue is with doing what is virtuous clearly contradicts the phenomena (*tois phainomenois enargōs*, 1145b27) of ethical life as we experience it. Peoples' actions may well fall short of what their convictions dictate about what is ethical.

In Heidegger's lectures courses of the 1920s, when he has not yet identified Platonism as the source of metaphysical nihilism,[18] he naturally gives due respect to the *idea tou agathou* as what Socrates in Book 6 of the *Republic* famously calls *epekeina tēs ousias*, beyond being (509b). In 1926, Heidegger defines it as follows: "*Idea of the good*: that from which everything becomes understandable, that towards which the various activities strive, *for the sake of* something, that *to which* something is suited and designated" (GA 22: 113). Heidegger assimilates the idea of the good to *Seinsverstandnis*, the understanding of Being that makes sense of a world and inner-worldly beings ontologically. To use his example from *Being and Time*, we understand the hammer *as* suited *to* the task of pounding nails *for the sake of* hanging a picture or building a house as governed by a fuller nexus of activities of making a home.

This nexus of ontological-hermeneutical understanding is inherently purposive for Heidegger, but not in the teleological sense that Plato or Aristotle would ascribe to the good of action. In this same passage Heidegger suggests "uncoupling the problem of Being from the idea of the good" and the "uncoupling of Plato's philosophy from Socrates and from his grounding in a specifically ethical orientation" (GA 22: 114). This is why, in his more elaborate analyses of the Cave Analogy starting in the 1930s, when developing the more radical critique of the Platonic roots of metaphysical nihilism as the source of modern "Liberalism," Heidegger defines the idea of the good as the *Ermächtigung*. This is what enables or empowers any and all beings and activities to be meaningfully what they are and thus empowers the opening up of truth as unconcealment, what Heidegger will soon be calling the *Ereignis*, the ontological event that establishes a meaningful world and allows human-being to own up to and inhabit it.[19] With this move, Heidegger effectively accomplishes the disjunction of ontology and ethics in his reading of Plato in which the idea of the good signifies Plato's failure to make that move himself. Heidegger still credits Plato with being responsive to the question of Being, but only partially and unthematically. The idea of the good points to the *problem* of how meaningfulness is possible for the understanding, which allows Heidegger to discern echoes of the question of being and truth as *alētheia* in Plato while also charging Plato with obscuring the question of Being and truth behind an ethical conception that links correctness and beingness. This obscuring of the Being question that allows Platonism over millennia to elide ontological universalism with ethical universalism is the root of Liberalism for Heidegger. By severing the link of the ontological and the ethical in the idea of the good as well as from its status as "beyond Being," Heidegger seeks to overcome what he deems the nihilism of a transcendent (*epekeina*) Good as the touchstone for both philosophical and ethical life.

As Robert Dostal points out in an insight he develops from Gadamer, even in granting the idea of the good the power of empowering the Being of all beings, Heidegger glosses over the special status of the idea of the good as distinct from all other ideas:

> The ideas are presented by Plato as true Being (*ousia*), but the Good is beyond Being. It is the very cause (*aitia*) of Being. As the source of light the sun is more difficult to see than any thing. Rather it lets things be seen for what they are, while it itself remains, for the most part, unseen. Though Plato does call the Good an idea, unlike the other ideas it is never in the *Republic* called *eidos* as the others are. Heidegger translated *eidos* as *Aussehen* or "appearance." In accord with this, the Good should not be understood as an appearance. Rather the Good presents no appearance. It is beyond the forms. It is their very ground.[20]

Note that the "beyond Being" of the idea of the good, unlike the other ideas, has no form.[21] This corresponds to what I will argue later is the Beyond of the idea of the good as what slips over the arc of the Divided Line. The Line in fact reveals itself as a Divided Ring where the idea of the good, as the formless source of form, allows image and idea to meet up in dialectic to draw meaning from unmeaning (see Figure 3). This, I will argue in chapter 8, is what happens when ethics as a set of established norms breaks down into a crisis of unmeaning, such as the one Thebes faced in the *Antigone*. A polemical ethics must draw upon the unformed but unshakable heart of what is ethical to re-form and reconstruct the meaning of ethics conceptually, in the given situation, with *phronēsis*.

This makes sense if the idea of the good, or the good itself, stands above not only all other ideas but if, in its "divine superiority" (509c) it also exceeds even truth and being itself. While Heidegger must have some sympathy for this, because he too seeks what it is that makes intelligibility and meaning possible, he must ultimately reject the *idea* of the good for the following reasons. The first is that what grants meaning cannot be some idea subsisting in some eternal, otherworldly domain, because Being is intimately bound to time and to the finite historicity of being-human. Second, while Heidegger might accept an implicit teleology of the *Woraufhin*, the projective upon-which of all meaningful activity as directed to some purpose which some thing or action might be good for, such purposes are always enclosed in a finite world of involvements, not in a teleology of the good that transcends historical situatedness.[22] Finally, because Heidegger rejects the transcendental universalism of the good in human existence, he must also reject moralistic claims about universalist ethics and political right.[23] I will argue against this that ethical life is the phenomenologically unavoidable conduct of fully being-human, and that to dismiss it as mere moralism is to belie our existential nature.

3.4 THE WRAITH OF THE NAME
ON THE DIVIDED RING

The following passage by Stanley Rosen on this subject comes close to my position but brings it into sharper relief, because we disagree on the idea of the good as *epekeina tēs ousias*, beyond Being:

> If *ousia* refers to the nature of being altogether, then "beyond" must mean here either that the Good is not, that is, not only is it not a particular being (*on*), it does not exist in any sense of that difficult word [i.e., "exist"]; or else the Good does exist, that is, "be," but it also goes beyond *ousia* into some higher domain. The former case is unthinkable, since for Socrates we cannot think of what is not; the latter case seems to conjure up a hybrid entity like a centaur or hippogriff, one which both is and is not. In this case, it seems to be a member of the domain of genesis, the members of which wander between being and nonbeing. We are here facing one of those points in Plato that are too cryptic to be amenable to an entirely satisfactory explanation. My own preferred view is that the Good is "beyond" being in the metaphorical sense that it is neither this nor that of a separate and definable kind but is rather a property or set of properties of Platonic Ideas, namely, intelligibility, stability, and eternity.[24]

Rosen is certainly right it would be "unthinkable" (nonsensical) that the good be "beyond" Being in the sense that the good simply does not exist. Rosen resists the alternative, though, that the good be some sort of contradictory hybrid between what "is and is not." In Rosen's solution, the "beyond" of the idea of the good describes the property or properties of the ideas as such. The good is what gives each idea its specific intelligibility (how it grants meaning to something in everyday life), its stability (how everyday life's meaning is reliably grounded, not chaotic), and its eternity (how meaning persists as universally normative across time and culture).

But what if the Divided Line were not simply a line but a Divided Ring? For echonic philosophy, the Line must be just that: linear (Figure 2). It rises from what is least in Being, the shadows, reflections, and images, to what is most in Being, the ideas and forms; what lies beneath the images simply *is not* (*mē onti*; 477a–478d). So there is nothing beyond the idea of the good, which is itself beyond Being. The echonic philosopher would rise through the levels of the Line to arrive ultimately at certain knowledge of the ideas and the good, at which point the journey would "come to the end" (504d). For zetetic philosophy, by contrast, the journey does not end, at least not in this embodied existence. The triadic structures of wonder-question-response and de-, pre-, and reconstruction are cyclical, like a ring. For the zetetic philosopher, knowing is not a possession but a way of being that opens up in wonder, breaks down what is at-issue through formulating a question, and proceeds, if it can, to reconstitute a meaningful world through argument while leaving open the possibility of responding ever-again to new breakdowns of meaning.

Admittedly, to think of the Divided Line as simply the front of a Divided Ring seen straight on, along one half-edge of its circumference, is a departure from the text of the *Republic*. My contention is that such a departure in imagination is exactly what Plato's dialectical method encourages us to enact in ideational dialogue with him. As Julia Annas and others have pointed out, there are *many* "annoying" puzzles and problems in explaining the Line's details.[25] My claim is that such slippages and difficulties are not a flaw but feature of the Allegory (as of all allegories), because neither Plato nor Socrates is providing some utterly final and authoritative account of knowledge and reality. Rather, they offer through the Allegory a *preconstruction* of the articulation of our understanding of the world, a philosophical account that has been so fertile because intended for deconstruction and reconstruction. If a complete and final understanding of the linked natures of Being and knowing is not something we can possess totally in echonic vision, at the end of the line—but if, at the same time, the world always-already makes a provisional sense that we can analyze, interpret, and enlarge upon—then we are both condemned and liberated to use our imagination to put into image and word what is our best understanding in light of the intimation of an idea.

This is what it means to articulate an idea and why ideation and imagination are fundamentally two sides of the same endeavor. They are linked through the dark side of the Divided Ring, the half-arc of the circumference we cannot see when looking at it head-on, the part illumined by neither natural nor artificial light. Figure 3, superimposing the Divided Line on the Cave, illustrates this dark side of the Ring as the domain of unmeaning, or nothingness, as passing through the earth, that which is hidden and unexposed. As Richard Kearney puts it in a discussion of the Czech philosopher Jan Patočka's conception of "negative Platonism,"

> [I]magination is *the tracing of transcendence*. The Idea of the Good could not make itself manifest within our finite experience without the testimony of such imaginary traces. Consequently, if imagination appears to refer to a realm of non-being, considered from the standpoint of empirical experience, it succeeds in breaking through the closed horizon of objective entities and pointing to the Idea of the Good. Without this transcending power of imagination there would be no such thing as moral freedom. Freedom presupposes the everyday activity of imagination."[26]

The breakthrough occasioned by the meeting up of imagination and idea in ideation requires these traces, what I have called intimations, of the idea of the good to animate and guide the zetetic endeavor of reintegrative re-creation after a breakdown.

The cyclical nature of the Divided Line as Divided Ring is all the more appropriate if we consider the sun as image for the idea of the good. Socrates himself alludes to the cyclical rather than the stationary nature of meaning when he says that even after emerging from the cave (like the sun from the underworld), the escaped prisoner would make sense of the heavenly realm "more easily at night" and only after that "the sun itself by itself" (516a–b). The standard image, with the sun at the summit of the visible realm, can re-inforce the impression that the progress of the understanding is linear, finally reaching its echonic apogee in contemplation of the sun as allegory for the good, where the sun remains locked in place at high noon, just as "The sun stopped in the middle of the sky" for Joshua in his victory over the Amorites (Joshua 10:13). But even for Joshua, the sun finally did set. In Greek mythol-ogy, the sun-god Helios makes a cyclical journey, passing every day into the chthonic underworld of Hades and emerging again each dawn. As Mircea Eliade explains, "the entry into Hades is called 'the gates of the sun,' and 'Hades' as pronounced during the Homeric age—'A-ides'—also brings to mind the notion of what is 'invisible' and what 'renders invisible.' The swing between light and darkness, solar and earthly, can therefore be taken as two alternating phases of one and the same reality."[27] The dark side of the Divided Ring, as the hidden, under-earthly realm of Hades, is *a-eidetic*, the domain of unmeaning as the absence or undoing of ideas (*a-ides*), like the wraiths that gather and then dissolve at the visit of Odysseus to the underworld. It is where the intelligibility that grants meaning lapses into unmeaning.

That there is *nothing* beyond the idea of the good, and that *what is not* lies beneath images and shadow, indicates that the dark side of the Ring is Nothing itself, the counterpart to Being. But as Heidegger would remind us, this Nothing is not no-thing, the sheer absence of entities in "a realm of non-being," about which it would be non-sense to speak. Rather, if the question of Being is about how the world can make sense at all, how a meaning to things and actions is somehow always-already there for us, then we exist as much in a world that makes sense and has meaning as in a world that makes *non*-sense and frays into *unmeaning*. We will address this in more detail when we dis-cuss the breakdown that happens in the cave in chapter 4, but the fundamental point is this: If we do not possess final, echonic knowledge, then the possibil-ity of meaning breaking down is always impending whether it manifests in terror or in wonder, which the Greeks indicated with a single expression, *to deinon*. Plato understood just as well as Heidegger that being-human, in our finite historicity, involves the polemical negotiation of meaning and unmean-ing in taking up the dialectical cycle of the Divided Ring. After all, in Greek myth, the sun does pass through the underworld; the chthonic realm of darkness is not a total absence of light. Just as the sun may leave its trace behind in glowing embers, when a world collapses into unmeaning in a breakdown, inklings and intimations of meaning to-come may still beckon towards the world's reconstruction, just as the stars and moon illuminate the night, even in the absence of the sun.

We do not usually see the dark side of the Divided Ring because we usually do not want to see it. Unmeaning is ontologically *unsettling*, what Heidegger called *unheimlich*, uncanny or, more literally, unhomely. The Nothing of unmeaning casts our regular habits into doubt and sends tremors through our habitation of a world that, for better or worse, at least makes sense to us. To borrow from Roberto Esposito, the dark, under-earthly, semicircular arc of the Divided Ring is an image for the perennial problem of *negation* in Western thought and its irruption into ethics and politics. In the face of an anxiety about the finitude of the human condition and the ever-present threat of identity succumbing to unmeaning, the totalitarianism of the twentieth century arose

> as the attempt to eliminate negation by characterizing as universal a political, social, or racial type of particularity. The category of totality, from which totalitarianism takes its name, was nothing but the device used by those who aimed to eliminate anything that did not fit into their own self-affirmation.[28]

The metapolitical question then becomes not how to negate negation as a way to fend off all threats of unmeaning in some echonic, unshakable self-identity and self-certainty, which so easily degenerates into a pathology of annihilation of all potential threat and otherness, but rather how to recognize and accept negation and unmeaning as a potentially positive feature of the cycle of human historicity. To rely again on Esposito, we can understand the dark side of the Divided Ring as a *potentially* affirmative negative: "Conceived of in an affirmative form, the negative is the limit that cuts across our life, revealing what it could be and has never been. . . . For this reason, it can at the same time be actual and inactual—the inactual that continues to disrupt our actuality."[29] Openness to this cutting-across of negation in finitude is the starting point of a polemical ethics guided by a skeptical idealism.

To be human, as the Between, means always to be exposed to the earthquakes of unmeaning that threaten to upset a settled world. As we will discuss in the next chapter, we can respond with despair or outright nihilism to such breakdowns of unmeaning in our habitation. We can also respond, in zetetic philosophy, to the breakdown as a *break-in* of wonder, an opportunity for reflective knowing that might enlarge the sense of the world. If the finitude of human-being entails that we may never, in this embodied life, achieve a fully realized knowledge, then the cyclical irruptions of unmeaning must be an existentially constitutive feature of our dynamic *polemos* with the world and to which we are called to respond. This would be a Platonic version of Heidegger's call of conscience, with the difference that the struggle with un-meaning must be guided by the meeting of idea and imagination in the work of ideation as it strives to make reconstructive sense of the world. The mo-tion of this *polemos* between meaning and unmeaning in zetetic philosophy is helicoidal (which admittedly strains the metaphor of the ring to its limit), because, when successful, it returns to where it was before, but with a larger sense of the meaning of the world, much like the progress of Dante through all three domains of the Divine Comedy.

Finally, it is important not to leave the impression that unmeaning, the dark side of the Divided Ring, is simply obscure, or worse, an obscurantist mystical notion. In his Preface to Eugene Gendlin's *A Process Model*, Robert Parker quotes a wonderful passage from William James:[30]

> Suppose we try to recall a forgotten name. The state of our consciousness is peculiar. There is a gap therein; but no mere gap. It is a gap that is intensely active. A sort of wraith of the name is in it, beckoning us in a given direction. . . . If wrong names are proposed to us, this singularly definite gap acts imme-diately so as to negate them. . . . And the gap of one word does not feel like the gap of another, all empty of context as both might seem necessarily to be when described as gaps.[31]

What James here describes as the "gap" is what I am calling the dark side of the Divided Ring, the realm of unmeaning that negates a given understanding or seemingly withholds a new one. Forgetting a name is an everyday occur-rence, unsettling or unnerving, perhaps, but rarely traumatic; nevertheless, it illustrates the negational irruption of unmeaning into existence, what I will call the breakdown. As James says, the gap is "no mere gap," nothingness as sheer void; it "is intensely active" in prodding us to mind the gap and fill it; it is an experience of the inactual that can either dismember the actual or, if grasped positively, that can evoke the hidden potential of the actual that is only as-yet inactual.

James brilliantly calls this a "wraith of the name" in the gap, a ghost both present, because I feel its lack, and absent, because I cannot fulfill it, at least not immediately and at will. This "name" can stand not just for the name of a person but for a word or concept for anything at all. Anyone who has tried to speak a new language surely has had this experience: struggling and fumbling to bring forth a word for what you know you mean but cannot express. Gend-lin calls this experience the "dot-dot-dot" ("[. . .]"), the powerful embodied sense that there is a meaning to convey, but it lies just beyond articulation in that "gap" of unmeaning—until one finds the word, or the image, or the brushstroke, or the musical note to express it, in the appropriate context.[32] The wraith of the name hovers in unmeaning, "beckoning us in a given direction"; this is what I have been calling the *intimation* of an idea. The wraith is whatever is at-issue in a question opened by wonder, from the everyday to the earth-shattering. It is a *pre-conceptual*, as-yet-unarticulated sense of a meaning, or what Parker calls a "more-than-conceptual knowing" that guides the work of imaginative articulation.[33] We can close the gap on the dark side of the Divided Ring between the beckoning of the wraith and the fulfillment of meaning through the dialectic between imagination and idea.[34]

Taken as a whole, this is the process of ideation. It is akin to what has long been called the hermeneutical circle, the problem of how, in interpretation, to relate part to whole, for each element must be related to an overarching context, but each such whole must encompass each of its constitutive parts. The problem of part and whole is not merely an issue for an obscure field of interpretive studies. Factically, as a feature of our existential-hermeneutical nature, the circle obtrudes upon us as finite beings because the coherence of part and whole inevitably frays. The understanding collides with breakdowns and propels us into the gap of unmeaning that demands our attention in re-interpretation on the dark side of the Divided Ring, what Gadamer describes as being "pulled up short" in any interpretive context, be it scholarly, ethical, or everyday. The figures of both circle and ring are somewhat misleading, though, because, as Gadamer also says, the existential-hermeneutical "task is to expand the unity of the understood meaning centrifugally," which is why the work of reinterpretation "is never finished; it is in fact [for finite human-being] an infinite process."[35] The circle or ring operates "centrifugally" when properly engaged because, as when we learn a new language, the process of ever-again reintegrating part and whole is expansive. It enlarges the understanding even if never complete. Its motion is helicoidal, not a vicious circle that merely ends up where it began.

To bring this full circle to the idea of the good, it is the good that prompts the imagination to conjure possibilities of meaning, which either come or do not. But without the idea of the good, no name, no concept, no word could be found to fit the purpose in any particular context hovering between meaning and unmeaning. This is why I disagree with Rosen that the "beyond Being" of the idea of the good is only "a property or set of properties of Platonic Ideas, namely, intelligibility, stability, and eternity." Because it straddles the preconceptual and the conceptual, the idea of the good is the "beyond" that elides the border between the realm of the intelligible (meaning) and unintelligible (unmeaning) in ideation. The idea of the good is indeed "unthinkable," as Rosen puts it, in purely conceptual terms, because it animates the ideational process between the conceptual and pre-conceptual (or more-than-conceptual) life of the mind. It is what makes the "beckoning" of the wraith of the ideas, which have not yet fully taken on form (*eidos*), meaningfully promising to the imagination. It is the idea of the good that engenders the trust of Socratic piety in a skeptical idealism that seeks the light at the end of the upward path from the cave, guided by the glimmering intimations that may be discerned in an earthen darkness nevertheless rich in possibility.

NOTES

1. For a critical assessment of *theoria*, see Andrea Nightingale, *Spectacles of Truth in Classical Greek Philosophy*, especially chapters 2 and 3 on its role in Plato and the *Republic*. Nightingale's analysis is explicitly sociological, at least in part, in tracing the transition from ordinary Greek language usage to philosophical knowing in Plato and Aristotle as *theoria* (beholding, contemplation). She rightly observes the potential distortion this may occasion, especially if visual "spectacle" is conceived as the only way of knowing, but this does not conflict with my claim that *some* metaphor for knowing is necessary and that any such metaphor, by the nature of language, is distorting. The Socratic journey of zetetic ascent to seek the best vantage for seeing fully is compatible with critical reflection on the vision-metaphor itself, too, as a ladder to be kicked away at the end of the climb.

2. On the latent nihilism of theory and of scientism as indifferent to the human scale of existence, see Reid, *Heidegger's Moral Ontology*, 29–49. For critiques of ocularcentrism, see David Kleinberg-Levin *Modernity and the Hegemony of Vision* and *Sites of Vision*, as well as essays by others in his edited volume, *Modernity and the Hegemony of Vision*, for a wide-ranging critique of vision in Western thought; see also Martin Jay, *Downcast Eyes: The Denigration of Vision in Twentieth-Century French Thought*. For a feminist critique targeted on Plato's Cave, see Luce Irigaray, "Plato's *Hystera*" in *Speculum of the Other Woman*. For a decolonial and antiracist critique of ocularcentrism, see Franz Fanon's appropriation of Sartre on the gaze to explore the fixation of identity upon the colonized and racialized, chapter 5 of *Black Skins, White Masks*, Helen Ngo's lucid overview of the topic of the racialized gaze in "The White Gaze, Being-Object, and Intercorporeity," in Pfeifer and Gurley, *Phenomenology and the Political*, as well as Iris Marion Young, *Justice and the Politics of Difference*, 125ff. For a defense of the vision metaphor, see Hans Jonas, "The Nobility of Sight."

3. See Drew Hyland on Plato's "complex irony" in *Finitude and Transcendence*, chapter 3, especially 101–3; also, Roochnik, "Socratic Ignorance as Complex Irony."

4. On the difference between Plato's and Socrates's irony, See Griswold, "Plato's Metaphilosophy," in *Platonic Writings/Platonic Readings*, 161. On the irony of language as such, see Kenneth Sayre's "Plato's Dialogues in Light of the *Seventh Letter*," also in *Platonic Writings/Platonic Readings*.

5. See Bloom, *The Republic of Plato*, 445fn34.

6. Consider Strauss, *The City and Man*, 119: "The doctrine of ideas which Socrates expounds to his interlocutors is very hard to understand; to begin with, it is utterly incredible, not to say that it appears to be fantastic. . . . No one has ever succeeded in giving a satisfactory or clear account of this doctrine of ideas." Rosen attacks Strauss for what he takes to be his esoteric anti-Platonism: "I suspect that Strauss did not take seriously the doctrine of the noetic perception of pure form [because] for Strauss, philosophy is discourse. Or in slightly different terms, I suggest that Strauss regarded philosophy as finally impossible because of the impossibility of furnishing the discursive validation of the foundations"; Rosen, "Leo Strauss and the Quarrel between the Ancients and the Moderns," in *Leo Strauss's Thought*, 141.

7. Consider Nietzsche, "How the 'True World' Finally Became a Fable" in *Twilight of the Idols*, 23–24, as well as 14 and 21; also *The Will to Power*, §1067.

8. For a trenchant discussion of this theme, see Hyland, *Finitude and Transcendence*, chapter 5, "The Whole Tragedy and Comedy of Philosophy."

9. See Klein, *A Commentary on Plato's* Meno, 119fn27, and Annas, *An Introduction to Plato's* Republic, 247.

10. Compare the differing illustrations in the text notes of C. D. C. Reeve's translation, which places ideas in the largest realm (Plato, *Collected Works*, 1130), and in Bloom's translation in *The Republic of Plato*, 445fn34, which finesses the ambiguity by not distinguishing the proportions of uppermost and lowermost zones.

11. Santas, *Understanding Plato's* Republic, 133, also 143.

12. In what follows, I differ from Annas, who claims that the scheme of the Line "breaks down" because the analogy of proportion between imagination to trust and thought to intellection does not hold. This issue is too complex to address here, but my position turns on how just as thought uses objects "as images" (510e) to arrive at the mathematicals, intellection uses the mathematicals, which are 'forms' only in the allegorical sense of seen by the mind's eye, to intuit the forms. See Annas, *An Introduction to Plato's* Republic, 251–52.

13. For *hypothesis* as "supposition" and its relation to thought (*dianoia*) on the Line and in the cave, see Klein, *A Commentary on Plato's* Meno, 120–25.

14. This is illustrated in Figure 2 by the depictions of non-Euclidean triangles at the level of intellection; it is not the illustrations we understand at this level but rather the *idea* that allows making sense of 'things' that indeed are also triangles, even if unexpectedly so according to our prior perceptions and conceptions.

15. Aristotle, *Nicomachean Ethics*, 5.2–4; Rawls, *Justice as Fairness*, §§13–14.

16. See Pierre Duhem, who traces the expression back to Plato's methodology on the testimony of Simplicitus, *To Save the Phenomena*, 5–6.

17. On *ousia* as is-ness, see Sheehan, *Making Sense of Heidegger*, 33–34.

18. Which is not to say that there are not hints of what will develop into this critique. In his 1920 lectures, Heidegger identifies Platonism's fixation on *a priori* knowledge as responsible for the neglect of the situated historicity of life as lived; see GA 59: 23, 71.

19. See GA 34: 99; GA 36/37: 200–204; cf. GA 9: 228 and 232, where he calls it the *Ermöglichung*, "the making-possible of the correctness of knowing and the un-

concealment of what is known." Heidegger had employed the term *Ereignis* as early as in his 1919 *Kriegsnotsemester* lecture course, but there the "event" refers to lived experience as integral to the life-world of historical being-human, not to the breaking open of truth as unconcealment that confers the life-world as such upon us; see GA 56/57: 75.

20. Dostal, "Heidegger's Plato," 82; I have amended the passage so that "Being" conforms with my capitalization. Dostal cites Gadamer's *Die Idee des Guten zwischen Platon und Aristoteles* (20-21) as his inspiration here.

21. For this reason, it is striking that some scholars call it the *form* of the good, for example, Annas, *An Introduction to Plato's* Republic, 251; Santas, *Understanding Plato's* Republic, 137ff.

22. For Heidegger's implicit but limited teleological normativity, see Reid, *Heidegger's Moral Ontology*, chapter 3.

23. See Fried, "Whitewashed with Moralism."

24. Rosen, *Plato's* Republic, 262.

25. E.g., Annas, *An Introduction to Plato's* Republic, 251; cf. 256.

26. Kearney, *The Poetics of Modernity*, 122.

27. Eliade, *Patterns in Comparative Religion*, 143–44.

28. Esposito, *Politics and Negation*, 4.

29. Esposito, *Politics and Negation*, 207.

30. Robert Parker, preface to Eugene Gendlin, *A Process Model*, xiii.

31. James, *Principles of Psychology*, 251.

32. For a discussion of the "[. . .]" device, see Greg Madison, *Theory and Practice of Focusing-Oriented Psychotherapy*, 37.

33. Parker, Preface to Gendlin, *A Process Model*, xiii.

34. For a phenomenological interpretation of "paying attention" that treats what is at issue here but proposes a rather different path from mine, because he effectively denies that that genuine attention can be guided by *phronēsis* and ideation as I interpret them, see S. West Gurley, "Attention Is Political: How Phenomenology Gives Access to the Inconspicuously Political Act of Attending," in Pfeifer and Gurley, *Phenomenology and the Political*.

35. See Gadamer, *Truth and Method*, 280, 302, 309; on the history of the hermeneutical circle, 302–4.

Chapter Four

Breaking Down in the Cave

If you do not expect the unexpected, you will not find it, for it is hard to find and out-of-the-way.

—Heraclitus, Fragment 18[1]

There is a pathway through Plato's Cave. In fact, there are two, and what is most important about them at this point in the argument is their intersection. This chapter will provide a roadmap for navigating the geography of the Cave in order to make sense of how its features accord with the hermeneutical, existential, and ethical dimensions of our situated transcendence. In previous chapters, I have argued that the ideas are a phenomenological given of ethical engagement with the world and that they animate the piety of zetetic philosophy. The ideas, in the process of ideation that mediates between our intimation of the truth and imagination of alternatives to a world that has broken down, draw us out of the cave to transcend its finitude, requiring and enabling us to return to reconstruct the historical world with a greater perspicacity, or what the Greeks called *phronēsis*, to be addressed in chapter 7. The intersection of the two pathways is the point at which the finitude of human historicity and the transcendence of a skeptical idealism confront one another and may reconcile in a polemical dialogue. At the crossroads of the cave Plato provides us with the resources to respond to Heidegger's critique that Plato fails to account for the finite temporality of being-human.

4.1 THE GEOGRAPHY OF THE CAVE

Of the two pathways in the cave, one is more familiar to readers of the *Republic*, as it bears the burden of the philosopher's ascent from opinion, error, and delusion to insight, truth, and wisdom. Many, if not most readers, take the journey up this path as the main meaning of the Allegory. Socrates calls it "the rough, steep upward way" (515e) that leads from the lower cave out into the light of day. It is the road less taken in the allegory, though it plays the most obvious role in the narrative. Very few manage to navigate this upward way, and in the *Republic*, Socrates treats them as the true philosophers, the echonic ones who eventually come to possess truth in its fullness. We have also seen why this portrait of what constitutes real philosophy is more complex, involving a dialectic between the zetetic and echonic modes.

But there is another road in the cave, one that has received little attention but which carries far more traffic and is critical for the meaning of the Allegory. It is a pathway that transects the cave rather than leading up and out. I will call this the *lateral path*. Socrates refers to this lateral path when he first presents his parable:

> Make an image [*apeikason*] of our nature in its education and want of education, likening it to a condition of the following kind. See human beings as though they were in an underground cave-like dwelling with its entrance, a long one, open to the light across the whole width of the cave. They are in it from childhood with their legs and necks in bonds so that they are fixed, seeing only in front of them, unable because of the bond to turn their heads all the way around. Their light is from a fire burning far above and behind them. Between the fire and the prisoners *there is a road above* [*epanō hodon*], along which we see a wall [*teichion*], built like [*hōsper*] the partitions puppet-handlers [*thaumatopoios*] set in front of the human beings and over which they show the puppets [*thaumata*]. (514a–b, tm; my italics)

This "road above" cuts across the cave, we can presume, laterally from side to side while remaining underground. The cave-dwellers do not ordinarily see the lateral path. Their bonds force them to look the other way, to the cave wall opposite them. Also, the pathway is not just behind but "above" them, screened by the constructed wall (*teichon*), making it all the more inaccessible and invisible to them. The lateral pathway's position in the cave, above the prisoners, also points to the overarching metaphor of the directionality of philosophy as transcending from one's embedded origins in the particularity of a historical world, with its own traditions, beliefs, opinions, and norms.

Glaucon says that "I see" (*horō*) the image Socrates has conjured up, and so Socrates continues:

> Then also see along this wall human beings carrying all sorts of artifacts [*skeuē*], which project above the wall, and statues of men and other animals wrought

from stone, wood, and every kind of material; as is to be expected, some of the carriers utter sound while others are silent. (514b–515a)

First, we should note that the language of image-making and seeing with the mind's eye evokes the language of imagination, which is technically that segment of the Divided Line furthest from the truth. Yet Socrates conjures an image to craft this powerful account of the nature of philosophizing and expects his companions to exercise their imagination to envision it, too. Within this parable intended as an allegorical image of the human condition, Socrates says the dividing wall between the prisoners and the lateral pathway is "*like* [*hōsper*] the partitions puppet-handlers set" up for their performances. More on this later, but it is important to underline that this puppet-wall is an analogy within an analogy. It is not the case that the travelers carrying things along the road actually (or, even more emphatically, necessarily) *are* puppeteers, which is a common misunderstanding of the allegory.[2] In fact, these passers-by (*pariontōn*, 515b) seem largely or wholly unaware that the objects they carry project shadows onto the wall of the cave, images that the prisoners see and interpret. Socrates does not say if the passers-by even realize the impact they are having. As he says nothing about their behavior other than that they pass on the road, carrying objects and making noise, they may well be either indifferent to or entirely unaware of the cave-dwellers.

So now we have the familiar picture, or image (*eikōn*), as Socrates explicitly calls it (517a). (See Figure 1.) But what does it mean? As we have noted before, Glaucon calls Socrates's depiction of the cave "A strange image [*atopos eikona*] and strange prisoners [*desmōtas atopous*] you are telling of" (515a). The connotations of the Greek *atopos* (strange) suggest more about *how* this image is strange. The adjective is formed from the alpha-privative and the word *topos*, which means "place," not in the sense of merely indifferent coordinates on a topological grid, but rather place as an abode, a locale one might inhabit and feel at home, as when we say, "Come over to my place for dinner." To be *a-topos*, then, means to be strange in the sense of out-of-place, unfamiliar, or displaced. In Greek, *topoi* can mean the way of doing things specific to a place, time, and culture, so to be *atopos* is to be estranged from the local traditions, practices, and understanding of one's community. Of persons, being *atopos* can mean eccentric, weird, or even disturbing. Socrates's contemporaries saw him as *atopos*, and Alcibiades, in the *Symposium*, treats his *atopia*, his bizarreness, as a defining feature of Socrates's singularly wondrous nature (221d).

We have seen that in response, Socrates says the prisoners in the cave are "like us" (515a5). Despite the everyday appearance of normalcy, we are all somehow *atopos*, out of place, even when we fail to own up to this. As something latent to the human condition, and represented paradigmatically by Socrates, *atopia* resembles what Heidegger in *Being and Time* calls our *Unheimlichkeit*, our uncanniness (SZ, §§40, 57–58), or in his interpretation of the Ode to Man in Sophocles's *Antigone*, the *hupsipolis-apolis* character of human-being, at once rising high in the city, deprived of the city (GA 40: 161ff). We will return to this theme in chapter 8, but Heidegger's point here is that while our understanding usually finds its home in the world (to be *heimisch* is to be at home, familiar, homey), lurking always at the edges of this familiarity is the possibility of a breakdown of meaning, because our understanding cannot maintain a final and total interpretation of all things and all possibilities.

In our finitude, time always frays the understanding. When Socrates asks (524e) what "compels" the intellect to "turn around" from its prior under-standing and make its zetetic inquiry, he answers that "some opposition" (*ti enantiōma*) and "strange interpretations" (*atopoi hermēneiai*, 524b) in things are "apt to summon or awaken the activity of the intellect" (523e). Contradictions in things inevitably arise to disturb our interpretations of the world. Even if we try to repress these oppositions back beneath our homely everydayness, they break forth occasionally in the mood of angst, that sense of dislocation and homelessness in the face of all our usual possibilities and understandings, or they break in on us in sudden disruptions of life. At-issue for us is what philosophy can or cannot accomplish in the oscillation between familiarity and uncanniness.

Back to the cave, then. The prisoners are "like us" because theirs is a world of shadows that grant a certain intelligible familiarity, but which can also in-timate a much fuller and richer world of understanding beyond. I agree with the standard view that the prisoners' perception of these shadows corresponds to the *opinions* people hold about both the moral and the natural world they share as members of a given community. We share a community of opinions and norms, in the Greek sense of *nomoi*, which includes both custom and positive law, all the familiar *topoi* that encompass, enable, and restrict the social, political, and cognitive contours of our historical world like the walls of the cave. The budding philosopher is someone whose bonds to the reigning opinion about these are broken, by luck or accident, by nature, or by delib-erate intervention, human or divine, in noticing the contradictions in some phenomenon and feeling compelled to resolve them.

She or he next painfully stands up, flexing long-cramped limbs, then turns around and, again with great effort, ascends past the barrier-wall, makes it to the road, and after recovering from the blinding light of the fire, makes sense of the fire's relation to the shadows projected by the various artifacts being carried along the lateral pathway. You can understand why this would be painful: think of turning around in a dark theater and looking straight into the light of the projector. Beyond this stage, the former prisoner must make yet another painful journey "along the rough, steep upward way" (*dia tracheias tēs anabaseōs kai anantous*, 515e), the other pathway in the cave that rises up beyond the fire, out into the open world and the light of day. Even that ultimate escape for the prisoner causes pain, as the former prisoner is "dragged" out along the upward path "into the light of the sun," all the while "distressed and annoyed," and when finally emerged, to have "eyes overpowered by [the sun's] beam and be unable to see even one of the things now said to be true" (515e–516a, tm). It is like attending a daytime screening of a film, then being herded at its end to exit immediately from the theater, emerging into a daylight quite blinding and disorienting as you gain your bearings to make your way home. All this echoes the epistemic and hermeneutic distress entailed by reconfiguring an interpretation of one's world.

4.2 BREAKDOWN AND TRAUMATIC RUPTURE

As any reader of Plato knows, the Cave Allegory is supposedly a story about the arduous process of exchanging opinion for knowledge—shadowy, fleeting images for shining, eternal ideas. But the meaning of the details can be elusive, because the allegory, as an image we envision in our own internal theater of the imagination, is so compelling as narrative. The details of the story make sense in terms of the parameters of the allegory and follow a logic internal to its narrative. People long chained would naturally find it painful to rise and move, to climb an unpleasant and difficult ascent, and to look into various blinding sources of light. Of course, once they get used to the outside, they would be loath to return back down to the cave, as Socrates says is the responsibility of the philosophers trained by Kallipolis. And no doubt they would look ridiculous, in their fumbling, bumbling comings and goings out into the light and then back into the dark.

But what is the meaning of all this pain and difficulty? Why would the ascent and descent be hard, even dangerous? Isn't knowledge a sweet and a good thing, desired by us all, as Aristotle says in the *Metaphysics* (980a21)?

A clue lies in how the whole process of liberation gets started, which is an image for how philosophy gets started. Having set up his picture of the prison-cave, Socrates says, "Look now. . .what their release and healing from the bonds and folly would be like if something of this sort [i.e., the narrative to follow] were by nature to happen to them" (515c, tm). Again, we are instructed to examine the meaning of the image with the mind's eye and the imagination, and at-issue here is how this liberating "release" (*lusis*) from the bonds were to happen *by nature* (*phusei*). What is natural about the liberation? Socrates immediately shifts from "them" (*autois*), the prisoners in the cave taken as a whole, to an individual: "Take someone who is released and suddenly compelled to stand up, to turn their neck around, to walk and look up toward the light; and who, moreover, in doing all this is in pain and, because of the flashing [of the fire], unable to see distinctly those things [i.e., the artifacts being carried along the road] whose shadows he previously saw" (515c–d, tm).

First to note, the release *and* healing (*lusin te kai iasin*) from the bonds is a two-step process. The release alone from the bonds is not sufficient for genuine liberation. In fact, the release or break is only the first step in an arduous process of healing and recovery. The bonds, as it were, cast their own lingering shadow. It is also striking that Socrates uses the passive voice to indicate how the prisoner "is released [*lutheiē*] . . . and compelled [*anankeizoito*] to stand up"; he does not say *who* or *what* does the releasing and compelling. One might assume that it must be some person who does the releasing, because soon Socrates will ask: "And what if someone dragged him away from there [the stage of the lateral road and fire] by force along the rough, steep, upward way [the pathway up into the open light of day] and didn't let him go before dragging him out into the light of the sun?" (515e, tm). Later Glaucon objects to Socrates's proposal that their "job as founders is to compel the best natures to the study which we were saying before is the greatest, to see the good and go up that ascent" (519c–d) of the Divided Line, and then compel them again (520a) to "go down" back into the cave to govern it. Glaucon says it would "do them an injustice" to force such refugees back into the cave and "make them live a worse life when a better one is possible for them" (519d).

Socrates has a telling response. He says, "We won't be doing injustice to the philosophers who come to be among us" (520a), that is, the educators of the next generation of philosopher-kings and queens, because they owe their liberation precisely to the founders and therefore owe a debt of service in return. But: "We'll say that when such men come to be in the other cities it is fitting for them not to participate in the labors of those cities. For they grow up spontaneously [*autophues*: by their own nature, *sui generis*] against the will of the regime in each; and a nature that grows by itself and doesn't owe its rearing to anyone has justice on its side when it is not eager to pay the price of rearing to anyone" (520b). This indicates two possible modes through which the liberation may occur "by nature": spontaneously or by deliberate education. This is illustrated by the two lower panels in Figure 4.

The educational system for the rulers of Kallipolis proposed by Socrates is remarkably detailed, but someone must have started it and so at least someone must get free spontaneously without it. Socrates says that the onset of philosophy happens "suddenly" (*exaiphnēs*, 515c). That word, *exaiphnēs*, is an important one for Plato. In the Seventh Letter, he says that the heart of philosophical insight is not something he can write up in a treatise: "For in no way can it be put in words as in other fields of learning; rather, from long communion with the matter itself and by living with it, it comes to be suddenly, like a light is kindled from a leaping flame, it emerges in the soul and then nourishes itself by itself" (341c–d). There is also the passage in the *Symposium*, where Diotima tells Socrates that at the end of the ascent of the ladder of love, proceeding from loving the many beautiful things at its start, "suddenly" (210e) the seeker is granted the wondrous vision of the "singular, ever-in-being form" (*monoeides aei on*, 211b) of Beauty itself that encompasses and gives being to all transient, beautiful things. What happens *exaiphnēs* happens by surprise, like the thief in the night. We might possibly prepare for it, but it comes unbidden, of its own accord and all of a sudden. We cannot make it happen, and we cannot predict when or what it will be.[3]

The sudden onset of philosophy begins as this unbidden, unexpected release of the prisoner from the bonds (515c), whether by someone else or spontaneously. In Greek, release from bonds, or manumission, is *lusis tōn desmōn*. A *lusis* is a release, a loosening, a dissolution, and an *ana-lusis* is a dissolution of something into its component parts, a breaking down of the bonds that hold it together. But what are the bonds that get broken down at the onset of philosophy?

The Greek word *desmos*, bond, is a ligature or connection that holds things together in ways that can be positive, negative, or both. It can be a simple strap or chains or an imprisonment. A *desmōtēs* is a prisoner, someone in bonds. In English, we speak of the *bonds of marriage*, of being *duty-bound*, of *the ties that bind*, and of *bondage*. These English usages correspond closely to the sense of *desmos*. We are *bonded* to a world in ways that free and fulfill us as well as constrain and diminish us. To use Heidegger's terms, we always find ourselves already immersed in a world about which we care, either positively or negatively; its meaning, and what we can do and accomplish within that meaningful world, *concerns* us. As we go about our business, we are bonded to and bounded by the meanings we inhabit in our historical location, our heritage, our community: our cave. These bonds and bounds grant connection, structure, and intelligibility to things, and they usually allow us to understand our involvements and to function without having to reflect upon that understanding in some detached, theoretical pondering. Our finitude means that we are bound to be bound, but freely to confront or to accept those bounds, as situated wisdom requires, also can free us for the choices available to us within those boundaries.

As Heidegger points out, sometimes the self-evidence of all these filiations breaks down. His famously prosaic example is the hammer. The hammer *is* a hammer for me because I interpret it as such for the sake of a purpose (hammering a nail to a wall for the sake of hanging a picture), and it comes ready-to-hand *as* hammer in the filiated web of purposes, procedures, and all the other things (nails, walls, pictures, and so on) interpreted in the as-structure of a particular, bounded world of meaning (SZ, 93–94). But if my hammer breaks, suddenly—*exaiphnēs*—there is a *breakdown* in the fabric of the system of references that makes meaningful action possible (SZ, 98). In English, a breakdown can be several quite different things: a collapse of a system or organization ("The government's system of monitoring environmental pollutants has suffered a breakdown"); a personal psychological or physiological collapse ("He had a nervous breakdown last week"); an intentional analysis of something into its most significant elements, usually for examination and then action ("The coach wants a breakdown of the opponent team's defensive strategy"). What unites them is the sense of a reduction of something to its elementary components. The first two are negative events that impede or prevent functioning in a given world-context; the third is usually positive. Breakdown is in fact a quite direct English correlate to the Greek *ana-lusis*, the dissolving of something previously cohering into component parts, the root of our word *analysis*.

The hammer is a commonplace example, but breakdown can happen in contexts from the mundane to the cataclysmic. In *Radical Hope*, Jonathan Lear analyzes the ontological bereavement of the Crow Nation of Native Americans in the nineteenth century, facing cultural and physical genocide. The disruptions of their way of life became so devastating that an entire world of meaning for things and practices faced complete breakdown. Lear quotes the last great chief of the independent Crow Nation, Alaxchiiaahush, Man-of-Many-Acts-of-Valor, speaking of the disappearance of the buffalo: "After this nothing happened." This is not a declaration of a Hegelian end of history but of ontological catastrophe where the good no longer orients action and meaning no longer inhabits things: "when the buffalo went away, the hearts of my people fell to the ground, and they could not lift them up again."[4] The buffalo did not just represent, they *were* the way of life for the Crow, so after their disappearance, cultural practices, ritual objects, everyday implements, norms, and traditional virtues lost their meaning and collapsed into indifference and unmeaning. As Heidegger puts it, "Where struggle ceases, beings indeed do not disappear, but world turns away. Beings are no longer asserted [that is, preserved as such]. Beings now become just something one comes across; they are findings" (GA 40: 67; Heidegger's interpolation)—inert "findings" in the sense of pots or arrowheads one might dig up, or see in a museum, or buy in an antiques shop, but no longer inhabiting a living world. Struggle, *polemos*, is what drives the hopefulness of the reinterpretive reappropriation of meaning, but when that "struggle ceases"—and now I draw instead on Plato—the good no longer inhabits a historical world. As Alaxchiiaahush puts it, that world falls "to the ground," the earth of a tradition that had sustained its significance but now swallows it up, as it did Oedipus.

In every context of breakdown, a domain of signification either temporarily or irrevocably dissolves. The breakdown announces what Karl Jaspers called the "limit situation" (*Grenzsituation*), a moment that both threatens and promises an existential transformation that we can either evade in bad faith or engage in hermeneutic struggle.[5] When a breakdown occurs, a web of signification ruptures, leaving one momentarily flustered or profoundly traumatized or potently awestruck. Some one thing, or perhaps a whole constellation of objects and social practices, seems to flop about, obtruding upon awareness but no longer fitting in. The world goes out of joint. Whether trivial or devastating or awe-inspiring, a breakdown presents an irruptive *opportunity* to notice the web of intersecting meanings that define the contours of things and the significance of the world. In prosaic cases, this window of opportunity may close as quickly as reaching for a different hammer or allowing a moment of idle curiosity to pass by. Nevertheless, the opportunity for the examined life beckons, even in everyday breakdowns, to see *how* things have been interpreted and to consider *that* they might be interpreted otherwise and then to consider *how*.

A *desmos*, a bond or tie, gets loosened, cut, or broken, *lutheiē*, as strands in the web of interconnected meanings that form the complex structures of a historical world. In Heidegger's language, the breakdown points to an event in the fore- and as-structures of the understanding and interpretation of a world that brings these up short. What breaks are the bonds of signification and reference that allow us to place things in the nexus of meaningful objects and practices that define a hermeneutically habitable world, the world as we live it on the historical, human scale. There are two levels to seeing the bonds: one grasps the fact *that* something has been interpreted in such and such a way, leaving a space for a new interpretation; another seizes upon the interpreted-ness of things as such, breaking open the possibility of the question of the meaning of Being itself that asks how it is possible that we can understand anything as what we take it to be.

The breakdown happens to us, but we can also take it up, following its drift in interpretive analysis. *Ana-lusis*, breaking down, therefore has both passive and active aspects. Even the devastation of a world of meaning can become an opportunity for transformation. Indeed, how a community responds in such a moment of crisis can mean the difference between cultural oblivion and cultural resilience and adaptation. As passive, a breakdown can happen to us, of a sudden and against expectation, interrupting the ordinary course of things. As active, a breakdown is something we do and produce by analyzing something confronting us as a problem or a challenge, although the impetus to do so first happens to us. In either case, passive or active, the breakdown occurs because something calls for interpretation and reintegration into meaningful context, but we heed this call, we do not make it. The process of analysis and reconfiguration can succeed or fail, or never even get started, but it is always *occasioned* by something out of joint, something that the previously operative understanding cannot fully make sense of, either any longer or not yet. These are the "strange interpretations" (524b) and oppositions in things that Socrates says summon the intellect to reconstructive dialogue. We can shunt that call aside and repress it, going about our business as best we can—if the moment of meaning-displacement is relatively trivial, we can usually do so—or we can endeavor to be as open as possible to noticing and then taking up the call. But in neither case do *we* make it happen that something about the world calls for reinterpretation.

The possibility and inevitability of breakdown is grounded in the finitude and temporality of human understanding. We are not capable of complete vision, entire comprehension. Furthermore, the understanding we do have is discursive: it unfolds, develops, or decomposes, through the *dia-logos* with our contextual environments, with both persons and things. The dialogue itself is motivated at its most energetic by the various breakdowns, from the petty to the all-encompassing, that impinge upon us and call upon us to revise our understanding through new interpretations. The breakdown of the bonds of understanding is therefore another way of describing what we addressed as *deconstruction* in the previous chapter, what Heidegger called *Destruktion* and *Abbau*, destruction and dismantling. Indeed, deconstruction is simply another way of saying breakdown. Both operate on the metaphorics of taking apart an existing assemblage, and the assemblage, the *logos* as a gathering, is the nexus of significations and referents among things that constitutes a meaningful world. This is why Jacques Derrida would say, in discussion with Gianni Vattimo, that:

> "I ought to have specified that what happens deconstructs itself in the process. It is not I who deconstruct; rather something I called 'deconstruction' happens to the experience of a world, a culture, a philosophic tradition: 'it' deconstructs, *ça ne va pas*, there is something that budges, that is in the process of being dislocated, disjointed, disadjoined, and of which I begin to be aware. Something is 'deconstructing' and it has to be answered for."[6]

Heidegger's *Destruktion* might seem more intentional and deliberate than this; however, I think he would not claim the deconstruction as his but as something happening within thought and meaning in a historical world and that he simply notices and articulates.

While I have disagreed emphatically with aspects of Derrida's postmodernist political understanding of deconstruction, largely because it downplays or ignores the Platonic ideation necessary for *reconstruction* of a world in favor of a too one-sidedly anarchistic conception of liberation, his succinct description of deconstruction is a splendid explanation of the point I want to make about the breakdown, the *lusis desmōn*, that occurs as the starting point to the internal action of the narrative of the Cave.[7] *Ana-lusis* is first and foremost something that *happens*, not something that we make happen, to the warp and woof of the meaning-structures of being-human in a historical world, which necessarily frays as a function of our finite temporality, but which we may reweave reconstructively. When Derrida says that "'it' deconstructs," the "it" is the hermeneutical nexus of the fore- and as-structures of our understanding and interpretation within which things, practices, and actions ordinarily find their meaningful place, or *topos*. Certainly "I" can follow the lead of this happening of deconstruction by taking up the *ana-lusis* as my own, but the "it happens" of the breakdown in meaning is *a priori*. Derrida says that the fraying of meaning-structures "has to be answered for," and this is another way of expressing the *dia-logos* that human beings are or can be in the life examined, our polemical confrontation with our finite understanding of the world.

The "has to be" of answering in this polemical dialogue has both an ethical and an existential aspect. We have a calling to answer the *atopoi* disjunctions that arise in the world, and we risk an increasingly incoherent cognitive existence if we evade responding to them. Nevertheless, Derrida's claim that the breakdown of meaning "has to be answered for" puts it too categorically: we are always *free*, at liberty, to ignore the call to respond; we can live the unexamined life, both ethically and cognitively, by sweeping the fraying threads of the textile of understanding under the rug of our consciousness, unless and until the incoherence of our historical world becomes so extreme that the everyday reliability of this world we inhabit becomes unsustainable. As Polemarchus responds in Book One of the *Republic*, when Socrates attempts to persuade him and his friends that he and Glaucon should be left alone to return to Athens rather than go with Polemarchus to his father's home, "Could you really persuade if we don't listen [*mē akousantas*]?" (327c). In the refusal to listen, we are borne along passively by the currents of the breakdown of the world rather than having an active role in its reconstruction. In other words, the *breakdown*, the deconstructive moment of *ana-lusis*, does not necessarily result in a full-blown *rupture*, at least not immediately, if it is repressed and ignored. The rupture is the breakdown fulfilled in the call that *demands* a dialogical response and *is* addressed through a reconstructive interpretation.

4.3 HEALING FROM THE BREAKDOWN

We will return to the active features of this reintegration. For the moment, recall that Socrates distinguishes between the breakdown of bonds, the *lusis*, and the healing from them, the *iasis* (515c). The healing is the much lengthier process. While the breakdown occurs *exaiphnēs*, of a sudden, the healing requires the arduous process of ascent—and, I will argue, return. To be healed, one must move up from the lowest cave floor where the bonds bind the prisoners, to the lateral path and the fire, and then up the steep, upward pathway into the open light of day—and after that, perhaps, *back* down into the cave.

The Greek noun *iasis* derives from the verb *iaomai*, a middle-voice verb that means to heal in both the passive and active senses: to heal *from* something and to heal someone *of* something. It also has a secondary meaning of *repair*, which corresponds to the reweaving, or perhaps *ad hoc* patching, of the fraying textile of the meaning-structures of an intelligible world. In contrast to the breakdown as *ana-lusis* that happens of a sudden, breaking in unbidden upon the understanding, the healing repair as the active analysis through reconstruction takes time, as well as courage and perseverance, in the life examined. Furthermore, its success is not guaranteed.

If the prisoners are "like us" and we are therefore in bonds as well, what is the symbolic meaning of the *pain* associated with the process of the healing from the bonds, as well as the risks Socrates ascribes to the recovery? The prisoner going through the healing process of liberation "is in pain" (*algoi*, 515c) at each station of the ascent: at the very first removal of the bonds and the flexing of the long-constrained limbs; during the ascent to the lateral path and when confronting the fire; during the ascent up the steep, upward path from the fire to the outside world; upon emerging into the blinding light of day once finally outside; and then, for some, in going back down into the cave, readjusting alternately to the darkness and the firelight. Socrates is candid about the risks for those returning from the light of day back to the cave. While their eyes are adjusting to the darkness, they will suffer disorientation and a new kind of blindness, the obverse of suddenly emerging from dark into light. In this condition they may stumble, and the inhabitants of the cave might ridicule them or even try to kill them or their former mentors as potential corruptors of the eyesight of others (516e–517a).

To make sense of this dual pain and risk, we can turn to Socrates's more formal discussion of the education of the philosophers in Book 7. There, he describes dialectic as the last and most dangerous study (537d–539d). It must come after the other studies, such as mathematics and geometry, which are preparatory for dialectic in method more than in content. In those prior studies, the rising philosopher learns to make and discard explanatory hypotheses, but the stakes are abstract, a matter of pure knowing or not knowing about things magnificent and beautiful but remote from human affairs, such as the Pythagorean theorem. But in dialectic, the hypotheses presented—and discussed, refuted, and reconstructed—are opinions not only about mathematics and the grand abstractions about truth or Being, but also about life on the human scale. Such questions involve piety and impiety, right and wrong, justice and injustice, courage and cowardice, and all the vices and virtues that orient and pinion us to our lives and attachments.

As we will see below in the discussion of the seduction by rhetoric, power, and pleasure, these normative convictions (*dogmata*) are the hypotheses that dialectic about ethical life threatens to destroy in its acts of deconstruction. The young, not yet matured to philosophy but who learn dialectic, "misuse [arguments] as though it were play, always using them to contradict . . . like puppies pulling and tearing with argument at those who happen to be near" (539b). More seriously, someone may deploy dialectic to refute the laws, traditions, and convictions "about the just and good and the things he held most in honor" (538d–e), all that restrains willful and predatory behavior. Such a person may then turn to lawless self-indulgence or manipulative sophistry. Dialectic is safe only in the hands of someone "who's willing to discuss and consider the truth rather than the one who plays and contradicts for the sake of the game" (539c). Of course, for us as for Athens, once the Pandora's box of dialectic is opened, its power disperses indiscriminately, and it is hard to imagine even Socrates's ideal city managing to keep it in bounds, however carefully guarded. Even the most just and judicious dialectician would face tremendous obstacles convincing ordinary citizens by argument alone.

Within the narrative of the Allegory, Socrates suggests this when he asks about the prisoner just released:

> What do you suppose he'd say if someone were to tell him that before he saw silly nothings, while, now, because he is somewhat nearer to what *is* and more turned toward beings, he sees more correctly; and, in particular, showing him each of the things that pass by, were to compel the man to answer his questions about what they are? Don't you suppose he'd be at a loss and believe that what was seen before is truer than what is now being shown? (515d)

The parallel is unmistakable between asking the ascending prisoner about what the shadows really "are" shadows *of* and Socrates' own questioning people about "what is" love, or justice, or piety, or any of the usual, human-scale topics of his inquiries. Equally unmistakable is Socrates's self-portrait of the liberated prisoner returning back to the cave to address its inhabitants:

> And if he once more had to compete with those perpetual prisoners in forming judgments about those shadows while his vision was still dim, before his eyes had recovered, and if the time needed from getting accustomed were not at all short, wouldn't he be the source of laughter, and wouldn't it be said of him that he went up and came back with his eyes corrupted, and that it's not even worth trying to go back up? And if they [that is, the perpetual prisoners] were somehow able to get their hands on and kill the man who attempts to release and lead up, wouldn't they kill him? (516e–517a)

As other commentators have suggested, this portrait of the returning liberator's travails obviously maps onto the fate of Socrates: first being ridiculed by the likes of Aristophanes as an absurd and corrosive wise-guy, and then his actual prosecution, conviction, and execution for impiety and corrupting the youth.[8] While Athenians might have laughed at Euthyphro for his overly pious and pompous claims to prophetic insight into the will of the gods—because he was so manifestly ludicrous in his extremity—at least Euthyphro accepted the prevailing myths about the nature of the gods, and so was probably no serious threat. But Socrates laid claim to a piety that would inspire not laughter but fear and pain. He did not question that the gods existed but whether the stories told about them were accurate—that they committed the rapes and castrations and violence attributed to Zeus, Chronos, and Ouranos, as well as all the other disputes among the gods (*Euthyphro*, 6a–c).

What does it mean to have "vision still dim, before his eyes had recovered"? It is the obverse of how dialectic guides the healing process. Dialectic "compels" the prisoner, as the method of recovery from the bonds of opinion, to confront the dogmas inherited from the happenstance of their particular location in a specific historical context. This is the meaning of the "rough, steep, upward way" (515e) from the stage of the lateral path to the outside world. It is "rough" (*tracheias*) because dialectic *is* the deconstructive path by which the bonds of received opinions are broken up into shards through the *polemos* of identifying contradictions among them, leaving the ordinary vision of the world in lesser or greater states of demolition. It is "steep" (*anabaseōs*) because dialectic is inherently precipitous, disorienting, and vertiginous; it risks a fall by deconstructing how our ordinary views grant us a coherent vision of our context, so that we can no longer navigate our historical world effectively. It is "upward" (*anantous*), most obviously in the context of the Allegory, because progress from imprisonment is up and out of the cave; but analogously because dialectic compels us to emerge, up and away, from the views that had previously grounded us in our happenstance. Now again, we run up against the inherently metaphoric nature of language. Why should this deconstructive process of breakdown, analysis, and dialectic be an *upward* motion, and why should that be *painful*?

As several readers of the *Republic* have noted, the imagery of upward and downward motion plays a central role in the narrative and the arguments of the dialogue.[9] The first word of the dialogue, narrated by Socrates, is *katebēn*, "I went down"—down from Athens to the port of Piraeus. When Socrates tells the story of the cave, he says the newly minted philosophers, after emerging into the light and growing accustomed to it, must each "go back down" (*katabateon*) into the cave to lead the people there. And as we have seen, the process of breaking free of dogmatic opinion involves an ascent up through several stages of increasingly greater understanding.

Why should greater understanding be associated with upward movement? Hikers are told that if they get lost in the wilderness, an important step for getting reoriented is to find a higher vantage point, especially if lines of sight are obscured, because from a height the prominent features of the landscape come into view as landmarks, and the more proximate details of one's location can be related meaningfully to them so that one can make progress. Similarly, when a breakdown of meaning occurs, it is important to step back from the details, away from the nitty-gritty of one's ordinary involvements, because these are the things that either overwhelm us with their multiplicity so that we cannot reorient our understanding or lull us into complacency with their everydayness so that what had once stood out in the breakdown as demanding attention recedes and gets covered over. Abstracting oneself, figuratively pulling oneself back from immersion in the details, grants the opportunity to discern new patterns and to reintegrate a broken-down sense of meaning into a provisionally navigable whole.

But why this should be painful is not yet clear. One obvious clue is the response that the Socratic method generates among some of his fellow Athenians—and which students and teachers alike can observe when using the method in the classroom. As Socrates reports in the *Apology*, many of the artisans, poets, and politicians, whose claims to knowledge he examined and usually demolished, reacted in anger (*Apology*, 21d–24a). Anger is a natural response to pain. One aspect of this is vanity. Few who profess a claim to knowledge, especially if that claim supports their social, professional, or political prestige, enjoy a public refutation. We see this in the *Republic* itself, where Thrasymachus reacts first in disdainful rage (343a–344d) and then in humiliation (350d) to Socrates's demolition of his definition of justice, because he wanted to "win a good reputation" (338a)—and presumably the fees he might have earned from Cephalus if his sons, Polemarchus and Lysias, had chosen him for their teacher after witnessing him defeat Socrates in elenchus. Indeed, one reason Polemarchus might have been so eager to get Socrates to come back to his home is because he knew Thrasymachus was already there and that he could pit him against Socrates as an impromptu audition or job interview (327c–328b).

Vanity and humiliation are important because they might inhibit the dissolution of the bonds of opinion, but they are not the only source of pain in the breakdown and subsequent healing process by which one ascends through the various stations up and out of the cave. Much more painful is that sense of *aporia*, of no-exit, that crawls over you when a belief that anchors some vital aspect of your life in place crumbles. This aspect is not about interpersonal status but rather your own sense of orientation within a world that had made sense up to that moment of breakdown. Opinions are binding because they are so often bound to our most intimate attachments, as to friends, family, faith, and country, and to our most defining activities, such as profession, work, and play. Heidegger's name for this attachment to the involvements of the historical world we always find ourselves in as pre-given is *care (Sorge)*. This is not necessarily care in the sense of affectionate or dutiful solicitude for things or people; it is care in the larger, existential sense that being-human means having a meaningful world oriented for us by what matters to us, including things that burden or frighten us, as well as those that bring comfort, joy, or satisfaction. When Heidegger says that Dasein *is* care in *Being and Time* (§§41–42), he means that to have a world involves having an understanding of things, persons, and activities that make sense because they matter to us in some way *as* what we take them *to be*. Breaking the bonds of opinion threatens to disrupt whatever illumination of the world we thought was sufficient to function within it.

Emotional pain can be as phenomenologically real as a blow to the face. Human beings generally desire to operate within the norms of the social group that is dispositive for them. That group may not be one that the individual loves, likes, or even tolerates—it may even be hated—but its norms have defined the contours of acceptable behavior for the individual that she relies upon to get through the day with minimum anxiety and distress. This corresponds with the experience of breakdown in the cave. The pain elicited by the threat or fact of breakdown of the bonds could result in a variety of responses: fending off the perceived attack on the bonds of belief by ignoring or repressing the potentially liberating person or event (in the case of persons, repression can extend to oppression and even elimination, as it did with the execution of Socrates by Athens); repairing the bonds in a slapdash manner that does not really address how badly they have been damaged, but does enough to restore an illusion of restraint for a while; pretending that the bonds have not been broken and continuing to function 'as if' they were still there; and, finally, engaging in the process of what Socrates calls the healing (*iasis*) from the bonds, which is separate from the release and which the other responses avoid. The healing process takes time to work through the pain of the dissolution of formerly orienting beliefs and then to reintegrate the contours of a meaningful life. The healing is education in the sense that Socrates gives it: a "turning around" (*metastrophē*, 518c, 532c) from the shadows as the ascent up through the stages of the cave, and then the subsequent return (to which we will return). This healing is necessarily polemical, because it must confront the prior convictions that occasioned the painful breakdown in the first place, deconstruct them, construe a new meaning, and reintegrate it.

The *Republic* addresses the two-phased pain of release and then healing from the bonds of opinion, most notably in the discussion of dialectic as the final stage in the education of the philosopher-rulers in Book 7, which Socrates explicitly calls the "journey" (532b)—the Greek is *poreia*, as opposed *aporia*, a pathway with a destination rather than one with no exit. This is the journey of healing from the bonds after the initial release, a journey that takes time and changes place, going through differing scenes and perspectives. While dialectic has the power to test (537d) the character of prospective philosopher-kings and queens as to the virtue of their initial opinions and to lead their souls upward in the cave and on the Divided Line (532a–c), in this passage on education Socrates also warns about "how great is the harm coming from the practice of dialectic these days" (537e). Dialectic can have this negative effect because of its power to unsettle and break the bonds of received opinion. Dialectic works its power "these days" (*to nun*) in cities that have no proper principles or superintendents for the education of its young in dialectic, "a job requiring a great deal of guarding" (*pollēs phulakēs ergon*, 537d), which otherwise produces adults "filled full with lawlessness" (*paranomias empimplantai*, 537e).

4.4 PHILOSOPHERS MISFIRED

This misfiring of dialectic recalls Book 6, where Socrates describes the two types of failed philosophers, the useless and the vicious. Both may be understood as resulting from a failure to grasp the importance of the idea of the good. If a person has all the raw talent needed for a philosopher-ruler—a quick learner; intrepid in spirit; having a good memory, brilliant insight, and sharp analytical skills—that person is also very attractive to those who would put those talents to use for purposes far less noble than philosophy or just rule. Such purposes involve all the arts of persuasion, the tricks of argumentation and rhetoric, that can sway people in the city's assembly, the law courts, or in the market place. We today would call this the work of public relations and marketing, including all the subtle arts of modern advertising, branding, consumer data analysis, political consulting, and so on. These seducers of the potential philosopher-ruler have no actual regard for the common good of the community. They seek to recruit the talents of the potential philosophers for factional purposes. This *potential* philosopher-ruler turns vicious by being seduced away from two things: healthy philosophy and the youthful virtues instilled in them by a traditional upbringing that directed them to the common good. The seducers win potential philosophers over by flattering them with the prospect of status and power for the vicious pseudo-philosophers (494c) and pleasures (538d) for the hedonist, each of which will flow from wielding their talents for refutation and persuasion without concern for the good apart from a distorted view of their own good. Such use of refutation and persuasion *resembles* philosophical dialectic in its method but not in its purpose. It seeks a partisan or private good rather than justice.[10]

When the once-naive but increasingly worldly youth discovers that the decent but perhaps boring, restrictive, and unsophisticated family that raised him is not really as reliably authoritative as he once thought, then according to Socrates, "unless he is by nature particularly decent" (*panu phusei epieikēs*, 538c), he will be sorely tempted to cease honoring them and begin listening to the flatterers and "to live according to their ways" (538b–c). Socrates says, "Surely we have from childhood convictions about what's just and fair by which we are brought up as by parents, obeying them as rulers and honoring them" (538c). These convictions—he uses the word *dogmata* here, which has a more binding normative force than *doxa*, opinion—seem to make us generally but unreflectively decent by fending off the passions, desires, and actions that would otherwise seduce us into injustice. But because these norms are unreflective, unexamined, and unsupported by argument, they are vulnerable to dialectic or eristic. Socrates asks:

> When a question is posed and comes to the man who is so disposed [that is, to honor and obey "the ancestral things," 538d], "What is the fair [*kalon*, also the noble]?"—and after answer that he heard from the lawgiver [i.e., the ancestral norms], the argument refutes him, and refuting him many times and in many ways, reduces him to the opinion that what the law says is no more fair than ugly, and similarly about the just and the good and the things he held most in honor—after that, what do you suppose he'll do about honoring and obeying as rulers the things he heard from the lawgiver? (538d–e)

The answer is obvious to both Glaucon and Socrates. To be refuted over and over again by arguments that deprive the ancestral convictions of their affective and binding force leaves a person feeling foolish for once having honored them and opens him up to all kinds of "outlaw" (*paranomos*, 539a) opinions and ways of life. This is particularly likely if, having lost his un-reflective but once-instinctive convictions, he "doesn't find the true ones" (538e). Without using the word, Socrates describes this state of mind, which views "what the law says as no more fair than ugly," as a form of nihilism: "Then when they themselves refute many men and are refuted by many, they fall quickly into a profound disbelief of what they formally believed"—which is a great cause for why "they themselves and the whole activity of philoso-phy become the objects of slander among the rest of men" (539b–c).

Nihilism may arise at the lowest level of the cave when the bonds of conventional convictions break down and the now released prisoner is left abandoned in that state, without hope of finding truth. Stumbling around in the darkness, no longer oriented by the naive but uncomplicated bonds of ancestral conviction, startled occasionally by the flare of the fire that now merely distorts their apprehension of the shadows on the wall, the released prisoner is disoriented and displaced, *atopos* with no way out, no exit— brought to *aporia* through argument.[11] As for members of the Crow Nation after its devastation, this condition of release unaccompanied by healing from the bonds, especially if extended into hopelessness, can be ontologically traumatic.[12] It leaves the prisoner deprived of a sense for living a meaningful life. Although the shadows remain, just as feelings and objects and people and norms remain in the world after our convictions break down, they have lost their prior significance for us. This deprives us of an understanding of our possibilities for engaging with them—just as one might continue to vote in elections even if convinced that voting makes no difference; as one might continue regular religious observations to please one's parents, even if one no longer believes. The released but lost, semi-blind, and abandoned prisoners cannot even ascend to the lateral road above the lowest floor of the cave and the fire burning there. The ascent and the bright firelight seem only to cause more pain and disorientation, and there is no one to guide and reassure them.

This trauma, caused by an unfulfilled tutelage and healing in dialectic that must be developmental and not merely sudden and episodic—*exaiphnēs* like the breaking of the bonds—leaves the released but not-yet-healing prisoner extremely vulnerable to the "flatterers": the allures of power and pleasure, fame and status, to supply meaning in life. For the shaky and only potential philosopher, such flatterers promise fulfillment through sophistry, in its an-cient and modern forms, as a way to manipulate others with argument and information. Power, pleasure, fame, and status have a very natural appeal.

Especially if one has been lost long enough without hope of an exit, a person becomes cynical about the possibility of any argument providing the orienting principles for a meaningful life. This nihilism is what Socrates means by the danger of *misology*, the hatred of argument. A person gripped by misology "no longer makes any use of persuasion by means of speech but goes about everything with force and savageness, like a wild beast" guided by the instinct for power and pleasure (411d–e). He also brings it up in the *Phaedo*, where he likens misology to misanthropy: "For misanthropy insinuates itself from trusting someone too much but naively [*aneu technēs*]" and then having that experience repeated over and over so that he ends up "hating everyone and believing there is nothing sound in anyone at all" (89d–e). So, too, the misologists, "by dissipating themselves in disputatious arguments, end up believing that they have become most wise and that they alone have had the insight that there is nothing sound or firm to anything or any argument, but all being [*panta to onta*] blithely fluctuates up and down, like in the [violent currents of the tidal straits of] Euripus, and nothing remains anywhere for any time" (90b–c; tm).

Socrates suggests that hating people and hating argument both issue from a nihilism that arises from a sense of trust betrayed, born of a naive confidence in one's own powers of judgment. We might modify this misological form of nihilism to a more sophisticated version. The corrupted nascent-philosopher, the one abandoned at the lowest floor of the cave, might still use argument for the sake of power and pleasure but forsake the promise that argument once seemed to make at the moment of initial release: that a noble and inspiring understanding of the world might be found, confirmed as true by dialectic rather than as arbitrarily binding by mute tradition. Despite having forsaken this noble aspiration for philosophical inquiry, the misologist might still make nihilistic use of argument (in eristic rather than genuine dialectic) to deconstruct any other argument that claims to have discovered what truth, virtue, justice, and the like really *are*, because to be absolutely free of normative fetters is preferable for the misologistic anarchist to being taken in again by illusions of righteousness that interfere with the naturally obvious attractions of power, pleasure, and prestige. This is not even the worst that can happen. The breaking down of the bonds can result in an ontological trauma so profound that it can cause a complete breakdown, unable to cope with reality.[13] Socrates acknowledges this danger at every station of progress out of the cave, where the former prisoner is exposed to various forms of pain and disorientation (515c–516a). While the bonds of opinion bind us, they do still give us the semblance of a stable, intelligible world, and to lose that sense of grounding can be devastating, because even if that present world is full of injustice and suffering, it is at least predictable.

All this suggests that the transitional moment between the release from the bonds, or the breakdown, and the healing from the bonds, or the ascent that completes the rupture from them by providing a genuine alternative, is an extremely sensitive one in education as the "turning around" of the soul. If the prisoner is abandoned here, or if the supposed liberator is in fact a sophistical manipulator or propagandist rather than a trustworthy mentor, the results may be disastrous, and from the perspective of the newly released, it may well be impossible to discern a philosophical mentor from a sophistical preda-tor. Unlike a passive stuffing of the mind with information or the training of the body with physical skills, the required turning (*periacteon*, 518c) of the soul towards the light requires a careful and respectful deployment of what Socrates calls the journey of dialectic (532d) as an active polemical engage-ment with the beliefs of the person ascending the pathway up and out of the cave. But first, the true mentor must earn the trust of the one dislocated and traumatized by the release, perhaps by showing how even the broken shards of the bonds of previous opinion may intimate unexpected meanings and a reintegration of the understanding.

This dialectic has a distinctly polemical character, in our larger sense of the polemical. Because it is not a formulaic insertion of information into the soul, but rather a learning and a teaching how to live the examined life of ques-tioning seeking, Socrates calls dialectical education an "art of this turning around" (*technē tēs periagōgēs*, 518d). On the one hand, the pedagogical art of polemical dialectic must bring the pilgrim-philosopher into confrontation with mere opinions, to analyze, refute, or confirm them. On the other, it must avoid allowing this confrontation to lapse into despondency and hopeless-ness about ever making progress. The seeker must learn how to internalize and integrate this dialectic actively as a feature of the life worth living, as a polemical ethic. Otherwise, whatever insights it produces will be short lived. They will fade with what Socrates describes as the misological effects of refutation after refutation of received opinion (537d–539c).

Socrates says emphatically that "this power [of sight] is in the soul of each" (518c) and that "this art takes as a given that sight is there, but not rightly turned nor looking at what it ought to look at, and accomplished this object" (518d). He directly links turning this power for "sight" (*opsis*, 518c) in the allegorical situation of the cave, from the shadows up into the light, to the image of the Divided Line, as the sight of the mind's eye turning around "from what is coming into being" (*ek tou gignomenou*) by learning "to endure looking at that which *is* [*eis to on*] and the brightest part of that which *is*—and we affirm that this brightest part is the good" (518c–d, tm). In principle, if not realized in practice, this power of polemical turning and ascent is latent in each of us, as vision is in the eye. Although its actualization may be risky and delicate, Socrates's maieutic drawing-forth (*anamnēsis*) of mathematical insight from an enslaved boy in the *Meno* suggests that a responsible, phronetic pedagogy may elicit the polemical turning to zetetic philosophy as a cast of mind as democratically as a population can embrace it. Short of a full embrace of zetetic philosophy by an entire people, responsible pedagogy, at the level of the fire, projects narratives, legends, and norms that lend salutary images of justice to some and leave the door to philosophy open to any who can take the upward way. Responsible guidance, responsive to the understanding of historically situated human beings, that leads up to the lateral pathway and the fire, and then up the steep, rough, upward way and out into the light of day, is vital if the released prisoner is not to suffer trauma and fall victim to despair, manipulation, nihilism, or a complete breakdown.

To put all this another way, the proper use of dialectic, for oneself and with others, expands upon Socrates's claim in the *Phaedo* that "those who engage in philosophy correctly study nothing other than dying and being dead" (64a). Dying and the prospect of death cause the greatest fears and the greatest pain for most. As the end of life, death seems to be the ultimate separation from all that we are and could be, all that we know, and all that matters to us. But breaking the bonds and bounds of the cave, the release from opinions about what we have held dear or what we have simply relied upon to navigate an uncertain world, can be a kind of death as well. To cease to believe what friends or family or mentors or other one-time paragons believe can be like dying to a whole world of commitments, concerns, affections, and expectations. To learn how to live with this possibility of dying to one's familiar world is a key feature of the pedagogy of dialectic, and so to a polemical ethic. It requires learning how to let go of opinions without falling into the despair of utter disorientation or nihilism. It means learning again to trust in trust, even after an initial, naive trust in the transparency of the world has been shattered. This means engaging in the zetetic life of philosophy, a life that embraces the helicoidal, triadic unity of wonder-question-response by trusting one's intimations but being willing to discard them if they fail in the *polemos* of interpreting the world with both honesty and charity. To see how this is possible requires understanding what happens after the initial release as the escapee ascends, past the fire and up the steep, rough, upward path to the light and back down again into the cave.

NOTES

1. This is my translation; see Kirk, Raven, and Schofield, *The Presocratic Philosophers*, 193.

2. For example, see Annas, *An Introduction to Plato's* Republic, 255.

3. For a thorough treatment of this theme, see Joseph Cimakasky, *The Role of Exaiphnēs in Early Greek Literature*, chapters 3–5.

4. See Jonathan Lear, *Radical Hope: Ethics in the Face of Cultural Devastation*, 2.

5. See Karl Jaspers, *Basic Philosophical Writings*, 96–104.

6. Jacques Derrida, in conversation with Gianni Vattimo, in J. Derrida and M. Ferraris, *A Taste for the Secret*, 80.

7. For my critique of Derrida, see *Heidegger's Polemos*, chapter 5, and "*Inhalt unzulässig*."

8. Consider Bloom, "Interpretive Essay," 307–10, 390, 399–400; Strauss, *The City and Man*, 62.

9. See Strauss, *City and Man*, Bloom, "Interpretive Essay," 310; for a sustained analysis of the "upward way" and its place in the motif of the Socratic "I went down" (*katebēn*) in the *Republic*, see John Sallis, *Being and Logos*, chapter 5.

10. For an incisive analysis of this theme, see Marina McCoy, *Plato on the Rhetoric of Philosophers and Sophists*, especially chapter 5.

11. For a valuable discussion of how *aporia* and *atopia*, lack of a way out through argument and finding oneself out of place in understanding, arise together in the liberation from the cave, see Andrea Nightingale, *Spectacles of Truth in Classical Greek Philosophy*, 96–107.

12. For a phenomenology of ontological trauma, see Polt, *Time and Trauma*, especially chapter 4.

13. For a perceptive phenomenological analysis and narrative of breakdown and healing in mental health, see Kevin Aho, *Contexts of Suffering*, especially the afterword.

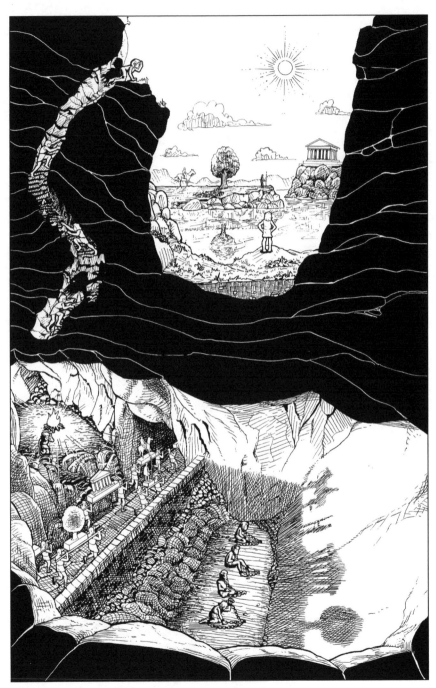

Figure 1. The Cave. Illustration by Marc Ngui.

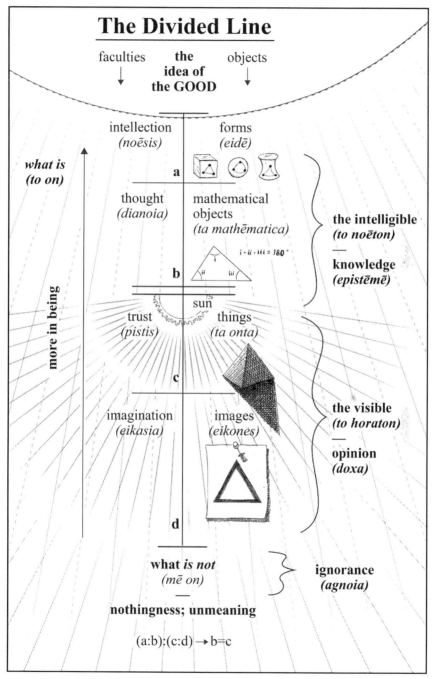

Figure 2.   The Divided Line. Illustration by Marc Ngui.

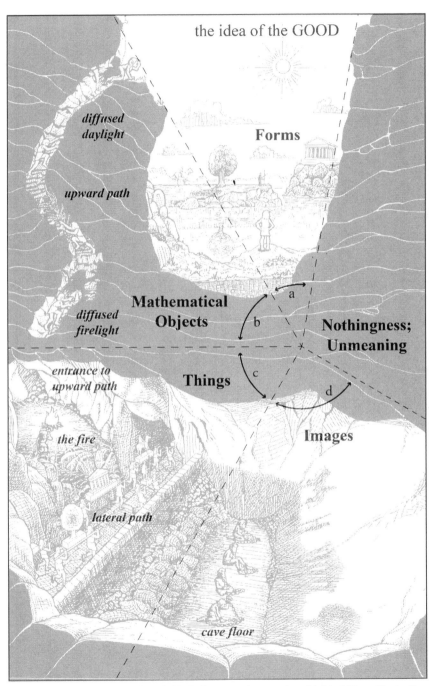

the idea of the GOOD

diffused daylight

Forms

upward path

Mathematical Objects

diffused firelight

Nothingness; Unmeaning

a

b

entrance to upward path

Things

c

d

the fire

Images

lateral path

cave floor

Figure 3. The Cave with the Divided Line superimposed as Divided Ring. Illustration by Marc Ngui.

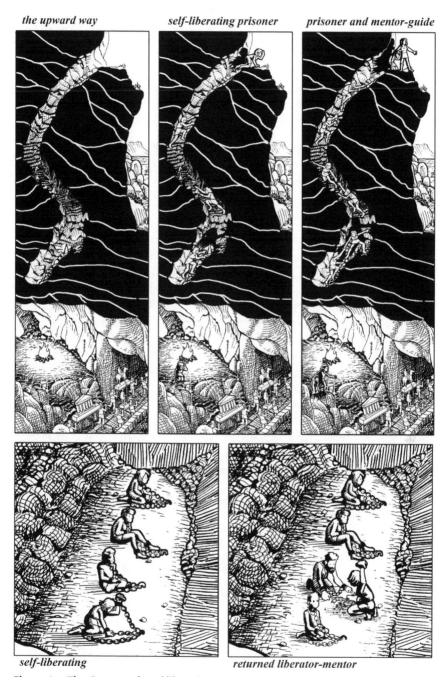

the upward way   *self-liberating prisoner*   *prisoner and mentor-guide*

self-liberating   *returned liberator-mentor*

Figure 4.   The Cave, modes of liberation and ascent. Illustration by Marc Ngui.

Chapter Five

Ideation and Reconstruction

Healing from the Bonds of the Cave

The road up and down is one and the same.

—Heraclitus, Fragment 60[1]

In the previous chapter, I argued that phenomenologically the breakdown of the bonds of opinion is not yet a breaking-free, because the healing from the bonds must also happen as a feature of genuine liberation. Deconstruction of some authoritative, authoritarian, or simply erroneous construal of meaning, however oppressive or limiting it might have been, is only the beginning. This beginning may easily falter and lead to despair, or fall into a new form of ideological manipulation, or into outright nihilism. The breakdown is not liberation itself, only its inception that can easily go astray. Socrates distinguishes the release that takes place in breaking the bonds from the healing from the bonds. Freedom is fully achieved by taking the path of recovery, which is the polemical, philosophical life.

5.1 LIGHTING THE WAY ON THE UPWARD PATH

In Socrates's allegory, the upward pathway in the cave represents the process of healing that is critical for philosophy and a life well lived. That upward pathway has several stages: first, to the level of the lateral pathway and the fire; second, up the steep, rough, upward pathway from the lateral pathway and the fire and out into the light of day; third, outside of the cave; fourth, back down into the cave (see Figure 2).

First, the lateral pathway and the fire. I will address this stage only briefly here because I will treat it separately in chapter 7 as the pivot between Plato

160

and Heidegger. What the escaped prisoner learns at this level is that the shadows cast upon the wall of the lowest level are *projections*, very much like the ones we see cast by a projector in a slide show or movie theater. They are not the things themselves. The shadows, the fleeting shapes that the prisoners' former opinions were *about*, now become newly comprehensible as produced by a cause beyond themselves. This accounts for them in a fuller sense than what is accessible from the lowest floor of the cave. Socrates says that, from the perspective of the lowest cave-dwellers, the shadows are not simply meaningless and arbitrarily chaotic. There are patterns to the shadows and when they appear, allowing the prisoners to hold contests for who can predict what will come next (516c). What the escaped prisoner may come to understand at the fire is that opinions and their objects are not merely arbitrary; there is something that gives them sense. Nevertheless, if the prisoner does not ascend further, then the realization that the *shadows themselves* are not arbitrary risks being replaced by the view that their *cause* is arbitrary, and this has its own dangerous consequences.

In the second stage, dialectic marks out "the rough, steep, upward way" (515e). Socrates says nothing more about the upward way than that it is rough and steep and leads out "into the light of the sun" (515e). Still, if this way is an image for dialectic, as he indicates, it is difficult and painful because it involves more than the deconstruction of individual opinions about some particular shadows, which can bring on the first release. It is a systematic and comprehensive deconstruction of opinions as well as accounts for the basis of opinion (call these accounts *theories* or *ideologies*, as we will discuss in chapter 7). This is all in the service of preparing the upward-bound prisoners for the true and fully integrated account of all that is, which will finally come to light out beyond the cave after they emerge, and that will also account for how this knowledge relates back to all the opinions and accounts of the shadows seen in the cave.

What lights the way on this upward path? Is it light from the fire, reflecting upward, or light from outside, seeping downward? Socrates does not say. Perhaps this is fitting for the practice of this comprehensive dialectic as the training of the philosophers, because it is potentially so disorienting and unpleasant that few will even attempt it. Few can withstand the wholesale deconstruction of their understanding of the world with only the promise of its reconstruction. As Socrates says to Glaucon, it is really only safe for those who have proven themselves mature enough to maintain the salutary opinions that make them suitable for citizenship in the city, even while putting those opinions to the most rigorous tests of dialectic (539c–540a; cf. 413c–414a).

Still, even for those resilient few who maintain that Socratic piety, that trust in the meaning of the world may ever-again be reconstructed, what keeps them going? What prevents them from remaining in or plunging back into the despair or nihilism that first appears at the original release from the bonds, when the prisoners cast off the certainties of naive opinion but have not yet found anything in its stead? At this point of decision for continuing on the upward path, the misology and nihilism could be all the more furious and acidic, armed with the systematic techniques of dialectic, now degenerated to mere eristic after giving up on the truth as dialectic's goal. Even though Socrates does not say what lights the way up, we are entitled to fill in the details from what he says elsewhere, because the logic of the Platonic dialogue itself, by implicit intention, calls upon us to enter the dialectic and use our own imagination in ideation.

For one thing, there are the intimations of the truth that dialectic can produce. As discussed in section 2.4, 'intimation' is my rendering of Plato's *anamnēsis* in the *Meno*, where it serves as the Socratic version of the hermeneutic circle. No inquiry can even begin without prior understanding of an intelligible world that undergirds any question *as* a question worth pursuing. There are two sides to these intimations. One comes from the act of questioning as such, the other from its direction or goal. Without the prior contextual understanding that makes a question arising from that context intelligible, there would not be the incendiary wonder and then the question that guides the inquiry. We can say this illumination of the dialectical upward way is provided in part by the light the fire casts upward, rather than the light it casts downward on the cave wall that produces the shadows the prisoners see. The upward firelight would not cast shadows of the artifacts upon the upward way, because the passers-by carrying them walk between the fire and the wall that separates them from the prisoners. Instead, what this upward firelight provides is simply illumination upon the upward path, which, while still very difficult, becomes potentially navigable.

But surmising this from the Allegory is still figurative, and does not explain what it means in terms of the practice of dialectic as productive discernment. Here, Heidegger's term *Lichtung* is particularly well suited to making sense of this because it has both a visual (*Licht*: light) and a spatial meaning: it is an area, a clearing, that is lit up and thus open to our understanding, involvements, and purposes. It is the *Da* of our Da-sein, the *here* of our being-human, the situated emplacement that defines our historical world. Our understanding has the potential to make sense of a world and all the things in it, but without that world already having been opened up for us, lighted up in advance, as it were, we would be blind—whatever our capabilities. The way we experience this opened-up-ness of a world is by having been always-already thrown, in Heidegger's idiom, into a particular *historical* world, whose overall sense grants meaning to most, if not all things, that we encounter within it. This is what the light of the fire provides for those living in thrall to the shadows on the cave wall. But the firelight provides something different for those setting out on the journey upon the upward way out of the cave. Due to the orientation of the fire, it no longer provides the shadowy shapes of the artifacts within a particular historical understanding. What it does provide is enlightenment about the casting (the thrown projecting) of historical understanding as such, which is how it conditions, or causes (as *aitia*), the opinions that human beings hold about the nature of the things they perceive.

This is the light that opens up and illumines the entrance to the upward way. While apprehending the role of the firelight in projecting historical opinion does not simply obliterate these opinions for a prisoner healing from the bonds and the trauma of release, it does hint at the possibility of something beyond received opinion other than despair, sophistry, or nihilism. The firelight, cast upward rather than downward, provides the inkling of hope. It grants a discernment for opinion as such, as the wellspring of the potential contradictions and questions that inevitably arise in our polemical confrontations with the world. Even the simple recognition of opinion *as such* provides the opportunity and impetus to seek something beyond opinion. The fire casts light upon and through the opening to the upward way.

Socrates in the *Meno* says that no inquiry, no hunt, would be possible without some prior scent of the quarry to be found.[2] This is the intimation granted by the downward-filtering light from outside, the second form of illumination on the upward way. It may be utterly inchoate at first, but it sheds just enough light to make the act of questioning and inquiry possible, so that the upward ascent can begin through an intimation of what transcends opinion. We receive *confirmations* of these intimations in dialectic when the dialectic produces insight, as in the *Meno* where Socrates shows that the slave boy can elicit a knowledge he had no notion he possessed. Even if such insights are only temporary as confirmations of intimation, as each may come under further dialectical inquiry ("they must all be returned to many times in the future," Glaucon says [532d]), such insights provide encouragement that the way up is not in vain. We will say more about the role of this upward firelight in the discussion of the crossroads of the cave in chapter 7, but the *responsible* use of a polemical dialectic derives from Socratic phenomenology. What people *say* when giving their opinions can guide the inquiry upward, because what they say already contains meaning even if they do not directly grasp its fuller significance. Otherwise, communication would not be intelligible at all. Opinion should be respected for that reason, not simply cast aside, as the newly released but unhealed prisoner might be inclined to do in an initial burst of resentment. Opinions are not nothing. They contain the first impulses of understanding that can lead to productive questions. As we shall see, this has to do with the integrated character of the Divided Line and with the fact of our finite embodiment.

Although Socrates does not describe this, the only shadow cast by the firelight that the ascending seeker now must contend with *as a shadow* is their own, cast up ahead along the upward path. By contrast, it is fair to assume that in the state of bondage, with the fire blocked by the wall running alongside the lateral path, the prisoners see not their own shadows, but only those projected by the artifacts passing in front of the firelight. The prisoners have little or no *reflective* sense of themselves. Unable to see even their own shadows, unable to move because of their bonds as do the shadows they see cast on the cave wall, they have no notion that they are implicated in the world of shadows, artifacts, and passers-by. Taking the shadows as the only things that are, they have no sense of their own perspective but rather inhabit their received opinions like a second skin. But at the level of the fire and the lateral road, the healing prisoner must become familiar with her own shadow while she comes to understand the relationship of the projecting firelight and the shadows of artifacts cast on the wall.

The former prisoner's realization that she herself also casts a shadow is a moment of self-discovery to which we will return in the discussion of the lateral path. The former prisoner now does have the ability for self-reflection and can realize that her embodiment and her situatedness are implicated in how opinion is projected upon things, including herself. This realization about the nature of opinion as cast or projected by a situated context in which one is oneself implicated opens up the question of whether one can rise above the situatedness of opinion, if there is a knowledge beyond the happenstance of opinion. This is the moment that the former prisoner may notice the opening to the upward way, lit up by the firelight, and consider taking it, despite how unpleasantly rough and steep it might appear. As she enters upon it, her own shadow, cast by the fire, would loom large, making the initial climb all the harder. What does this mean? If, as we have argued, understanding the relation of firelight, artifacts, and shadows corresponds to insight into how the bonds of historical opinion are forged from a forced perspective upon what *is*, then a recognition of one's own perspectival opinion, even as one seeks to climb beyond it, can be the greatest impediment to that progress. Socratic phenomenology begins with opinion because, even when faulty, there is something inherently meaningful to opinion. The shadow cast by the fire along the upward path is how one's own embodiment and the perspective it brings with it can distort and obscure a proper understanding of the nature of opinion, making it harder to grasp what is really at issue in a confrontation with the meaning inhering to a particular opinion. We are likely to overcompensate for our own perspectival happenstance, discounting the intimations of meaning, or we are liable to insist upon our own convictions and resist dying to them. Even if that is in principle what we want, the shadow of our selves gets in the way. This is why climbing the upward path within sight of a friend or mentor might help to alert us of our limited ways of seeing.

But if the seeker does not give up at the start of the upward way, frightened off, as it were, by her own shadow, we can surmise that intimations also must come from above on the upward journey. After all, the tunnel must eventually open to the light of day, and this daylight will filter downward along the upward way, just as the firelight seeps upward. As the seeker climbs higher, the firelight ebbs away and the diffused daylight penetrating the upward way increases.

If the light of the fire cast upward represents the dialectical understanding of how opinion forms our historical world as something we are contingently thrown into, and for that reason not utterly meaningless, the daylight filtering down must represent something else. In the context of both the Divided Line and the Cave Allegory, the daylight represents the absolute enlightenment of knowledge, which the seeker does not yet have, but which beckons along the upward path. Intimations of such knowledge might come from the study of mathematics, for example, which are positioned at the third level of the Divided Line, though still below ideas and the idea of the good. While not yet the fullness of a comprehensive knowledge that would shed light on things both human and otherwise, mathematics, when studied properly, has the power to ignite the mind with the beauty of an understanding abstracted from contingent particulars and historical opinion.

If the firelight intimates our situatedness, our rootedness in a historical emplacement that entails all the already-having-been-interpreted of a world we did not choose, the filtered daylight intimates our potential for transcendence, the possibility of rising above the contingent to the universal and perhaps to the eternal. Though the diffusion of upward firelight and of downward daylight may overlap, in inverse proportion, all along the upward way, the seeker climbs from the initial guidance of the firelight, which teaches about the hold that opinion as such can have over us, to guidance from the daylight, which promises a universal knowledge that will put all particular opinion in its correct place, rather than simply obliterate it. Indeed, as she climbs further upwards, the seeker's shadow will gradually be displaced as the diffused daylight from above slowly overpowers the firelight, casting the shadow back, rather than forward. The shadow of the self ceases to obscure the way up and forward and instead marks what the seeker is leaving behind, if she looks back on her progress.

But on the upward path we now run into a serious difficulty that derives from the distinction between the zetetic and the echonic philosopher. Within the narrative of the Allegory as Socrates tells it, the aspiring philosopher does indeed emerge from the cave's dark passageways into the light of day. Once outside, the former prisoner completes her liberation as the fulfillment of the hope and trust that guided the way along the upward path through the upward and downward intimations of knowledge. The outside world, illumined by the light of the Sun rather than by a feeble fire, constitutes the next stage of the journey, after the upward path, and before that, the lateral path and the fire, and before that, the initial release from the bonds. In the narrative, the knowledge gained outside, by the light of the Sun, reveals things as they really are, not merely as the artifacts of contingent, historical human representation as seen at the level of the lateral path in the objects carried by the passers-by. This corresponds to an apprehension of the ideas, with the Sun as the idea of the good that is the source of the meaning for all the ideas and so of everything else, down the Line. It is this knowledge that entitles the philosopher-rulers to govern, and to do it effectively once they return and adjust to the darker illumination of the cave. This is the echonic vision of philosophy, the one that lays definitive claim to the truth, that has it, holds it, and wields it to govern in the city "in a state of waking, not in dream as the many cities nowadays are governed by men who fight over shadows with one another and form factions for the sake of ruling, as though it were some great good" (520c).

Socrates does not make this claim for himself. It is one of the most famous things about Socrates that he claims that the extent of his wisdom is knowing that he does *not* know. As we have seen, he is a zetetic philosopher, one still seeking that complete illumination, still ascending the upward way. But this throws the whole narrative of the Allegory into confusion. It is deeply puzzling that Socrates would propose a conclusion to the philosophical journey that not even he has attained. That he has not reached the end brings into question whether the destination is as he describes it and whether a final, absolute knowledge is even achievable. That in turn calls into question the notion that philosopher-rulers could even come into being, let alone return back to the cave to lead the city in a state of waking. The threat of misology and nihilism, which first arose at the moment of release and confusion for the prisoner at the lowest level of the cave, returns now with a vengeance.

The promise implied by embarking upon the journey of the difficult upward pathway was that the intimations of truth would lead, in the end, to an apprehension of the truth, a way really *out* from opinion, deception, illusion, confusion. That hope seems dashed if even Socrates cannot fulfill this promise. If so, what justifies bothering to attempt the painful and exhausting upward pathway? It seems to be a fraud, one even more crushing than the initial confusion at the first release, because it is a betrayal, a promise broken. If not a fraud, then perhaps it is a delusion bordering on psychosis to believe that an imaginary set of ideas and ideals, beyond sensory verification and subsisting in some timeless zone accessible only to the mind, is the *ontōs on*, what is really real, most truly in being. This fraud, delusion, or psychosis threatens a breakdown as a decisive end of philosophy.

Here we reach a stage tangential to the Allegory and unspoken within it, but nevertheless essential to its meaning. We can be confident that this stage is there because Plato himself must certainly have been aware of the contrast between Socrates as zetetic philosopher and the echonic philosopher-rulers of the *Republic* that Plato depicts Socrates asking his companions to imagine. Plato thus calls *us* to consider this apparent paradox in connection with the narrative of the Cave, and with the argument more broadly, that on the surface *seems* to seek to establish the legitimacy of philosopher-rulers. This confrontation between the Socratic *context*, that Socrates is not a knower, and the argument's narrative *within the text* is Plato's masterstroke as the meta-teller of the tale: of the Cave, the Divided Line, and the *Republic* as a whole. It is how he can speak with us, without speaking directly to us, by drawing us into the *polemos* of philosophizing and about philosophy itself as way of life, through both the said and the unsaid. It is precisely the *contradiction* between echonic and zetetic philosophy that sets the *polemos* of interpretation on edge with his text. It is here, reader, that you are invited back into the picture, the *eikōn* that both Socrates and Plato have drawn.

5.2 IDEATION AND SOCRATIC PHENOMENOLOGY

The key is Socrates's phenomenology, his commitment to an interpersonal dynamic of asking people for and then conversing with them about their opinions. Of course, you can always refuse that call or refuse the conversation after giving an answer, but if you take it up, then Socrates has also committed himself to his piety in the dialectic: that what you have to say, your opinion, is already rooted in meaning, even if deeply obscured and requiring extensive deconstruction to make it more visible and intelligible. Socrates's piety, as a trust in trust, remains resilient even if a particular conversation results in *aporia*. This phenomenological piety about the meaningfulness of what people have to say was discussed just above as the intimations produced by the light shed by the fire upon the upward path. It entails the assumption that whenever you honestly give an opinion, it is somehow rooted in a meaningful historical context that illumines it. But what about the downward intimations, the ones from the daylight filtering in from above? If the zetetic journey has no end, are these not just will-of-the-wisps, luring us into miasmic bogs of ill-founded and imaginary ideas that will separate us from the only firm ground

we can trust for our everyday existence, the settled convictions of the historical communities to which we belong?

We have already seen that Socrates orients his phenomenology of conversation on what he readily calls a hypothesis, not a doctrine or a settled
theory: the ideas or forms. He has said that *something like* the ideas, "some
such something" (*toiouton ti*, 533a), must *be* if meaningful dialogue is to be
possible at all, because *something* must have already lent intelligibility to the
world we share in speech as meaningful, because it is simply manifestly so
that there is meaning. Plato makes this point when he has Parmenides, in the
dialogue of the same name, say the following about ideas and the very possibility of speech:

> If someone were not to grant that forms of beings exist, nor to demarcate [*horie-
> itai*] a form for each one, he would have nowhere to turn his thought, for he does
> not grant that there is an idea that is always the same for each of the various
> beings, and in this way he would completely destroy the power of talking things
> through [*dialegesthai*: dialectic, discussion]. (135b–c)

Our *logos*, our giving of accounts in speech and in dialogue, the power of
words as such, is grounded in a larger *logos* that has always-already gathered together a world of meaning, making any given conversation at least
provisionally intelligible. Even to doubt meaning is to assume it in the act of
doubting. The 'idea' is itself an image, a metaphor, based on the operation of
human vision. It is not the thing itself, even if "some such something" *like* it
must be. The Socratic metaphorics of vision, by focusing on the Greek word
idea as what-has-been-caught-sight-of, tries to address what is at-issue in the
problem of how meaning, truth, and knowledge can be possible. Just as we
do see things as distinct and separate from one another (and to go beyond
ocularcentrism, also the blind, using Braille maps, for example, *discern* the
meaningful differences among things), so also we *do* understand things, in
advance, even if often blurred and mistaken, without the account that philosophy latterly seeks to give them. Otherwise, we would have no world at
all, only William James's "blooming, buzzing confusion," a mere manifold
of sensations, to use Kant's terminology, which we could not even begin to
articulate in understanding, let alone in language.[3] Even mistakes presume, as
the background to identifying them as mistakes, a context of an understanding of meaning that allows us to discern truth from untruth, and so go about
our business.

For Socrates, the ideas are a heuristic for engaging in the dialectical
polemos of conversation, because they allow him to draw the conversation
partner from opinion to analysis by relying on the inchoate sense of meaning
that we already inhabit by using words. The key to the Divided Line is that it

is *an image*: literally—if we assume that Socrates could have been drawing it in wax or sand for the young men in Cephalus's house—and figuratively, as something *we* must imagine as we read or hear about it. The same is true of the Allegory of the Cave. It is an *image*. We must imagine it to understand it as Socrates narrates it. We employ precisely that power of imagination which Socrates places at the lowest level of the Divided Line, in order to make sense of the idea of the ideas, which reside at the highest level, supposedly the furthest removed from images, reflections, and representations, as well as the shadows on the cave wall. Image and idea both partake in the same metaphorics of vision. We must not forget that the Divided Line is not divided by actual barriers, any more than are the modes of understanding the world, from imagination, to trust, to the thought that can perform mathematics, to the insight that grants the ideas. The cave itself is a continuum, from lowest depths to the outside, and even if it contains obstacles to the ascent (and return), no stage is completely walled off from the others. To say that the ideas are on a continuum with images and imagination is not to denigrate the ideas but to fulfill their meaning.

Thus, the term *ideation* is apt for what is at-issue in countering the nihilism that threatens the upward path on the zetetic model of philosophy. *Ideation* captures the sense of imagination and idea as deeply connected, as well as the sense of a verbal process and not just a thing, an engaging in the activity of philosophizing as an ongoing confrontation with meaning. The Socratic insight is that meaningful existence requires ideation, whether as something we do implicitly or something elicited by philosophy. What Heidegger critiques as metaphysics, as the oblivion of what it means to be, is in fact a phenomenological necessity for our understanding of a meaningful world and for ethics more particularly.

To illustrate why ideation is a necessary feature of our hermeneutical existence, I will now appeal directly to you again, reader. Without you, these words and pages are just ink on cellulose or pixels on a screen, or soundwaves played by a book-on-tape, or digital data stored in a server. Indeed, without you and the rest of us, who have the kind of hermeneutical understanding that you share, words and ink and pixels and screens have no meaning at all. They are just stuff, uninterpreted and meaningless. And yet, I only *imagine* you as reader, whether a friend or colleague whom I know, or a stranger far off in place or time. As discussed in my address to you, even if you were here, right in front of me, I would still have to imagine you, because *personhood* is nothing I can touch or see or hear, even if I had you in an MRI machine to see your brain in action as we speak. Being-a-person is nothing empirically verifiable; it is something that only the person that I am can experience as my own, in a cave of selfhood. Unless there is a form of consciousness I have never known,

I cannot experience being-you nor you being-me. Yet without the idea of you, the activity of conversation, or of writing, would be unintelligible.

The presence to me or to you of the other person as person is not ordinarily a *concept*, although we can certainly make it a matter of theoretical concern, as we are doing right now; rather, it functions phenomenologically as an *a priori* feature of our interpersonal dealings. It is more fitting to call our apperception of the personhood of the other an *ideation* than a concept, because if we do reflect on our everyday assumption that it is persons, rather than, say, robots or mirages, that we interact with, then we see that this being-with-others-as-persons is simply a constitutive way of our being in the world. Through ideation, we *see* the person there, despite the fact that there can never be any sensory or empirical evidence of personhood. The idea of the other-as-person is a transcendental condition of the possibility for discourse of any kind. It is a phenomenological given of the activity itself, because discourse of any kind entails that other nodes of thought, feeling, and self-awareness are 'there' to us, in various ways. Otherwise, what we take to be dialogue would only be the projections of a solipsistic monologue, and this runs up against the reality of *discovery* through conversation: that there are understandings of the world that I myself did not create.

I bring up the idea, or the ideation, of you—and of others—as persons because it is phenomenal evidence that the ideas are indeed connected with imagination. Far from making the ideas delusional, this connection is what makes them a constitutive feature of our understanding of a meaningful world. The ideas are a metaphor, and as such imagined, but so too are all concepts. The question is whether they, or "some such something" by whatever name we call them and whatever metaphor captures their role, are *necessarily* constitutive of a meaningful world and, more specifically, to a philosophical life. The ideas are the heuristic that Socrates turns to, because he refuses misology and nihilism; he *trusts* that even when the world breaks at one of its joints, asking "What is X?" (*ti to on*) and employing the idea of X as a prompt to investigation and discussion will possibly illuminate the meaning already inherent to our understanding. In asking the "What is X?" question, the definition of X (justice, piety, love, etc.) would not itself *be* the idea of the thing. That is because only in the light of the idea could the definition make sense and be correct, just as it is only because of the idea, if still only dimly sighted and intimated, that Socrates or we discern hermeneutically that a given definition is *incorrect* and that the polemical work of interpretation and dialogue must continue. The idea informs linguistic articulation and definition, but the idea itself straddles conceptuality between the domains of meaning and unmeaning.

5.3 OUT OF THE CAVE: THE ECHONIC VISION

In the Allegory of the Cave, the culmination of the ascent from the cave is to emerge from the upward pathway into the broad light of day. I will not tarry here, for reasons to be made clear in what follows. Emerging from the cave, as usually interpreted, represents the realization of the complete liberation of the mind in light of ultimate truth. The sight acquired once out of the cave is the *echonic vision* of the truth: once beheld, this vision is absolute, without need for re-vision. As we have noted before, understanding the ideas, which grant intelligibility to each instance of the particulars, and grasping the idea of the good itself, which clarifies what ideas such as justice, wisdom, moderation, and courage are *good for* as human virtues for a life well lived, is what justifies the rule of the echonic philosophers as legitimate. There is an absolute self-sufficiency to the vision of the echonic philosopher, akin to the wisdom of the divine.

A key detail requires attention at this point. Even upon emerging from the upward pathway into the open, the escaped prisoner's vision is not immediately healed and made whole. At first, asks Socrates, would not the disoriented prisoner coming into the light "have his eyes suffused by the sunbeam and be unable to see even one of the things now said to be true?" (516a, tm). What follows is a period of habituation, where the prisoner completes the process of healing from the bonds:

> At first he'd most easily make out the shadows; and after that the phantoms [*eidōla*] of the human beings and the other things in water; and, later, the things themselves. And from there he could turn to beholding the things in heaven and heaven itself, more easily at night—looking at the light of the stars and the moon—than by day—looking at the sun and sunlight. [...] Then finally I suppose he would be able to make out the sun—not its appearances in water or some alien place, but the sun itself by itself in its own region—and see what it's like. (516a–b)

The final mark of healing and liberation is that the former prisoner would conclude that the sun "is in a certain way the cause of all those things he and his companions [back down in the cave] had been seeing" (516b–c). The seeker would arrive at the end of seeking "by making out the sun itself." We should keep in mind that this is a healing in the echonic account, where philosophy comes to an end by being able to behold the sun, the image for the idea of the good. As all know, we can only make out the sun itself directly for a brief moment, or risk temporary or permanent blindness where the distinct intelligibility of things gets overwhelmed and erased. The danger in gazing directly upon the idea of the good is that contemplating the source of all meaning might overwhelm one's sense of the specific meanings that things happen to have in one's particular circumstances and why these should even matter to us.

On my account, any actual healing must transpire through the life of zetetic philosophy as skeptical idealism, a life that mediates between the longing for transcendence and knowledge and the rootedness of finite human understanding. What is remarkable about the account Socrates gives is that even outside of the cave, the features of the cave remain present. There are shadows of things themselves, such as of trees; there are *eidōla*, phantoms, or less dramatically, reflections of things and people in water. An *eidōlon*, from which we have our word "idol," is like a shadow of an *eidos*, a form, as when you look in a mirror. By itself, it is not the thing (the you, for example, which is only reflected as a "phantom" in the mirror), but very close to the thing in its delineations (a reflection bears an eerie resemblance to what it reflects, without actually being it). As part of the Allegory, the sun is itself an *eidōlon* of the idea of the good, just as the *image* of the Divided Line is an *eidōlon* of the structures of intelligibility as such. The Divided Line bends back upon itself again, so that images, the lowest level, are part of the ideas, the highest, and vice versa. If this involution were not the case, if the divisions of the Divided Line were not integrated with one another—making it in fact an Integrated Line, or a Divided Ring—then knowledge of the apex would be useless at the base, and the base would find no resolution at the apex. Indeed, even after emerging into the open, even after getting accustomed to the daylight and coming to look upon the sun itself as a source of all that is, the prisoner is still in a cave, one enclosed by the cosmic vault of the sky like the natural earthen walls of the cave, a point that Heidegger also makes (GA 24: 403). Transcending the cave, in the Latin sense of *trans-scandere*, to climb across or above or to surpass, is a compromised undertaking.

Even so, the Cave image is not compromised in the purely negative sense of irrevocably flawed, because, as with all great images and metaphors, its failings point beyond itself so that it can transcend itself. No word, no metaphor, no image *is* the same as the thing itself. That would be idolatry. Instead, each word, metaphor, and image is an *eidōlon* in that larger sense of something that points beyond itself, that is not simply *equivalent* to what it is about, and therefore cannot represent it in its fullness. Full meaning always escapes us. The *eidōlon*'s flaws, as with any breakdown in understanding, are the clues to what can only be apprehended by entering into the *polemos* of confronting the image through interpretation and reinterpretation as provoked by the flaws, inconsistencies, and inadequacies of what has been said or depicted. As such, the Allegory, as any word or metaphor or image, is a compromise in the

Latin sense of a *com-pro-mittere*, a sending-forward-together that impels the intimations of ideational thinking with the deferred promise of fulfillment.

The *eidē* and *ideai*, forms and ideas, that Socrates promotes as a way to make sense of our sense-making as such, are themselves images and *eikones*, but so is everything we say. All language is cave-like, being just such a compromise between the meanings we have inherited, the breakdowns in those meanings we inevitably run up against, and the reintegrations we achieve if we can navigate the ongoing ascent to heal the breaks. To compromise after a confrontation is to project forward a meaning into the future that we can trust and share in together for a while, until the next breakdown of meaning requires another breakthrough from unmeaning. Compromise is futural; it retains the grounds of confrontation as a trust that when breakdown in meaning breaks out again, the ongoing process of dialogical *polemos* will strive to reknit the frayed and always fraying fabric of understanding, a fabric whose evolving patterns intimate its mending.

5.4 TRANSCENDENCE DEFERRED: PRECONSTRUCTION AS ENVISIONING

What I have called the implied or tangential contradiction between the echonic and the zetetic conceptions of philosophy in the *Republic* raises a decisive question about the upward pathway. On the narrative surface of the Allegory, echonic philosophers do indeed manage to emerge into the light of day and come to grasp the truth about reality as their absolute possession. They achieve an absolute transcendence from mere opinion into complete knowledge, gazing upon the sun. The same cannot be true of the zetetic philosophers, whose mode of philosophizing is an ongoing seeking for truth, knowledge, and wisdom.

At the lowest level of the cave, we interpreted the breakdown of understanding that initially cuts the prisoner loose from the bonds of received opinion as a *deconstruction,* both of specific opinions and of the modes of interpreting what the opinions are *about*, namely, the shadows, what it is we believe we have understood as this or that thing. At the level of the lateral pathway and the fire, escaped prisoners may come to understand that what had conditioned their way of seeing and interpreting these things is the projection of opinion by our historical situatedness. So, what happens on the upward pathway, between the recognition of the contingency of opinion and the realization of absolute knowledge? What is the healing prisoner doing and learning there by climbing upward?

I have suggested that on the upward path, diffused firelight from below at first guides the seeker, which gives way to the diffused daylight from above, and that the former decreases and the latter increases in proportion to how far the seeker has climbed (see Figure 4, upper panels). The illumination provided by the firelight represents an understanding of how historical contingency mediates the influence of opinion, while still preserving the phenomenal content of opinion. For Socrates, this is the meaning inherent but often unsaid in what people say, but which needs fuller elucidation to guide the upward way, an elucidation provided by dialectic and dialogue. This is an understanding that might transcend but does not obliterate mere opinion. That greater understanding, though not yet realized, still beckons upward. We will illustrate how this happens in the next chapter with various examples.

In chapter 1, we discussed the triad of *construal* of a meaningful world in Heidegger's 1927 lecture course: a moment of *deconstruction*, which frees up historically ossified concepts for new use; a moment of *construction*, which starts construing a new way of potentially understanding and employing the historical concepts now unlocked and made available by the deconstruction; and a moment of *reconstruction* that brings the new understanding to bear on how we understand and live in the world. After the historical meaning of contingent opinions, norms, concepts, and the arguments for these has been deconstructed, new possibilities of meaning may be imagined. This is the moment of construction, or what I have called *preconstruction*, but because the latter is an unwieldy term, and the former probably too vague, I also call this the moment of *envisioning*.

This envisioning involves the intimations of another possible world, a future meaning that could be integrated into life, combining imagination and ideas in polemical dialogue with the received but now deconstructed opinions inherited historically. It is a version of *ideation* that can range from daydreaming to complex and systematic philosophical arguments in the light of the ideas that beckon. To en-vision, as with many words with the prefix *en-*, means *to place oneself into the context* of a vision, a seeing of a future possible world of meaning and imaging oneself living within it. While envisioning may be delusional (and we will address this later), it is also something we are doing all the time, in the little everyday struggles where we have to plan ahead due to circumstances we had not predicted. Hence, envisioning is something futural that we are always already doing as a feature of our finitude and existential temporality, but we can elevate it to a self-aware activity.

With respect to the triad of wonder, question, and response, envisioning takes place at the level of response, when we address a question occasioned by the breakdown of understanding marked by the moment of wonder that gives us pause and disrupts our usual ways of seeing, in situations ranging from the trivial to the momentous, from the rapturous to the traumatic. At its most elaborate, preconstruction as envisioning involves what we would usually recognize as a philosophical argument, most obviously in political philosophy, but not only in that context. As one response provoked by the breakdown and the wonder and questioning it involves, philosophical argument engages in the dialectical, reinterpretative *polemos* with deconstructed concepts and arguments in order to justify and legitimize an alternative understanding as fully and as comprehensively as possible. An example would be the cynical realist Thrasymachus, who nevertheless cannot avoid getting embroiled in a debate about the nature of an *ideal* ruler "in the strict sense" (341b). Such polemical work of reinterpretation is how imagination locks horns rigorously with the past for the sake of a future. This envisioning, in all its forms, is what transpires through the intimations of the diffused daylight of the ideas, filtering down from above, in recuperative confrontation with the relevant patterns of received opinions illumined by the firelight of historical insight.

But now we must ask why it matters if one understands progress up along the upward path on the zetetic rather than the echonic model of philosophy. Presumably, the seeker destined to emerge as a thoroughly complete echonic philosopher would arrive in a position where she could confirm that the intimations of her envisioning of alternatives to the contingent opinion she had been born into—intimations that led her upward on the pathway—were indeed correct, or at least could be adjusted to fit with the absolute truth, given the final vision that she would come to apprehend in looking upon the sun of the idea of the good. For such a philosopher, a philosophical argument, once made and understood, would be final and decisive, no longer subject to revision. So, for the echonic philosopher, the truth realized in argument would provide the irrefutable legitimation for rule. It would not be dogma, it would not be opinion (even if it might seem so to the uninformed), but rather the exact representation of what *is* that provides the template for all appropriate action in the world, a technology for rule and for education and for engineering both the human and the natural environments.

While the zetetic philosopher engages in exactly the same dialectical activity as the prospective echonic philosopher, who after all is still seeking while on the upward path, the difference is that the zetetic does not emerge into the light of day to behold that final, all-encompassing vision of the truth. But why would the zetetic philosopher not fall into the trap of despair, produced by a realization that insight into the historicity of opinion is not enough to lead one out into the light of a transcendent truth, a truth whose beckoning intimations on the upward path turn out to be nothing more than delusional phantoms projecting upward by some phosphorescence within the cave but never leading out of it? This is the second occasion for nihilistic despair. The first is the initial and potentially traumatic breakdown of the bonds of received opinion. The second is the belief that there may be no escape from the contingency and divisiveness of historical viewpoints.

Notice that this same danger threatens the prospective echonic philosopher, whose journey upward through dialectic may also be very long, and whose literal out-come is no more or less assured while still on the journey. The journey of philosophy provides no prospective guarantee of success. That is the risk of embarking in philosophy, that combination of hubris and humility in facing *to deinon*, the awe-inducing terror of the limits of our understanding. Nihilism always lurks at the edges of the recognition that opinion is in some sense historically conditioned and contingent, but that there may be no alternative, and so no certain knowledge.

So, why would Plato set up the Cave Allegory in such a way that brings that tangential divide into play between the zetetic and the echonic philosopher: the philosopher that Socrates claims to be, a seeker who does not know the truth, and the philosopher-rulers that Socrates posits in his narrative of the city in speech, whose completely realized knowledge entitles them to rule? It might seem that Plato risks undermining the whole philosophical enterprise by obliquely suggesting that the philosopher-rulers are purely a figment of Socrates's philosophical imagination, exposing the attentive reader to the corrosive risk of nihilism.

Several responses might save Plato, and by extension Socrates, from this charge of promoting nihilism, a version of the charge against Socrates for corrupting the youth by unsettling their convictions as provided by the gods and traditions of the city. One is that Socrates himself was no such nihilist and seemed content to live a life entirely upon the upward path, never laying claim to that final, comprehensive wisdom about all that is. Presenting the example of Socrates would be a mere appeal to the authority of Socrates as philosophical paragon, were it not for the Socratic defense of his activity as a kind of philosophical piety. As we have seen, that defense is more than bald assertion of the merits of the philosophical life. It involves both an argument immanent in texts, such as the *Phaedo* and *Republic*, and an extrinsic argument that, I would claim, Plato encourages us to develop for ourselves in confrontation with the meaning of both the texts and the example of Socrates's philosophical life as such. This is the brilliance of Plato's dialogue form, which raises these questions for the attentive reader and provides resources to address them, thereby coaxing us into the dialectic that constitutes the polemical life of philosophy by kindling the meeting of imagination and idea in ideation.

Another response has to do with the role of *envisioning* as the form philosophy takes as a mode of construction, or the preconstruction of a new way of understanding constructed from the elements analyzed, broken down, by deconstruction. I have argued that it is a phenomenological given that we simply *do* this preconstructive envisioning as a feature of our existential structure as beings who interpret themselves and the world, in both everyday life and in those extraordinary circumstances that mark the breakdown of understanding. To use Heidegger's terminology from *Being and Time*, envisioning is an *existentiale*, a mode of our polemical human-being that makes the world intelligible to us as we confront the breakdowns of our understanding and endeavor to reinterpret the world. Our finitude requires this, because no understanding will be final and complete, as imagined in the vision of the echonic philosopher who comes to the end of philosophical seeking in a full and exhaustive illumination of the understanding.

So why project the echonic vision to our imaginations at all? The young men in the *Republic* long to know if the imagined city is possible. Philosophical *eros* longs to know if an imagined ideal can ever be made real (471c). Why should Plato have Socrates invite us to imagine the philosopher-rulers, who, as the response to the third wave threatening to engulf the city in speech, take up a major portion of the *Republic*, from the latter part of Book 7 (473c) through the end of Book 7 as the ideal rulers of the ideal city? Surely the simplest answer is that imagining what it would be *like* to know is one of the most natural acts of philosophical reflection. The breakdown in opinion gives rise to this desire. Even if that desire cannot be fully realized, a responsible defense of the philosophical life must address the desire to know without either killing it off or inspiring unrealistic hopes of complete satisfaction. That is a feature of the zetetic healing from the bonds: a reconciliation of hubris and humility, a reconciliation that is an ongoing activity of reconstructive interpretation of the world, not an eradication of the tension between them. The ambition inspired by the desire to know provides the fuel to philosophical ideation, especially in its initial stages, after the first dislocations of deconstructive breakdown. The more mature zetetic philosopher has learned to temper this hubris with a humility that accepts our finitude and fallibility, but without falling into nihilistic despair. That combination is what I have been calling skeptical idealism as the healing from the bonds. Next I will address what compels this balancing of hubris and humility in the life of zetetic philosophy.

NOTES

1. In Curd, *A Presocratics Reader*, 48.
2. For the role of the hunt as metaphor for philosophy in Plato, see Mary Townsend, *The Woman Question in Plato's* Republic, 60–61 and passim.
3. Kant, *Critique of Pure Reason*, B218–19.

Chapter Six

The Compulsion of the Body

Why after all this one and not the rest?
Why this specific self, not in a nest,
but a house? Sewn up not in scales, but skin?
Not topped off by a leaf, but by a face?
Why on earth now, on Tuesday of all days,
and why on earth, pinned down by this star's pin?

—Wisława Szymborska, from "Astonishment"[1]

The nature of skeptical idealism becomes clearer if we consider the distinction between how echonic and zetetic philosophy would function at the next stage of the Allegory: the return of the philosopher back down into the cave. The context is the founding of legitimate, wise, and just rule for the presumptively ideal city that Socrates and his companions are building through discussion. In describing the aspiring seekers who have arrived at the conclusion of their ascent from the cave and their education in philosophy to become possessors of truth, Socrates says that he and his interlocutor friends, as the founders of the imagined Kallipolis, must not "permit them what is now permitted," namely for the realized philosophers "to remain there" outside, beyond the cave in the open light of day, as if they had "emigrated to a colony on the Isles of the Blessed while they are still alive." Instead, Socrates says, "Our job as founders is to compel the best natures to go to the study which we were saying before is the greatest, to see the good and to go up that ascent" (519c–d) and then again "by persuasion and compulsion" (519e) to "be willing to go down again [*palin katabainein*] among those prisoners" and "share their labors and honors, whether they be slighter or more serious" (519d). According to the surface narrative of the Allegory, these "best natures" must be the prospective and then fully realized philosophers, the echonic philosophers who know the full truth of the forms and the idea of the good after their ascent from the cave. Only full possession of truth grants their legitimacy and ability for completely just and wise rule.

We must contend again with the metaphorics of the Allegory, and in two ways. First, what is the meaning of this *compulsion* (*anankē*) to go back to the cave, apart from the logic of the narrative? In that narrative philosophers would owe their enlightenment to the education provided by the city and therefore owe that community a debt in a way that philosophers arising spontaneously (again, *exaiphnēs*) in other societies unfriendly to philosophy would not (520b). After all, the circumstances of philosophers returning to Socrates's Kallipolis are so extravagantly unlikely, as he himself acknowledges (502c–540d), that we are left wondering what this compulsion would mean outside of the allegory.

Second, there is an even greater difficulty posed by what I have called the tangential but nevertheless essential narrative: the conflict in principle between the philosophers of the Allegory, who are echonic possessors of wisdom, and Socrates himself, who is a zetetic seeker. What would it mean to go back to the cave if you have never properly made it out at all? The answer to both questions involves one thing: the body.[2] It is the compulsion of the body, as a feature of the finitude of being-human, that necessitates zetetic philosophy as the actual practice of a philosophical life, rather than echonic philosophy as the end of philosophical life.

6.1 OUR BODIES, OUR CAVE[3]

The echonic philosophers of Kallipolis and of the Allegory of the Cave are *imagined* as a mode of the Socratic *ideation* of the idea of justice. They are ultimately figures or figments of Plato's storytelling that we also must imagine to get the idea, as it were, of the allegory. As imagined figures, these philosophers have bodies that we also can imagine. We can imagine the escaped and healing prisoners ascending from the cave to the open. They obviously would bring their bodies with them, which is why it is at least possible that once they have fully escaped into the light of day, they could feasibly go on living up there, contemplating in both relief and horror the dark hole from which they had emerged through a disorienting, painful, and sometimes traumatic process. But because we the readers, as well as Socrates and his friends, exist only *metaphorically* in a cave, what would it mean to emerge from this metaphorical cave of the world we inhabit with our actual bodies, not just imagined ones?

Socrates gives some indication when he says that the fully realized philosophers of the Allegory would not normally want to engage in politics for the sake of the city because they would regard themselves as emigres to the Isles of the Blessed, with far better things to do. Greek mythology treated the Isles sometimes as a place in this world reserved for the most virtuous and sometimes as a kind of heaven in the afterlife. Socrates speaks of the philosophers as believing themselves there "while they are still alive," rather than dead but rewarded in the next world, which implies that their ordinary expectation would be that this paradise is only accessible in an afterlife. This echoes the sense from the *Phaedo* that the only good philosopher is a dead philosopher, because only then would she avoid the distractions of living that led Thales to fall into the well. It is because the body is mortally vulnerable that we must look out for its needs, even if we wish to lead the life of the mind.

As Socrates points out in Book 2 of the *Republic*, such needs of the body and our incapacity to tend to them adequately as lone individuals is what gives rise to human community in the first place: "a city, as I believe, comes into being because each of us isn't self-sufficient [*ouk autarkēs*] but is in need of much" (369b). The needs of the body are a decisive constraint on human freedom. We are mortal and finite rather than immortal and infinite beings, which means we cannot be entirely self-sufficient, as immortal divinity can be. Our need for one another extends to things beyond the body, too, such as the need for friendship and love, as well as for the dialogue necessary to enlarge our understanding in everything ranging from training and basic education to philosophy. But these features of a good life depend on first fulfilling the needs of the body, and the contingent facticity of the body and its needs binds us in our factical situatedness, in this body, in that context of its requirements.

To care for the body therefore requires caring about the community. This may be in some minimal or passive way, such as wanting the community's continued support. But to take for granted the contributions of the community to one's own well-being is to rely on luck or privilege, and neither is particularly stable. For this reason, we all owe a debt to the community that sustains us, even if it is a rather bad community, as Socrates, arguing in the *Crito*, diplomatically describes Athens (51c–d). This debt is analogous but not identical to the way that the philosophers owe a debt to Kallipolis for educating them out of the cave of received opinion. Even in a quite unjust community, to which we may owe very little indeed, we cannot afford to be indifferent to how that society impacts our embodiment, because we cannot reliably live in our heads if a dictatorship confiscates our subsistence, enslaves us, or outright kills us. The good life for human beings, as Aristotle argues in the *Politics* (1252b27–32), is not the same as sustaining mere life, even if it requires the latter, and sustaining the good life of philosophy requires doing what one can to make one's community the best it can be as well, even if it starts out quite badly.

This is the "compulsion" we all endure to go back to the cave, not only to make life better and more just, but to stay engaged in a *constructive* polemical way with those who, like Thrasymachus, either passively or actively seek to make it worse. To ignore that compulsion is to risk falling down the well, like Thales, or flying too close to the sun, like Icarus. Even for those who live the lucky life of leisure, to ignore this compulsion is to live in bad faith and to do injustice both to all those people who fulfill the needs of their bodies and to the institutions of society as a whole that make such a life possible. In our finite embodiment, such neglect is just reckless, like stargazing at night without looking where you are going.

The body also provides a response for the second problem: the metatextual clash between zetetic and echonic philosophy. Our embodiment is the concrete fact of our finitude. We are not gods. We cannot simply transcend the body to emerge into an immortal existence of pure life of the mind, Aristotle's thought thinking itself (*noēsis noēseōs noēsis*, *Metaphysics*, 1074b36). More emphatically, the body *pins* each of us *down*, as Szymborska's poem at the head of this chapter says, to our individual historical site. This includes the habits, affects, affections, inclinations, aversions, loves, and hatreds, as well as the features of face and limb and health and voice and gait and brain and on and on that simultaneously enable and delimit our possibilities, whether social or occupational or simply physical. This being-pinned-down involves everything physiological that defines us in our unique specificity and everything that happens to us as physical beings whose existence is never fully at our own command. The body is the cave made flesh.

The Allegory of the Cave hints at this hypogean embodiment when Socrates begins telling it. He instructs Glaucon and the others to "See human beings as though they were in an underground cave-like dwelling" (514a). "See" here is the Greek *ide*, which is the imperative form of *eidon*, an irregular verb that means "to behold," "to look," but also "to have the look of" something, and, as early as in Homer, "to see with the mind's eye" (e.g., *Iliad* 21.61) and "to know." This verb *eidon* is complex, having as its infinitive *idesthai*, "to see," and in these various forms we ourselves can see how both *eidos* (form, shape, look of a thing) and *idea* (that which has been seen) are united closely in the Greek, bringing together seeing, looking like, knowing, and imagining. So, Socrates is asking his companions to see with the mind's eye, to imagine, to *envision*. What they are to envision is *anthropous*, for which the best translation is "human beings," because this Greek word refers to us all, irrespective of gender or other distinctions. We must see these human beings living *hoion*, "as if," in an *oikēsis*, a noun formed from *oikos*, a house or home, but mean-ing more broadly the act of inhabiting, which is captured well by the English gerund, "dwelling," a habitation. This dwelling Socrates wants us to see is both *spēlaiōdēs* and *katageios*, cave-like and underground. The former com-bines two words: *spēlaion*, cave, and the suffix *-eidēs*, meaning "-like" but more specifically, "having the form of—," because it derives from the same root as *eidos*, "form." Once again, the Divided Line is involuted, folding back upon itself from idea to imagination, with the highest level, that of knowledge of the forms, meeting up with the domain of image at the lowest level in a reflection of reflection.

The latter word, *katageios*, also combines two words, the preposition *kata*, "down" or "under"—as in Socrates's first word of the *Republic*, the *katebēn* of "I went down" to the Piraeus—and *gaia*, the word for both "earth" and the primal goddess, Earth, Gaia. So, Socrates invites us to envision a dwelling that is cave-like in form and beneath the earth. In the parable, the true echonic philosophers emerge from Earth into a domain under the bright dome of Sky, the heavenly realm far removed from all the messy specificity of earthy particularity, but they always begin as earthly—and must return to earth. The English "human being" reminds us of the fundamental bondedness and boundedness that defines the human condition. "Human" is from the Latin *humus*, earth, which in term derives from the Indo-European root *dhghem-*, Earth, which is also the root for the Greek *chthon*, earth in the sense of land, the country, the place on the surface of the earth where one is from or abides as home. Calvert Watkins explains this filiation as follows:

> We normally think of *earthling* as a word useful for distinguishing humans from invading Martians or other extraterrestrials. Words meaning "earthling" have been around for millennia, however, and in Indo-European distinguish humans from gods—celestial beings of a different sort [than science fiction extrater-restrials]. The root *dhghem-* "earth" furnished the base for a number of words meaning "human being" in the daughter languages.[4]

Something very similar happens in Hebrew, where "Adam" derives from the word אדמה, *adamah*, the earth, the soil or dirt or dust, from which God first formed us, and to which Adam and we all return. The body itself is *spēlaiōdēs*, akin to a cave, because we, as earthlings, as human, are pinned to a specific time, place, and homeland of meaning into which we are born and then borne along as historical beings. We can never fully emerge from this earthly habitation, unlike the echonic philosophers that Socrates invites us to imagine who escape the cave. But the earthly bondage of the body should not be mistaken for something simply negative. It is, after all, what enables life for mortals, who must naturally *be somewhere*, grounded in a physicality and materiality and historical situatedness that we do not choose.

For all these reasons, there is no possibility *except in imagination* for embodied beings such as ourselves to do what Socrates describes as an option for some who escape from the cave: to live entirely outside the cave in the life of the mind. The body, as the inescapable situatedness of an existence we cannot choose or fully master, prevents the total fulfillment of philosophy in the echonic sense. It is not simply that we must occupy ourselves with the private and the civic labors of maintaining the body. The body itself compels us to have a view from somewhere, to paraphrase Thomas Nagel.[5] We cannot simply eliminate the distortions of perspective and inclinations that the shadows of the bodily cave lock us into as the medium of our historical situatedness. We cannot reach a perspective of absolute objectivity, the view from nowhere, because we are embodied.

Again, this is not simply a negative condition. Just as the cave-dwellers necessarily begin somewhere, in the radical specificity of the cave they find themselves born into, so too does each of us start from our own unchosen embodiment. All the involvements and moods and projects and needs and aptitudes that our individual bodies grant us, refracted by how that individual specificity means something different in different historical contexts, is what grants us opportunities for coming up against the contradictions of the world, without which the triadic cycle of wonder, questioning, and response could not get under way. It is only because we naturally care about the owned specificity of our embodied, situated existence that a breakdown of that existence can matter to us, be it in an everyday challenge or a catastrophic event, and so provide the impetus for the *polemos* of making sense of the breakdown and reintegrating the world through a response to it. Caring about the body, in its largest sense as our situated embodiment as earthly, historical beings, with all the worldly involvements this implies, is what can potentially open us to the inception of philosophy. The actual polemical work of this philosophizing must always take place in the zetetic, reconstructive striving of that same cave-like embodiment.

In narrating the Allegory, Socrates says that "we," that is, he and his companions as founders of the city in speech, must "compel" the completed philosophers to go back down into the cave to rule it. But it is our embodiment that compels us to do this outside of the Allegory. We cannot exist without the body and all the extended relations with other embodied human beings who form the communities that fulfill the body's material needs. We are individuals, but nevertheless interdependent as political-social-ethical beings.

These human relations also provide the context for a life beyond mere necessity, the larger fulfillment of a good life, including philosophy, as well as the nobility of an ethical life and political activity. Even more fundamentally, the body compels us back into consideration of the materiality, the finitude, and the specificity of the opinions and habits that have always-already formed the provisional meaning of things and the world as whole.

To ignore this cave-like embodiment as the way we always-already understand ourselves and the world is like what Socrates says about staring into the fire after first breaking free of the bonds (515c), or into the Sun when first emerging from the cave (516a), or again at the fire when descending back down into the cave (516e–5717), or at the idea of the good itself when ascending the Divided Line (506e). To gaze this way risks blindness, either temporary or permanent, because staring directly into the source of illumination overwhelms vision. Looking at the light source overpowers the capacity to differentiate among the things made clear and distinct by the light, just as contemplating what makes intelligibility possible at all can obscure the meaning of the things and practices that are historically given to us in our everyday existence.

Again, this is why Socrates begins with what people *say*. His phenomenology assumes a meaning to the understanding, if only because the world is always-already given to us in some provisionally intelligible way. It helps to take seriously this word: *pro-visionally*. We already see forward, ahead of ourselves, prospectively and circumspectively, as Heidegger would say (e.g., SZ, 150 and 69, 80–81), or else the world would not be navigable. At the same time, our seeing is provisional in the sense of temporary and open to revision. We are vulnerable to the *exaiphnēs* interruptions, the sudden and unexpected breakdowns that threaten to undo the structures of familiar meaning. Those structures are provisional because they are temporary, and they are temporary because our mode of understanding is temporal and finite. What is provisional in our seeing is therefore also potentially *revisionary*, not as a vindictive or timorous evasion of reality, but more literally as a seeing-anew that reintegrates a world of meaning after a breakdown. Our embodiment is cave-like because we always begin where we are situated in a given world of meaning, even if we seek to transcend and reconstitute our understanding of it. But we can never entirely transcend our finite, historical human-being, because we cannot leap over our own shadows, the sheer facticity of our always-already emerging in a world of meaning as historically given to us. Self-sufficiency is necessarily incomplete for finite beings like ourselves. It requires the polemics of reintegration in the encounter with what upsets our provisional expectations. This is why being-human requires the social friction, as well as the cooperation, of ethical life.

6.2 THE RETURN: RECONSTRUCTION AS REINTEGRATION OF THE LINE

So far, we have discussed two aspects of the construal of meaning that can be mapped to two phases in the ascent from the cave. Deconstruction occurs when some contradiction provokes a breaking of the bonds of opinion that tie the prisoner to seeing the world in a certain way. Preconstruction occurs when the ascending prisoner envisions an alternative way of seeing, composed in part from the deconstructed conceptual elements of the prior belief, through the dialectical process of the upward pathway, which corresponds to the refining of the alternative through the rigorous examination of arguments, hypotheses, definitions, and so on. We also have discussed how the complete fulfillment of the echonic philosopher is impossible due to our historical and physical embodiment, our being pinioned in time and place. Now we turn to the journey back down into the cave that the compulsion of the body forces upon the supposedly liberated prisoner, and I will argue that this corresponds to the *reconstruction* of meaning.

In describing the moments of transition for both the prisoner and the philosopher, Socrates suggests that someone possessing insight (*noun ge echoi tis*)

> would remember that there are two kinds of disturbances of the eyes, stemming from two sources—when they have been transferred from light to darkness and when they have been transferred from darkness to light. And if he held that these same things happen to a soul too, whenever he saw one that is confused and unable to make anything out, he wouldn't laugh without reasoning but would go on to consider whether, come from a brighter life, it [that is, the disoriented soul] is in darkness for want of being accustomed, or whether, going from greater lack of learning to greater brightness, it is dazzled by the greater brilliance. (518a)

We have discussed the pain involved in such disoriented or disturbed seeing in the pivotal moments of transition during the prisoner's ascent: the moment of initial release in the breakdown of the bonds; the moment of confrontation with the fire on the lateral pathway; and the moment of emergence in the light of day. The first represents the dislocation of meaning to things and world when received opinion falls into contradiction and no longer provides guidance; the second, how historical contingency projects received opinion; the third, how the ideas provide the foundation for a knowledge that both transcends and explains contingent opinion. These each involve progress from darkness into light, from the most naive opinion to the fullest understanding, and each transition involves painful reorientation.

You have probably experienced what it is like to go suddenly into a dark place from a brightly lit one or vice versa: the meaning of things turns hazy, and you have to grope your way around while your eyes adjust. The descent back to the cave is a transition "from light to darkness," and Socrates's account suggests that even for the wisest, the echonic philosophers fully enlightened by the absolute knowledge of the ideas and the idea of the good beyond the cave, there can still be a kind of ignorance. This is not ignorance about what the truth is but rather about how truth may be integrated with the contingency of opinion that orients most of us, most of the time, to the meaning of the lives we inhabit. This dynamic of reintegration is something that Heidegger misses in his lectures on Plato's Cave. Socrates's warning that anyone with insight would not laugh at a person stumbling in such a moment of transition recalls the distinction that Socrates draws in the *Euthyphro* between the laughter of his fellow Athenians at the eccentric pretentions of Euthyphro—claiming to be a prophet and knower of the will of the gods—and their anger at himself, Socrates, whom they were now prosecuting for the capital crimes of impiety and corrupting the youth (3c–d). It is one thing to appear laughably buffoon-ish due to outlandish notions, which is inherently possible or even probable for philosophy; it is quite another to seem a mortal threat to a society's most cherished norms *and* to lead astray the people's children, their most cherished hope for continuity in the affections, connections, traditions, and memories of what makes life most meaningful to them.

As we have seen (4.3), Plato hints at Socrates's fate in Athens when he has Socrates ask Glaucon about the former prisoner, now enlightened, who returns to his seat at the bottom level of the cave. To review, the liberated prisoner, now returning to the lower cave, would undergo intense disori-entation because of the effects of the darkness on eyes now accustomed to sunlight; the prisoners would ridicule him, saying that "he went up and came back with his eyes corrupted" (517a) and they might get angry enough to try to kill whoever has been releasing their fellow cave-dwellers to this fate. The Greek for having one's eyes "corrupted" (*diephthapmenos*) is a form of the same word used in the city's charge against Socrates for corrupting the youth (*Euthyprho*, 2c); it means to utterly (*dia-*) destroy (*-phtherein*) something, to kill, and, in moral matters, to corrupt someone, whether by seduction or bribery or some other nefarious means. Laughter against the outlandish philosopher can quickly shift to persecution or outright violence if shaming the corrupting influence with ridicule fails to end the threat, as Aristophanes's *Clouds* and Socrates's actual fate illustrate. Both failures, imagined in the *Clouds* and actual in historical Athens, were confirmed for the public by Socrates's hold on some of the city's most promising youth, most famously Alcibiades.

In the context of the Allegory, the disturbances (*epitaraxeis*) of the eyes are not an irrevocable corruption, as the cave-dwellers assume it to be from their perspective, having never made the ascent themselves. The disturbances are a temporary but still dangerous condition. The prisoner, in the extreme disorientation which comes when the bonds are first broken at the lowest level of the cave, would then be most susceptible to the despair of believing that the illness in seeing might be permanent. With each iteration of disorientation in the stages of ascent, however, the healing prisoner can (but does not necessarily) gain more confidence that such episodes are transitory.

As ever, we have to interpret these details of the allegory, which is powerful enough that it can make us forget the narrative is an allegory. The disturbances are dislocations of the meaning-structure that all human beings find themselves always-already inhabiting. The understanding of what things and practices most properly are gets knocked out of joint. A person finds it difficult or even impossible to function in the usual way. At each stage of the ascent, the healing prisoner must wait for their eyes to adjust. Similarly, after some aspect of our understanding of meaning has been thrown into confusion by a rupture in our opinions, we must find a way to reassemble the broken-down elements of our world in a manner that can once again make sense, but, in the helicoidal structure of polemical philosophy, on a higher level that can still account for what we had seen and believed before. According to the Divided Line, those higher levels include making sense of opinion, manifested by what we imagine and what we trust in our everyday worlds: from the perspective of knowledge, manifested by thought, which reveals the universal principles of mathematics operative in things; and by intellection, or insight, which grants access, even if only partial or provisional, to the ideas.

There is an important distinction to draw between the disturbance of the eyes in the ascent from the cave and the disturbance in the descent back down into the cave. The former is largely a private matter, experienced by a single individual who has or has been broken loose from the bonds of received opinion. There may or may not be a mentor to guide the prisoner upward through a form of teaching in dialectic that assists in the prisoner's own "turning around," as Socrates calls it, rather than simply imposing some new vision. (See the various panels of Figure 4, which illustrates possible modalities of release and ascent in the cave.) But still the released prisoner seems to experience this privately, or at least only with a mentor, without involving the other prisoners who remain in their bonds.

By contrast, there is a very public aspect to the descent back to the cave. The returning philosopher, in Socrates's descriptions, necessarily comes to the attention of the cave-dwellers, either because his initial, clumsy fumbling around in the dark before his eyes have adjusted causes a commotion, or because his job, if he has been educated as a philosopher-ruler, is precisely to interact with the cave-dwellers. This is why Socrates asks,

Do you suppose it is anything surprising if a man, come from acts of divine contemplation to the human evils, is graceless and looks quite ridiculous when—
with his sight still dim and before he has gotten sufficiently accustomed to the
surrounding darkness—he is compelled in courts or elsewhere to contest about
the shadows of the just or the representations of which they are the shadows, and
to dispute about the way these things are understood by men who have never
seen justice itself? (517d–e)

The parallel here to Socrates's own fate in Athens, forced to defend himself at his trial, is unmistakable.[6] As we have seen, Socrates describes the
cave-dwellers as potentially wanting to kill the awkward and graceless zetetic
philosopher who threatens the community's order and its children with his
outlandish but somehow alluring ideas. That fate only sharpens the question
about the distinction between the zetetic and the echonic philosopher in returning to the former habitation at the bottom of the cave. Socrates does not claim
to be an echonic philosopher who possesses the truth, and so his awkward-
ness among the Athenians would make sense. But the philosopher-rulers are
supposed to lead in the cave, and being ridiculed and scorned hardly seems a
promising start. Socrates imagines the pep-talk the city's founder would give
to the newly minted echonic philosopher about to return to the cave:

So you must go down, each in his turn, into the common dwelling of the others
and get habituated along with them to seeing the dark things. And, in getting
habituated to it, you will see ten thousand times better than the men there, and
you'll know what each of the phantoms is, and of what it is a phantom, because
you have seen the truth about fair, just, and good things. And thus, the city
will be governed by us and by you in a state of waking, not in a dream as the
many cities nowadays are governed by men who fight over shadows with one
another and form factions for the sake of ruling, as though it were some great
good. (520c)

The key phrase here is "in getting habituated" (*sunethizomenoi*). The
Greek adjective *synēthēs*, habituated, is composed from *sun-*, together, and
ēthos, habit or custom, the basis for our word 'ethics' and most famously
discussed in Aristotle's *Nicomachean Ethics* as the foundation of a virtuous
character. It is significant that *ēthos* also means 'a usual place,' as in the haunt
of animal or person, an abode one is accustomed to in-habit. 'Habituated' is
therefore a particularly good rendering for *synēthēs* and its related forms, and
we might go further to say what Socrates is describing here is a habituation
as *syn-ēthēs* in the sense of a *co-habitation*, a getting-used to living with others and seeing things in the way they are accustomed to understanding them.
Someone who is a *synēthēs* is a friend, an intimate, someone whose character
and habits are congenial enough to make a shared life feasible. As habituated

cohabitation, *synēthēs* is akin to *Mitsein* in Heidegger: being-with others in being-*in*-the-world, in-habiting it as the space of meaning that we can share with others in a life that makes a kind of provisional sense, although *Mitsein* has no necessary ethical meaning, only the ontological-hermeneutical one.

Even the echonic philosopher does not possess this *synēthēs* directly as a result of the presumptively complete enlightenment provided out in the light of day. This is perhaps a reflection of the Greek sense, exemplified by the story of Thales and the well and addressed directly by Aristotle in the *Nicomachean Ethics* (1140a33–1140b3), that there is a difference between theoretical and practical wisdom. The knowledge of abstract, universal truths does not itself give direct insight into the unpredictable contingencies of the historical situatedness of human existence. The ability to integrate the two requires *phronēsis*, practical wisdom, and this form of wisdom requires intimate, embodied co-habitation with the particulars of a specific historical way of life—the essence of habituation. This cannot be taught in the abstract. It must be lived affectively, and because it is not calculable in advance, it must be risked as a matter of *tolma*, daring, and of courage (see chapter 8).

A difference between the zetetic philosopher who happens to return to the habitation of the cave-dwellers and the echonic philosopher who returns purposefully to rule it is that the latter, as an aspect of the training for rule, could have been instructed to expect this particular "disturbance" of the eyes, the turbulence of adjusting from the dark to the firelight. Even so, no amount of study of the theory of leadership or case studies in 'applying' philosophical insight or role-playing such scenarios can prepare the one who is returning for the contingencies of the actual, affective, embodiment of the process of habituation. In this regard, echonic philosophers might be no better prepared than zetetic ones in making themselves at home among those who have not made the philosophic journey. Indeed, it might be harder for the echonics, who have supposedly achieved such an absolute epistemological transformation that it would fundamentally estrange them from the cast of mind of the cave-dwellers' life-world. By contrast, the zetetics remain closer to the cave-dwellers in living with shadows and uncertainty. Still steeped in the polemical dialogue with the given historical world as they make their philosophical journey, the zetetics are potentially more alive to the practical wisdom needed to interact reconstructively with that world.

We must ask what is the disturbance of the eyes during the return to the lower levels of the cave and how it differs from the disturbances of vision during the ascent. *What is at-issue is that even for the echonic philosopher, emerging into the light of day and learning all there is to know about the ideas and the idea of the good itself is not yet complete wisdom and therefore not yet a complete healing from the bonds of the cave.* If the Cave Allegory is a story about liberation, then that liberation is not complete without going back to the cave. As we have seen, Heidegger recognizes this too. We must ever-again refresh the *logos* by returning to *dialogos*. That necessity is confirmed by the argument that our actual embodiment means that we always have our cave with us, that there is no absolute emergence from the cave of historically habituated opinion, at least not in this life, and that care of the body and attentiveness to the finitude of our own understanding demands that we inhabit a world with others, also embodied, sharing an *ēthos* as our common ground for an understanding potentially open to mutual revision in a polemical, ethical dialogue. Our unshakable embodiment, our inevitable situatedness, makes us return to the fuller task of liberation in ethical and political life.

In this messy work of embodied reconstruction of the world, the actual zetetic philosophers might be more adept than the imagined echonic ones. The zetetic philosopher is a skeptical idealist: *idealist*, because still faithful to the piety that the transcendent ideas provide crucial guidance in the search for a better understanding, even if this understanding cannot result in the absolute possession of a final truth that ends philosophy as a seeking; *skeptical*, because with the recognition of human finitude and the nature of our discursive, temporal, dialogical understanding, the zetetic recognizes that such philosophy must ever-again engage in *re-vision* of what we had thought true, submitting our understanding and interpretation to *skepsis*, to investigation, inquiry, and critique, but not for the sake of a sheer nihilistic destruction of meaning. This is the Socratic version of the Judaic *tikkun olam*, the duty to repair the world.

If the zetetic does not seek to destroy meaning, then what deserves this *skepsis*? Potentially anything and everything, but not *simply* anything and everything, because that is just willful destructiveness and nihilism. Here, we must let our embodiment, in its fullest sense, be our guide in practical wisdom. We must attend to how the meaning of the world shows up, phenomenologically, as breaking down in *what matters* to our situated existence. This involves a phronetic *discernment* for what we care about in what we say—not just random nitpicking, but what announces itself in the contradictions in things that impinge upon us in wonder. By following Socrates's lead in roving among and talking with all kinds of people in his homeland, zetetic philosophers may make what people *say*, about what truly matters to them and how they understand and justify it, a guide to the inquiry after a meaning that is always-already operative, but usually hidden, in our everyday lives. Because the zetetic philosopher is always on-the-way, attentively on the lookout for the *polemos* of contradictions in meaning, he or she lives closer to the habituation of the cave, in all its murkiness, than does the imagined echonic philosopher.

I have argued that the echonic philosopher is an ideation, an idea we can imagine as we wonder about what it would mean to know, but that the echonic philosopher is *only* an idea, an idea of reason, as Kant might say.[7] This idea, this *eidos*, of the echonic philosopher becomes an *eidolon*, an idol, if we treat it as an ideal to be realized as the only legitimate qualification for ethical authority and political rule. As an idea, though, the echonic philosopher serves a dual purpose: positively, for inspiring the ascent on the upward way, because even if absolute knowledge eludes us, greater understanding can come to us as a form of provisional wisdom; negatively, for reflecting upon what it means that we cannot attain this ideal absolutely. As embodied, situated beings, we cannot overcome our finitude and enter unconditionally upon the view from nowhere, to borrow again from Nagel. But this does not render the zetetic philosopher's activity pointless, because that activity is necessary to the ever-ongoing confrontation with the temporal world, whose unpredictable contingencies and contradictions impinge suddenly, unexpectedly, and unavoidably upon the finitude of complete understanding.

Concretely, this means that any deconstruction of a given understanding or received opinion, followed by the preconstruction or envisioning of an alternative as a philosophical response to a question at-issue, must still return, as it were, to the actual lived historical context from which what is at-issue first arose. Deconstruction alone, treating the breaking of bonds of received opinion as the final form of liberation, leaves the freed person uprooted, unable to fit into and inhabit a world. This *deconstructive* nihilism as a corrupted form of freedom has a counterpart in a *preconstructive* nihilism, a free-floating, visionary imagining of alternatives. A very elaborate, philosophically sophisticated, and meticulously argued treatise on justice, for example, may fly off into a Cloud-Cuckoo-Land of speculation untethered from historical reality or any reasonably imaginable context for implementation. But note, this too is *a form of nihilism*, an Icarean escape into hyper-abstraction that leaves behind the situated historical existence of being-human, of being-here.

If there is no actual possibility of attaining the complete knowledge of the echonic philosopher, then a complete healing from the bonds of received opinion also is not possible. We are never entirely free of the past and its conventions and convictions. What is possible is a life of zetetic philosophy, a skeptical idealism that serves as a necessary therapy for—and perhaps even a reconciliation to—the bondage that is our embodiment in the cave of ourselves, without which we would not be at all. In a real sense, then, zetetic philosophy *is* the healing from the bonds of the cave. This entails a freedom that includes not just a deconstructive liberation from the bonds of the given, and not just a preconstructive envisioning of an alternative, but also a *reconstructive* reintegration of what could be with what has been, and with what is. This is precisely what transpires in the *synēthēs* of philosophy. It is the becoming at-home with the ever-ongoing *polemos* with the given as both a deep famil- iarization with the historical specifics of how a particular world construes its meaning and as a well-developed practical wisdom for how to integrate new understandings with the ones already at work in a historical community. To be able to navigate with this situated, habituated, practical wisdom is key to the healing from the bonds and to recovering from the disturbances of the eyes, namely, an inability to pivot between abstract ideals and the practical interpretation and realization of those ideals in a specific context.

6.4 ONE'S OWN AND THE BODY POLITIC

Socrates's arguments for features of the ideal city, Kallipolis, provide evi- dence internal to the *Republic* for the dynamic of the triad of construal. For example, Socrates asks, "Is, then, that city in which most say 'my own' and 'not my own' [*to emon te kai ouk emon*] about the same thing, and in the same way, the best governed city?" (462c). This point harkens back to what is at-issue in the origins of any human community: the fact that we are not self- sufficient organisms and therefore have a need for one another (369b–c). But the motivating discussions of the *Republic* suggest something more. Thrasy- machus claims that injustice and tyranny are the greatest good for a human being, and Glaucon's thought experiment of the Ring of Gyges purports to show the weakness of any social contract. Therefore arises the question of what prevents individuals from exploiting the cooperation of the community to fulfill their private desires, with as little sacrifice as possible of their own needs, as far as they can get away with it—if they have the strength of body and mind to do so. This possibility, the source of exploitative criminality, lies hidden in every community.

When Socrates takes up this problem, he asks, "Have we any greater evil for a city than what splits it and makes it many instead of one? Or a greater good than what binds it together and makes it one?" (462a–b). For a com- munity to provide for the needs of all of its members—the reason they would be part of it in the first place—each member must *trust* that their contribu- tions and sacrifices will be reciprocated rather than exploited. The motto of the United States, approved in 1782, echoes this point: *E pluribus unum*, Out of many, one. Socrates asks further, "Doesn't the community [*koinonia*, the sharing] of pleasure and pain bind it [the political community] together when to the greatest extent possible all the citizens alike rejoice and are pained at the same comings into being and perishings?" (462b). These "comings into being and perishings" involve all the changes of a contingent world that might convulse our affective lives: births and deaths; victories and defeats; harvests and droughts; and so on. As Socrates then says, "the privacy of such things dissolves" the community (462c); here, "privacy" is *idiōsis*, from which we have words like "idiot" and "idiosyncrasy," and it means "making private" in the sense of a peculiar or eccentric way of doing things particular to oneself in isolation, without regard to others.

The individualization of desire, pleasure, and pain is a carrier for spreading the disease of injustice in a community, which is why Socrates goes on to suggest that "that city is best governed which is most like a single human being," illustrating as follows:

> For example, when one of us wounds a finger, presumably the entire community—that community tying the body together with the soul in a single arrangement under the ruler within it—is aware of the fact and all of it is in pain as a whole along with the afflicted part; and it is in this sense we say that this human being has a pain in his finger. (462c–d)

Glaucon and Socrates agree that the "city with the best regime is most like such a human being" (462d), because its citizens would rejoice and lament, feel pleasure and pain, for the same things, "to the greatest extent possible" (462b). This qualification points to what is at-issue, what does *not* go without saying: that the political community *is* not by nature a single body. This is the core of the political problem, because we do not necessarily feel the same joys and disappointments as others at the same things. What is most immediately "my own" is *my* body and all *my* needs and desires and all of the relationships—to friends and family—that are mine in an exclusive sense, rather than in an inclusive one that embraces the community as a whole. The loves and attachments that we naturally feel are generally private and exclusive, and yet this is what makes injustice not just possible but likely in the body politic.

The conception of a single 'body politic' is itself an *ideation*, an ideal that we can imagine, just as the ideal city Kallipolis is an ideation that unites private and collective identity in a single whole. This ideation has drastic implications in the *Republic*, because to overcome the gulf between "my own" as a private and a common good, Socrates makes some very radical proposals, the "three waves" that threaten the plausibility of the ideal city. The first is providing equal opportunity of profession and education to women and men, so that women may do any job that men do, and vice versa, if they prove their merit, including serving as soldiers and rulers. This is necessary because the city must overcome all merely contingent differences of the body so that each individual's talents most fully serve the needs of the city. The second wave is the abolition of the private family, of private erotic love, and of monogamous marriage; this includes the eugenic breeding of children according to a scientific plan, separating them from their mothers at birth, and raising them in common, apart from their biological parents—who will not even know them as their own, other than knowing all the city's children as "their own." This is necessary because, more than anything else, "my own" body individuates my needs to what my erotic longings are, to the progeny of that longing in the form of children, and the division of "my own" interests in raising those children from what might be in the best interest of all children in the community. Finally, the "third wave" requires that philosophers rule the city, so that knowledge of the good can provide unity to the city, rather than self-interested, unreflective opinion dividing it into factions.

Once again, the *Republic* acknowledges the profound political and existential importance of the body. It is the body that pinions each of us to a private, idiosyncratic, nexus of needs, desires, attachments and therefore prevents us from simply existing outside of the cave altogether. The body is the inevitability of our thrown situatedness, a perspective that binds us tightly to what we think we want and know. This embodiment gives meaning to all that matters to us in a world that makes sense on the human scale. The body is the home of the *Jemeinigkeit*, the always-my-ownness of individuated existence. We bear the cave with us so long as we are embodied, and to be embodied is what and how we are as finite beings.

But does this mean that Socrates's ideation of Kallipolis as the community that overcomes the division between "my own" and "ours" is simply an illusion, a phantom of an overactive philosophical imagination? Does it mean that his philosophical arguments and his policy proposals for gender equality, family equality, and enlightened rule based on this ideation are entirely implausible or ridiculous?

Some readers, such as Allan Bloom, have gone so far as to argue that the three waves serve as a tragi-comic *reductio ad absurdum* to warn against the overweening and naive ideological ambition for a political community that would finally and utterly overcome the injustices and inequalities fostered by the division between private and public good.[8] Bloom is certainly right that the measures needed to fully overcome the private interests fostered by the body would be so extreme as to defy any reasonable expectation of what human nature is capable of accomplishing. The erotic longings of the body are not simply up to us to govern as individuals. They descend upon us unbidden as a decisive feature of our personal, situated thrownness. To expect that a government of enlightened technocrat-philosophers could tame these erotic necessities, so that we could not love those we feel impelled to love, would be asking a great deal of human nature, just as it would be asking rather too much to take newborn children from their birth mothers and separate them forever as a family unit. For Bloom, the lesson of the *Republic* is a negative one of moderating such imprudent ambitions by showing just what would be necessary to achieve them, and how unlikely and undesirable that would be.

But if we understand the policy proposals that Socrates envisions through philosophical argument in the sense of the *preconstruction* that follows upon a *deconstruction* of what is problematic about current institutions, we can interpret them as part of a larger dialectic with what is at-issue within the text, as well as a larger dialogue that Plato invites us to join.[9] The ideation of a community that completely reconciles public and private interest, just like the ideation of echonic philosophers who come to grasp the entirety of the truth, serves an important role in rousing the interpretive polemics of philosophy. If complete justice in a community entails the noble idea that all citizens should care for the whole as much as for themselves in order to prevent faction and to cultivate a dauntless public spirit, then we must consider what price we would have to pay to achieve that complete unity of "mine" and "ours." One does not have to go so far as to interpret Kallipolis as the antithesis of what a sensible society would look like to reflect dialectically upon how far it makes sense to go with Socrates's proposals. The fact that we are each individuated in our own bodies sets a natural, if somewhat historically flexible, limit to the complete identification of my own embodiment with the body politic. A dialectical reading of Plato suggests that not only does Plato expect us to notice the difficulties immanent to the arguments as the dialogue unfolds, but he also expects us to take up the polemical work of philosophy in confronting how these proposals might relate to our own ethical, social, and political lives. That is because justice depends on this ongoing, situated reconstruction of what is at-issue, rather than on applying some definitive, trans-temporal blueprint of the ideal.

For example, Socrates argues that for the sake of the unity of the city and for finding an appropriate path in life for each child, justice requires that all children in Kallipolis receive equal opportunity in education. This applies to more than absolute equality of educational and professional opportunities for girls as well as for boys (457b–c). It also means that the children of the gold ruling class should get no special consideration over children born of silver or bronze parents. In this absolute meritocracy, no matter your birth, you should be able to attain whatever position, high or low, your talents and virtues allow, both for your own sake and for the sake of the city (415b–c). This seems entirely just, a matter of fairness for children who had no choice in being born male or female, rich or poor, high status or low.

If such fairness and equality truly matter, then there are many flaws in the American educational system, for example, that would demand attention. Should expenditures for primary education be based on local property taxes, which disproportionately disadvantage children born into poorer neighborhoods through no fault of their own, often ones redlined for gen-erations by race? Should parents be free to send their children to private schools which charge hefty tuition, or should education, as Socrates in the *Republic* and Aristotle in the *Politics* (1337a21–27) argued, be universal and public only, so that all citizens have the same stake in ensuring both that it be excellent and that it unify rather than divide the people by class? To push the argument for fairness and equality even further: Even if there were public education equally funded for all children, would not the children of the wealthy and successful still have major unfair advantages provided by the high socioeconomic status of their parents, which gives their children an unearned advantage in obtaining tutoring, finding internships and jobs, feel-ing at ease with the manners of the important and the powerful, and so on? Why not do something like what Socrates suggests by making citizens all live together in dormitories and eat together in common dining halls so that all socialize with all, thus diminishing the effects of differences in status? And, in fact, we do something that *resembles* this policy suggestion in college dorms and dining halls.

The limit to such measures, once again, is the body, as well as all the ma-terial reality that it represents. The love that parents generally feel for their own children can be an overwhelming impetus to ensure that "one's own" do well, even when this is not fair to other children. The extremity of the measures that Socrates suggests—abolishing private property and private homes, abolishing private families and private love among couples in favor of temporary, arranged marriages for eugenic breeding purposes, separating babies permanently from their mothers at birth—points to how far a society would have to go suppress these claims of the body. Such measures promote the kind of absolute unity that Socrates's envisioned just city would require in order to erase all distinctions of personal preference and private good in favor of a total identification of all citizens with the good of all. But the skeptical idealist approach is an inherently recursive, reiterative process in which the imagined ideal is brought into polemical dialectic with the situated givens of a particular historical context.

Here I am close to Hermann Cohen, who argued that Plato's ideas are akin to Kant's regulative ideas, that the ideas are not intended to extricate us from the life of empirical existence but rather to provide us with a necessary and therefore unavoidable *a priori* heuristic to assess and refine our understand-ing of that existence: "that reason and embodied sensory experience should ever remain blood-relations, so that the distinction between them should not mislead us into a total separation between them, by which only rhetoric and not the longing for truth would triumph."[10] This involves interpreting the lived context and then reinterpreting it again and again through the process of integrating actual changes in the meaning of things, institutions, practices, and even language, all in the light of the ideated ideal. We need the ideal of unity as a regulative idea to illuminate and counteract the meaning of disunity when it threatens to pull us apart entirely, even if the ideal is unrealizable in absolute terms. This dialectical negotiation of ideal and real requires *phronēsis*, which will be discussed further in chapter 8.

This polemical process may also force a reinterpretation of what the ideal is. For example, the difficulties inherent to the implementation of social equality as an ideal might provoke a reconsideration of the ideal or even of the idea of justice animating it. This is consistent with the conception of a skeptical idealism, one that posits the idea as necessary to the ethical, political, and thoughtful life, but does not lay claim to an absolute knowledge of the idea or of how to implement it as an ideal. For educational equality, what might be possible in the context of an Israeli kibbutz is probably quite different from what would be in the United States or in the Japanese educational system. The historical situatedness of American traditions and character places constraints on what is possible in light of the ideal—not rigid constraints, but elastic ones, whose resistance is proportional to the distance it pulls institutions and beliefs from their historical embeddedness. American individualism, which resists governmental involvement in family matters; the separation of church and state, which has permitted the private development of both secular and religious schools; the federalism that differentiates tax policy both among states and within states: these and other factors constrain what is possible in promoting educational equality. That does not mean these constraints cannot be managed or even broken, but doing so requires perspicacious discernment in practical wisdom.[11]

6.5 THE CONFRONTATION OF IDEATION AND MATERIALITY

Socrates is explicit about the regulative function of the idea or ideal as a feature in the full process of ideation, which involves imagining an alternative and considering how to apply it, and then actually doing so. In his general description of selecting and appointing guardians from among the silver class in the city through a process of testing to see if under pressure from pleasure, fear, or pain they maintain "their conviction that they must do what on each occasion seems best for the city" (413c), Socrates says the process must be "something like this, not described precisely, but by way of a model [*hōs en tupōi*]" (414a). He makes this point even more vividly when discussing the purpose of justice itself with Glaucon:

SOCRATES: But if we find out what justice is like, will we also insist that the just man must not differ at all from justice itself but in every way be such as it is? Or will we be content if he is nearest to and participates in it more than the others?

GLAUCON: We'll be content with that.

SOCRATES: It was, therefore, for the sake of a pattern that we were seeking both for what justice by itself is like, and for the perfectly just man, if he should come into being and what he would be like once come into being. Thus, looking off at what their relationships to happiness and its opposite appear to us to be, we would also be compelled to agree in our own cases that the man who is most like them will have the portion most like theirs. We were not seeking them for the sake of proving that it's possible for these things to come into being. (472b–d)

Granted, in this case Socrates is not interested in actually implementing some version of Kallipolis. The whole purpose of imagining Kallipolis as a city in speech was as a metaphor for the psyche of a human being and whether being just is indeed a virtue that conduces to the human good. But even so, the context of the *Republic* demonstrates that there is a political and practical aspect to what Socrates is doing in producing "a pattern" (*paradeigma*) of a just person: He seeks to steer these promising young men away from arguments that favor a tyrannical injustice whose principles they certainly could have implemented in public life as a very different paradigm. The historical Polemarchus and Lysias were leaders of the democratic revolt against the oligarchic tyranny imposed by Sparta at the end of the Peloponnesian War.[12] Whether they did so as a result of a conversation with Socrates we cannot know, but even if not, through the dramatic features of the dialogue Plato shows us Socrates precisely as modeling reconstructive intervention with his own historical situation by defending justice as an idea and ideal, through the construal of Kallipolis as an ideation that can address the lived concerns of *these* companions, *there*, at *that* time and place.

Socrates asks later, when the young men, with all the enthusiasm of youth about an ideal, insist on knowing if Kallipolis is possible: "Can anything be done as it is said? Or is it in the nature of acting to attain less truth than speaking, even if someone doesn't think so?" When they agree that the ideal can be truer than the real, he says: "Then don't compel me necessarily to present it as coming into being in every way in deed as we described it in speech. But if we are able to find that a city could be governed in a way most closely approximating what has been said, say that we've found the possibility of these things coming into being on which you insist" (473a–b). Here, the decisive term is *engutata*, "most closely approximating"—closest to, nearest to. In the process of ideation, which includes action to change the world—including changing the minds of influential future leaders of society—the ideal must be approximated due to the situated contingencies of historical existence. As regulative, the idea guides the polemical dialectic with historical actuality, compelling the actor to account for the contingencies that inhibit or assist the approximative realization of the ideal. Under favorable conditions, with political action guided by a discerning practical wisdom, the real might then make asymptotic progress towards the ideal. This is the responsible answer to Glaucon's question, "Is it ever possible for this regime to come into being, and how is it ever possible?" (471c). As Socrates asks, "[W]ill we be content if [the just man, or the just regime] is nearest to it [namely, the imagined ideal—the preconstruction] and participates in it more than the others?" (472c).

Another way of saying this is that the obverse of a skeptical idealism is a reconstructive realism. In the cycle of ideation, reconstruction is the encounter between material reality and projected ideal. *Material* here means not only physical objects as governed by natural laws and the natural resources at hand to implement policy, but also means the opinions, institutions, traditions, and all the unspoken practices that habituate us to the meaning of a specific historical world. Material reality, understood ontologically as well as ontically, is anything about the always-already givenness of the world that offers *resistance* to what we can envision and hope to implement or produce. It is akin to what Heidegger calls *facticity*. I can envision flying like a bird, but if I don't take into account all the physical laws and material constraints, I will never come close to approximating flight. We can, like Socrates, envision a world in which women have the same opportunities as men, including serving in the military and in ruling. That Socrates took this seriously, I do not doubt, given his own acquaintance with Aspasia, often credited with the success of Pericles, and Plato's portrayal in the *Symposium* (201d–212c) of a younger Socrates gaining insight from Diotima into the one thing he did claim to know about: love (177d).[13] Assuming that this specific ideal is in fact in accord with the idea of justice, achieving the ideal of gender equality requires an exquisitely fine-tuned understanding of the historical constraints and opportunities for action and change.

6.6 IDEAL AND ILLUSION

This discussion has broached specific questions about *enacting* a polemical ethics, which will be the subject of future volumes in this project. Our main task here is to flesh out a metaethics of polemical, skeptical idealism as a way of being-human and of doing philosophy, but it is impossible to do that without providing some initial sense of how metaethics filters into an engaged life, where the confrontation between the ideal and the real takes place. This is crucial to understanding any genuinely iterative process of ideation because it explains the difference between ideals that are fantasies that we can only imagine—at least if we don't want to cause terrible damage—and ideals that can serve as regulative ideas or paradigms for an asymptotic approximation in the praxis of ethical and political life.

Without developing a detailed metaphysics of the real, we can say that in a polemical ethics, the real is how the world brings us back to earth, to what is given factically as unavoidable, to what constrains us both interpretively and practically in the always-already of a historical world. The difference between a delusional fantasy and an envisioned ideal is that the latter is able to engage in dialogue with the resistance offered by the world, whether it be in trying to find a way to fly, for example, or in achieving gender equality in society. It can be hard to distinguish delusional fantasy from brilliance of imagination because true visionaries can seem utterly unhinged from the earthy realities of their situated existence. The dream of flight may have seemed fanciful before the Wright brothers, but we have indeed brought the fantasy of flight into reality, even if not in the form imagined by the myth of Icarus, but only because human ingenuity slowly came to grips with the material reality constraining the possibility of flight. But, even if we cannot (yet!) fly quite like a bird, or like Icarus, understanding the ontic materiality of flight (gravity, aerodynamics, engineering, etc.) allows us to reinterpret what 'flying' might mean, to reimagine it, and then to realize it. The goal of gender equality certainly seemed as improbable when proposed by Socrates more than two millennia ago, or when advocated by suffragettes one hundred years ago, or as tested when women serve in combat or run for president to-day. We can tell the difference between illusion and ideal only by entering in good faith the polemical activity of attempting to realize or prove unfeasible the vision proposed by confronting the prevailing material reality.

This has implications for how we should understand truth in a polemical ethics. Are the ideals we envision in the light of an idea true? Or, as Nietzsche might say, are they just lies we concoct to make life bearable, to fend off for a while the chaos of a cosmos in flux? For Heidegger, truth happens in the *polemos* between earth and world. This is truth in his ontological sense of *a-lētheia, Unverborgenheit,* unconcealment, the truth that makes meaning possible. It is easy to misunderstand this unconcealment as some act of discovery by some intrepid explorer or researcher, uncovering some new fact about the world. But as discussed earlier, unconcealment for Heidegger has to do not with a given ontic array of facts (*alētheia*-3), known or unknown, but rather with our ontological openness to a meaningfulness of world and things in which discovery in the mundane sense is possible in the first place. In a polemical ethics comprising the full and reiterative cycle of construal—deconstruction, preconstruction (or envisioning), and reconstruction—human beings, as interpretive beings, confront truth dynamically in both senses: ontological truth as unconcealment and ontic truth as matters of fact about what is.

In the moment of the breakdown, the irruption of unmeaning that is either positive in opening us to new possibilities of meaning or negative in collapsing the sense of a world in despair, we come into conflict with the unconcealment of the world as it has been opened up to us in the happenstance of our historical situatedness. This confrontation with unconcealment is rarely thematized as such when it happens, but it is happening nevertheless whenever we pause in wonder, formulate a question, and forge a response to some phenomenon that brings us up short. It begins as the deconstructive loosening and release of ways of seeing, interpreting, and understanding, and can proceed either into nihilism or into the attempt at reconstruction. This may happen in contexts from the humble to the overarching: When a tool breaks and a person seeks a way to make up for its loss in getting on with a task. When someone's patience breaks with a job and he reconsiders his path in life; when someone's forbearance with injustice breaks and she starts to envision a different kind of world. Or even when one looks to the night sky and wonders why there is a world as such rather than nothing, and wonders why, in that world, they are someone rather than no one—and "Why on earth now, on Tuesday of all days"? In each such case, we run up against how we understand and interpret the way the world opens up to us, what the things within it are, and what we can do while we are here. Granted, such moments can rise up suddenly and just as quickly fall silent, without so much as an echo in our lives. But each such moment is a call, an appeal to confrontation with unconcealment. Even the tiniest incident or observation can precipitate a *polemos* that transforms one's world.

From the moment of breakdown, even in otherwise everyday routines, to avoid falling into complete despair and *aporia*, one must envision an alternative and then implement that alternative in one's lived existence, even if that implementation is incomplete. It is never enough to envision some alternative in theory (preconstruction); one must *implement* it by reintegrating the invention into the practice at-issue. This is the moment of reconstruction. It is where, as the expression goes, the rubber meets the road. The new dispensation must gain traction in a way that its meaning can make sense and take hold in the world as it is given, because we cannot create all meaning *ex nihilo*. This is how the *polemos* with the meaning of the world, in order to open a new pathway in it, comes into confrontation with the construal of the world as it is. Each creative act, even the most soaring revolutionary change, depends on its reconstruction, its reintegration, into the always-already subsisting context of a world of meaning, opened up to us in its unconcealment.

The new tool I have invented may fail to meet its purpose. Perhaps it is too heavy, or not heavy enough, or the materials I have chosen cannot bear the stress of the task. A new move in a sport—a new pitch in baseball, for example—must be tested in the field, and it may fail to challenge the batter. A new way of playing the guitar might fail to provide the flexibility needed to play many compositions, or it may fail to please the audience. A new rule for a game may fail to make it any more fun or fair. At the grander level, a revolution may fail to achieve even its most modest policy goals, let alone alter the whole habitus of human beings in society. Even if envisioned changes do work largely as hoped, the historicity of human-being, the ever-fraying nature of our inhabiting a meaningful world, will mean that another breakdown, another irruption of unmeaning, will arise and that we must renter the polemical circle again.

Here a respect for truth has its place in the more mundane, ontic sense (again, *alētheia*-3). For empirical truth to play a role in the polemical cycle, we do not have to settle the grand metaphysical question of whether facts are real as such or if they are always mediated in their meaning for us as conceptual constructs. What matters is that in any given way of meaningfully construing the world, the vast preponderance of elements is simply not up to us. Human innovation cannot be creation *ex nihilo* because the world of meaning—the historical world within which we enter the cycle of construal by breaking with the past, envisioning some alternative, and then implementing it through reconstruction—is what provides the context for innovation. At most, our confrontation with a given world of meaning can prepare us and even spark the emergence of a transformed world of meaning. But as inworldly beings, this is never something we can control.

The polemical process of reconstruction can allow us to discern the difference between a delusional ideation and one that can approximatively realize a newly envisioned meaning that is genuinely visionary rather than merely fanciful. Facts and truth in the conventional sense matter. This should not surprise us, but philosophers sometimes forget. To draw from Heidegger, there is an earthiness to the world of meaning: "World grounds itself upon earth, and earth protrudes into world" (GA 5: 35). Any world of meaning depends upon a given sense of the things that we did not make and cannot completely remake; at the same time, the giving keeps happening, jutting up unexpectedly into our experience and understanding, unsettling the world of meaning as it is, either bringing it down or opening it up to new constellations of meaning. In the *polemos* with any given meaning of things, the earthiness of the world offers a resistance to our attempts at reinterpreting it, not just conceptually but also actually, in implementation. A hammer made of papier-mâché will not function well as a hammer—unless it is a prop in a play. To throw a pitch using just thumb and index finger is unlikely to work in a baseball game—unless it is a burlesque. To play an electric guitar at a folk concert in 1965 is unlikely to go over well with the audience—even if you happen to be Bob Dylan. To make it a rule in bridge that you may play your hand only after setting your cards on fire is unlikely to make the game more fun or fair—unless you are at a party with surrealist artists. A revolution with aspirations that stretch human nature past its limits is unlikely to succeed—unless the goal of revolution is *Götterdämmerung*.

There is a dialectic, a dialogue, to the process of reintegrative reconstruction that keeps the helicoidal cycle of the *polemos* in motion. To take another familiar example, consider the history of the introduction of the three-point shot in basketball. For much of its early history, scoring a basket in gameplay, rather than by a penalty shot, awarded the team two points. Slowly, it dawned on many in the sport that awarding three points to successful baskets shot from a designated arc of distance from the net would improve the game, because it would allow players of differing skills and attributes to score in different ways with different techniques, and it would improve the pacing of the game by allowing quicker turn-arounds and scoring attempts. Some colleges made experiments with the rule in the 1940s and 1950s. The American Basketball Association adopted the rule in the 1960s, and the rest of the world followed by the 1980s. But the *calibration* of the rule continues even now, with different diameters of distance for different leagues, skill levels, and genders. The argument for the rule change was based on the insight of some that there was something *at-issue* in the game, something in breakdown, that was preventing the game from being its best. Advocates envisioned a rule change that would address what was at-issue, and then had to convince others to apprehend the problem and to accept their solution. Then, officials and coaches had to implement that rule change. In the process of reconstructing the meaning of the game while integrating that change, they have had to calibrate the rule-change to different contexts, because these contexts confronted them with successes and failures for what is at-issue for different constituencies of players, audiences, coaches, team owners, sporting events, and so on. The material dialogue is not just with the human beings involved in the game about what the game is about, it is also a dialogue with the physical facts of the game—what the court design is, the physics of making a shot, the physiognomy of players (by age, gender, and skill level) in different leagues of play, and so on again.[14]

Much the same happens in the dialectical process of philosophy. The moment of wonder exposes something at-issue in the world that seems worthy of thought. The thinker then construes what is at-issue in the form of a question that can be addressed intelligibly, based on existing understanding, but that may also potentially transform that understanding. The thinker then responds to the question with an answer that is as rigorous and systematic as the subject requires. Even then, no serious philosopher would consider the work done, because now come the critiques and responses and revisions and retractions. The polemical circle reiterates the moment of wonder in which what is at-issue arises *exaiphnēs* in unexpected ways and presses ever again for response.

Any philosophical argument that envisions an alternative way of making sense of things, as preconstruction before the enactment of reconstruction, is a standing challenge to reenter the *polemos* of thinking, dialogue, and reformulation of argument. The argument itself provides the material invitation for further deconstruction, revisioning, and reconstruction of itself, all guided by what is at-issue. In fact, much the same happens in any human endeavor of interpretation and reinterpretation, because no extant understanding stands forever against the fraying of meaning by unmeaning and the subsequent call to respond. It happens in all domains of design, for example, from mechanical to architectural to sartorial, as the fashions and the facts demand an adaptive response. It happens in lawmaking, when the public and legislators come to realize that there is something at-issue in existing statutes or the constitution itself that needs amending in light of changing circumstances (such as traffic laws to account for cell phone use while driving) or an ideal not yet realized in the fundamental principles of the polity (such as a constitutional amendment to end slavery or to grant women the vote). Reconstruction is how the polemical cycle keeps itself honest by bringing the ideal into confrontation with the real. The rigors and discoveries of an ongoing zetetic struggle is the only healing available to us. If engaged properly, with Socratic piety, it opens us up to the wonders and discoveries of life rather than to the anxieties and traumas that the inevitable dislocations of meaning would otherwise bring.

NOTES

1. Wisława Szymborska, *Poems New and Collected*, 128.

2. Bloom is particularly good on the meaning of the body, although my account here of the body as cave would moderate the conclusions he draws; see especially *The Republic of Plato*, 362–64.

3. With respect for *Our Bodies, Ourselves*, originally published in 1970 by the Boston Women's Health Book Collective, which had such an important impact on the understanding and the politics of embodiment and gender.

4. Watkins, *Dictionary of Indo-European Roots*, 20.

5. See Thomas Nagel, *The View from Nowhere*, especially chapter 11, section 2.

6. Cf. Bloom, "Interpretive Essay," 307–10.

7. See Kant, *Critique of Pure Reason*, B383–84. Kant also takes Plato's *Republic* as itself an example of an idea of reason, in this case, of freedom (B372–73); other examples include virtue (B371–72), plants, animals, humanity, and even the cosmos (B374).

8. "Book V is preposterous, and Socrates expects it to be ridiculed"; Bloom, "Interpretive Essay," 380. Cf. Strauss, *The City and Man*, 61–62.

9. For a subtle reading of the intentionally dialectical structure of the *Republic* taken as a whole, see Roochnik, *Beautiful City*.

10. Cohen, *Kants Theorie der Erfahrung*, 12. I am also indebted to Lucas Fain's as yet unpublished paper, "Plato after Marburg: Rethinking Forms and Ideas through the Inspiration of Hermann Cohen," which takes up Cohen's salutary distinction between *eidos* and *idea* but argues that "*idea* asks a question to which *eidos* gives a response."

11. For a rich, meticulous treatment of this theme, see Patrick Byrne, *The Ethics of Discernment*, especially chapter 1, Discernment and Self-Appropriation.

12. See Bloom, *The Republic of Plato*, 440–41n3.

13. For a plausible account of the connection between the historical Socrates and Aspasia and the speech of the Platonic Socrates about Diotima's teaching about love in the *Symposium*, see Armand D'Angour, *Socrates in Love: The Making of a Philosopher*.

14. For the early development of basketball's rules, see the book by the inventor of the game: James Naismith, *Basketball: Its Origin and Development*; for the modern history, see W. G. Mokray, L. W. Donald, et al., "Basketball," *Encyclopaedia Britannica*.

Chapter Seven

At the Crossroads of the Cave

'

You must see the infinite, *i.e.* the universal in your particular or it is only gossip. Did I ever remark to you that philosophy after its flights ends in a return to gossip? It goes ahead and formulates as far as it can the laws of the cosmos, but it ends in the purely empirical fact that the cosmos is this and not otherwise—an unrelated, unexplained datum, which is gossip and nothing else.

—Oliver Wendell Holmes to Harold Laski, 1926[1]

Heidegger's critique of Plato implies that Plato has no sense of the historicity of human-being and that time plays no role for Plato in the way meaning is constituted for human beings—at least, not time in Heidegger's ontological sense as the horizon of Being. Ontological temporality entails the embedded, projective historicity of being-human that establishes a meaningful world. To employ a contrast that Heidegger would not himself use, this would make Plato an inheritor of Parmenides, who, in the prevailing interpretation, argued that being is one, eternal, and unchanging; rather than Heraclitus, who argued that all being is plural, impermanent, and in flux. But is this characterization of Plato's neglect of the temporal historicity of human beings true? Because if not, then Plato might well offer a way to understand how to mediate our historical situatedness and the call to transcendence. The intersection of the two pathways, the lateral and the upward, is the place to inquire further. The logic of situated transcendence works its way out at the crossroads of these paths.

7.1 THE LATERAL PATH

As we have seen, Socrates describes the travelers on the lateral pathway, the ones who carry objects that end up getting projected on the cave wall, as "passers-by" (*pariontōn*, 515b). Passing-by is a temporal activity, and a pathway implies temporal transition and trajectory. Unlike the prisoners in the cave, the passers-by are not locked in place. They have a degree of freedom of movement, constrained by the bounds of the pathway's contours. Presumably they could leave the lateral pathway, either by descending into the lower cave or by ascending the upward pathway, but it does not seem to occur to them to do so. Also, unlike actual puppeteers, the passers-by do not seem aware that they are projecting images to the cave-dwellers, whom they also seem not to notice. Socrates says that every now and then, "one of the passers-by happens to utter a sound" (515b, tm), which the prisoners interpret as coming from the shadows they see on the wall. What do these features of the allegory *mean* beyond the tale itself?

One clue is that while the comings and goings of the shadows may be somewhat haphazard, they are not simply random. Socrates suggests this when he says that among the cave-dwellers, there might be "honors, praises, and prizes for the man who is sharpest at making out the things that go by, and most remembers which of them are accustomed to pass before, which after, and which at the same time as others, and who is thereby most able to divine what is going to come" (516c–d). There seem to be temporal patterns in movements of the objects carried and then projected on the cave wall, almost as if there were regular transports of statues, furniture, and other goods along the lateral pathway. But what does this mean about our lived reality, if the cave-dwellers are, as Socrates says, "like us"?

The shadows correspond to how we interpret beings as we do, given our bonds to prevailing, given opinion about both things and norms. The objects carried by the passers-by would then correspond, in the Allegory, to actual things themselves. The shadows of the artifacts being carried are *projected*, thrown forward, to the prisoners, as if the cave were a primitive movie theater, with Plato as the first cinematographer of our imagination as readers. The prisoners interpret these projections according to the understanding they have as formed by their particular cave of received opinion. At issue here is the *qualified arbitrariness* of this received opinion. Each cave has its cultural norms for making sense of sociality, as well as its traditions for making sense of the physical reality of the nonhuman world. While not simply random, these understandings are *historically contingent*. They are largely the result of historical accidents that often do follow patterns but are not governed by some overarching intention or providential history, in the more literal sense of a Providence that sees ahead and plans accordingly and intentionally. Again, Socrates gives no indication that the passers-by are aware of how the fire casts shadows of what they carry or, more significantly, of the effect their passing-by and the projected shadows has on the cave-dwelling prisoners.

Two things in this depiction deserve immediate attention. What do things that the passers-by carry signify, and what does it mean that the passers-by have no awareness of their impact upon the prisoners? Socrates says the passers-by carry "artifacts . . . and statues of men and other animals wrought from stone, wood, and every kind of material" (524c–515a). The Greek word used here for the things carried is *skeuē*, which Bloom properly renders as "artifacts," but which has a broad range of meanings, including: vessel, implement, accoutrements, equipment, baggage. Most broadly, then, what they carry is *stuff*, but this stuff is all human artifacts such as "statues of men and other animals." What is common to all of this stuff is that it is the product of human making—in Greek, *poiēsis*. The artifacts are not all statues and other representational objects, although Socrates does single out statues as a prime example of *skeuē*, perhaps because they are so obviously the workings of human artifice. So, the passers-by do not carry things themselves, the *auta eikeina* as the products of nature, *phusis*. The decisive question is why they do not carry natural objects, such as animals or plants or stones, but only artifactual constructs of them (see Figure 7.1).

Concerning "the things that are carried by" (*parapheromenōn*), Socrates asks, "If [the prisoners] were able to discuss things with one another, don't you believe they would hold that they are naming these things going by before them that they see?" (515b).[2] The prisoners name (*onomazein*) the shadows that they see passing by, and the verb here for "they would hold" is *nomizein*, which is related to *nomos*: norm, custom, convention, or law. It therefore can also mean to adopt as a custom, to enact as a rule, and, as we would say, to coin, both in the literal and figurative sense that a 'coinage' can mean establishing something—a kind of metal, a type of shell, a specially printed piece of paper—as the customary currency for commerce. It can also mean fashioning a new word as valid currency for the exchange that takes place in language. This is why Hermes was the god of travelers, merchants, and messengers as well as translators and interpreters, and from whom we have our word, *hermeneutics*, the study of the making and communicating of meaning. Hermes was also the god of thieves, who conduct their own form of commerce both within and against a system of rules. Similarly, coining a new word both works within a language and appropriates elements of it against customary usage, but also reintegrates the new word with that usage, if the 'theft' is successfully laundered in the commerce of language.

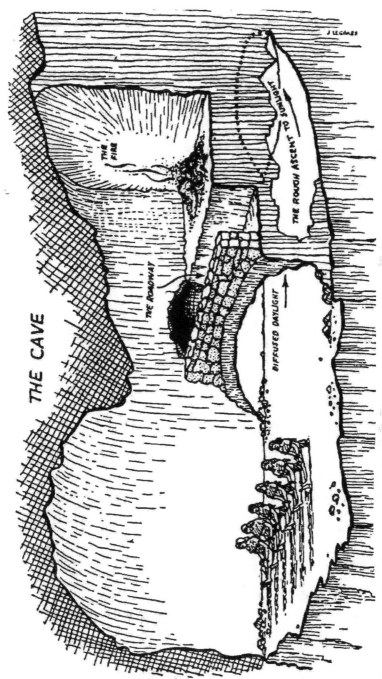

Figure 7.1. The Cave, from Rouse, *Great Dialogues of Plato*. Illustration by J. Legakes, courtesy of Penguin Random House.

The prisoners forge a meaningful world by naming the shadows, which allows them to delineate them, identify them, remember them, and communicate about them. Naming, then, is a form of *poiēsis*, poetry in its most elemental sense as a making that makes up a meaningful world by making it intelligible and communicable in language. This is as ancient an insight as Adam naming the animals that God parades before him after creating him last (Genesis 2:19). Although such naming is organic and necessary to the life of the cave as community, it is nevertheless a *skeuē* itself, an *artificial* imposition of *nomos*, custom or convention, upon *phusis*, nature, that may very well distort and misapprehend what is. The artifice of naming is never simply delusional, though, because in the integration of the Divided Line and the Cave, the apprehension and comprehension of shadows and images is not divorced from things or beings, *ta onta*. The shadow is still a shadow *of* something, even if the prisoners "would hold [*nomizoien*] that the truth is nothing other than the shadows of artificial things [*skeuastōn skias*]" (515c).

7.2 ARTIFACTS AND UNINTENTIONAL *POIĒSIS*

This brings us back to why Socrates says the passers-by on the lateral road carry artificial and not natural things, because this is clearly not an oversight or accident on his part, nor on Plato's. All human *hermeneuein*, all of our understanding, interpretation, communication, and translation of things and experience and action is necessarily mediated by the *poiēsis* of historical language. We do not have immediate access, as historical beings, to the things themselves, and when we endeavor to communicate our understanding as individuals, we also cannot provide immediate access to others of the my-ownness-ness of that experience and understanding of things. No word is simply a substitute for the thing itself, even if we must rely on words to mediate, always pro-visionally, the meaning of things. Instead, both our individual understandings and our discourse with others is mediated, primarily and for the most part, by how things are named and presented to us by contingent human *artifice*. Our predecessors handed down such meaning-making artifacts (which include practices as well as things) often unintentionally as they engaged in the most fundamental form of *poiēsis*, the poetry of language that named and secured such innovations in the nexus of historical meaning. They endeavored, as now we in turn take up that endeavor, to 'make sense' of a historical world. All language and representation as sense-making is broadly poetic, and words themselves are *skeuē*, artifacts borne and projected to us in the passing-by of a particular linguistic community's history that provide form and conceptual intelligibility to the manifold and shared experiences within that community. To the extent that we are born and borne into a world of meaning, thrown into it as a given matrix of received opinions and under-standings, language is the inherited artifice that mediates that world.

This is the meaning of the *projection* of the artifacts, casting shadows thrown by the fire against the lowest cave wall. Historical *poiēsis* in language as the *logos*, as the construal of meaning in the broadest sense of making a world intelligible, is *cast forward* in the traditional practices and received opinions of a linguistic community. The passers-by on the lateral path carry artifacts because human tradition does not convey and project historically the things themselves but rather how those things have been mediated intergen-erationally in the formations and mutations of language, technological prac-tices, and social customs, seen in this broad sense as poetic sense-making. After all, in the Cave parable, the supposedly actual things reside not on the lateral pathway but outside, in the light of day. As is frequently the case in the inherited traditions of a community, actors who establish lasting conven-tions and practices and then secure them in language often do not realize at the time that they are doing so, just as the passers-by on the lateral path do not realize the effect they are having on the prisoners. Actors whose acts be-come historical in this sense are usually responding to the exigencies of the moment, without any particular intent to pass along a new custom. The ser-endipitous poetry of their success, call it unintentional or spontaneous *poiēsis*, that establishes the meaning of new words, works, practices, and institutions. For an everyday example of such sedimentation of meaning and practice in language, consider the residue of both Norman French (Latinate) and Saxon terminology in legal documents, such as when we "devise and bequeath" an estate in a will, where "devise" derives from the Norman, meaning to bestow real property, and "bequeath," from the Old English, to grant personal prop-erty. We understand this expression's oddness in this specific sedimented usage, even though we rarely use these words in this archaic way in any other context in ordinary language.[3]

This point draws inspiration from the concept of *sedimentation* in Hus-serl's later work. There, sedimentation is a name for the process of how in-novations of any kind—in language, social practices, concepts, tool-making, and so on—accrue in layers over time and become part of the background understanding for how both individuals and entire cultures operate in a meaningful historical world. Each new layer of sedimentation enables more complex structures to emerge. As Dermot Moran and Joseph Cohen have explained, the development of sedimented techniques for playing the guitar, for example, form the basis for playing ever more naturally and fluently. Similarly, in learning a language, the original acquisition of habits falls into the background of the activity and becomes largely unconscious as one incrementally improves. Otherwise, the activity itself would be impossible, like trying to skate or run by intently remembering how to flex each muscle and make each movement. One would simply fall. At the societal level, practices, concepts, language, and, most importantly, society-organizing goals, says Husserl,

> live on in sedimented forms yet can be reawakened again and again and, in their new vitality, [can] be criticized; this manner of inquiring back into the ways in which surviving goals repeatedly bring with them ever new attempts to reach new goals, whose unsatisfactory character again and again necessitates their clarification, their improvement, their more or less radical reshaping.[4]

This is another way of describing the de-, pre-, and reconstructive construal of meaning, which depends on the prior sedimentation of meaning. 'Sedimentation' fits well with the metaphor of earth as the ground for the openness of world. 'Sediment' is itself earthy, accumulating in layers of practices and language upon which a meaningful world is grounded. But we can *delve* into this layered earth, even if we cannot unearth it entirely, for otherwise it would be the strip-mining of a tradition that leaves no lived practice behind. Delving may unearth strange things caught in sediments of a shared history, the fossils of linguistic and cultural practices that shaped the conceptual schemes of our modern selves. The deeper we delve, the more challenging it is to bring this background—or *underground*—to light. We can endeavor to do this by making ourselves aware of personal or societal assumptions and habits, then critically engaging and reformulating them, all in terms of the goals we set for living and thinking well. Those goals necessarily follow from an implicit or explicit conception of the good, for self or society. This is why Husserl says that "all prejudices are obscurities arising out of a sedimentation of tradition" that we can never unearth totally, because situated life always depends on a ground of habituated practices and opinions that recede into the background of awareness.[5] Nevertheless, it remains the duty of every thinker and every ethical actor ever-again "to carry out a *responsible critique,* a peculiar sort of critique which has its ground in these historical, personal projects, partial fulfillments, and exchanges of criticism rather than in what is privately taken for granted by the present philosopher."[6]

7.3 HISTORICITY AND THE CROSSING OF THE PATHWAYS

In his interpretation of the *Republic*, Allan Bloom depicts the founders of cities as deliberately and comprehensively responsible for the details of ethical, institutional, cultural, and material life: "Legislators and poets are the makers of these horizons; or, to use the symbols of the cave image, they are the men who carry the statues and the other things the reflections of which the prisoners see. These objects are not natural; they are themselves images of natural objects produced with cunning art so as to look like their originals, but are adapted to serve the special interests of the artists."[7] This is the portrait we get from Plutarch of figures like Lycurgus, who, as lore would have it, deliberately and with careful intentionality reconstituted the customs and institutions of Sparta in a comprehensive way, including property division, marriage and sexual relations, education and military training, music, clothing, political institutions, dining and food, and even rules for how to craft the woodwork on homes so that it would be as functional and unpretentious as possible. The deliberately intentional and comprehensive (even totalitarian) influence of a founder like Lycurgus does occasionally intervene in human history, but this is quite rare and not how the texture of meaning usually arises and endures in human communities, due to human finitude and the accompanying slippage of meaning. Even Lycurgus, according to legend, did not create his customs from scratch, but first traveled Greece seeking models and grafted these onto existing traditions in Sparta.[8] Bloom's depiction of the passersby as always the deliberate manipulators of the projected shadows gives the lawgivers and the poets of custom, language, and belief too much credit for an ability to create and manage opinion both comprehensively and from scratch. It also neglects the fact that much of the development of concepts, language, and tradition is unintentional and haphazard. Most importantly, it obscures the ontological point that the Divided Line is a continuum and that the shadows are still shadows *of* things themselves, not simply illusions. The shadows can grant access to what transcends them, and natural things exercise constraints on how the artifacts, as representations, can be fashioned, and so how the shadows can be projected.

The conception of the absolute creator-founder is partly justified, though, by Socrates's insistence that the founders of Kallipolis would exercise an absolute censorship over music, which Socrates explicitly understands in its largest sense to include not just what we think of as music, but *every* artifact and artifice of human *poiēsis*. Socrates indicates that not just the songs we hear and sing, not just the stories that inspire us the most, but also the *musikē* of everyday artifacts can have a profound effect on how we are attuned to the meanings of a shared existence. He asks:

> Must we, then, supervise only the poets and compel them to impress the image of the good disposition [*tēn tou agathou eikona ethous*] on their poems or not to make them among us? Or must we also supervise the other craftsmen

[*dēmiourgois*] and prevent them from impressing this bad disposition, a licentious, illiberal, and graceless one, either on images of animals or on buildings or on anything else that their craft produces? Mustn't we . . . look for those craftsmen whose good natural endowments make them able to track down the nature of what is fine and graceful, so that the young, dwelling as it were in a healthy place, will be benefited by everything; and from that place something of the fine works will strike their vision or their hearing, like a breeze bringing health from good places; and beginning in childhood, it will, unawares, with fair speech lead them to likeness and friendship as well as accord? (401b; tm)

The music of everyday artifacts, from clothing to public buildings to the implements we eat with, attunes us "unawares" to the norms and meanings of an *ēthos*, an interwoven text of significations that binds the understanding to a way of life and expectations of behavior. Hence, Socrates's famous pronouncement that "a change to a new kind of musical training is something to beware of as wholly dangerous. For one can never change the ways of training people in music without affecting the greatest political laws" (424c). In American history, perhaps there is no better illustration of this than the 1960s, when profound shifts in musical tastes accompanied equally profound shifts in dress, sexuality, gender roles, politics, and many other aspects of social and cultural life.

This is how history is present in the cave: as the contingent but not purely random source of the particular constellation of meaning of a human society, its being-a-world. As human-beings, we always already find ourselves *situated* in a particular nexus of historical meaning whose totality can never be fully planned in advance. We can also call this *happenstance*: we always happen to find ourselves standing *in situ*, situated in a site of presumptive meaning that grounds the involvements of our everyday going-about-our-business. Our location, our standing, in a particular concatenation of the nexus of history provides us with the horizon and landmarks of meaning by which we orient our individual lives. The history of our individual and collective happenstance is contingent, but it nevertheless projects, as it were, over the wall that separates us from an intimate familiarity with how the sedimentation of generations of historical practices supplies us with the patterns of meaning by which we cobble together a meaningful world. That dividing wall (*teichion*, 514b) over which meaning projects is the barrier between the present and the past, which is a natural barrier in one sense, because ontically we cannot time-travel. It is also an ontological-hermeneutical barrier that being-human artificially erects to conceal the nature of what transpires behind it along the lateral pathway. The construct of the barrier-wall prevents us from being overwhelmed all the time by the past and by the realization of the continency of our historicity; but ontologically, it is not an impermeable barrier, as time's arrow is for us ontically in the physical universe: some can escape to climb over it to confront what happens in the background to history.

Hubert Dreyfus, one of Heidegger's most influential readers, described this attunement to the music of meaning as the *background practices* of our being-in-the-world.[9] The practices that inform the meaning of our existence, in the practical sense of granting access to the significance of things, activities, and even concepts, lie in the *background* because we can never fully get behind them; they quite literally *in-form* the intelligibility that makes any inquiry possible in the first place. To be human is to be subject to and product of a formation of the understanding that happens "unawares," as the cumulative effect of generations of meaning-making shared practices. We all are musical; we are attuned to and entranced by the rhythms of meaning and action that define the sedimented reception and interaction of personal and cultural practice. Even a founder as profoundly innovative as Lycurgus must rely upon a vast, pre-existing weave-work of intelligibility—linguistic, institutional, technological—to implement changes that, while transformative, are small compared to this always-already comprehensive attunement to practices. This sedimentation informs our understanding unawares through the cumulative influence of a history of unintended, spontaneous, innovative acts that project over the wall of time separating us from the past. This is a wall we ordinarily do not see behind and often are unaware of in our everyday activity, like the *techion* separating the prisoners from the lateral path, with our attention glued to the images of meaning projected before us in the world we habitually inhabit.

Remarkably, in the geography of the cave the lateral and the upward pathways *intersect*. While Socrates does not explicitly say this, the logic of the cave's geography implies it. If they did not cross, then the seeker for truth who emerges from the cave would not have a full understanding of how each 'station' of the cave integrates within the whole of the truth revealed by the journey. That is why an illustration of the cave such as the one found in the edition of the Platonic dialogues by W. H. D. Rouse cannot be right (Figure 7.1: The Cave, from *Great Dialogues of Plato*).[10]

In this illustration, the lateral "roadway" before the fire and the "rough ascent" do not meet up at all. The latter passes under the former. This does not conform *narratively* with the Allegory, because Socrates describes the escaping prisoner as encountering the fire. On my interpretation, that encounter is symbolically important because if philosophical understanding must become familiar with and integrate all levels of the Divided Line and the cave as the world of human habitation, as illustrated in Figure 4, it cannot simply bypass the fire and the lateral pathway. It is a feature of the proper pedagogy of the cave, as well as of that pedagogy's potential failure, that the liberated can only rise to the light of day by first confronting and making provisional sense of the fire and lateral pathway, only then returning to inhabit and rule the cave by encountering them again in the light of the greater understanding won by ascending the upward path.

The two paths must therefore intersect precisely at the point where the lateral road passes between the fire in the cave and the wall blocking the lateral pathway and the fire from the view of the prisoners. Although Socrates does not describe how this happens, if the cave-dweller who escapes the bonds is to make any progress to a fuller liberation, she or he must first get past the wall, arrive at the lateral pathway, and encounter and make sense of the fire. Socrates says that while the newly released prisoner would now be "somewhat nearer to what *is*," to Being (*nun de mallon ti eggutero tou ontos*, 515d2–3), this liberated cave-dweller would still be in pain and dazzled by the fire until his or her eyes adjusted to its light. Only then would the freed prisoner begin to understand the relation of fire and light, objects and projection.

I suggest that this initial adjusting of the eyes to the fire is the dawning of historical consciousness: the realization that ways of understanding, both of ethical norms and of the world itself, are historical; that our opinions, our *ideology* (in the sense of an integrated whole of opinions), are to some significant extent historically contingent. For Heidegger, they must be *entirely* historical if there are no transcendent ideas that apply universally. The escaped prisoner may grasp this at the level of the fire burning above and beyond the lateral pathway. This is what authenticity (*Eigentlichkeit*) means for Heidegger; it is a moment when one recognizes the entirely groundless contingency of the everyday meaning of the world one inhabits. Confronting the existential anxiety provoked by this realization of historical contingency, authenticity entails being able to return to and embrace that world through revitalized interpretations, realizing meanings implicit but previously unrealized in one's given existence. The fundamental difference between Heidegger's view and my own is this: I believe Plato's teaching that without the intimation and ideation of the ideas, the polemical cycle of de-, pre-, reconstruction would be unhinged from the genuine phenomena of human ethical life and the practical wisdom needed to guide it.

7.4 SOPHISTRY AND PHILOSOPHY AT THE CROSSROADS OF THE CAVE

What Socrates does not directly say here, but what may plausibly be extrapolated from other passages in the *Republic*, is that this crossroads is the place where a sophist may set up shop. In Book 6, Socrates responds to Adeimantus's challenge that philosophers are either useless or vicious: *achrēstous*, without profit, or *pamponerous*, utterly depraved (486d). Adeimantus seems to have in mind either pasty intellectuals, such as the hapless denizens of the Thinkery in Aristophanes's *Clouds*, or malignant subversives, such as Thrasymachus or perhaps Unjust Speech in the *Clouds*, who would undermine wholesome traditional beliefs and practices in order to make a profit, justify their vices, or seek power. This is consistent with our previous discussions of the two poles of the more jaded Athenian perception of philosophers: the laughably eccentric, such as Euthyphro, and the genuinely dangerous, such as Socrates himself, accused of impiety and corrupting the youth. In reply, Socrates lays the blame not on genuine philosophy as such, but on the community that does not know either how to recognize it or how to cultivate it. True philosophers appear useless only to those who do not understand things well enough themselves to discern what proper knowledge looks like or how to wield it. Communities of this sort are like ignorant sailors on a ship who cannot grasp the knowledge of astronomy necessary for navigation, and who would ignore the recommendations of a true pilot as unintelligible (488a–489c).

But it is the vicious who are most significant for our purposes, because Socrates associates them with the sophists as the ones with the most pernicious effect on the young and on society as a whole. As we have seen, Socrates describes the sophist as a failed or corrupted almost-philosopher, someone who has all or most of the qualities of mind and character that would make for a genuine philosopher. Such a person, says Socrates, is exceedingly rare (491a–b), because the qualities required are so unusual: they must be erotic in the sense of utterly longing for learning, for the truth, and for what *is* (485b–c); they must be self-controlled, forsaking pleasures of the body and other distractions for the sake of learning (485d) and not overly concerned with money (485e); they must be courageous, not petty but instead magnanimous in their aspirations, able to endure adversity, not even fearing death (486a–b); they must also be fast learners with good memory, given the rigors of their search (486c–d); finally, they must be graceful and charming, able to attend to the music of inspiration and thereby led "easily to the *idea* of each thing that itself is" (485d), but also so that they can communicate effectively with the inhabitants of the cave when returning to lead them.

Socrates then says, "What is most surprising of all to hear is that each one of the elements we praised in that nature has a part in destroying the soul that has them and tearing it away from philosophy"—and here he means not only the features just enumerated but also all the virtues—"And what's more besides these, all the things said to be good corrupt it"—that is, the soul of the potential philosopher—"and tear it away—beauty, wealth, strength of body, relatives who are powerful in the city, and everything akin to these" (491b). Here, Socrates is speaking directly to and about the most promising youth of Athens, such as Glaucon and Adeimantus, and perhaps even more so Alcibiades, who had generous endowments of mind combined with all the privileges of birth, wealth, beauty, health, vigor, education, and connections to power. The danger is that "the best nature comes off worse than an ordinary one from an inappropriate rearing" and that "the best natures become exceptionally bad when they get bad instruction" (491d–e). Everything, therefore, depends on the careful and proper *cultivation* of this exceptional potential, because such rearing does not happen by accident, "unless one of the gods chances to assist" (492a). Socrates asks whether it is even worth mentioning, because so obvious, that "certain young men are corrupted by sophists"—as the youths gathered there in Cephalus's home might have been by Thrasymachus before Socrates's intervention (492a–b).

But at this point, Socrates says something even more perplexing to Adeimantus: that it is not the professional sophists who are the greatest threat, but rather the public, when it gathers "in assemblies, courts, theaters, army camps, or any other common meeting of a multitude" (492b). The multitude deflects attention from its own pernicious influence on the promising young by condemning the individual sophists. Nevertheless, argues Socrates, it is the crowd, with its "great deal of uproar" of praise and blame, its "shouting and clapping" that rock the very stones of a gathering place, that can exert the greatest effect of sophistry on the young (492b–c). What, asks Socrates is "the state of the young man's heart" in such venues and events? "Or what kind of private education will hold out for him and not be swept away by such blame and praise and go, borne by the flood, wherever it tends so that he'll say the same things are noble and base as they do, practice what they practice, and be such as they are?" (492c). The allusion to the career of someone like Alcibiades is unmistakable.

Lest we imagine that this dynamic is an anachronism specific only to the direct democracy and relatively small population of ancient Athens, consider the effects today on the young, and not just the young, of attending a concert, megachurch, or sport event, political rally, with massive screens and sound systems projecting images and saturating the body with music, crowds roaring and swaying together. Or consider the mania for self-curation on Twitter, Facebook, or YouTube, with the craving for 'likes' and for the possibility of becoming 'an influencer' or the next internet sensation, perhaps garnering an invitation to the White House as the newest alt-news media star in a post-truth world.[11]

The greater sophist, then, is public opinion, which exerts a powerful gravitational pull, especially on the ambition and imagination of the young as they begin to find their way in the world. Socrates says that "each of these private wage earners whom these men"—that is, the public in its multitude—"call sophists and believe to be their rivals in art, educates in nothing other than these convictions [*dogmata*] of the many, which they opine when they are gathered together, and he [that is, the professional sophist as a private teacher] calls this wisdom" (493a). The skill of the private sophist is to understand and teach with great precision the disposition, opinions, and passions of the particular public that is dominant, as well as those of relevant sub-populations that play important roles in a particular community at a specific moment in its history. Then, says Socrates, it is like:

> [A] man who learns by heart the angers and desires of a great, strong beast he is rearing, how it should be approached and how taken hold of, when—and as a result of what—it becomes most difficult or most gentle, and, particularly, under what conditions it is accustomed to utter its several sounds, and, in turn, what sort of sounds uttered by another make it tame and angry (493a–b).

The community has its particular, historically contingent passions and convictions, and it will applaud or reject, perhaps violently, proposals, representations, and actions that confirm or conflict with these. By understanding such proclivities in detail, perhaps by using all the tools of modern social science, the sophist "calls it wisdom and, organizing it as an art, turns to teaching" (493b).

Nevertheless, the disposition of the multitude is not infinitely malleable. In fact, Socrates recognizes that sophistry depends on grasping what a phenomenologist would call the background practices of a people's ethos, its convictions and habits, just as the beast has its natural proclivities. What the sophist's expertise can teach is how to *manipulate* these proclivities. We see this all the time in our era: how Google and Facebook manage the personal data their users provide, usually inadvertently, to target advertising to those very users on both an aggregate and an individual level, or how firms such as Cambridge Analytica or the secret services of hostile nations can use such data to micro-target voter populations to attempt electoral manipulation or to compromise political figures.[12] These are just the recent egregious examples. Advertising and marketing firms have for decades used sophisticated methodologies, including neuropsychology, to understand and then corral consumers' purchasing behavior, just as social science can assist in learning, predicting, and interfering in the voting behavior of populations.[13] But such information tells marketers, public relations experts, political consultants, and advertisers nothing about what is good for people or for a community: "Knowing nothing in truth about which of these convictions and desires is noble, or base, or good, or evil, or just, or unjust, [the sophist] applies all these names following the great animal's opinions—calling what delights it good and what vexes it bad" (493b–c), all as part of the project of manipulation. This is how to win votes, ratings, 'likes,' and purchases. So, while unable to create the disposition of the public *ex nihilo*, the skilled sophist can present things in a way most likely to enthrall and thereby gently nudge public taste and public opinion in the desired direction. In extraordinary moments where the opportunity occurs for a new founder to reconfigure a radical departure in society—a "new prince," as Machiavelli would say—the sophist might be able to do more than just nudge. Even so, there is a kind of hermeneutical circle of desire, opinion, and action that begins with a historical people's most entrenched proclivities and convictions. The sophist must find the right way to engage these in order to nudge, to budge, or perhaps even to transform them in some revolutionary way.

The young potential-philosopher is therefore in a precarious position if deprived of the proper education, mentors, or companions. All of the magnificent aptitudes and virtues—being intelligent, charming, quick to learn, and so on—make such a person a promising target for "kinsmen and fellow citizens" who "will surely want to make use of him, when he is older, for their own affairs" (494b). As the promising youth enters adulthood—say, embarking on college and then graduate education in law or business—those who want to use his talents will "lie at his feet, begging and honoring him, taking possession of and flattering beforehand the power that is going to be his"; they will offer him, or her, loans, scholarships, internships, fellowships, then well-paying jobs with attractive bonuses, all to develop their skills in managing the beast, not for what is just or right or noble, but for what enhances power, prestige, and wealth. What will such a young man do, asks Socrates, "especially if he chances to be from a big city, is rich and noble in it, and is, further, good-looking and tall? Won't he be overflowing with unbounded hope, believing he will be competent to mind the business of both Greeks and barbarians"—like Alcibiades, again—"and won't he, as a result, exalt himself to the heights, mindlessly full of pretension and empty conceit?" (494c–d).

Now we must map this account of the descent into the viciousness of sophistry back onto the narrative of the cave. Where on the upward journey does this corruption transpire, and how?

We have seen in chapter 6 that the released prisoner first stumbles around in a daze, unable immediately to reconcile the shadows that she had previously always seen with the blinding light emanating from the fire. If she does not fall victim to nihilism or despair at this point, she might make her way up to the level of the lateral pathway, with the passers-by carrying artifacts, and to the fire itself. This, too, will be a traumatic dislocation, but the former prisoner may come to understand the relation between the fire, the artifacts, and the projection of the shadows, as well as how the bonds of the prisoners force them to see nothing but those shadows.

It is at this point, upon arrival at the lateral pathway and the fire, that the incipient philosopher faces the greatest temptation and most defining decision. At this delicate crossroads in life, Socrates says, the released wanderer might encounter a mentor who would "gently approach the young man in this condition and tell him the truth—that he has no intelligence in him [that is, no *nous*, no genuine insight and comprehension] although he needs it, and that it's not to be acquired except by slaving for its acquisition"; Socrates then asks, "do you think it will be easy for him to hear through a wall of so many evils?" (494d). The "evils" Socrates means are all the inducements of power, prestige, pleasure, and wealth the youth will be promised by society if he will only bend his prodigious talents and labors to the interests of those who already enjoy such things. The truth told by the gentle mentor is not easy to hear, in part because the mentor says that genuine insight will only be won by "slaving" for it. Translating this to the imagery of the Cave Allegory, this gentle admonition by the mentor would be a way of pointing out the opening to the "rough, steep, upward way" (515e) that leads away from the fire and the lateral path up to the light of day, where genuine insight is possible. The Greek here for "slaving" is *douleusanti*, a word directly related to the bonds, the *douloi*, that bind the prisoners in place at the lowest level of the cave (514a–b, 515c). For the newly escaped prisoner, embarking upon that upward path might sound like trading one form of bondage for another. The youth will have only just emerged from the original trauma of dislocation from habitation on the floor of the cave, which, as miserable as it might have been in retrospect was apparently stable—until it was not. Now, at the level of the fire and lateral path, the talented youth is offered a new stability and a new hold on power, both visible in the light of the fire. The opening to the upward path, by contrast, promises only more toil and instability. The youth will not actually *see* the light of day from this vantage point, the supposed insight promised by the gentle mentor, only the harshness of the ascent, lit up in its first stages by the fire through the opening to the upward path. The inducement to choose that path rather than to stay in place, in the comfort of the fire, might be weak indeed.

The mentor thus carries a great deal of the burden if the youth is to make the right decision. The mentor must convince the youth to trust that there is indeed light at the end of the upward tunnel. This involves successfully kindling that Socratic trust or faith in a transcendent truth. Socrates asks:

> But if, thanks to his good nature and his kinship to such speeches [namely, to the suggestions of a benevolent mentor that he lacks genuine insight "although

he needs it" (*detai de*, 494d)], one young man were to apprehend something and be turned and drawn toward philosophy, what do you suppose those will do who believe they are losing his use and comradeship? Is there any deed they won't do or any word they won't say, concerning him, so that he won't be persuaded, and concerning the man who's doing the persuading, so that he won't be able to persuade; and won't they organize private plots and public trials? (494d–e).

Plato's allusion here to the persecution and trial of Socrates himself is unmistakable.[14] If the mentor fails to teach the incipient philosopher diplomatically, so that the powers-that-be in the cave do not suspect or fear that they might be losing a talented future ally, the mentor and student will likely fall victim to persecution. The mentor must be a zetetic, like Socrates, whose skeptical idealism can persuade the incipient philosopher to embark up on the upward path, whose gentleness offers a supple, phronetic balance between a daring that verges on hubris (because willing to depart radically from received opinion) and a modesty that remains prudently aware of the limitations of human finitude and the indebtedness of understanding to received opinion. The mentor's persuasion must therefore consist in three things: convincing the youth that "he needs" to embark upwards; that there is some reason to hope that this need can be fulfilled, even if only in part; and that the departure from received opinion and norms must be handled with tact.

The need, the *detai*, is grounded in the verb *deō*, to need, to lack, to want, and is related to a cluster of words for what is required, what is fitting or proper (*dei*), from which we have *deontology*, an account of what we ought to do as a matter of duty. The young philosopher must be made phenomenologically aware that there is something lacking at the level of the fire, despite its apparent allures, and that an ethical and good life requires embarking on the upward path, despite its apparent toils. At the same time, the young philosopher must have some reason to believe that the search upward is not pointless, or else the endeavor will tumble back down into a deeper despair or nihilism from a still greater height than in the initial dislocation of the lower cave. The failed philosopher might then retreat to the inadequate but comfortably tangible inducements of the sophistic life at the level of the fire, which will seem to outweigh the empty promise of a supposedly transcendent alternative.

Here again we must avoid getting mired in the details of the Allegory, as if the logic of that narrative alone were enough to establish its truth. An allegory's power lies in how well it can goad us into examining and reexamining the phenomenon it is about. No allegory, just as nothing in language, can map the thing itself perfectly, but the most powerful uses of allegory and language push us to think all the more deeply about what does not fit. We must consider, then, how the prisoners are still "like us" if they ascend to the level of the fire, and why that situation is so precarious.

On the lateral path, the anonymous passers-by carrying artifacts are like the succession of generation upon generation of historical human beings. The smaller and greater innovations, usually quite unintentional and spontaneous, generated by these ancestors in language, technologies, institutions, norms, and cultural practices get projected—anonymously for the most part, in sedimented layer upon layer—onto the life-world of a particular historical community. This community is a specific 'cave' of bounded cultural meanings in which we are, at least at first, entirely immersed and bound up. The tact of the aspiring philosopher involves a recognition of how the historicity of meaning forms the bonds and bounds of a world that, however flawed, is home for those with whom she shares a community. Tactful empathy grasps that breakdowns of this meaning can be deeply traumatic, and so both the departure and return must be negotiated with care and compassion.

The fire itself as allegory is harder to understand. Socrates says it represents the sun (517b), but that hardly sheds light on what the fire represents in the production of historical understanding. It helps to think in terms of seeing *in the light* of fire: the projection of the *artifacts* against the cave wall would not happen without the light cast by the fire, an *artificial* light, compared to the sun, because it does not present the things themselves but rather how they are mediated by historical understanding. Each historical community, in order to function, must share in the construal of a meaningful world, for community requires communication. Those who dwell together must see together to be able to speak together, and their mutual needs form the basis of what matters to them *as* meaningful. The fire is the source and *condition* of the possibility of a shared intelligibility that can be projected communally and intergenerationally. The fire is the *eventuation* of shared meaning in a particular historical world, in the light of which the spontaneity of invention can adjust and pass down an evolving, temporal understanding.

As we have discussed above in our exploration of a broad definition of sophism, whoever comes to understand the mechanism of the production of historical meaning is in a position to wield considerable social and political power. Those who reach the level of the lateral path may gain this historical awareness. Instead of change and the projection of change in historical understanding within a community occurring by happenstance, as it generally does in the naive, pre-historical consciousness, they come to realize that what people see as real, as well as their opinions about that reality, while not infinitely malleable, is susceptible to manipulation. Existing concepts and constructs can be deconstructed and reconstructed with intention, and with a greater or lesser degree of formal methodology, in order to rearrange peoples' desiring, understanding, and interpreting.

As ancient religions have long recognized, human beings are profoundly vulnerable to the charms of the graven image. This is amply illustrated in our times by the pervasiveness of advertising of all kinds, commercial and political, the moving images of modern narratives in film and television, and the ubiquitous and profoundly addictive presence of handheld screens. The image is powerful because it can serve as a substitute for the thing itself, and also because it excites the power of the imagination in the individual. When presented with skill, images projected by the sophist can convince people that what they imagine is in fact a world they inhabit, and that because they have imagined it, it is their own creation, something they have freely chosen, rather than being a mere projection imposed on them by someone else. The most convincing tricks are the ones the tricked believe they have accomplished themselves. The sophist therefore incites the illusions of ideology, rather than the ideations of philosophy.

The sophist, in contrast to the philosopher, abandons himself to the power of the image. The sophist traffics back and forth over the wall and between the fire and the prisoners chained to the floor, rather than along the upward path. What the sophist traffics *in* are shadows and their projection. Although their ancestors mostly had no awareness of what they were projecting to their communities and descendants, like the passers-by on the lateral path, the sophist intentionally becomes a puppeteer, casting shadows and projecting images deliberately as a way of crafting historical understanding. The sophist understands the relation of fire, object, light, and the projection of shadows on the wall.

In short, the sophist understands the distinction between *phusis* and *nomos*, nature and convention. Just as Thrasymachus, for example, understands justice to be nothing more than the advantage of the stronger—defined as whatever ideology serves the interests of the ruling body that happens to hold power—so does the sophist more generally understand that opinions are contingent, historical constructs. The sophist is the puppeteer, the *thaumatopoios*, the wonder-worker who knows intimately the moods and opinions of the audience of cave dwellers, as well as what it is they *think* they see, and who can thereby manipulate them by doing deliberately and consciously what before had happened unawares: projecting images against the cave wall.

It is remarkable that the sophist shares to some degree in the *wonder* that also gives rise to philosophy. This is a further indication of the unitary phenomenon of questioning as liberation. Both the sophist and the philosopher originate from a breakdown in the received way of understanding the world, but the sophist gives up on ascending the upward path or sending others up along it, from wonder to wisdom, in favor of manipulating wonder for personal and political gain. As we have discussed, the sophist degrades wonder into a tool for domination in the spectacle of propaganda. At the most accomplished level of sophistication, the skilled sophist can do more than manipulate isolated elements within the confines of a population's existing desires and convictions. The arch-sophist becomes so adept at broadcasting shadows that she or he can reconfigure an entire ideology.

Propaganda as *technē*, as skillful mastery over images and shadows, is what fascinates the sophist, who falls in love with the power of ideas (in the conventional sense) to weave a world of meaning for a population, a meaning to be manipulated almost at will. Ideas and their historically situated efficacy can never be more than ideological tools for the sophist, who remains fixated at the level of the fire, obsessed with casting shadows over the wall and observing how the crowd of prisoners will react in order to refine the skills of projection. The sophist finds joy in the power of propaganda, not in truth as such. While the sophist takes up position on the lateral pathway where it passes by the fire and intersects with the upward pathway, she either does not notice that the upward path is there or scorns it as a "rough, steep upward way," hardly worth the bother. Or worse: he realizes that ascending the upward path might empower some to expose him, and so he might be tempted to wall it off altogether, to prevent escape from the cave.[15] Translating from the allegory, this walling-off would involve arguments, propaganda, threats, and inducements to convince anyone who might be tempted by the idea of transcendent ideas that such things are futile delusions and that the only thing that matters is what people can be made to believe is true. As Socrates says, the sophist cares nothing and knows nothing about which of the cave-dwellers' "convictions and desires is noble, or base, or good, or evil, or just, or unjust." These are all just labels of convenience to the sophist, for he does not believe in a noble, or a good, or a just in itself as independent ideas; he only believes in these things as constructs to be manipulated.

Marina McCoy, in her insightful study *Plato on the Rhetoric of Philosophers and Sophists*, makes a compelling case that, from the perspective of the cave-dwellers, there is no obvious difference between sophistry and philosophy. At-issue is whether a putative teacher is a mentor or manipulator. Plato does not distinguish between philosophers and sophists as using different technical methods. Eristic, arguing for the sake of winning the argument, can look much the same as dialectic, arguing for the sake of reaching the truth. The distinction lies in "differences in character and moral intention," as McCoy puts it, which is also what makes it so difficult to distinguish between the sophist and the philosopher in practice, because doing so requires acute skill and judgment in observing that intention in the speech and deed of the person in question, and presumably one would already have to be wise to do so. McCoy's argument about the sophist in the *Republic* "as an incomplete philosopher, skeptical of opinion (*doxa*), freed from the chains within the cave, but not yet oriented toward the forms" and therefore "the most dangerous sort of character in the city," supports the analysis here. Both sophist and philosopher, when engaged in civic life, employ rhetoric and argumentation at the crossroads in the cave, deliberately managing how the fire casts its shadows.[16]

The philosopher's recognition of the necessity of rhetoric is a recognition of the inevitability of human communal understanding as inflected by history and the fact that all rational accounts must also contend with the affective truth of human situatedness and embodiment. McCoy rightly argues that Thrasymachus is an ambiguous figure, for while he clearly seeks status, and probably employment, by promoting his immoralist view of justice, he does also seem to have what looks like a philosophical commitment to his position. He believes it to be true—and important because true.[17] On the interpretation of the crossroads of the cave, this would be Thrasymachus not having previously realized that there is the upward path leading out, which would explain why he would stay and listen after his humiliation by Socrates. His *eros* for knowledge wins out over love of honor and gain, allowing him to take that other path seriously, at least for the rest of that nightlong discussion. This suggests that even a quite cynical sophist may be redeemed by a highly effective and genuine mentor who can reignite both the liberation and the sense of wonder necessary for the hard work of ascending the upward path.

At the same time, this account suggests that the philosopher, who loves the truth for its own sake but who must return to the cave, must also find ways to present the truth in a form perhaps quite far removed from philosophy, such as myth and story, that can reach the cave's inhabitants. While this might seem to collapse philosophy into the deceptions and manipulations of sophistry, it is important to consider here what Richard Kearney, drawing on the work of Paul Ricoeur, discusses as the positive potential of *the social imaginary*. Against thinkers like Marx and Feuerbach who argue for a science of a social *truth* against the mystifications of legend, lore, and ideology as false consciousness, Kearney argues for a hermeneutics of a social *imaginary*, defined as comprising "the interplay of ideals, images, mythologies, and utopias informing our cultural and political unconscious. Here we are concerned with ways in which a poetics of imagination operates in our everyday lives, often anonymously, to produce collective narratives—stories we tell ourselves in order to explain ourselves to ourselves and to others." Those stories are open to the *polemos* of retelling, We see this now, in the debates over national founders, monuments, symbols, and even the names of sports teams in the United States. As we have discussed, no community can exist without this sedimented background of shared and largely unconscious meanings and practices. A social imaginary is a repository of a community's "myths, ideals, and rhetorics" that allow it to share a formative past and ideals of the future. But more than a repository, it is a treasury from which a community may draw, in politics most especially, for the founding stories that members must revisit and renew to maintain their unity and resilience as a community.[18]

The philosopher at the level of the fire also draws from this positive store-house of the social imaginary to reinterpret and reconstruct a community's way of seeing its history, itself, and its possible futures, all assuming some viable understanding of the good. The echonic philosopher would lay claim to total possession of the good as well as to the social truth of historical human beings, such as those who have claim to practice a genuine science of history that holds the hermeneutical key to unlock with finality the whole of meaning and to tell a story that would never need revision. The zetetic philosopher would have only intimations of truth and the good and so would depend, as do the rest of us, on the social imaginary for the historical narratives, symbols, and images that mediate the meaning of a shared world. At the fire, the zetetic would draw on this treasury to reconstruct the social imagination in ways that direct the people more towards the good, justice, and virtue, using practical wisdom to reimagine and revise stories and images as the situation requires. The sophist, by contrast, draws on false credit in order to manipulate the public for private or sectarian ends, depleting the treasury until the community's funds of imagination are exhausted by cynicism.

The question is how a genuinely philosophical mentor can induce someone to leave the light of the fire and attempt the difficult upward journey through, away from, and back to this social imaginary to engage constructively with it. This cannot be understood in terms of what Socrates says is the false view of education: that some echonic philosopher, in total possession of the truth, would simply pour learning into the mind of the student, like pouring water from a full jar into an empty cup, or, as Socrates says like "putting sight into blind eyes" (518b–c).[19] Rather, the zetetic philosopher, as mentor, must be able to model her own manner of truth-seeking and draw the student into the search. The crucial phrase in the passage cited above, where the student arrives at the crossroads of life between the lateral path and the upward path—between sophistry and philosophy and between cynical manipulation of images and trusting engagement with ideation—is that Socrates says that this departure upward can happen if a youth (or someone still young in mind) "were to apprehend something and be turned and drawn toward philosophy" (494e). The Greek here is instructive. What Bloom renders as "apprehend" is *eisaisthanētai*, to perceive, to understand, to 'get' something conceptually; "turned" is *kamptētai*, which can have an even stronger sense of bending dramatically, as when a charioteer pivots a horse team around a turning post in a race; "drawn" is *helkētai*, which also can have a more vivid sense of being dragged or pulled with force.

That last word is the same one that Socrates uses to describe the last stage of the prisoner's emerging from the cave, starting from the level of the lateral path and fire: "And if someone dragged [*helkoi*] him away from there by force along the rough steep upward way and didn't let him go before he had dragged him out into the light of the sun, wouldn't he be distressed and annoyed at being so dragged?" (515e–516a). As we have discussed, the difficulty and distress come from having one's opinions challenged through dialectic, which is not simply a threat to personal vanity but potentially to one's whole orientation to the world in what it has meant and how it has mattered. Presumably, anyone who has managed to get as far as the fire would have already come to terms with having their initial and naive opinions as a cave-dweller disrupted, perhaps traumatically, by the original release from the bonds. If they have accustomed themselves at the level of the fire to these disruptions of the social imaginary, they will have understood the relationship of history to the way opinion is projected over generations to establish norms. The task for the genuine mentor is to lead the potential philosopher away from the twin lures of historicist relativism and manipulative sophistry. Thrasymachus revealed himself to be a kind of cultural relativist about the nature of justice and power. As his case demonstrates, the opinions formed at this level of sophistication can arouse just as much passion, possessiveness, and defensiveness as those naive opinions of the prisoners still bound to the cave floor.

Socrates causes Thrasymachus considerable discomfort and humiliation in refuting his positions. Before giving up to Socrates, Thrasymachus sweats and blushes while being "dragged [*helkomenos*] with considerable effort" (350c–d; my translation) through the argument's dialectic. This introduces the same language of compulsion and resistance as in the Allegory for this stage of philosophical progress. But Thrasymachus becomes tame. He does not leave in a fit of wounded vanity but stays to listen, because Socrates has indeed rekindled his wonder for something more than the power of rhetoric and the wages or prestige it might provide.[20] This means that the potential philosopher, in order to embark upon the upward path, must do so voluntarily by *internalizing* the compulsion of the dialectic, by coming to feel at home with it as a zetetic seeker. The being *turned* here must be an expression of the existential freedom to choose a way of life. Otherwise, as Polemarchus suggests in a playful seriousness (327c), one could simply refuse to listen to the *logos* of dialectic. The *polemos* of dialectic with one's situated, received opinions or with one's more sophisticated 'theoretical' ones, must be free. It must sublate the compulsion and make its energy one's own.

What the skilled mentor does with dialectic is first to point out the entrance to the upward path, the opening to the possibility of something more than historical consciousness. Through dialectic with the mentor, this involves the incipient seeker's apprehending something, somehow (*eisaisthanētai pēi*, 494e), about his inadequacy and ignorance that opens him up to the possibility of this something more in philosophy. We see this happen through the debate with Thrasymachus, where, whatever we might think of the arguments Socrates uses to achieve his victory, he at least succeeds in showing the young people present that Thrasymachus's relativism about justice is not adequate to making sense of what it means to live a good life. It certainly happens with Glaucon and Adeimantus. Not only does the mentor indicate the possibility of this alternative. The mentor must also guide the student far enough along the upward path that she or he begins to discern another source of illumination, the daylight filtering down from above, rather than the light from the fire, which now burns below and behind as the student ascends.

Absolutely crucial here for understanding the upward pathway is that, as Heraclitus has said, "The way up and the way down are one and the same" (Fragment 60). The philosopher, recall, must go back down into the cave, and the pathway for escape out is one and the same as the one for return. The Cave, just as the Divided Line, is an integrated continuity. We have interpreted this to mean that embodiment, in its fullest sense, is not something a human being can simply leave behind and transcend entirely. This embodiment includes not simply the individuation of the body, with its physical limitations and its sensations and its needs, but also the embeddedness of human understanding in a specific cultural-linguistic historical context. *Transcendence is situated.* It begins in the shadows of received opinions, makes its progress by confrontation with them, and must return to them. Zetetic philosophy must reconcile itself to this embodiment, to the understanding that mortal transcendence is necessarily encumbered with the embodied and the historical and that it must speak in their language.

This is another reason that McCoy is correct to say that the sophist and the philosopher can appear identical from the perspective of the cave-dweller. Both employ the tools of rhetoric. Both must be able to speak fluently the language of their specific embodiment, as situated in a particular place and time, among a people with their characteristic passions and propensities, their mindsets and opinions formed by a deeply sedimented history. Just as Socrates makes use of images, such as the Noble Lie of the three metals of the soul, the Divided Line, and the Allegory of the Cave, and just as Plato uses the images of narrative setting and characters in the dialogue form as such, so too must the returned philosopher master the projection of shadows for the prisoners, from the fire, over the wall bordering the lateral path, and onto the cave wall. Because the Cave and the Line are each integrated wholes, even the dimmest image is still an emanation of the truth. We can only make sense of our world, as a world that matters to us, through narrative, where the interlacing textuality of meaning captures our imagination and connects us more vividly to the world.

But the use to which the philosopher puts image, rhetoric, language, and narrative differs in kind from the manipulations of the sophist. The philosopher's mastery must entail a *phronēsis*, a practical wisdom, about which images and narratives and arguments will best reach a specifically situated individual or audience *for their own good*. It means which stories and arguments are most likely to liberate with the least amount of trauma and, even if they do not liberate, will be the best imagistic renderings of a more abstract truth, and therefore least likely to harm individuals and the community. The sophist's rhetoric seeks only manipulation for the sake of power, prestige, pleasure, or wealth. It uses word, image, and argument to direct desire and mold ideology, but without any sense that there might be more to wisdom than a method of manipulation. This is true whether or not the sophist is aware of and intentionally manipulating historical consciousness as such, just as a skilled archer can hit a target using physics without knowing about physics thematically. The sophist does not care for the well-being of the target audience, except perhaps in the transactional sense that Thrasymachus suggests: as a shepherd tends the flock for eventual shearing and slaughter (343a–344c). The sophist, as sophist, has no concern for anything but situated embodiment in flesh and ideology, has no awareness of the opening to the upward way that beckons beyond—or else is aware of it, but walls it off as a threat to their own power or in spiteful regret for this path not taken.

Now, Heidegger may not be a sophist, but he does share with the sophist a distinct hostility to the ideas in their Platonic sense. Heidegger also shares with Thrasymachus the rejection of a justice that transcends historicity and contingency, and both end up endorsing tyranny, but Thrasymachus only in theory, Heidegger in actual practice. Thrasymachus turns out to be potentially redeemable in the *Republic* (498c–d), but Heidegger never retreats from his embrace of the "inner truth and greatness" of National Socialism as he envisioned it (GA 40: 208). For Heidegger, the notion of eternal ideas as the touchstone for meaning, for what we take things to be, is an anathema, because all meaning is historical, finite, transient and rooted, not fixed and eternal as the basis for an ethics and a politics that he rejects as a Liberalism stretching from Plato through Christianity to the Enlightenment. But might Plato in his allegory also account positively for the *historicity* of meaning and the *situatedness* of human understanding? The analysis of the lateral pathway and its relation to the fire and the projection of the shadows shows that Plato does provide room to think about the interweaving of rooted historical particularity with a universalism that transcends contingency. We always begin within a constellation of meaning that is historically given: the cave and the opinions projected into it by the activity along the lateral pathway.

7.5 THE UPWARD PATH

But why is this not enough? Why do we also need the upward path? It *could* be enough to say that some of the opinions in the cave are simply false (say, that the world is flat or that three million illegal votes were cast in California in the 2016 presidential election), and that the upward path intimates a truth we can attain that transcends historical accidents and ignorance. This will hardly satisfy Heidegger, though, who holds that truth is interpretive all the way down, that there is no emergence into a total, complete, and final enlightenment, not even as a regulative postulate, that requires no further *re*interpretation.

The test of the upward path is whether the ideas are needed to make sense of moral phenomena. Socrates claims that the sophist does not care whether a conviction is actually noble, good, or just. Can we really live as if this were true? Well, yes, we can, but the price we pay is that we can no longer say that anything is just or unjust in itself. Moral judgments become a gambit in the ideological game-play in a discourse of power. This is why Jan Patočka says that a negative Platonism, one that leaves us open to the idea of the good but without metaphysical dogma pretending to ultimate knowledge,

> preserves for humans the possibility of trusting in a truth that is not relative and mundane, even though it cannot be formulated positively, in terms of contents. It shows how much truth there is in man's perennial metaphysical struggle for something elevated above the natural and the traditional, the struggle for the eternal and supratemporal, in the struggle, taken up ever again, against a relativism of values and norms—even while agreeing with the idea of a basic historicity of man and of the relativity of his orientation in his context, of his science and practice, his images of life and the world.[21]

Radical historicism denies what is essential to the phenomenon of ethical judgment: that rightness and wrongness are meaningful to us absolutely and not just contingently and that justice transcends the arbitrary givens of a particular historical context. For Heidegger, Platonism is nihilistic because it sacrifices the only existence we have, the one of historically given finitude, on the altar of transcendent, eternal ideas; idealism negates the given, the only world of meaning we can actually inhabit. By contrast, Patočka reminds us that the meaningfulness of human freedom and ethical life depends precisely on this struggle, which he explicitly calls a *polemos* in other writings, to negate without annihilating, to step back and away from the embeddedness of our historicity precisely as the way to embrace it again.[22] I differ from Patočka when he says that truth "cannot be formulated positively, in terms of contents"; on my account, the zetetic trust in truth, pledging troth to truth, requires making the preconstructive attempt to envision an alternative to the meaning of a world we find drifting into unmeaning. This is a facet of the reintegrative healing of polemical philosophy.

Recall that the upward path of the ideas and the lateral path of history intersect, and they do so at the point of the fire, which must be close by the lateral path and not far from where the upward, outward path begins. This suggests that historical consciousness, which the liberated prisoner may achieve at the level of the fire, is itself a preliminary form of transcendence, a necessary way station along the upward path to the exit. A good history teacher may have intimations of the upward path and point the way without going up it herself.[23] To see by the light of the fire is to recognize the contingency of the shadows in the cave. This realization of the cave's historical contingency is what constitutes authenticity, the only form of liberation possible for Heidegger. It means forever losing the comfortable, naive (*heimlich*) understanding of meaning, handed down by tradition as simply and incontrovertibly true. For both the sophist and the historicist, this awakening from innocence is the end of the story. It means giving up on truth altogether, as truth is conventionally understood. Heidegger calls this the *Unheimlichkeit* of human existence: the uncanny realization that all meaning is contingent, grounded on nothing (SZ, 188–89).

At stake here is the role of *wonder*. Socrates, remember, says that "Between the fire and the prisoners *there is a road above*, along which we see a wall, built like the partitions puppet-handlers set in front of the human beings and over which they show the puppets." In Greek, the word here for puppeteer is *thaumatopoios*, literally a wonder-worker, and the puppets are *ta thaumata*, the wonders. These wonders are tricks and illusions, a semblance that takes on the air of reality, made possible by the wall that separates and hides the technical trickery of the wonder-worker from the audience. Yet, both Plato (*Theaetetus*, 155d) and Aristotle (*Metaphysics*, 982b) say that wonder is the beginning of philosophy—not wonder in the sense of idle curiosity or listless pondering, but rather wonder in the Greek sense of *thaumazein*: a wonder that knocks you back and brings you up short in the encounter with something unexpected. Such wonder sets your world on fire because of a contradiction and a puzzle that demands your attention and thought in order to restore meaning and integrity to the phenomena.

What do these two wonders share, puppetry and the birth of philosophy? We may think of a puppet show as mere amusement, but seen with the eyes of a child, it is an astonishing transformation of the nonliving into the living. It provokes the tantalizing awareness that this transformation is at once mysterious and potentially explicable as a performance, which explains the enduring appeal of the tale of Pinocchio. The puppet show is more than amusement, then, for it kindles both delight and the intimation that there might be more to the world than one had once thought. Just so, philosophical wonder sets the world on edge with an admixture of dismay and joy and hunger, a driving desire to see behind the wall that separates transient opinion from echonic knowledge. The danger is that this longing can give way to frustration and so to the temptation of dogma as a way of claiming an echonic knowledge to which one is not entitled. This is a form of nihilism, because it denies aspects of the given phenomena to arrive at an illegitimate certainty, such as when some philosophers of mind argue that consciousness can be reduced to purely physical events, because they have a doctrinal commitment to a form of naturalism that refuses to admit the existence of phenomena that cannot be explained without resorting to what transcends material processes.[24]

The challenge to zetetic philosophy as the *iasis*, the healing after the break (*lusis*) from the bonds of the cave, is to reconcile the seeker of truth to a journey that may not end with echonic possession, at least not in this life, because a reconciliation to longing is also reconciliation to our inherent finitude. Socrates does this in the *Symposium* (203b–c) by suggesting that as an *erōs*, an overwhelming, longing love for wisdom, philosophy is born of two parents: *Penia* and *Poros*, Need (or Poverty) and Resource. Zeteticism as healing means a reconciliation to *erōs*, to longing as never entirely fulfilled and yet nevertheless and as such fulfilling as this ongoing journey. The poverty of philosophy is the recognition of its separation from absolute knowing; its resource is the givenness of intimations of the truth, which light the way with the distant daylight, refracted down from beyond the upward way. It is worth remembering that in ordinary usage, *poros* in Greek means a way to pass over or through, such as a ferry or ford, and our English word *pore*, which provides a passage from body to world. In the language of Sophocles's Ode to Man, we are *pantaporos-aporos* (*Antigone*, 359), everywhere with a way through, yet without a way through. Once again, the phenomenological given that some meaning is given to us, in the sheer fact that the world makes provisional sense, provides Socrates with his phenomenal resource for the ongoing journey, despite his poverty: exploring what people *say* as the avatar of the givenness of a meaning beyond us. Even in our poverty, the word is the richest source of meaning available to us, because in language and in speaking with others we touch upon meaning and upon the personhood of the Other—as I now do with you and you with me—despite never possessing either definitively and echonically.[25]

The upward path in the cave points to another layer of transcendence: one that goes beyond the realization of historical contingency and apprehends the ideas that are imperfectly refracted in the shadows of the cave, the historical opinions of a given community. The fire of history on the lateral path is a prefiguration of the sun of the ideas at the end of the upward path. Both on the Divided Line and in the Allegory of the Cave, the shadows and images, the cultural givens of opinion, are not simply nothing. They are not merely contingent. They are reflections of the chain of meaning up through the ideas in the light of the idea of the good, and their significance depends upon that chain. If that is right, then nihilism would consist not in rejecting and thereby utterly negating the shadow-world of the cave but in denying that it is ultimately connected to what transcends the cave. Once again, Patočka puts this well:

> The problem of ethics, the problem of *essential meaning of human beings* is to be sought in the ultimate kernel of human life. This kernel concerns the donation of intentional meaning which unfolds into the world without actually being reducible to it. It implies a transcendence beyond all reality. [What I have called *intimation.*] We understand this transcendence through the experience of separation, of distancing ourselves, taking our distance. The ethical life is our first practical contact with the negativity inherent in our very essence.[26]

Patočka uses Husserlian language of "intentional meaning" to indicate that the world and things in the world have significance *to us*, even if that meaning *as* a "donation" *given to us*, cannot be reduced to an explanation based on anything we encounter empirically within the world. There is therefore a *positivity* to the negativity of the essential freedom of being-human: by entering into the interpretive *polemos* with both the given and the giving as such, such freedom has the potential to induce new meaning in a world breaking down into unmeaning. This positive-negative freedom emerges through and as ideation, which integrates a world as we envision it might be with the meaning of the world as it is.

Such reconstruction is a difficult freedom, requiring practical wisdom. This is why Socrates says that a person with insight (*nous*), "would remember that there are two kinds of disturbances of the eyes, stemming from two sources—when they have been transferred from light to darkness and when they have been transferred from darkness to light" (518a). Failure to recognize the danger of these disturbances, being "dazzled" (518a–b) by either sudden darkness or sudden light, can result in a disorientation amid opinions and norms that no longer make sense, leading to ridicule, persecution, or even execution. Those returning must learn to operate at the level of the fire, too, in order to translate their insights into the historically situated language of shadows that nevertheless are not nothing. According to the Divided Line's continuum, contingent historical opinion necessarily has some relation to a wisdom that transcends it, or it would be less meaningful than garbled echoes and dim reflections of truth.

Everyday, cave-bound opinion would otherwise be simply unintelligible, and that is manifestly not the case phenomenologically, for we self-evidently do function within a margin of meaning. If nihilism means losing a sense for how the world may be meaningful, then far from constituting nihilism as the forgetting of contingency as the source of meaning for human beings, Plato's intersecting pathways suggest that nihilism only sets in when we give up on the struggle with contradictions between the contingently given and the ideas that can draw us out from the contingent. The ideas can then lead us both out from and back to our situated belonging in the world in order to reconstitute that world's meaning responsibly, as best we can, in the refracted light of what transcends it. What we need to investigate next is how to conduct that responsive reconstruction responsibly, and that brings us to *phronēsis*, wisdom in action.

NOTES

1. Howe, *Holmes-Laski Letters*, vol. 2, 835.

2. An alternative manuscript does not include the *onomazein* in the sentence, and so, as Bloom notes, another rendering for this would be "they would hold that these things that they see are the beings" (*The Republic of Plato*, 465n1). I follow Bloom and Reeve here in including *onomazein*, but even without it, the sense of the claim is that the prisoners would take, and so mistake, the shadows as the beings (*ta onta*) themselves.

3. For a brief overview, see Paul Brand, "The Language of the English Legal Profession."

4. Husserl, *The Crisis*, 71; on sedimentation, see Moran and Cohen, *The Husserl Dictionary*, 289–91.

5. For a discussion of how such practices necessarily recede into the background of awareness so that awareness of meaning as such is possible, see Mark Wrathal's introduction and the essays by Hubert Dreyfus collected in Dreyfus, *Background Practices: Essays on the Understanding of Being*, especially chapters 3–6.

6. Husserl, *The Crisis*, 71–72.

7. Bloom, *The Republic of Plato*, 404.

8. See Plutarch's "Lycurgus," in *Lives*.

9. See Dreyfus, *Background Practices*.

10. Plato, *The Great Dialogues of Plato*, trans. W. H. D. Rouse, 314.

11. For example, see Katie Rogers, "White House Hosts Conservative Internet Activists at a 'Social Media Summit.'" To be clear, this is not a matter of 'left' or 'right,' even if supposed conservatives are currently the most adept at such projections.

12. See Confessore, "Cambridge Analytica and Facebook," and Helderman and Zapotosky, *The Mueller Report*, 587–618.

13. For example, see Shaw and Bagozzi, "The Neuropsychology of Consumer Behavior and Marketing," and the chapters collected in Suhay, Grofman, and Trechsel, *The Oxford Handbook of Electoral Persuasion*, especially Gilles Serra, "A Menu of Clientist Methods to Buy and Coerce Voters: The Dark Side of Electoral Persuasion."

14. Cf. Bloom, "Interpretive Essay," 399–400.

15. This is akin to what Leo Strauss says about "pseudo-philosophies" that frighten the cave-dwellers so badly about the upward path that they induce the prisoners to "dig a deep pit beneath the [natural] cave in which they were born, and withdraw into that pit." See Leo Strauss, "How to Study Spinoza's 'Theological-Political Treatise,'" in *Persecution and the Art of Writing*, 155.

16. See Marina McCoy, *Plato on the Rhetoric of Philosophers and Sophists*, 1 and 22.

17. McCoy, *Plato on Rhetoric*, 117.

18. Kearny, *The Poetics of Modernity*, 66, 67, and 70ff.

19. Even if an echonic philosopher were serving as mentor, as in the ostensible *narrative* of the cave, where echonic philosopher-rulers would be educating the next generation of rulers, they would also have to re-inhabit, as it were, the mindset of the zetetic seeker, because that is the present situation of the student being taught. This would not be impossible to imagine, as it would also be the situation that the now-complete philosopher-rulers had themselves experienced during their period of tutelage.

20. Cf. Bloom, who has a different reading of the meaning of the friendship established between Socrates and Thrasymachus: *The Republic of Plato*, 400–401. Bloom interprets Thrasymachus as a defender of the interests of the received opinions of the city for whom philosophy is a threat, but this is hard to reconcile with his initial teaching that the life of the tyrant is the best, for that is just as much a threat to the norms of Athens, if not more so.

21. Patočka, "Negative Platonism," 205–6.

22. For Patočka on *polemos*, see *Heretical Essays*, 42–43.

23. My thanks to Lauren McGillicuddy for this example.

24. For examples, see Paul Churchland, *Matter and Consciousness* or Daniel Dennett, *Consciousness Explained*; for a counterargument to reductive theories of consciousness, see Hubert Dreyfus and Charles Taylor, *Retrieving Realism*, 11–16, 51, 93, and for a critique of scientism, see Reid, *Heidegger's Moral Ontology*, 37–49.

25. On poverty, consider Meister Eckhart's sermon 52, in Meister Eckhart, *The Essential Sermons, Commentaries, Treatises and Defense*, 201–3, and Ian Moore, *Eckhart, Heidegger, and the Imperative of Releasement*, 24–28.

26. From an entry of 1947 in Patočka's journals, quoted in Kearney, *The Poetics of Modernity*, 121.

Chapter Eight

Retrieving Phronēsis

Antigone at the Heart of Ethics

See—there is a limit to looking,
and the world gazed upon
wants to blossom in love.

The work of vision is done,
now do heart-work
on the images in you, the ones imprisoned; for you
overpowered them: yet you do not know them.

—Rainer Maria Rilke, from "Turning-Point"[1]

Previously, I have argued that Plato provides a response to Heidegger's critique that idea-ism and idealism set the stage for a nihilistic human hubris that forgets our finitude and the embedded situatedness of our existence as what most matters to life. In this chapter, I will argue that in addition to misunderstanding the ethical meaning of ideation, as I have argued previously, Heidegger misunderstands a form of thinking vital to ethical-political life, *phronēsis*, generally translated as practical wisdom or prudence. Heidegger's radical historicism prevents him from seeing the intersection of principled norms with life as we find it and as we live it, at the crossroads of the cave. At-issue here is how ethical life proceeds from and reconstitutes itself according to insights and judgments that are *preconceptual*, that precede any specific conceptual formulation and argument. We have already encountered the preconceptual in various ways: as the earth that undergirds and sustains a meaningful world; as the background practices that make the world and action within it intelligible and navigable; as the sedimentation of personal habits and cultural routines that recede into the unconscious habituation of more complex and interwoven concepts, language, traditions, norms, and praxis.

What we will now address is what impels and informs the dynamic of delving into the preconceptual background of our mores, institutions, and behaviors when the world faces breakdown in unmeaning. *Phronēsis* is the heart that animates the polemical ethics of bringing the ideas into confrontation with the contingent, situated lives we inhabit. Understanding *phronēsis* as the pivot between transcendent idea and situated finitude brings us from Plato to Aristotle and, as we will see, to Sophocles's Antigone as champions of a nuanced conception of the situated transcendence of being-human. This initiates a turn to the next stage of the project: the question of *enacting* a polemical ethics in reading texts, in personal ethical life with others, and in political life with communities. That will be the substantive work of subsequent volumes, but in this and the final chapter, we will establish the transition. First, as a counterpoint, we will explicate Heidegger's understanding of the role of *phronēsis* as a feature of the preconceptual ethical life of politics, and then we will deconstruct his reading of the *Antigone* in order explicate phenomenologically the necessarily ideational aspect of *phronēsis* in ethical-political life.

The word *phronēsis* is related to a family of words in ancient Greek that illuminate its meaning. The *phrēn* is the midriff, the seat of an embodied knowing that is tied to the intuitive, intimate, and familiar, the furthest thing from the conceptual knowing of metaphysical philosophy. Hence, the verb *phronein* means to know in your gut, to have an instinctive feel for what fits with the familiar, as well for what breaks with it. It is a thinking that discerns the way to effective action amid the contingencies of life, and therefore it must be rational in the sense of being responsive and responsible to both the particulars and the principles of action. The noun *phronēsis*, in turn, refers to the capacity to make judgments that fit well with what a particular situation demands but is not *merely* instinctual or nonrational. As a form of reason embodied in practical judgments, it acts with an insight that, while in the moment of action may well be intuitive, can also be defended rationally in private reflection and in public dialogue with others as part of an ethical-political community. Convention translates *phronēsis* as 'practical wisdom' or 'prudence,' but these renderings lose the sense of the Greek connection to affective, embodied knowing that is not immediately conceptual. It is neither a form of abstract wisdom formulaically applied to practice, nor a prudence that calculates options according to principles of cautious moderation. I will leave *phronēsis* in the Greek, because its meaning is at issue for understanding ethical life as mediating the preconceptual with the rationally defensible.

8.1 HEIDEGGER'S POLEMICS OF *PHRONĒSIS*

From the ancient Greeks onward, the role of *phronēsis* has generally been understood as the virtue of mind required for sound judgment and action in ethics and politics. In *phronēsis*, judging and acting are not separate, as if one were first to make a cognitive assessment and then apply it in deed; rather, the two are united in the praxis of human embodiment amid the contingencies of temporal existence. In Aristotle, the divine would not need *phronēsis*. The divine has no need to match discursive rationality with finite embodiment, because the divine's intelligence is nondiscursive, self-sufficient, and non-embodied. By contrast, because we are embodied and not self-sufficient, and our intelligence is discursive, requiring time for learning and deliberation, the human good requires practical wisdom to manage the body, both through the moral virtues and through the everyday activity and political cooperation needed to secure the body's needs.[2] This does not mean that persons possessing *phronēsis* act instinctively in an irrational sense. The rationality of right action has been thoroughly habituated into their thinking and acting, and in a way that they could, in principle, explain, defend, and revise through rational discourse and deliberate re-habituation.

Phronēsis is therefore a distinct and defining feature of being-human as embodied and embedded in the sociality and rooted specificity of affective ethical life. We see this in Heidegger's lectures of the early 1920s where he endeavors to appropriate Aristotle's *phronēsis* phenomenologically. In a 1924 lecture course, he says, "The *aisthēsis* of *phronēsis*, as *phronēsis*, is related to the *prakta*" (GA 19: 163). Here, *aisthēsis* is perception as a taking-in, a making-sense of a domain of beings. In *phronēsis*, what one takes in are the *prakta*, the contingent contexts and ends of practical action, in contrast to the first principles of theoretical wisdom (as when one 'gets' the axioms of geometry). *Phronēsis* therefore depends on a rational insight (*nous*) into the radical specificity of a context: "*Phronēsis* is *insight into here-and-now* [*Diesmaligen*], the concrete here-and-now-ness of the momentary situation. *As aisthēsis, it is eye-sight, the seeing that in the blink of an eye takes in what is ever-always concrete and, as such, can always be otherwise*" (GA 19: 163–64). Heidegger takes up the metaphorics of sight, as did Plato. The 'looking' here is not physical eyesight but the ontological seeing of being able to make sense of a contingent context, all in the blink of an eye (*Augenblick*) so that practical action might be possible at all as befitting the situation.

Heidegger's ontological-existential appropriation of Aristotle is most apparent when he says that *phronēsis* is the mode of Dasein's Being that discloses our "Being-oriented to beings that are in each case themselves Dasein" (GA 19: 164; cf. 48). In Aristotle, that is because praxis as such is necessarily ethical. It has to do with the discernment that enables us to act ethically. This is a discernment that grants us the situated insight to live well as human beings, both with oneself and with others, not just instrumentally (which would be mere cunning), but as beings who flourish only by respecting ourselves and others as finite, embodied beings capable of shared rational discourse in the conduct of life. Heidegger recognizes that *phronēsis* has to do with *eu zên*, living well as being-human or Dasein (GA 19: 49), and that *eu prattein*, acting well for the sake of living well, depends on a perception of the good, *to agathon* (GA 19: 48), but he ontologizes the meaning of the good, as we have also seen in chapter 3 concerning his reading of Plato's idea of the good.

Heidegger takes a crucial passage in the *Nicomachean Ethics* defining *phronēsis* as *hexin alēthē meta logou praktikēn peri anthrōpō agatha kai kaka* (1148b4–5)—"a truthful habituated characteristic of acting rationally concerning practical matters of good and bad for human beings"—and he *glosses* it as *hexis alēthēs meta logou practikē peri ta anthrōpō agatha*. He then loosely renders this gloss to define the *telos*, the end or goal, of *phronēsis* as "*ein solches Gestelltsein des menschlichen Daseins, daß es über die Durchsichtigkeit seiner selbst verfügt,*" which may be translated as "a certain disposition of human Dasein that presides over its own transparency" (GA 19: 50). Heidegger's aggressive ontologization of this definition of *phronēsis* not only obscures the ethical *good* of the goal of practical action, it entirely eliminates the *bad* that virtuous praxis must also aim to avoid, all in favor of an existential-hermeneutical self-awareness that has no ethical *telos*. Mark Blitz succinctly addresses the stakes of this decapitation of the ethical good as the purpose of praxis:

> For all the ways in which we can speak intelligibly of guidance, direction, and authority, such that these are not ultimately relative, apparently depend on the kind of universality in possibility that Heidegger denies for man. This is even true of the non-absolute Aristotelian prudence [i.e., *phronēsis*] or the Platonic measure of the fitting, for in the last analysis these rely on an understanding of what is natural in the humanly noble, the humanly just, and the humanly good. . . [I]f "goodness" is grounded in what is not permanently possible, is it not finally reduced to the arbitrariness of one's own?[3]

What Blitz calls "one's own" are the finite concerns and involvements of historical facticity, which may both open up and obscure the possibility that Heidegger does posit as a measure for being-human: authenticity. Heidegger says, "A mood can close a person off from himself; certain things of peripheral importance can overwhelm him; he can get so caught up in himself so that he does not authentically see himself"; this means that *phronēsis* "needs ever again to be rescued," because "the insight into oneself must ever-again be wrested away from the danger" of this self-obscuring (GA 19: 51). Heidegger then says, "It is by no means obvious that Dasein be disclosed for itself in the authenticity of its Being" (GA 19: 51), and goes on to say, "Therefore, as soon as it is achieved, *phronēsis* is bound up in an ongoing struggle against the tendency to cover over that lies in Dasein itself" (GA 19: 52). "Struggle" (*Kampf*) is a word that within a decade will be one of Heidegger's translations for the *polemos* that lies at the heart of being-human, and here, the struggle of *phronēsis* defines Dasein's authenticity against what in *Being and Time* Heidegger will call those modalities of existence—such as idle chatter, ambiguity, idle curiosity—that the They-self throws up against Dasein's owning itself by owning up to itself in authenticity. Now, my own argument in this study includes the view that central to being-human is a polemical ethics that struggles to makes sense of its obligations in its own situated context.

The issue here, though, and where I claim that Heidegger and Plato part company, lies in how Heidegger interprets the truth-telling, the *alēthuein*, of *phronēsis*—the making clear of human-being to itself—as *conscience*:

> *Phronēsis* is nothing other than conscience set into motion that makes an action transparent. One cannot forget conscience, but one can certainly allow what the conscience discloses to be obscured and rendered ineffective by *hēdonē* [pleasure] and *lupē* [pain], by passion. Conscience [nevertheless] announces itself ever-again. (GA 19: 56)

In *Being and Time*, the call of conscience can be ignored, but it is what summons the human-being to seize upon its possibilities as its own, authentically, in a polemical interpretation of the meaning of its world, rather than allowing itself to be defined passively by the meaning it is caught up in by the trajectory of history.[4] Consistent with what Heidegger says here about *phronēsis* as ever-again returning to the struggle with its own existential features that obscure insight into a positive appropriation of its situated being, authenticity in *Being and Time* is necessarily a polemical "modification" of the way the world has always-already been interpreted (SZ, 130, 170), because we cannot recreate meaning as a whole *ex nihilo*. Being-human, for Heidegger, means resolving upon what the call of conscience, as *phronēsis*, discloses in the irreplicable situation of finite historicity as the space of one's interpretive decision in action. But famously, this call of conscience gives no *content* to the resolution, only the perspicacity for the situation that allows one to make it one's own.

This is the result of Heidegger's ontologizing conscience and *phronēsis*. Because there is no transcendence to the good, no *idea* of the good as either ethical or ontological, the meaning of action is always entirely immanent to the *ēthos* of the cave of a given historical world, even if merely as a deconstructive reinterpretation of it. The good to which conscience calls and *phronēsis* orients the human agent is always grounded in a historicity of a given community to which one belongs and whose *ēthos* is incommensurable with other communities, because the good cannot transcend historicity. Hence, at the level of political action, as an extension of ethical life as historical-communal *ēthos*, what *phronēsis* must discern is the context of decision that applies only to that people, rather than to human beings as such. This is at the heart of Heidegger's rejection of "Liberalism" as a modern extension of Plato's universalism. At-issue, then, for the meaning of political judgment in Heidegger, is discerning what is at stake in the particular historical fate in the essence of one's own community.

8.2 ESSENTIAL POLITICS

One of the most important texts for Heidegger's understanding of how political judgment and decision should take place is a seminar he held in 1933–1934, at the height of his involvement with National Socialism. Its title is *On the Essence and Concept of Nature, History, and State*. The seminar begins with an explicit attempt to distinguish *essence* and *concept* (Session 1): grasping the essence of a thing or domain in existential understanding, as situated historically, necessarily comes before grasping it conceptually. This follows the analysis set forth in *Being and Time*, where Heidegger argues that Dasein always already inhabits a world of understanding that makes sense pre-theoretically, that theory and explicit concepts always follow as a modification of or abstraction from Dasein's preconceptual understanding (SZ, 138). In this seminar, he calls this "the simple, prescientific beginning of the question of the essence of the domains at hand, which consists in the plain, uncomplicated, quite naive expression of how nature, history, and state are given to us" (NGS, 53–54). Theory and the definition of concepts are always derivatives of an understanding of meaning that must precede all formal articulation in conceptual terminology or theoretical detachment.

Here it must be understood that "essence" for Heidegger is not the *eidos*, *ousia*, or *substantia* of the metaphysical tradition, which would be essence in the sense of a permanent, metaphysical substrate to reality, more recently critiqued as *essentialism*, especially in feminism.[5] Instead, Heidegger famously says that "*The 'essence' of Dasein lies in its existence*" (SZ, 42). This means that *who* we 'are' does not reside in properties pertaining to a substance-essence as some *what-thing*. Rather, who we are depends on structures of our Being as existing, as hermeneutical beings who make sense of the world by polemically confronting and reinterpreting it, a position potentially consistent with contemporary anti-essentialism. Phenomenological analysis means getting at the essence of things as they appear in preconceptual understanding. In Heidegger, such understanding is always historical for beings such as ourselves, whose existence precedes their essence. In the seminar, the turn to what he calls the "naive" givenness of a meaningful world very quickly becomes a historical analysis of *phusis*, *natura*, and other key philosophical terms. That is because nature, as a *phusis* that brings meaning into manifestation and significance for us apart from our choosing or control, provides insight into essence understood ontologically rather than metaphysically. Essence in this reconstructed sense, for Heidegger, precedes a conceptual understanding detached from the embedded understanding that grants our primary grasp of the essence of things in the world as what matters to us in our situated existence. An excessive focus on conceptualization and theory risks flattening this more direct encounter with the essence of things.

"We begin," Heidegger says, "by clarifying the political as a way of Being of human beings and what makes the state possible" (NGS, 74). He explains as follows:

> The manner of our Being marks the Being of our state. In this way, every people takes a position with regard to the state, and no people lacks the urge for the state. The people that turns down a state, that is stateless, has just not found the gathering of its essence yet; it still lacks the composure and force to be committed to its fate as a people. (NGS, 74)

Heidegger connects politics with Being, which in turn connects with the radical historicity of a particular people. Politics cannot be understood in the ways familiar to the metaphysical tradition—say, in liberalism—as the arena for the protection of fundamental human rights, because human beings are not a what-thing with ahistorical, essential properties. Politics does not describe legitimate or illegitimate interaction based on some feature of human nature understood as a metaphysical essence. Instead, politics is "a way of Being of human beings." That seems hopelessly abstract until we realize that this "*way* of Being" is always a matter "of *our* Being"; it is always about how a particular historical people shares in an understanding of the world as a world that matters to them in its specificity and as intimately, even exclusively and incommensurably, their own. Politics must therefore be finely attuned to the historical meaning of a given community. Of course, the community Heidegger speaks of here as sharing "our Being" is the German *Volk*. To understand its radically historical, specific way of Being is to understand its shared "fate" (*Schicksal*), not a fate in the metaphysical sense of a predetermined future, but rather as an understanding of how the momentum and trajectory of its history presents that people with its particular challenges and tasks as what it must confront in the cycle of polemical reinterpretation (cf. SZ, §74).[6]

Heidegger says that a people that has not found its essence cannot form a state. To find its essence must mean to understand the singularity of its own historical mode of Being, including a mission, a "fate" as a guiding possibility, that defines it as this particular people, rather than finding its essence as some universal feature of a metaphysical humanity. The state, then, embodies the way of Being of a particular people that has found the strength *to* express itself in a state. Heidegger even goes so far as to identify the state *"as the Being of the people"* (NGS, 79), because even if the people is prior in having its own unifying historical task, only in having a state can it face that task, embody it, and protect and project its own identity in the community of peoples.

If the essence of politics is the formation of radically historical and incommensurable essence of a people in a state, there can be no universal conceptual standards for politics, no trans-temporal measure of legitimacy in a political theory. Heidegger intends this as a revolutionary departure from the metaphysical tradition of the essence of politics and state formation, a departure in keeping with the transformation of the thinking of Being that Heidegger has announced in *Being and Time* and that we have discussed throughout this volume as a departure from Platonism. To think politics without concepts, or at least prior to concepts, without metaphysical essences, means doing away with normative standards for legitimacy and justice. To think politics this way means no longer appealing to timeless principles, such as the social contract, human rights, or the rule of law in liberalism, and then applying them to particular cases, which is what Heidegger means by a conceptual approach to political thought. Post-metaphysical political thought would mean staying attuned to the unique historical circumstances and taking up the challenges so presented. This may all sound very abstract, but without universal principles, even as undogmatic postulates of a skeptical idealism to guide *phronēsis* in political life, one can hardly be surprised that the rejection of Enlightenment liberalism's discourse of rights, limits to power, rule of law, and so on, would lead to the barbarities of an atavistic ethno-nationalism, a prospect we still face today.

Being exquisitely attuned to historical contingencies might sound like Aristotelian *phronēsis*. But if politics, as essential in Heidegger's sense (linked to the singular challenges facing a distinct community's historical trajectory) has no ground in any transcendent ideal or principle, and if the good can only shed light on the particular cave-like historicity that is one's own, and not universally for being-human, what then is the measure for political action? This question will ultimately separate Heidegger from Aristotle on *phronēsis*, and it is one that drives Heidegger towards *decisionism* during this period. In *Nature, History, State*, Heidegger argues that this decision is one facing individuals as members of the people: "Every individual must now reflect in order to arrive at knowledge of the people and state and his own responsibility. The state depends on our alertness, our readiness, and our life" (NGS, 74). In *Being and Truth*, a lecture course later in 1933, he links this decision with essence: "not only is the question about essence not insidious, but it is the very questioning that unrelentingly holds us in actuality and impels us to a decision there" (GA 36/37: 88). Throughout the early Black Notebooks of the 1930s, Heidegger says that the epochal decision, the one that will define the fate of the National Socialist revolution and the fate of the West and indeed of the globe, is a "decision between beings and Being," by which he means deciding either to embrace the people's historical finitude as a bulwark against the oblivion of Being, as a "transformation of human being," or to join in with the nihilistic, global chase of the will to power to subdue all beings in a system of machination (GA 95: 117–201; GA 96: 16–22).

The preparation of individuals for this decision through openness to questioning is linked to the necessity of the leader (*Führer*) who takes the state in hand and directs its collective action:

> The Being of the state is anchored in the political Being of the human beings who, as a people, support this state—who decide for it. This political, that is, historically fateful decision requires us to clarify the original, essential connection between people and state. An understanding and knowledge of the essence of the state and people is needful for every human being. This knowledge, the concepts and cognition, belong to political education, that is, what leads us into our own political Being; but this does not mean that everyone who gains this knowledge can or may now act politically as a statesman or leader. For the origin of all state action and leadership does not lie in knowledge; it lies in Being. Every leader *is* a leader; he must be a leader in accordance with the marked form of his Being; and he understands, considers, and brings about what people and state are, in the living development of his own essence. (NGS, 73)

Once again, we see that post-metaphysical understanding of the Being of the people precedes conventional *concepts* about the state, its institutions, and so on. While such conceptual knowledge may be necessary for political education of citizens (so, on a par with *alētheia*-3 in Sheehan's typology), political action in its deepest origins "does not lie in knowledge [understood conceptually]; it lies in Being." So, a leader simply "*is* a leader"—or he is not. In this leader's "essence" existentially understood, he either succeeds in being that leader, and thereby is properly attuned to the decisions called for by the historicity of his people's Being in Heidegger's sense of *phronēsis*, or he fails to *be* a leader. No formula, no standard, determines this; only the *is* or *is not* of engaged action. Heideggerian *phronēsis* would guide the singularity of such ontological decision in the singularity of historical circumstance.

Heidegger clearly has a *Führer* such as Hitler in mind here. Note the first sentence of the following passage, but also the role that he assigns to himself:

> A leader does not need to be educated politically—but a band of guardians in the people [*eine Hüterschar im Volk*] does, a band that helps to bear responsibility for the state. For every state and all knowledge about the state grows within a political tradition. Where this nourishing, securing soil is lacking, even the best idea for a state cannot take root, grow from the sustaining womb of the people, and develop. (NGS, 73/45)

The resonance with Plato's guardians in the *Republic* is unmistakable. Heidegger advocates the formation of these guardians as a "political nobility" (NGS, 74) in the tradition of Bismarck's political class, but one more firmly rooted in the people; Bismarck's nobility collapsed with his death, thus proving its superficiality. While Heidegger's vision here is vague (though it suggests why he took the university so seriously during his political engagement), he clearly intends the political education of the guardians as not merely forming an understanding of the historical tradition as a series of dates and facts, or of the state as a collection of institutions and functionaries. Genuine political education must prepare these guardians for a post-metaphysical thinking about the *essence* of the people and the state so that they are prepared for the genuinely historical decisions that will face the nation and its leaders. If, as he says in *Being and Truth*, "essence cannot be brought together in thought and represented in empty concepts and displayed in a conceptual system" (GA 36/37: 86), then Heidegger's guardians are a radical departure from Plato's. Rather than apprehending the *idea* of the good as a trans-temporal source for justice as an ideal and standard, they would be attuned to thinking of the historical *destiny* of the people in its state as an ongoing ontological question, always open to further reflection while at the same time ready for decision but unencumbered by a universal teleology of the good or of justice.

8.3 *ANTIGONE* AND THE *POLIS* AS ESSENTIAL TRAGEDY

Heidegger's understanding of the essence of politics as preconceptual is connected to his interpretation of the grand sweep of the history of the West now become a planetary force in modernity both in modes of thinking and in historical forces more conventionally understood. This attempt to rethink the essence of politics is vivid in two lecture courses where Heidegger considers what it means to be human and to be a *polis* through a detailed analysis of the choral passage known as the Ode to Man in the *Antigone* of Sophocles (lines 332–75). These two are *Introduction to Metaphysics* (1935) and the course on *The Ister* (1942). Having written elsewhere on the former, I will confine my analysis to outlining its central elements.[7] It is in the latter that Heidegger explores more fully the person of Antigone and the kind of thinking she embodies, and that is what I most want to examine in terms of retrieving *phronēsis*.

In *Introduction to Metaphysics*, Heidegger sets the terms of what it means to be human and to be political in relation to the Ode (GA 40: 153–72). As befitting Sophocles's drama, Heidegger presents these as tragic modes of Being, and because of that, an illustration of what is most noble. It is crucial to underline that Heidegger interprets the Ode as a way to make sense of Parmenides's saying that "thinking and Being are the same" (GA 40:153–55), because it is precisely *phronēsis* as a mode of *thinking* that is at issue for us. Several Greek words and word pairings lie at the heart of Heidegger's reading of the Ode, especially *deinon*, *tolma*, and *hupsipolis-apolis*. In the two strophes and first antistrophe of the Ode, the chorus describes human beings as *deinotaton*, "most wondrous" (in many translations), because they venture out on land and sea, subduing the earth, capturing animals on land, sea, and air, stopping only at death as something they cannot master. For Heidegger, this *deinotaton* means that human beings are most *terrible* (*deinon*) because they are the "most uncanny" the "most unhomely"; they are restless among beings, always testing their limits, but they also necessarily run up against death as a limit that cannot be surpassed. Human beings are *violent* in their uncanny venturing amid beings: both ontically violent, in dominating animate and inanimate nature, and ontologically, in challenging the meaning and interpretation of what things are. But it is Being, as "the overwhelming sway" that governs all beings, that they run up against and risk shattering against, because Being establishes the meaning, and so the limit, of all beings as what historical humanity encounters. It is this *polemos* between Being and human beings that is most terrible, but also most productively tragic, because only by Dasein's daring to run up against the limits do history and the world remain meaningful through the *polemos* of reinterpretation (cf. GA 40: 170, 176–77).

In the fifth and final antistrophe (365–75), the chorus praises this restless human daring (*tolma*) and cleverness (*sophon*), but also fears these. For the chorus, the wondrous daring of human beings may also mean that those who dare might ignore the limits set by the laws of the land (*nomous chthonōn*) and the gods' sworn justice (*theōn t' enorkon dikēn*). Honoring (*geraiōn*) the laws and justice would elevate someone in the city (*hupsipolis*), but exiled from the city (*apolis*) is anyone who dares what is not right (*mē kalon*).

Heidegger, by contrast, reads the appositional use of *hupsipolis* and *apolis* as a properly paradoxical description of our uncanny essence. Only the *conventional* morality of a cowardly They-self dismisses the daring necessary to confront Being in the *polemos* of deconstructive reinterpretation and all the ontic disruptions that might follow, thereby risking disaster. This pacific ontological cowardice clings instead to morality as a "table of values that is attached to it externally," obsessed with "the cultivation of undisturbed comfort" that such imposed certainty brings (GA 40: 173). This is the *conceptual* approach to ethical life that Heidegger deplores as moralistic: a *theory* that one can *apply* to cases, thereby relieving oneself of the ontological responsibility of a genuine *polemos* with the rooted singularity of the situation one faces. A "table of values" may literally be written on tablets of stone to emphasize that there is no rewriting them, no rethinking them.

Heidegger explicitly proclaims that the creative few, who stand outside the city (*apolis*), employ a violence that is primarily ontological in confronting the established truth of Being, but also ontic in disrupting the conceptually settled norms and lives of the people, potentially with actual violence (GA 40: 159). In rising beyond (*hupsi-*) the existing norms of the city (*polis*), they are the only ones capable of founding and renewing the community (GA 40: 161–62). The essence of politics revolves around the *polis* as the site of both confronting the limits and reconstituting the meaning of a collective, historical way of Being. Such a "violence-doer knows no kindness and conciliation. . . . For such a one, disaster is the deepest and broadest Yes to the overwhelming" (GA 40: 172), because disaster reveals Dasein's finitude in Being, our incapacity to get behind all meaning and master it completely in a comforting forever-so.

Other commentators have argued that when Heidegger lectures on the Ode in 1942, he has softened his position.[8] There is some truth to this. Largely gone, though not entirely absent, is the valorization of creative violence. But our focus here will be on the last lines of the Ode, where the chorus seems to reject the one who violates the laws of god and city. In Greek, those lines read:

Mēt' emoi parestios
genoito mēt' ison phronōn hos tad' erdoi.

Heidegger renders the lines as follows:

Nicht werde dem Herde ein Trauter mir der,
nicht auch teile mit mir sein Wähnen mein Wissen,
der dieses führet ins Werk.

Such a one shall not be entrusted to my hearth,
Nor share his delusion with my knowing,
Who puts such a thing to work. (GA 53: 115)[9]

Heidegger rightly indicates that *parestios* is a combination of *para* and *hestia*: at the hearth. The *Herde*, the hearth, is the heart of the home, the most intimate, most literally familiar place, for it is where the family gathers for light, warmth, meals, and fellowship. At the hearth, the home is most homely. But can a *hupsipolis-apolis* person ever be trusted to share this hearth? Such a person, like Antigone, has broken away into the radically un-familiar, un-homely, and uncanny. Heidegger links *hestia* with the *phronōn* (GA 53: 133–34), which derives from *phrēn*, which in the introduction to this chapter we saw is core to an embodied knowing that senses implicitly what fits and does not fit with the reigning meaning of a given world. We speak of knowing in the gut, but also with the heart, especially when this preconceptual knowing touches on what is nearest and dearest to us, both affectively and in our way of interpreting what is most important to our world. Heidegger calls this knowing "a pondering and meditating . . . from the 'heart,' from the innermost middle of the human essence itself" (GA 53: 134; cf GA 8: 149).

The problem is the un-homely, the uncanny, the *hupsipolis-apolis* figure in the Ode. Being-at-home, having-a-home seems paradoxically to demand a dis-location. The city and the hearth, the communal and the familial, the political and the personal, are linked by this paradoxical feature of what Heidegger calls "the essence of the *polis*" (GA 53: 99) and of being-human. The home is secured only by the daring breakaway from established, familiar meaning, risking the potentially tragic demise of the familiar, which is en-tirely in keeping with what we have elucidated as the breakdown within the cave. "The *polis*," says Heidegger, "is the *polos*, that is, the pole, the whorl in which and around which everything turns" (GA 53: 100). The human world is historical; it "turns." The meaning of not just individual things, but also all things, beings as a whole, may shift and go out of alignment in this whirling "whorl" of history. The word *state* derives from the Latin *status*, standing. Heidegger insists that the essence of politics precedes the political in the de-rivative sense of institutions, constitutions, parties, and intrigues. It is what allows a historical community to take a *stand*, find a *pole*, around which the meaning of the world can orbit. The *polis* is "the site [*die Stätte*] of the abode of human history that belongs to humans in the midst of beings. . . . [W]hat is essential in the historical Being of human beings resides in the pole-like re-latedness of everything to this site of abode, that is, this site of Being homely in the midst of beings as a whole" (GA 53: 101).

Heidegger says that the uncanny, the *deinon* in the sense of a terrible un-homeliness is "the fundamental kind of essence belonging to human beings" (GA 53: 72–73). In contrast to a mere adventurer, who abandons the home, the truly unhomely person is *hupsipolis-apolis*: "Constantly on a path toward the homely site, and at the same time placed at stake in the play that repudi-ates the homely, human beings in the innermost essence are those who are unhomely" (GA 53: 111). Why this paradoxical drive that must fail? Because of the *deinon*: we are finite, we cannot get behind Being and bring beings as whole into a final perspective beyond perspective and bring historical mean-ing to a final stand. Human-being, as historical, *is essentially* paradoxical: thrown into a world whose meaning is always-already formed, that meaning is also on-the-move, unmasterable, impossible to grasp as a finished whole. Hence, the only way to be at home is to accept the tragic necessity of the paradox: "For this very reason the *polis* remains what is properly worthy of question, that which, on account of such worthiness, prevails in permeating all essential activity and every stance adopted by human beings" (GA 53: 101–2). Remaining *open* to what is most question-worthy grounds the para-dox: it is the ontological essence of politics before politics "in the derivative [ontic] sense" (GA 53: 102), because we thereby remain alive to what is most worthy of thought in a particular place and time. This is why Heidegger re-sists glib answers to the "Who are we?" question, such as biological racism.[10] To keep the historical task vibrant is to keep it question-worthy.

But then how to make phronetic ethical and political judgments in the "derivative" sense at all? For Heidegger, the answer lies in the Ode's final lines about *hestia* and *phronein*, hearth and knowing. To know the hearth as knowing from the heart means to know it as the intimately familiar, the world of meaning that constitutes the political as the preconceptual core of what binds a community together in its understanding of the world. But because to be human is to be historical, and because our historical existence is radically finite, the hearth and its familiarity are always exposed to incompleteness, challenge, and failure. Ontological earthquakes break down the most intimate structures of meaning. So, "if the 'hearth' determines the homely, and if the *deinon* is that which, in its supreme configuration, must remain excluded from the hearth, then the *deinon* can be the uncanny only if it has the essential nature of the *unhomely*" (GA 53: 133).

Human beings always-already reside in a meaningful world. Even if that world is exposed to ruptures in meaning, the breakdowns we analyzed in the cave, we still begin with what Heidegger calls knowing (*Wissen*) as *intimat-ing* (*Ahnen*, GA 53: 132) how the world makes sense; otherwise, *Being*-in-the-world at all would be impossible. Translating Heidegger's *Ahnen* as 'inti-mating' invites comparison with my use of 'intimation' in previous chapters.

To this extent, I agree with Heidegger: There would be no sense, no meaning, only a purely negative unmeaning, if we had no preconceptual intimation of the background sense of things as the way Being opens up a world for us to inhabit. Heidegger insists that this intimation is *not* some naive, unformulated presentiment of what might become some fully developed theory; rather, intimation is what grants us the pre-theoretical connection (*Vernehmen* as *noēsis*) to the world as meaningful, without which no theory would be possible at all. If it were not so, we could not experience the *deinon* as an uncanny break with the given sense of the world (GA 53: 133–34). Here, though, I agree with Plato. In Heidegger, the intimations of meaning enmesh us in a historical world, a cave without transcendence to the universal, whereas in Plato, the intimations of meaning do both by giving us an impetus to seek a fuller meaning that transcends our situatedness while also making us more discerning about how the universal is refracted in the contingencies of our rooted lives. Once again, the dynamic between transcendence and situatedness illuminates the proper role of *phronēsis*.

To make ethical-political judgments means to engage in a pre-theoretical thinking that reflects on what belongs to the hearth and home as constituting the life of the given historical community. While one does not have to disagree with Heidegger on this to embrace a Platonic polemical ethics that enlarges upon it, we first have to make better sense of *pre-theoretical* (or preconceptual) *thinking*, which sounds paradoxical, if not outright contradictory. Does not rational thought involve precisely the formation of concepts, the formulation of definitions, and the construction and analysis of theories and arguments, all in a manner that is deliberate and self-aware, rather than preconceptual? Those elements are certainly part of rational thought, the part that takes place in the moment of response in the triad of wonder-question-response. In ethical and political thought, it is most familiar to us in the work of a Locke, a Mill, or a Rawls. But is there not more to this in the human *logos*? Do we not also *think* when we wonder, or when we devise a question from that wonder? Does not an artist think, even if not in terms of definitions, concepts, and syllogisms, when using a brush, crafting a poem, molding clay, composing a score, or playing a composition? Plato, by inviting us to pay attention to the moments when erstwhile opinion breaks down in unmeaning or when the mind lights on fire in the diffused light of an idea, also invites us to contemplate this form of thought that is more properly non-conceptual than conceptual. It is what allows us to engage in *discernment* while Being-in-the-world, to *notice* when that world goes out of joint into unmeaning, to understand when and why that *matters*, so that we can engage in the polemical work of ideation that links imagination and idea to reconstruct the world of meaning.[11] Rationality, in the more familiar form of redefining concepts, reformulating arguments, and devising new theories, can only meaningfully happen if first one has some intimation of what *matters*. For anything to matter, we must be involved, rooted, in a world, and this too has its logic, its *logos*, in our situated existence, at the heart and by the hearth of the life we inhabit.

For Heidegger, our thinking from the heart-and-hearth cannot be subjected to ethical formulae or laws, be they 'natural' or 'positive' law. The ontologically ethical and political precede these ontic aspects of how we order our lives together. There is indeed a *phronēsis* in Heidegger: it is the work of *phronein*, thinking from the *phrēn*, the heart of our connection to a particular place, time, and community, even if that means breaking with all that, in uncanniness, to bring it back into joint. It is an intensely sensitive attunement to the radical finitude of historical situatedness in the *polis* as site, *polos*, around which the world takes meaningful shape. Understood in this way, *phronēsis* would be a form of care, *Sorge*, that reveals to Dasein the complexities of its situated Being-with-others in the *Da*, the unique Here of historical location (see GA 36/37: 87). Justice is then what Heidegger in *Introduction to Metaphysics* calls *Fug*, that is, "fittingness," or "fit" (GA 40: 168–69).

As Dennis Schmidt has described, this idea of justice as "fit" must mean something like the thinking of an artist who 'sees' what stroke of the brush will fit with a painting, or a composer who 'hears' what note is called for in a composition.[12] This cannot be derived from a set of rules, because in such cases, thinking is meditative rather than calculative: it ventures into unmeaning in the positive sense: following an intimation of meaning where there is nothing yet concrete. We may willingly enter into such thinking but cannot control it with logic as an algorithm, which is why the Greeks assigned its outcome to the divine intervention of the Muses. Only *phronēsis* in Heidegger's sense of thinking from the *phrēn*, from the heart or gut, can arrive at what justice demands, as what is fitting. But this ontological, radically historical notion of *phronēsis* seems to provide no guidance for ethical and political life. This is the whole point for Heidegger: to get past the metaphysical notion of ethics and politics as following some external (or indeed internalized) *idea* that sets a command and takes away the responsibility of "taking heart" oneself, of tuning in exquisitely to one's historical situatedness, to assess the historical fate of one's community, to allow that to guide one's sense of what may remake, restore, or sustain what fits with what matters.

Yet, in Heidegger's own case, this unmoored political thinking resulted in a disastrous decision in favor of the National Socialists, in part because he explicitly rejects, as a form of Platonic metaphysics, politics as guided by norms "in a juridical-moral sense" (GA 40: 169). Furthermore, in rejecting modern liberalism as a late form of Platonism, Heidegger also rejects all the protections attached to human rights, the rule of law, mixed government, and so on. Heidegger's anti-conceptual *phronēsis* leads to a radical relativism and an intense form of decisionism. While we might still have convictions, and while we might still make judgments, there is no longer any ground, any principle, we could base these upon, except for our own intimations of what "fits," and these are incommensurable, beyond *logos* in the sense of a shared political discourse that might settle our disputes.

8.4 *ANTIGONE* AND THE *POLIS* AS THE SITE OF POLEMICAL *PHRONĒSIS*

Having examined Heidegger's anti-conceptual thinking about the *Antigone* and *phronēsis*, let us recall the context for the Ode in the *Antigone*. It is often called the Ode to *Man*, but as Heidegger asks: To whom do those last lines apply? Whom would the chorus exile from the *polis*? For Heidegger, it is clear that *Antigone* herself is *hupsipolis-apolis*, the one who unsettles hearth and home (GA 53: 129).

Remarkably, Heidegger does not discuss in detail the actual ethical-political drama of the play, one that is rooted in questions of legitimate rule, obedience to law, and loyalty divided between city and family. Creon accuses Antigone of "daring to take the risk [*etolmas*] of transgressing [*huperbeinein*: overstepping; transcending] the laws" (449), norms in the conventional sense of juridical imperative. Creon has decreed that Polyneices must not be buried, for he had attacked his own city with an army that would have destroyed hearth and home. To violate Creon's law means death, but Antigone refuses to obey the decree. At first glance, this looks like thinking ethical life from the *phrēn*, from the heart—*phronēsis* in a Heideggerian sense. Antigone refuses to be governed by a normative ethics merely imposed as external rules and fiat. Instead, she insists on the freedom to consult her own *sense* of the ethical as what is fitting and proper to the situation: that she bury her own dead brother. Confronted by Creon with fact that Polyneices killed her other brother, she says, "It is my nature to nurture not hate but love" (523). Antigone makes her decision based on what heart-and-hearth call for, even if it seems imprudent and impractical to conventional practical wisdom.

But even if that is true, Antigone also does not simply stand her ground mutely, without the *logos* of argument. To Creon, she defends her decision, but not as an incommensurable, personal intuition of what is "fitting," as Heidegger requires in his sense of intimation as *Ahnen*. Instead, she appeals for justification to the "unwritten and unshakable laws of the gods" (*agrapta kasphalē theōn nomima*, 454–55). Recall that the chorus appeals to "the laws of the land" as a limit to human daring. Perhaps Heidegger does not mention this dimension of the drama because Antigone's position looks like an expression of natural right or natural law that trumps positive law: that ethics (in the ancient sense, comprising both morality and politics) cannot be fully determined by human "laws of the land," that there is a ground for ethics that transcends what happens to be written on the statute books by human hand. She says that the laws she obeys "live not for now or before, but for always, / and no one knows when they appeared" (456–57). She claims a ground for ethics that is timeless ("for always," *aei pote*), a direct contradiction of Heidegger's view that what governs human existence is radically temporal; indeed, hers is a pre-theoretical version of the Platonic *idea* of justice that Heidegger so vehemently rejects.

Antigone says these laws "live" (*zē*) in a form that is both "unwritten and unshakable" (*agrapta kasphalē*); the "unwritten" is the heart that gives life to the letter of the law, and to rewriting or even breaking that law when the letter fails. Against a Heideggerian rebuke that this recourse to timeless law is a way of avoiding one's own radical responsibility, Antigone says these laws *live* precisely *because* they are unwritten; their life resides in each person's having to make sense of them on their own, as she does, risking everything. They are *unshakable* because the mere givens of positive law, written in the codes of law or the common law of inherited norms, can never substitute for this personal responsibility to discern the ethical. Her declaration foreshadows Levinas's claim that "Universalism has a greater weight than the particularist letter of the text; or, to be more precise, it bursts the letter apart, for it lay, like an explosive, within the letter."[13] Antigone does shun judging the ethical by what convention happens to demand, what 'They' say must be done, just because 'it is written.' Crucially, Antigone's unwritten, unshakable laws are not simply the same as the modern idea of natural law or human rights, which we attempt to codify in a philosophical system. The meaning of any such system must be blown apart by the "explosive" of confrontation in the face of an unmeaning that may lead either to tragedy or renewal, depending on whether the confrontation succeeds in drawing new meaning for norms from the challenge of unmeaning. For Antigone, it is a matter of personal responsibility to a law she must discern for herself, not bound by tradition, yet still bound to answer to it. She makes her case to the community for what she discerns as eternal and universal, thereby answering the call of conscience both for herself and to the community.

What is *asphalēs* for Antigone, then, is her unshakable right to take a stand on the ethical and its demands for herself, risking the explosion of norms, even as she ascribes this appeal to the eternal laws of the gods. They are *unwritten* laws, therefore manifestly open to re-interpretation; they are precisely *not* a codified "table of values" or dictatorial norms. This is the core of ethics as what I am here calling *the ethical*, or simply ethical life, which is distinct from normative *ethics*, either as traditional codes of conduct or highly elaborated philosophical systems of ethics. What I mean by this distinction is similar to the one Levinas draws "between the ethical and the moral": "By morality I mean a series of rules relating social behavior and civic duty. But while morality thus operates in the socio-political order of organizing and improving our human survival, it is ultimately founded on an ethical responsibility towards the other."[14] *The ethical precedes ethics.* It involves our responsibility to *make sense* of an ethical challenge for ourselves while at the same time *making a case*, by rational argument, to those others with whom we share our world, both as a mark of respect for the fact of that interdependency and because intimations of the ethical must always start from given, traditional norms, even when in confrontation with them. Where I depart from Levinas is when he says that the ethical "is a form of vigilant passivity to the call of the other"; Levinas insists on this "passivity" as a way to avoid totalization and to remain open to what the call of the other might disrupt in the settled norms of established morality. But while a polemical ethics must be alive to this disruptive call, it must also *actively engage* in the dialectic between established meaning and a potentially fertile unmeaning that irrupts within it to spur the reconstruction of ethics in response to the call. Antigone insists on her ethical agency, but still in a form that appeals to a common understanding. She does not reject dialogue in favor of solipsistic, mystical insight; she engages in a dialectic between what is "unwritten" in the ethical and the norms that are written, in the extended sense of established morality and rules, in order to reformulate these norms. Both she and the chorus, as well as Creon, appeal to law. It is this double responsibility of the ethical that is *asphalēs*, the unshakable ground of responsibility to both self and community, bound together but distinct, in the polemical working-through of what is at issue in ethical life whenever existing normative ethics fall short.

The intense political drama of the *Antigone* arises through a shattering ethical conflict, the explosion that Levinas deems the heart of ethical life that must at times burst the confines of written norms, in that extended sense of "written" as meaning what has been established and set as normative, *nomos*, and seems to brook no defiance. The drama of the play centers on the clash of two domains of meaning that each lays uncompromising claim on the individual: family and community. This clash threatens the whole community with breakdown into unmeaning. But just as *to deinon* has a double aspect as the wondrous and the terrifying, so does the irruption of unmeaning: it is an opening to new constellations of meaning as well as to the collapse of meaning into despair. Antigone does not make her case in a philosophical form, but it is worth remembering that if she is the *apolis* figure at the start of the play, the one the chorus and Creon expel from the hearth as *deinotaton*, her position carries the day by the end, persuading both the chorus and Creon. Even if she herself dies, she dies a hero. By acting from the *phrēn*, the heart of ethical life, she lacks the *phronēsis* to negotiate the crisis in a way that would save herself, but she does show the way to saving the city. The awful tragedy of her fate is also awe-inspiring, because it opens up new vistas of meaning for both the legendary Thebes and the historical audience in Athens, as well as for us. Even if it is too late for Creon and Antigone, Sophocles's tragic lesson might well be that it does not have to be too late for us if we can enlarge upon the *phronēsis* needed to navigate ethical life.

We can have a politics that remains open to the polemical interplay between *the ethical* and *ethics*, or ethical life in conflict with customary normative ethics (*nomoi*). By *ethics*, again, I mean the established norms of personal and political life: constitutions, laws, mores, and so on—all that Heidegger scorns as calcified codification that allows us to evade our radical responsibility by simply obeying without thinking. By *the ethical*, I mean that heart of life to which we turn in thinking whenever we, like Antigone, discover that we cannot agree with what the statutes or norms dictate and find ourselves plunged into the awfulness of awe-inspiring unmeaning, with only our conscience as a guide to the intimations of a new or renewed meaning for reconstructing a shared world. Ethics is ontic: it is about having established norms for action. This is not to denigrate ethics, which is vital for being-human; but the ethical, or ethical life, is ontological: it is how we face up to the polemical task of reconstituting our ethics, because all established norms, all "letters of the law," fray in the face of our finitude and may fail to do justice to what is ethical and just.

8.5 RETRIEVING *PHRONĒSIS*

This discussion returns us to *phronēsis* and the essence of politics, and now we can no longer ignore Aristotle. Heidegger does discuss Aristotle briefly in his second reading of the *Antigone*. This comes during his analysis of the *essence* of the *polis* as the historically situated site around which the meaning of the world revolves. Heidegger cites Aristotle's description in Book 1 of the *Politics* of "the human being as *zōon politikon*," which he says is translated "in a superficial way" as "'the human being is a political being'" (GA 53:102). For Heidegger, to be a political being involves what Aristotle means by calling us "a *zōon logon echon*—a living being that has the word, which means: *that* being that can address beings as such with respect to their Being":

> Who or what the human being is precisely cannot be decided "politically" according to *that* thinker who names the human being the "political being," because the very essence of the *polis* is determined in terms of its relation to the essence of human beings (and the essence of human beings is determined from out of the truth of Being). (GA 53: 102)

Heidegger understands the essence of human beings and of politics as grounded in the "truth of Being": the way that a world of meaning opens up historically for us. As *logos*, this truth of Being collects the understanding of the world in a particular way for a historically located community, and so *logos* and *polis* are connected at the *polos*, the site around which meaning forms, differentiating one community from others in the *polemos*.

But in his ontologized understanding of politics, Heidegger leaves out what Aristotle says about the actual work of the *logos* in the *polis*. In Book 1 of the *Politics*, Aristotle says that human beings have the *logos* because, unlike any other living being we know of, we discuss and make determinations about what is just and unjust. We debate and then act on our *accounts* of what is right and wrong, and we give *reasons* for why we hold the positions we do (1253a8–18). The *logos* encompasses these dimensions of rationality—account, dialogue, giving reasons, argument—and more, because it also includes the possibility of contemplating *what as yet has no account*, that demands an account, but as yet only beckons by intimations through the explosion of unmeaning that a breakdown in norms induces. The conflict between Creon and Antigone epitomizes the political. Each articulates a position on a matter of decisive importance to the city. For them, politics fails; disaster overtakes the city. But it does not have to be so, and surely Sophocles sought to offer his audience in democratic Athens that possibility through the warning of the tragedy. We recognize that politics, as the domain of discourse about the just and unjust, is polemical, but that this conflict may be mediated by speech, not violence. Unlike social insects, we do not cooperate harmoniously by instinct alone. Heidegger is right about the *deinon* and the *apolis*; it is essential to being-human to disagree and to diverge from established justice. Our understanding of the social world is vulnerable to breakdown, never entirely set and secure. Rules, laws, and ethical codes are never final and adequate to every circumstance. But what is *asphalēs*, a firm foundation, is that as long as we remain human-beings, the call of conscience can summon us from the contingencies if our situatedness to confront the breakdown in de-, pre-, and reconstruction.

At stake here is what it means to *be* ethical. Heidegger is surely right that it does not simply mean conforming to the norms of the society into which we happen to be thrown by submitting to the dictates of whatever authority claims to command. To be ethically responsible is to be *alive* to conflicts and breakdowns in these laws and norms, to the need to *think* them through, and to the necessity of becoming *apolis* if one deems them unjust. This is what we learned about the breakdowns within the cave and what Antigone means by saying that the unwritten laws *are alive* (*zē*). It is not that they command us with yet another, somehow ultimate layer of authority, but rather that we are *called* by ethical life to think through for ourselves what we believe is just, and also to give an account of that determination. The break with Heidegger happens here, because this life of ethical *phronēsis* is not mere decisionism or intuitionism, even though the ethical is not a norm, and even if justice is higher than statutory law.

Ethical life is what calls for reflection beyond established concepts and norms, what we must think about polemically, whenever we discover that existing norms are somehow inadequate or unjust, even if, in reconstructing ethical life, we must translate the ethical into new norms, concepts, practices, institutions, and indeed systems of ethics. That is the work of preconstruction and reconstruction. But what does such thinking consist *in*? Heidegger rightly says that it cannot be simply another form of *ratio*, calculating from indubitable first principles and applying them to a new situation, because that would still be ethics in the metaphysical, conceptual sense (GA 53: 117–18). Later, in the discussion of ethics as *ēthos* in his "Letter on Humanism," Heidegger says that "there is a thinking that is more rigorous than the conceptual"; it is "a thinking that is neither theoretical nor practical. It eventuates prior to this distinction" (GA 9: 357, 358). But if ethical-political thinking is not about grasping conceptual norms from an authoritative dictate, tablet of commandments, law book, or philosophical theory and applying them, what is it?

One possibility is that ethical life, which includes the political in the ancient sense, involves reflecting on justice as what fits (the *Fug*) in the given unique situation, and this cannot be given in advance by a formula that takes away the responsibility for each such moment as decisively one's own. But this seems again to throw the measure for action back to thinking as a kind of *technē* of the *ēthos* that intuits without any capacity for giving reasons. This is ultimately why Heidegger links Parmenides's *noein* and *einai*, thinking and Being, as "the same," with both Heraclitus's *polemos* and *logos* as "the same" and with Sophocles's thinking of human beings as *deinotaton* and *hupsipolis-apolis*, because our ethical-political life is never fully at-home. Conflicts ever arise over the meaning of the world, over its Being as a collected *logos*, and the only way to break through is to accept the uncanniness of situated, historical life and take a stand. Heidegger thinks leaders do that: they take a stand where there is no calculable measure and thereby paradoxically "ground the abyss" (GA 65: 7).

Heidegger errs, though, by rejecting existing laws and norms as contemptible expressions of the They-self, as manifestations of metaphysical essentialism, or as derivative conceptual thinking. Just as "Being is always the Being of beings" for Heidegger (SZ, 37), we might also say that the ethical is always the ethical of an ethics, or the political is always the political of a politics, where 'the ethical' and 'the political' stand for a domain of polemical reflection to which we must turn when the meaning, purpose, or practice of existing *nomoi* have broken down. This is the heart of ethical life to which thinking must return when these norms break down in order to breathe new life into ethics, newly conceptualized and newly institutionalized. This liminal domain, where existing meaning threatens to collapse into unmeaning, is where imagination and idea meet in the apprehension of new or renewed insight into the ethical and political, insight that has the potential for the reconstruction of our social world. Unmeaning is never simply a naked nothingness, an ontic nullity where no-thing makes any sense. Understood ontologically and hermeneutically, unmeaning emits intimations of meaning, and thus is the counterpart to meaning, which is always fraying, never complete, always threatening a decay into unmeaning.

On the other hand, the fertile potential inherent to unmeaning, which is not simply the annihilation or lack of meaning, is that unmeaning is itself on the verge of mending, of becoming coherent at its edges, if only we take up the threads of the intimations that beckon in the call of conscience by exercising the ideation that mediates between idea and imagination. Both meaning and unmeaning are not attributes adhering to beings but modes of Being; they describe the way things do or do not *mean* for us as we take them to *be*, and we to each other as the beings for whom meaning and unmeaning is what we *do* in dialogue and what makes the world either matter to us or fade into insignificance. Just as we find ourselves always-already in a world of established meaning where beings are interpreted as what they are, so do we find ourselves always-already living in a world of established norms. But the *apolis*, *deinon* moment of human existence is always a possibility. We "apprehend" (*noein*) that in some particular case the norms do not "fit." This is that moment of breakdown for the prisoner in the cave. Just as we can challenge the interpretation of beings, so can we challenge the justice of norms. This is polemical justice. But we can only make this challenge in terms of the deconstruction, but not destruction, of the understanding we already have, as Antigone does with the chorus's understanding of law, even as we work our way to a new understanding through ideation.

In the *Nicomachean Ethics*, Aristotle singles out a moral virtue critical to justice: *epieikeia*, which might be translated as reasonableness, equity, or fair-mindedness (Book 5.10). At issue for Aristotle is that no rule can cover every possible contingency. For that reason, to do justice in a unique circumstance it may be necessary to ignore or break the standing rule. But the crucial question here is, *to what* does the rule-breaker appeal in such a case? Where does thinking *go* when existing norms and concepts no longer suffice? What justifies the decision made, both intellectually, as the ground for the rule-breaking, and politically to the community, as the legitimacy of such a violation of settled norm? As Aristotle suggests (*Politics*, 1287a19–32), such rule-breaking may easily tilt into lawless tyranny. It is necessarily *apolis* in two senses: as a departure from established norms and as a threat to the very life of the community. Nevertheless, Aristotle holds this *apolis* moment as essential to the political, precisely because of the finitude of human understanding and the necessary deficiency of all settled laws and norms, which cannot always fit the given situation. There can be no rule for when the existing rules do not apply, for that leads to an infinite regress (*Ethics*, 1137b14–30), and so *epieikeia* demands a mode of thinking other than merely interpreting or applying an existing rule, be it a human posit or a purported natural or divine law.

Corresponding to the moral virtue of *epieikeia* as the disposition to be mindfully flexible, rather than a narrow stickler about the rules, is the intellectual virtue of *phronēsis*, the thinking that discerns properly when and how to bend or even break the rules (and with whom, to what extent, in what way, and so on). As such, Aristotle's *phronēsis* seems very close to Heidegger's notion of the thinking, the *noein*, that intuits the just as the fitting and appropriate. This does not mean it is irrational or, worse, barbaric, according to Heidegger (GA 9: 346). But why is this not intuitionism and decisionism, a thinking that can give no account, no *logos*, of itself?

The answer may lie in Aristotle's concept of *noēsis*, an especially difficult word to translate. In Book 6 of the *Ethics*, it is the faculty that allows us to intuit the fundamentals of a science, such as the axioms of geometry, that are true but cannot themselves be demonstrated; one either 'gets it' or does not (1140b3–1141a9).[15] That is in the domain of theoretical wisdom (*sophia*), of eternal truths; but we could also say that *noēsis* plays a role in *phronēsis*, the domain of contingency, which is precisely the domain of historically situated communities. This noetic thinking must apprehend with exquisite finesse not timeless, indemonstrable axioms, but rather a situation's singular features to judge what norms must be broken to what extent, and how they can be rectified, reconstructed, and remedied.

Previously, we have called this openness to such finesse the *intimations* that unite us in our *situated transcendence*.[16] It is essentially paradoxical, like being *hupsipolis-apolis*, and yet essential to what it means to *be* human as open to the ethical. Because ethical life is always encountered through the ethical breakdowns of an ethics, that is, through the *polemos* that arises when we discover that established norms fall short in a given situation, political and ethical life can only rise high (*hupsi-polis*) when we have the insight (*noein*) for situations that call into question our established norms; such thinking transcends the community's givens and is therefore *a-polis*. Heidegger might be right in his "Letter on Humanism" to cite Aristotle's *Nicomachean Ethics* as saying that ethics is first and foremost about *ēthos*, a way of life shared by a community whose norms are *habitual*, and therefore largely preconceptual (GA 9:352–53). Aristotle therefore considers the lawmaking leader crucial, because lawmaking in the broad sense constitutes the institutions and practices that inculcate this *ēthos* (*Ethics*, Book 10.9).

But because politics is polemical in the deeper sense, we cannot always rely on ethics as simply the preconceptual "background practices," as Hubert Dreyfus would call them, of our life together.[17] When conflicts arise, if we are to resolve them through a shared human *logos* in the manner of human politics for Aristotle rather than through bestial violence, then in times of breakdown, we must make that ethics explicit. That is, *we must make it conceptual* so that we may talk through the ethical in our ethics. This means we must not rashly discard or scorn established ethics—as laws, rules, norms—when thinking the ethical, because that ethics is the only ground for discourse with our community about what the ethical calls for when the established norms break down. The shadows on the cave wall are not about nothing. Heidegger himself says that a community works out its collective fate through *Mitteilung und Kampf*, "communication and struggle" (*logos* and *polemos*), but he neglects the role that existing norms must play in structuring but not dictating how the reasoned discourse for resolving a confrontation must proceed if community is to be reconstructed after a breakdown (cf. SZ, 384–85). We *cannot* discard the existing discourse entirely, because all political-ethical discourse depends in advance in our sharing *some* grounds of understanding, the ethical life of any ethics, just as sharing a world depends on our having some shared understanding of the Being of beings.

8.6 EXAMPLES OF *PHRONĒSIS* IN ETHICAL LIFE

Let me give examples that illustrate where Heidegger goes wrong in thinking the ethical at the limit. In a book I wrote with my father about ethical, legal, and policy questions after 9/11, such as torture, invasions of privacy, and presidential power, we argued for such a situated transcendence (without calling it that) in facing limit situations in our norms through a form of Aristotelian *phronēsis*.[18] We cited political leaders who bent, or even broke, the law: Thomas Jefferson violated the Constitution when, as president, he authorized military expenditures without congressional approval when he thought war with Britain was immanent in 1807; Abraham Lincoln violated the Constitution by suspending *habeas corpus* without constitutionally mandated congressional approval when he deemed Washington under immanent threat in 1861 at the outbreak of the Civil War. On the citizens' side, oppressed people in America have resisted in a variety of ways. Civil rights activists deliberately violated long-established Jim Crow laws, especially in the 1950s and 1960s, to protest and overturn those laws as unjust.[19] More recently, women have challenged both unwritten norms of abusive sexual behavior and the written rules of precedent on assault and harassment through the #MeToo movement. Also, the Black Lives Matter movement, especially after the killing of George Floyd, has mobilized protesters of all races to demand substantive change to structural racism in policing, criminal justice, and the public memorialization of our shared history. For the most part, these movements have not bent or broken laws, but they have vigorously challenged norms in ways that portend genuine societal change. This is the hermeneutical-political polemics of ethical life confronting established norms to give new form to ethics, law, and institutions. It is polemical ethics enacted.

Essential to these examples of both officers and subjects of the law is respect for law even in bending or breaking the law. Ethical life cannot subsist without producing norms to live by, even if those norms may have to be confronted and reconstituted ever again, given our finitude. This underlines the *idea* of justice that transcends the existing conceptualization and institutionalization of justice, due to a crisis, a breakdown. Lincoln went to Congress to acknowledge a violation of the law, asking Congress to rectify the rupture by ratifying it *ex post facto*, risking impeachment if Congress would not. Civil rights activists showed respect for the law, even as they broke it, by risking prosecution. In each case, the actors took upon themselves the risk, the *tolma*, of *apolis* action that transcended established norms.

My father and I observe that in discussing his law-breaking, Jefferson "recognized that in an emergency, public servants must hold to the principle that the welfare of the people trumps the letter of the written law." In Jefferson's words: "The officer who is called to act on this superior ground [the welfare of the people; the common good], does indeed risk himself on the justice of the controlling powers of the Constitution, and his station makes it his duty to incur that risk." Jefferson also writes, "A strict observance of the written law is doubtless one of the high duties of a good citizen, but it is not the highest. . . . To lose our country by a scrupulous adherence to written law, would be to lose the law itself, with life, liberty, property and all those who are enjoying them with us."[20]

Like Antigone, Jefferson holds that the right to pass judgment on the adequacy of standing law is critical to justice. But that right entails a willingness to take upon one's own head, and as a *duty*, the risk of appealing to what Antigone called the *unwritten* ground of established, written law; this submission to judgment distinguishes such norm-breaking acts from the acts of tyrants who respect no established norms whatsoever. The political actors we cite appealed to their fellow citizens' *sense* of the ethical underlying the specific ethics of the established norms. They employed *phronēsis* in violating ethics as mere rules, but appealed to the intimation, defended in rational discourse, of a common good that lives (*zē*) at the heart of this ethics and without which it becomes mere fiat, incapable of discerning its own breakdowns. This concern and respect for norms as given makes possible, although not certain, the reconstruction of personal and political bonds after the disruptive rupture.

Acting beyond law for the common good must risk the ethical-juridical judgment of the community or else risks drifting into tyranny or anarchy. We may each appeal to an ethical life beyond established ethics and norms, but we must submit to the community to validate this appeal, or else dissolve communal life entirely into a sterile unmeaning. This dialogical responsibility saves reconstructive idealism from the "Because I said so!" of authoritarianism, decisionism, or crude intuitionism, none of which are able, or willing, to give an account of their determinations because they depend either on the arbitrary willfulness of the tyrant or on a refusal of responsive dialogue in favor of insisting upon incommensurable atavism. Avoiding this silencing of dialogue is the source for the responsibility to give reasons for one's *apolis* insight and expose oneself to the judgment of the community. It is an acknowledgment of one's own finitude, one's own fallibility, in passing judgment on the norms of the community. It is what keeps both leader and citizen from *hubris* in bending or breaking those norms through a polemical ethics. Heidegger entirely misses the *phronēsis* needed for negotiating the breaking and reconstruction of norms by championing only the *hupsipolis-apolis* creative few, which leaves him vulnerable to the despotic politics of National Socialism and the *Führerprinzip*.

Crucial to the *hupsipolis-apolis* action of norm-breaking actors, then, is this responsible appeal to the common good at the heart of ethical life beyond the given norms as well as to the very norms they live by every day. Unless the community is so unjust as to be irredeemable, requiring instead revolution or separation, the political actors present their law-breaking as a *responsive* loyalty to the spirit of the laws even if that spirit has not been realized, as with Antigone in legend and civil rights activists in history. Jefferson and Lincoln argued that the Constitution was established to preserve the community; their actions were a redeemable break to accomplish just that preservation. In civil disobedience against racist laws, activists argued that the founding principle of "all men are created equal," as well as the constitutional protections developed in the spirit of that principle, meant that the Jim Crow laws were themselves unlawful, even as they accepted legal punishment to demonstrate their allegiance to law as a fundamental principle of shared political life.

This is how ethics in the *norm-al*, situated sense inhabits ethical life in the *apolis* sense as transcending norms. That life beyond established norms must still must *account* for itself, for its *noēsis*, the rationally defensible intuition of what 'fits' justice as newly formulated in terms the previously normal ethics can understand. Thus *polemos*, as a conflict over what justice calls for, and *logos*, as accountability, bring ethical life and ethics together in situated transcendence. This is how metaethics, as a reinterpretive encounter with the foundations of ethical life, even if not explicitly thematized as such, comes into play with a given established ethics. There is no guarantee that this appeal to the community will succeed, but that is the *apolis* risk rule-breakers take upon themselves as the pledge of shared allegiance to a common good.

This is why, in his ontological interpretation of *polemos* in politics, Jan Patočka says, following Heraclitus, "*Polemos* is what is common"—*common* both in the sense of pervasive and of what we share: "*Polemos* binds together the contending parties, not only because it stands over them but because in it they are one." Politics, rather than brute violence, is the contentious but shared dialogue interpreting what constitutes the heart of the community, what is right and wrong, lawful and unlawful. That is why Patočka properly links *polemos* and *phronēsis*: "The power that arises from strife is a power that knows and sees: only in this invigorating strife is there life that truly sees into the nature of things—*to phronein*. Thus *phronēsis*, understanding, by the very nature of things, cannot but be at once common and conflicted."[21] Common and conflicted, *logos* and *polemos*, are united by *phronēsis* because only through discerning the historically situated particulars and how they matter as meaningful, does what is at-issue in the conflict for a specific community come to light in a way perspicacious enough for resolution through vigorous struggle in debate, dialogue, discussion, and the consequent reconstruction of norms, laws, and institutions. Otherwise, as Sophocles warns, disaster awaits.

In the analysis of the polemical cycle of exit and return in the cave, I have described the moments of this process as a triad of de-, pre-, and reconstruction of norms. In deconstruction, we run up against the limits of given norms and expose them; in preconstruction, we formulate a new understanding of what the ethical calls for, but always in terms of what 'normal' ethics involves as norms to live by; in reconstruction, we integrate those new norms in the life of the community. The danger of failure is alive in each moment, because *phronēsis* cannot eliminate the contingencies of human finitude. In deconstruction, the danger lies in going beyond identifying how a conceptual scheme we live by has broken down to promoting a nihilistic mistrust in meaning altogether; in preconstruction, or envisioning something new, it lies in imagining ideals and theorizing alternatives so remote from the given norms that they have no hope of dialogue with the situated existence of the historical community; in reconstruction, it lies in failing to integrate new insights and ideals with the existing institutions and practices of the community, from the most intimate habits to the most general principles, so that society might be reconstituted enduringly. Nevertheless, risking these dangers is necessary for ethical life to persist, precisely because that same finitude of human institutions, habitual practices, and ethical-political concepts makes breakdowns in meaning and the subsequent cycle of reconstrual inevitable.

To be *un*-ethical is to refuse the call of ethical life, the phronetic thinking as *noein*, the attentive, discerning perception that discloses the limitations of established norms. To refuse to *be alive* to the possibility that the given norms may be inadequate, that new interpretation is going always to be needed in the *polemos* of the historical situatedness of human political life, is a failure of responsibility. To believe that ethical life is only about calculating according to established rules and applying them, rather than thinking about what gives those rules their validity metaethically, is a failure to heed the call of conscience. Such rigidity in the face of finitude results only in tyranny and repression, which will inevitably corrode the affective sharing of norms that give life to the body politic. Still, the triad of de-, pre-, and reconstruction always transpires as an appeal to ethical life *through* a discussion of ethics and the principles as a community has understood them hitherto.

In this movement from *noēsis* to explanation, the conceptual is not alien to genuine ethical thinking. It gives that thinking a foothold in the situated life of the community. The articulation of principles, political and ethical theories, and systems of law is integral to how we give voice to ethical life, even if these conceptual schemes cannot exhaust it. I am arguing, then, for a polemical reconciliation of *idea* and *noēsis*, of reason and non-conceptual thinking, of concept and essence, of metaphysics and ontology, of Plato and Heidegger, in a situated transcendence that must ever-again work through the breakdowns and breakthroughs of our finite historical understanding.

Heidegger failed to respect ethics as the concrete experience of ethical life, and this left him with an unhinged *phronēsis*. In his rush to overturn metaphysical thinking, Heidegger uprooted everything he took as an expression of Platonic "Liberalism" and moralism. This led him to contribute in a significant way to some of the most abhorrent impulses of one of the most barbaric movements in human history, such as the valorization of transgressive violence and leadership beyond law. No reader should forget that in a lecture course as early as 1933, Heidegger told students that proper understanding of the *polemos* involves detecting or even *fabricating* an enemy that has burrowed into the "innermost roots" of the *Volk* and that this enemy must be attacked "with the goal of total annihilation" (GA 36/37: 91). A properly attuned *phronēsis* is moderate even in its radical willingness to depart from the norm; it respects the givens of ethics as the only living context for how the historically situated community comes to terms with the ethical as the ground for ethics—even if that be the supposedly metaphysical understanding of norms in the Western tradition.

Heidegger welcomed tragedy as the human condition, as the experience of our limitation in the face of Being, but he failed to notice that Greek tragedies often ended with a satyr play and that the festival of Dionysus included comedy as well as tragedy. The comic is not merely the ridiculous or the funny, but another way of seeing the finitude of human existence in another register than tragedy.[22] Joy and reconciliation are possible conclusions of our *polemos* with our situatedness, not just the disaster faced by Antigone, Creon, and Thebes. To *be* ethical, to live the ethical life, rather than living passively by inherited or imposed codes of ethics, we must face possibilities of both disaster and breakthrough as we work for the ever-reconstructing existence of the community. We cannot do this without rethinking ethical life by confronting ethics as we find it and live it in our given historical world. In turn, we must be ready to reconstitute that ethics in the light of ideas we can articulate for one another by reflecting on ethical life as what transcends the here and now.

NOTES

1. Rainer Maria Rilke, "Wendung," 52; my translation.

2. On embodiment and the difference in Aristotle between divine and human wisdom, see *Nicomachean Ethics*, 1141b4–13, 1143b17–23, 1177b27–32, 1178b17–1179a2.

3. Mark Blitz, *Heidegger's* Being and Time, 201.

4. For a detailed account of the Dasein as polemical in its existential structure, see Fried, *Heidegger's Polemos*, chapter 2, "Polemos as Da-Sein."

5. For example, see Allison Stone, "Essentialism and Anti-Essentialism in Feminist Philosophy."

6. In *Being and Time*, Heidegger distinguishes between the fate (*Schicksal*) of the individual and the destiny (*Geschick*) of a people (*Volk*) that encompasses individual fates (SZ, 384–85), but in *Nature, History, State*, he speaks of the singular fate of an individual people, embodied in its state, among other peoples.

7. See Gregory Fried, "*Introduction to Metaphysics*," in *The Bloomsbury Companion to Heidegger*; also, *Heidegger's Polemos*, chapter 4.

8. See Clare Pearson Geiman, "Heidegger's *Antigones*," in *A Companion to Heidegger's Introduction to Metaphysics*; Theodore Kisiel, "The Seminar of Winter Semester 1933–34 within Heidegger's Three Concepts of the Political," in *Nature, History, State*.

9. I employ the excellent translation by William McNeill and Julia Davis in what follows, but I have amended it here. I will render *Sein* as "Being" rather than "being."

10. Consider Heidegger's attack on Erwin Kolbenheyer (GA 36/37: 209–15). This does not mean that Heidegger cannot subscribe to an *ontological* racism. See *Heidegger's Polemos*, 227–28.

11. For an insightful treatment of discernment in the light of Aristotle's *euphuia* as deepened through iterative self-reflection and dialogue in community, see Byrne, *The Ethics of Discernment*, 304–6.

12. Dennis Schmidt employed this analogy in his July 2013 lectures for the Collegium Phaenomenologicum, "Idioms of the Ethical in Heidegger: From the Rectoral Address to 'Letter on Humanism.'" Of his published work, Schmidt's essay, "Heidegger and the Call for an Original Ethics," most succinctly captures his critique of ethics as "applied" theory in favor of a way of thinking about ethical life as attuned to the singularities of existence.

13. Emmanuel Levinas, *Nine Talmudic Readings*, 39.

14. For this and the quote below, see Levinas, "Ethics of the Infinite," 80.

15. On *noēsis* as thinking that 'gets it,' see Fried, "A Second Letter to Emmanuel Faye," in *Confronting Heidegger*, 218–25.

16. See also Fried, "Heidegger and Gandhi," 60–61.

17. See Hubert Dreyfus, *Being-in-the-World: A Commentary on Heidegger's Being and Time*, 4–5.

18. Charles Fried and Gregory Fried, *Because It Is Wrong*.

19. Fried and Fried, *Because It Is Wrong*; see especially the chapters on "No Beginning or No End" and "Learning Not to Be Good."

20. Quoted in Fried and Fried, *Because It Is Wrong*, 155, 136.

21. Patočka, *Heretical Essays*, 41.

22. See Hyland, *Finitude and Transcendence*, 137.

Conclusion

Towards Enacting a Polemical Ethics

Poets, prophets, and reformers are all picture-makers, and this ability is the secret of their power and achievements: they see what ought to be by the reflection of what is, and endeavor to remove the contradiction.

—Frederick Douglass, "Pictures and Progress"[1]

The task of this book has been to lay the metaethical foundations for a polemical ethics upon the ground cleared by enacting a confrontation between Plato and Heidegger. We can agree with Heidegger that being-human is essentially hermeneutical in its understanding of the world and that we enter into the *polemos* whenever we engage in a genuine, authentic interpretive struggle, without following his rejection of Plato's idealism. My reading of the Cave Allegory argues that ethical life, which includes political life, requires the projection of the idea as a constitutive feature of our polemical, hermeneutical, and historical existence. If this reading is sound, it can build the metaethical foundations of a polemical ethics by accounting for the historicity of being-human without discarding either our situated awareness of meaning or the ideas that transcend it. The next steps involve enacting a polemical ethics upon this foundation.

A reconstructive view of history can help us to embody this polemical ethics and lead to a new understanding of freedom. For now, I want to underline the presuppositions and arguments of my ongoing project. Heidegger is in part correct to say that big-L Liberalism has its roots in Plato, but this Liberalism is not a nihilistic dead end. Rather, this larger Liberalism, which includes but exceeds the classical liberalism of modernity, offers the best hope for the polemical freedom and situated transcendence of being-human. This more encompassing Liberalism posits freedom as the starting point of philosophy as a way of life that all can potentially share in varying degrees.

Four types of freedom are described by the Greeks. The first three are: *autarcheia*, or autarchy, meaning freedom as self-sufficiency (usually but not necessarily in an economic sense); *autonomia*, or autonomy, which means being free to govern oneself and to set one's own rules; and *exousia*, license, or the freedom to do as one pleases because one holds the authority or simply the sheer power to do so—the power of tyrants.

The fourth freedom is *eleutheria*, freedom from being subject to the arbitrary will of another. *Eleutheria* is the opposite of slavery, *douleia*.[2] The Greek *eleutheria* might seem to have no direct counterpart in English, but in fact there is an etymological connection. The Latin *liber* and the Greek *eleutheria* both derive from the same Indo-European root, **(e)leudo* and variants, which is also related to the root **leuth*, which means to grow, and is related to words such as the German *Leute*, the people, and the Roman deity Liber, god of plant growth and viniculture.[3] This freedom, this *liberty*, can be described as the freedom to flourish where one is planted, as opposed to being forced to grow against one's will in a strange land. In short, the English word *liberty* is an etymological cousin to the Greek *eleutheria*. Ancient linguistic usage echoes the claim of Heraclitus that there is an ontological distinction between the freeborn, the *eleutheroi*, or the *liberi*, and the slaves and captives, the *douloi*, or the *servi*. In such a conception, the human social world would include both as a simple fact of the natural order of things. In the ancient slave societies that were bound by this master-slave ontology, *eleutheria* required the forced labor of the enslaved to free up time for the free to enjoy liberty, both as private persons and as participating members in the civic life of a free but exclusive society.

But we can manumit the vital core of liberty as *eleutheria*: we can recognize that personal liberty is both secured by and fulfilled through civic liberty. This *eleutheria*, unbound from the binary of free and slave, may encompass a conception of liberty as a positive realization of human-being without a concomitant repression and exploitation of others. That is the ideal proposed by the proponents of modern liberalism, who hold liberty and equality to be compatible, even if their balance must regularly be negotiated in practice.

Liberty as *eleutheria* means that our private liberty, our independence from arbitrary impositions upon our freedoms, is protected, fulfilled, and enlarged by our civic liberty. Civic liberty, the active, willing, and honorable participation in the political life of an independent polity, is necessitated by our finitude, because we are not wholly independent individuals. Eleutheric freedom, as an interdependent independence, is a feature of the paradoxical

Between of human-being: between the earth-bound dependency of embodied situatedness and the sky-bound longing for separation and individuation. Such freedom completes us as individuals, to the extent possible in a shared human finitude, by allowing us to contribute both individually and collectively to sustaining the intertwined independence of self and community as an expression of human freedom. The necessity of returning to the cave because of our dependent embodiment bears witness to this intertwining of self and society in eleutheric liberty.

And so a key feature of enacting a polemical ethics will be to delineate an eleutheric liberty, or *eleutherism*, as the kind of reconstructive liberalism I hope to develop and defend. At the same time, like all constructs limited by human finitude, eleutheric liberty includes unresolvable tensions and problems. Thus, it must be a reconstructive liberalism paired with skeptical idealism that lays itself open to correction, reinvention, and renewal. No political system and certainly no magical political concept will settle once and for all the political problem while we remain human.

The tyrannical in spirit try to evade finitude by treating our interdependence as an embarrassment, something to be overcome for oneself or exploited in others. But this evasion is in bad faith, for it denies the most evident fact of our finitude: our mortal limitations and dependencies. We are not gods. We are finite beings, frayed by our contingencies and mortality. We cannot be entirely self-sufficient, because we cannot survive, let alone flourish, by supplying all of our needs by ourselves or from ourselves, as does the divine. Living in bad faith is illiberal, because it poisons and precludes the fuller freedom we can attain, in constructive dialogue with others and the world, in ethical life, in political life, and in the life that acknowledges its codependency with a natural world that no human ingenuity can fully master. License craves an unachievable and tyrannical mastery over human finitude. This will to mastery is futile, because it ruins the true liberty that only the interdependent life can provide. If left unchecked, this will degenerates into a hubristic will to power, as history teaches only too well.

If our historicity and embedded finitude as members of particular historical worlds is fundamental to being-human, then eleutherism must account for how this situatedness may be compatible with the universalism of liberal ethical and political thought. It also means reconciling three dimensions of freedom: freedom from, freedom to, and freedom for. The first suggests liberation from as many constraints as possible, including the bonds of belonging and tradition in a particular historical community; the second, the autonomy to pursue opportunities as one sees fit; the third, embracing the bonds of identity in community as what frees us for a belonging that transcends the limitations of a cramped and cyclopean individualism. These three dimensions may well conflict, but if polemical being-human is riven by such tensions, then recognizing and balancing these tensions through *phronēsis* in a responsible response to ever-changing contexts is what makes this difficult freedom (to borrow from Levinas) an inevitable feature of ethical-political life.[4] This in turn requires that the safeguards of negative freedom in traditional liberalism—especially rights, popular sovereignty, limited government, the separation of powers, and the primacy of the rule of law—be reconciled to a positive freedom that entails a more affective and reflective sense of belonging, identity, and responsibility to one's own historical community. Finally, eleutheric liberty, as a feature of reconstructive liberalism, must account for how an autonomous, self-sufficient, and independent individual can be reconciled to the third dimension of freedom: the understanding that we are ultimately dependent upon a world of meaning not of our making, even if we may, at our most venturesome, envision and prepare the reconstitution of that world. Such forms of reconciliation must be a recognition and embrace of the ongoing struggle, through practical wisdom, to balance universal and situated freedom, not a reconciliation that pretends to settle the problem forever.

As the polemical task of ideation and reconstruction necessarily unfolds through a situated transcendence, a confrontation with something at-issue in one's own embedded existence, my future work will focus on a confrontation that claims me: the meaning of the American experiment in liberal democracy. As anyone who has taught the founding texts of the American experiment can attest, the meaning of the Founding, especially as exemplified by the Declaration of Independence, remains contentiously at-issue, especially the egalitarian principles of the proclamation that "We hold these truths to be self-evident, that all men are created equal, that they are endowed by their Creator with certain unalienable Rights, that among these are Life, Liberty and the pursuit of Happiness."

In a context of vast inequalities separating those in a position to proclaim such principles and to frame institutions and those without a voice—the enslaved, women, native peoples, unpropertied classes—can we believe that "all" really means *all*, and all *persons*, and not just *men*? At-issue in this *polemos* is the *idea* that animates these words—*all*, *men*, *created*, *equal*, and even *are*—and how to interpret that idea in its ideation, both historically and in our own construal of it. Do these words truly declare a universal human equality? Or, do they bear witness to the specific civic equality of a very particular set of human beings, the ones who framed the founding documents: wealthy white men? This interpretive confrontation with the text leads to a *deconstruction* of the meaning of the Declaration, and that deconstruction can bring about at least two outcomes: a complete breakdown of its meaning so that it can no longer provide legitimation for a political community grounded in its claims, resulting in the death of the body politic; or, an opening for *reinterpretation* of its elements, such as "all," "men," and "equal"—perhaps even "are" and "created" as well. What would serve as the basis for such a deconstruction and reinterpretation?

In support of the latter restrictive view is the simple historical fact that many of the Founders owned slaves and that slavery was perfectly legal before, during, and after the American Revolution and in the Constitution of 1787. Furthermore, the Founders *say* "men" in the Declaration, so why not believe that they meant *only* men? As a matter of historical fact, women had vastly inferior civic, educational, professional, and property rights before, during, and after the Revolution, so why not take the Founders at their word, *this* word: "men"?

Charles Mills makes exactly this point in *The Racial Contract*: The *idea* of the founding and of those words was to institute a body politic in which white males, particularly propertied white males for whom other human beings could *be* property, would share equal civil rights in a master-race polity that would exclude all other people as persons rather than (potential) property. Hence, in contrast to idealized conceptions of the meaning of the Founding, writes Mills, "the notion of a Racial Contract might be more revealing of the real character of the world we are living in, and the corresponding historical deficiencies of its normative theories and practices than the raceless notions currently dominant in political theory."[5] Historical reality tells us what the idea truly *is*, and the words of the Declaration take on meaning as a tool of partisan propaganda, not an ideal we can live by or live up to.

And yet, in the same passage, Mills writes, "Insofar as contractarianism is thought of as a useful way to do political philosophy, to theorize about how the polity was created and what values should guide our prescriptions for making it more just, it is obviously crucial to understand what the original and continuing 'contract' actually was and is, so that we can correct for it in constructing the ideal 'contract.'"[6] This follows from the distinction Mills draws between his *descriptive* account of the historical reality of the racial contract and a *prescriptive* account of what a presumably just social contract would legitimately endorse. At-issue in the confrontation between the grim historical reality and a brighter alternative—a *subjunctive* reality, as it were—is whether the idea is limited by its historical expression or if polemical ideation might reveal what remains productively and positively *unsaid* in what was said. Mills implicitly concedes that the meaning of the founding is *not* limited to its historical instantiation when he speaks of "constructing an ideal 'contract.'" These few words unite ideation, the preconstructive envisioning and thinking-through of an alternative, with reconstruction, the implementation of that alternative given the historical realities, all grounded in a deconstruction of the historical failure *properly* to understand and enact in norms and institutions the idea once imperfectly expressed but nevertheless sent on its way on the upward path.

To put this another way, on what basis can we object to the slavery, the racism, and the sexism inherent in the American founding? If I proclaim, "These words *say* that 'all men are created equal,' but that is clearly hypocrisy, because these *men* held slaves and subjugated women," then what is it about those words that I can declare hypocritical as the obfuscation of an unjust historical reality? To interpret that reality *as* unjust, I must have an *idea* of why it is unjust and what would be more just, either implicitly as an unspoken intimation or envisioned in a political theory. Only in the downward-cast light of the idea does the upward-cast firelight of the historical context and its attendant opinions about the nature of equality come into view as something meaningful that *matters* to us. It is through the conflict, the contradiction, the *polemos*, between the historically situated and the ideated transcendent that the difference gets worked out. In fact, it is the very *inadequacy* of those words in their historical context—*all* men; all *men*: really?—that provokes the deconstructive breakdown, ignites the philosophical reflection into what has been left unsaid, and motivates the polemical pursuit of a new understanding and *implementation* of equality in the light of the idea of justice. Otherwise, the deconstructive breakdown results only in nihilist unmeaning.

This, then, is the Socratic phenomenology of seeking the meaning of an opinion both *through* what people say and *beyond* to what is unsaid. To object to the historically situated interpretation of "all men are created equal," the idea, as something intimated that we can still imagine and refer to as a guide in an ongoing dialogue about justice, must break through and, as it were, shine through these specific, historically determined words. Across generations, Americans have imagined how things *could be* in light of what the idea seems to imply as the ideal. They fought and struggled according to that idea and made progress towards the intimated ideal by ending slavery, granting women the vote, winning civil rights, and continuing in struggle today—as of this writing, most notably in the multiracial movement to end structural white supremacy that erupted after the murder of George Floyd. Such living history demonstrates both the power and the phenomenological necessity of the idea in its confrontation with its always-imperfect historical expression in language, institutions, law, and customs. If we believe human freedom can have anything to do with history at all, then that confrontation, the ideation that pivots between imagination and ideal in collision with the real, is what serves as the motive force of historical change.

All this suggests that it is precisely the slippage and splintering of language in polity-defining texts such as the Declaration that ignites the contradictions, setting the *polemos* of history in motion about what those words *could* mean and *should* mean, despite and even because of whatever they *have* meant historically. In this case, the breakdown in language involves the ambiguity of "all men" and whether it applies prescriptively to *all* human beings *in principle*, even if not descriptively as historical *fact*. Also at-issue is whether new wording, such as *all persons*, might be needed to bring the idea from intimation to actual expression and social, political, and legal implementation. In this case, both the "all" and the "men" incite the *polemos* over the scope of the meaning of these words that goes beyond these words themselves.

Socratic phenomenology tells us that what people say can have a meaning that extends beyond what they have said, how they have said it, and even beyond how they thought they had meant it. This unsaid, this excess of meaning beyond its historical entrenchment, must be elicited through a dialogue that may bring the participants up short in *aporia*. It may even provoke a breakdown in the way we had been seeing that meaning as a prelude to its reconstitution. Meaning can be elicited in dialogue and implemented in political action through the activity of polemical confrontation about the slippage of meaning. We find such reconstructive reinterpretation of history in the battles over flags and monuments in America today, especially those that valorize the Confederacy.

Throughout our shared, situated, and provisional understandings of and confrontations over what "all men" means, we have harkened—and in some cases, been justly forced to harken—to those who expanded our understanding of the possible meaning of our founding texts. There is the example of Frederick Douglass, former slave and fierce abolitionist, who adamantly opposed the Garrisonian interpretation of the nation's founding as an irredeemable compact with slavery. In his 1852 address, "What to the Slave is the Fourth of July?" Douglass insisted that "America is false to the past, false to the present, and solemnly binds herself to be false to the future."[7] Still, Douglass meant that this falseness is predicated on a betrayal of the underlying truth of the 4th of July, a meaning both spoken and unspoken that exceeds the intent of any individual founders or any of the Americans of his own day who perpetuated that falseness. Douglass went even further than almost any of his contemporaries, making common cause with the nascent women's rights movement to interpret the "all men" as meaning all human beings, not just white males.[8]

Douglass serves as a paradigmatic exemplar of the polemical Platonist: someone who enters into a deconstructive and, most importantly, a reconstructive dialogue with his tradition. Douglass lays bare the deficiency and ambiguity of the intended meaning of the "all men" of the Declaration as well as the excess dormant within it, and he can do this because he is a

Platonist about the ideas that animate meaning. He seeks a reconstituted polity grounded in a reinterpretation faithful to the meaning polemically latent in the Founding. The Declaration's "all men" phrase is deficient because it fails to articulate adequately the universal ideal of equality; it is excessive, not because it says too much too radically, but because its unspoken but ideated meaning exceeds the inadequacy of its expression as "all men." Moreover, despite this inadequacy, that excessive, latent meaning remains available through the "all men" and perhaps even because of it. For the phrase itself is a stumbling block, not in the purely negative sense of the biblical commandment, "Thou shalt not . . . put a stumbling block before the blind" (Leviticus 19:14), but in the positive sense that stumbling across an obstruction lodged in language brings us up short, compelling us to confront a challenge in the meaning of a shared world—in this case, the historical contradiction of a slaveholding nation dedicated to liberty and the proposition that all men are created equal.

If this were not so, how would the idea occur to Douglass, or to any of us, that "all men" fails to articulate the idea fully? It is through the constructive *polemos* with that failure that we can rearticulate the meaning at–issue in the Founding in a way that is not "false" to the past, present, and future. Such falseness—a violation of the Socratic trust necessary for honest societal and political dialogue—denies the facts of historical injustice and the ambiguity of the founding principles, denies how that history thoroughly pervades the challenges facing the contemporary body politic, and denies how a viable future demands standing up to this confrontation with historical meaning to reconstruct self-understanding for a resilient community. Without some intimation of the idea of justice, in this case as including a form of human equality, the polemical work of such a reinterpretation could not even begin. That is the difference between the Platonic *polemos* and the Heideggerian. It is the glimpse of the 'ought' that transcends our finite embodiment, a glimpse engendered by confronting that historical situation reflectively to tease forth its unfolding meaning in both its excess and its deficiency, but with faith in the ongoing work of removing the contradictions.

That the efforts and successes of a Frederick Douglass, or more recently a Martin Luther King Jr., were not complete does not diminish their example or that of all those who worked with and after them. The polemical confrontation between ideal and actuality is a cyclical hermeneutic, helicoidal in form if done properly. Each iteration of the cycle may bring the real closer to the ideal, although nothing guarantees this will be so. Much depends on the *phronēsis*, the practical wisdom, of reconstructive action in ethics and politics to align an envisioned ideal with the radically situated historical actuality that must be engaged to accomplish anything lasting. The question, to paraphrase Heidegger on the hermeneutical circle (SZ, 153), is how to break into the polemical cycle in the right way so that reconstruction can prepare the ground for the next inevitable confrontation to bear fruit, rather than to collapse in nihilistic despair when progress falters or seems to fail altogether. That reconstructive work is at-issue now in the United States, embodied in questions of affirmative action, police-community relations, mass incarceration, educational and economic redlining, and many others. To be a founding ontologically, our Founding, just as any founding, must remain a living touchstone for the polemical reinterpretation of its meaning; otherwise, it will ossify as a historical dead letter. A founding, to retain its inceptive force, must be *found* again in the *polemos*. That is why figures like Douglass are as much Founders, or more properly *Refounders*, as the so-called Founding Fathers. Because being-human and language are finite and fragile, no human community can survive intact as a body politic without such refounding.

Furthermore, because the cycle of de-, pre-, and reconstruction is an existential feature of being-human, it does not operate only on this grand scale of major historical change, but also locally. Consider policy making and, as an example, transportation policy. In my city of Boston, the traffic patterns and commuting conditions have become so problematic as to verge on systemic breakdown. To truly address this problem properly requires more than breaking down what is going wrong through a deconstructive analysis. It also requires an ideation, a reimagining and reconceptualization of what movement in a zone of human habitation can and should involve. But even more, a genuine polemical confrontation with what is at-issue in the patterns of human movement in one's city requires the informed and engaged savvy, the practical reason, to implement what improvements can be accomplished, given the situated potential of the historical contingencies of that specific community, which in this case also means confronting patterns that both accidentally and deliberately divide Boston's citizens by class and race. An ethical polemics requires attention to everything at issue in a city's transportation: social and political dynamics, geography, laws, the economic system, the available material resources, the labor and skills necessary for the job, and so on.

Or consider how our laws—intended to protect citizens as they live in freedom—have become weapons used against citizens to limit their private opportunities, extract wealth from them in the form of fines and legal fees, and expose them to unjust harassment and death. And yet, to be free we need laws as the framework within which to flourish in eleutheric liberty. To repair and reconstruct our laws—even such minor laws as those regarding jaywalking or bail posting—we must first be alive to what has broken down in current law and confront it. Only if we can ideate what a better law would be can we then propose a specific statutory change that fits with the legal regime as it now is to bring it closer to what it should be. If this were not possible, then all positive law would be as immutable as the laws of nature. The life of the law, as we saw with Antigone, transcends the written letter of the law, but also cannot subsist without it.

This is how practical wisdom participates in the reconstructive realization of the ideal, and it happens on the grand historical scale, the local, and the purely personal, because it is a defining feature of polemical human-being. Our relation to the truth and to language is zetetic rather than echonic. We may mean more than we say, and we can always question our works, our words, and ourselves about the truth of what we mean. The future requires us to undertake such questioning if we are to refound our democracy by embodying a polemical ethics.

NOTES

1. Douglass, "Pictures and Progress," in *The Portable Frederick Douglass*, 357.

2. Recall that in Fragment 53, Heraclitus says that "War . . . makes some slaves, others free [*tous men doulos epoiēse tous de eleutherous*]."

3. See the discussion of the link between *eleutheria*, plant growth, and freedom as a member of one's kinship group in Emile Benveniste, "The Free Man," *Indo-European Language and Society*.

4. Levinas, *Difficult Freedom*.

5. Charles Mills, *The Racial Contract*, 7.

6. Mills, *The Racial Contract*, 7; see 5–7 for the distinction between prescriptive and descriptive.

7. Douglass, "What to the Slave is the Fourth of July?" in *The Portable Frederick Douglass*, 205.

8. See David W. Blight, *Frederick Douglass: Prophet of Freedom*, 196–97.

Bibliography

Aho, Kevin. *Contexts of Suffering: A Heideggerian Approach to Psychopathology.* London: Rowman & Littlefield International, 2019.

Annas, Julia. *An Introduction to Plato's Republic.* Oxford: Oxford University Press, 1981.

Arendt, Hannah. *The Human Condition.* 2nd ed. Chicago: University of Chicago Press, 1998.

Aristotle. *The Complete Works of Aristotle: The Revised Oxford Translation*, vols. 1 and 2. Edited by Jonathan Barnes. Princeton: Princeton University Press, 1984.

———. *Ethica Nicomachea.* Edited by I. Bywater. Oxford: Oxford University Press, 1920.

———. *Metaphysica.* Edited by W. Jaeger. Oxford: Oxford University Press, 1957.

———. *Politica.* Edited by D. Ross. Oxford: Oxford University Press, 1957.

Auden, Wystan H. *Collected Poems.* New York: Vintage International, 1991.

Backman, Jussi. "All of a Sudden: Heidegger and Plato's *Parmenides*." *Epoché* 11, no. 2 (2007) 393–408.

Badiou, Alain. *Plato's "Republic": A Dialogue in 16 Chapters.* Translated by Susan Spitzer. New York: Columbia University Press, 2013.

Benveniste, Emile. *Indo-European Language and Society.* Translated by Elizabeth Palmer. Coral Gables, FL: University of Miami Press, 1973.

Blight, David W. *Frederick Douglass: Prophet of Freedom.* New York: Simon & Schuster, 2018.

Blitz, Mark. *Heidegger's "Being and Time" and the Possibility of Political Philosophy.* Philadelphia: Paul Dry Books, 2017.

Bloom, Alan. Interpretive essay in *The Republic of Plato*, 307–436. Translated by Allan Bloom. 2nd ed. New York: Basic Books, 1991.

Blondell, Ruby. "Where Is Socrates on the 'Ladder of Love?'" In *Plato's Symposium: Issues in Interpretation and Reception*, edited by J. Lesher, D. Nails, and F. Sheffield. Cambridge: Center for Hellenic Studies, 2006.

Blumenberg, Hans. *The Laughter of the Thracian Woman: A Protohistory of Theory.* Translated by Spencer Hawkins. London: Bloomsbury Publishing, 2015.

Brand, Paul. "The Language of the English Legal Profession: The Emergence of a Distinctive Legal Lexicon in Insular French." In *The Anglo-Norman Language and Its Contexts.* Edited by Richard Ingham. Woodbridge, UK: York Medieval Press, 2010.

Braver, Lee. *Groundless Grounds: A Study of Wittgenstein and Heidegger.* Cambridge, MA: MIT Press, 2012.

Byrne, Patrick B. *The Ethics of Discernment: Lonergan's Foundations for Ethics.* Toronto: University of Toronto Press, 2016.

Carnap, Rudolf. "The Elimination of Metaphysics through the Logical Analysis of Language," translated by A. Pap. In *Logical Positivism*, edited by A. J. Ayer. Glencoe, IL: Free Press, 1959.

Cimakasky, Joseph. *The Role of* Exaíphnes *in Early Greek Literature: Philosophical Transformation in Plato's Dialogues and Beyond.* Lanham, MD: Lexington Books, 2017.

Cohen, Hermann. *Kants Theorie der Erfahrung.* 2nd ed. Berlin: Dümmlers, 1885.

Confessore, Nicholas. "Cambridge Analytica and Facebook: The Scandal and the Fallout So Far." *New York Times*, April 4, 2018. https://www.nytimes.com/2018/04/04/us/politics/cambridge-analytica-scandal-fallout.html.

Crowell, Steven. "Why Is Ethics First Philosophy? Levinas in Phenomenological Context." *European Journal of Philosophy* 23, no. 3 (2015) 564–88.

Curd, Patricia, Editor. *A Presocratics Reader: Selected Fragments and Testimonia.* Translated by Richard D. McKirahan and Patricia Curd. 2nd ed. Indianapolis: Hackett, 2011.

Dahlstrom, Daniel. *Heidegger's Concept of Truth.* Cambridge: Cambridge University Press, 2009.

D'Angour, Armand. *Socrates in Love: The Making of a Philosopher.* London: Bloomsbury Publishing, 2019.

Derrida, Jacques. *Dissemination.* Translated by Barbara Johnson. Chicago: University of Chicago Press, 1981.

———. "Force of Law: The Metaphysical Foundations of Justice," translated by Mary Quaintance. In *Deconstruction and the Possibility of Justice*, edited by D. Cornell, M. Rosenfeld, and D. G. Carlson. New York: Routledge, 1992.

Derrida, Jacques, and M. Ferraris. *A Taste for the Secret.* Cambridge, UK: Polity, 2001.

Descartes. René. "Meteorology." In *Discourse on Method, Optics, Geometry, Meteorology.* rev. ed. Translated by Paul J. Olsamp. Indianapolis: Hackett, 2001.

Donne, John. "The Anatomy of the World" (Poem 155). In *The Complete Poetry of John Donne.* Edited by John T. Shawcross. New York: Anchor Press, 1971.

———. *The Complete Poetry and Selected Prose.* Edited by Charles M. Coffin. New York: Modern Library, 2001.

Dostal, Robert J. "Beyond Being: Heidegger's Plato." *Journal of the History of Philosophy*, 23, no. 1 (1985): 71–98.

Douglass, Frederick. *The Portable Frederick Douglass.* Edited by John Stouffer and Henry Louis Gates Jr. New York: Penguin Books, 2016.

Dreyfus, Hubert L. *Background Practices: Essays on the Understanding of Being.* Oxford: Oxford University Press, 2017.

———. *Being-in-the-World: A Commentary on Heidegger's Being and Time, Division I.* Cambridge, MA: The MIT Press, 1990.

Dreyfus, Hubert L., and Charles Taylor. *Retrieving Realism.* Cambridge, MA: Harvard University Press, 2015.

Duff, Alexander M. *Heidegger and Politics: The Ontology of Radical Discontent.* Cambridge: Cambridge University Press, 2015.

Duhem, Pierre. *To Save the Phenomena: An Essay on the Idea of Physical Theory from Plato to Galileo.* Translated by E. Dolan and C. Maschler. Chicago: University of Chicago Press, 2015.

Dussel, Enrique. *Ethics of Liberation: In the Age of Globalization and Exclusion.* Translated by Eduardo Mendieta. Durham, NC: Duke University Press, 2013.

Eliade, Mircea. *Patterns in Comparative Religion.* Translated by Rosemary Sheed. Cleveland, OH: Meridian Books, 1967.

Sextus Empiricus. *Outlines of Pyrrhonism.* Translated by R. G. Bury. Cambridge, MA: Harvard University Press, 1933.

Esposito, Roberto. *Politics and Negation.* Translated by Zakiya Hanafi. Cambridge, UK: Polity Press, 2019.

Fain, Lucas. "Plato after Marburg: Rethinking Forms and Ideas through the Inspiration of Hermann Cohen." Unpublished paper, 2020.

Fanon, Franz. *Black Skins, White Masks.* Translated by Richard Philcox. New York: Grove Books, 2008.

Fried, Charles, and Gregory Fried, *Because It Is Wrong: Torture, Privacy and Presidential Power in the Age of Terror.* New York: W. W. Norton, 2010.

Fried, Gregory. *Heidegger's Polemos: From Being to Politics.* New Haven, CT: Yale University Press, 2000.

———. "Heidegger and Gandhi: A Dialogue on Conflict and Enmity." In *In the Wake of Conflict: Justice, Responsibility and Reconciliation*, edited by Allen Speight and Alice MacLachan. New York: Springer, 2013.

———. "How Dare We Read Heidegger? After the Black Notebooks." In *Jenseits Von Polemik Und Apologie: Die 'schwarzen Hefte' in Der Diskussion*, edited by Alfred Denker and Holger Zaborowski. *Heidegger-Jarhbuch*, vol. 12. Freiburg: Karl Alber, 2020.

———. "*Inhalt unzulässig*: Late Mail from Lodz." In *Heidegger and the Holocaust*, edited by A. Milchman and A. Rosenberg. Amsterdam: Rodopi, 1998.

———. "Introduction to Metaphysics." In *The Bloomsbury Companion to Heidegger*, edited by François Raffoul and Eric S. Nelson. London: Bloomsbury, 2013.

———. "A Letter to Emmanuel Faye." In *Confronting Heidegger: A Critical Dialogue on Politics and Philosophy*, edited by G. Fried. London: Rowman & Littlefield International, 2019.

———. "Odysseus on the Beach: Humanity between the Anthropocene and the Hubriscene." In *The Task of Philosophy in the Anthropocene: Axial Echoes in Global Space*, edited by Richard Polt and Jon Wittrock. London: Rowman & Littlefield International, 2018.

———. "Retrieving *phronēsis*: Heidegger on the Essence of Politics." *Continental Philosophy Review* 47, no. 3 (2014): 293–313.

———. "Peter Trawny: Freedom to Fail: Heidegger's Anarchy." *Notre Dame Philosophical Reviews*, June 13, 2016. Accessed May 23, 2020. https://ndpr.nd.edu/news/freedom-to-fail-heideggers-anarchy/.

———. "A Second Letter to Emmanuel Faye." In *Confronting Heidegger: A Critical Dialogue on Politics and Philosophy*, edited by G. Fried, 209–36. London: Rowman & Littlefield International, 2019.

———. "What Gives? Heidegger and Dreyfus on the Event of Community." In *Being Shaken: Ontology and the Event*, edited by Michael Marder and Santiago Zabala. London: Palgrave Macmillan, 2014.

———. "Whitewashed with Moralism: On Heidegger's Anti-Americanism and Anti-Semitism." In *Heidegger and Jewish Thought: Difficult Others*, edited by Elad Lapidot and Micha Brumlik. London: Rowman & Littlefield International, 2017.

Friedman, Michael. *A Parting of the Ways: Carnap, Cassirer, and Heidegger*. Peru, IL: Open Court, 2000.

Gadamer, Hans-Georg. *Die Idee des Guten zwischen Plato und Aristoteles.* Heidelberg: Winter, 1978.

———. *Truth and Method.* 2nd rev. ed. (1st English ed. 1975, translated by W. Glen-Doepel and edited by John Cumming and Garret Barden), revised translation by J. Weinsheimer and D. G. Marshall. New York: Crossroad, 1989.

Geiman, Clare Pearson. "Heidegger's *Antigones*." In *A Companion to Heidegger's Introduction to Metaphysics*, edited by Richard Polt and Gregory Fried. New Haven, CT: Yale University Press, 2001.

Gendlin, Eugene T. *A Process Model*. Evanston, IL: Northwestern University Press, 2018.

Gilbert, Jack. *Collected Poems*. New York: Knopf, 2012.

Gray, Jesse Glenn. *The Warriors: Reflections on Men in Battle*. Lincoln: University of Nebraska Press, 1999.

Gonzalez, Francisco J. "Confronting Heidegger on Logos and Being in Plato's Sophist." In *Platon und Aristoteles—sub ratione veritatis: Festschrift für Wolfgang Wieland zum 70. Geburtstag*, edited by Gregor Damschen, Rainer Enskat, and Alejandro G. Vigo. Göttingen: Vandenhoeck and Ruprecht, 2003.

———. "Dialectic as 'Philosophical Embarrassment': Heidegger's Critique of Plato's Method." *Journal of the History of Philosophy* 40, no. 3 (2002): 361–89.

Gordon, Peter. "Heidegger in Purgatory." In *Nature, History, State*, by Martin Heidegger. Translated by G. Fried and R. Polt. London: Bloomsbury, 2015.

Griswold, Charles L. Jr. "Irony in the Platonic Dialogues," *Philosophy and Literature* 26, no. 1 (2002): 84–106.

———. "Longing for the Best: Plato on Reconciliation with Imperfection." *Arion: A Journal of Humanities and the Classics* 11, no. 2 (2003): 101–36.

———, editor. *Platonic Writings/Platonic Readings*. University Park, PA: Pennsylvania University Press, 1988.

Habermas, Jürgen. "On the Publication of the Lectures of 1935." In *The Heidegger Controversy: A Critical Reader*, edited by Richard Wolin. Cambridge, MA: MIT Press, 1993.

Hatab, Lawrence J. *Proto-Phenomenology, Language Acquisition, Orality, and Literacy*. London: Roman & Littlefield International, 2020.

Heidegger, Martin. "Drei Briefe Martin Heideggers an Karl Löwith." In *Zur philosophischen Aktualität Heideggers,* vol. 2, *Im Gespräch der Zeit*, edited by Dietrich Papenfuss and Otto Pöggeler, Frankfurt am Main: Vittorio Klostermann, 1990.

Note: All other original texts by Heidegger, as well as the English translations of those texts consulted in the course of this work, are listed in the Abbreviations section, immediately after the Acknowledgments.

Helderman, Rosalind S., and Matt Zapotosky. *The Mueller Report.* New York: Simon & Schuster, 2019.

Henry, Michel. *The Essence of Manifestation*. Translated by Girard Etzkorn. The Hague: Martinus Nijhoff, 1973.

Hesiod. *Works and Days*; *Theogony*; *Testimonia*. Translated by Glenn Most. Cambridge: Loeb Classical Library, 2018.

Hofstadter, Albert. *The Basic Problems of Philosophy.* Bloomington: Indiana University Press, 1982.

Hoffmeier, James K. *Akhenaten and the Origins of Monotheism*. Oxford: Oxford University Press, 2015.

hooks, bell. *Belonging: A Culture of Place*. New York: Routledge, 2009.

Hornblower, Simon, and Antony Sparforth, editors. *Oxford Classical Dictionary*, 4th ed. Oxford: Oxford University Press, 2012.

Howe, Mark DeWolfe. *Holmes-Laski Letters: The Correspondence of Mr. Justice Holmes and Harold J. Laski*, vol. 2, *1926–1935*. Cambridge, MA: Harvard University Press, 1953.

Husserl, Edmund. *The Crisis of European Sciences and Transcendental Philosophy*. Translated by David Carr. Evanston, IL: Northwestern University Press, 1970.

Hyland, Drew. *Finitude and Transcendence in the Platonic Dialogues*. Albany: State University of New York Press, 1995.

———. *Questioning Platonism: Continental Interpretations of Plato*. Albany: SUNY Press, 2004.

Irigaray, Luce. *Speculum of the Other Woman*. Translated by Gillian C. Gill. Ithaca, NY: Cornell University Press, 1985.

James, William. *The Principles of Psychology*. Vol. 1. New York: Cosimo Classics, 2007.

Jaspers, Karl. *Basic Philosophical Writings*. Translated by E. Ehrlich, L. Ehrlich, and G. Pepper. Atlantic Highlands, NJ: Humanities Press, 1994.

Jay, Martin. *Downcast Eyes: The Denigration of Vision in Twentieth-Century French Thought*. Berkeley: University of California Press, 1993.

Jonas, Hans. "The Nobility of Sight." *Philosophy and Phenomenological Research* 14, no. 4 (1954): 507–19.

Kamm, Frances M. *Intricate Ethics*. Oxford: Oxford University Press, 2007.

Kant, Immanuel. *Kant: Critique of Pure Reason.* Translated and edited by Paul Guyer and Allen W. Wood. Cambridge: Cambridge University Press, 1999.

Kearney, Richard. *The Poetics of Modernity: Toward a Hermeneutic Imagination.* Atlantic Highlands, NJ: Humanities Pres, 1995.

Kellerer, Sidonie. "Rewording the Past: The Postwar Publication of a 1938 Lecture by Martin Heidegger." *Modern Intellectual History* 11, no. 3 (2014): 575–602.

Kirk, G. S., J. E. Raven, and M. Schofield, editors. *The Presocratic Philosophers.* 2nd ed. Cambridge: Cambridge University Press, 1983.

Kisiel, Theodore. "The Seminar of Winter Semester 1933-4 within Heidegger's Three Concepts of the Political," In *Nature, History, State*, by Martin Heidegger. Translated by G. Fried and R. Polt. London: Bloomsbury, 2015.

Kisiel, Theodore, and Thomas Sheehan, editors. *Becoming Heidegger: On the Trail of His Early Occasional Writings, 1910–1927.* Evanston, IL: Northwestern University Press, 2007.

Klein, Jacob. *A Commentary on Plato's Meno.* Chicago: University of Chicago, 1965.

Kleinberg-Levin, David, editor. *Modernity and the Hegemony of Vision.* Berkeley: University of California Press, 1993.

———. *Sites of Vision: The Discursive Construction of Sight in the History of Philosophy.* Cambridge, MA: MIT Press.

Klemperer, Werner. *The Language of the Third Reich.* Translated by Martin Brady. London: Bloomsbury Academic, 2013.

Lapidot, Elad, and Micha Brumlik, editors. *Heidegger and Jewish Thought: Difficult Others.* London: Rowman and Littlefield International, 2017.

Lash, Joseph P. *Helen and Teacher: The Story of Helen Keller and Anne Sullivan Macy.* New York: American Foundation for the Blind, 1981.

Lear, Jonathan. *Radical Hope: Ethics in the Face of Cultural Devastation.* Cambridge, MA: Harvard University Press, 2008.

Levinas, Emmanuel. *Difficult Freedom: Essays on Judaism.* Translated by Seán Hand. Baltimore: Johns Hopkins Press, 1990.

———. *Nine Talmudic Readings.* Translated by Annette Aronowicz. Bloomington: Indiana University Press, 2019.

———. "Ethics of the Infinite," in Richard Kearney, *Debates in Continental Philosophy: Conversations with Contemporary Thinkers.* New York: Fordham University Press, 2004.

Liddell, Henry G., and Robert Scott. *Thesaurus Linguae Graecae.* Oxford: Oxford Clarendon Press, 1940. Available online through The Perseus Project, edited by Gregory Crane et al. Accessed April 23, 2020. https://www.perseus.tufts.edu/hopper/.

Locke, John. *Second Treatise of Government.* Edited by C. B. Macpherson. Cambridge, MA: Hackett, 1980.

Love, Jeff, and Michael Meng. "Heidegger's Metapolitics." *Cultural Critique* 99 (Spring 2018): 97–122.

Madison, Greg, editor. *Theory and Practice of Focusing-Oriented Psychotherapy: Beyond the Talking Cure.* London: Jessica Kingsley Publishers, 2014.

Marion, Jean-Luc. *Negative Certainties*. Translated by Stephan E. Lewis. Chicago: University of Chicago Press, 2015.

McCoy, Marina. *Plato on the Rhetoric of Philosophers and Sophists.* Cambridge: Cambridge University Press, 2008.

McGuirk, James N. "*Alētheia* and Heidegger's Transitional Readings of Plato's Cave Allegories." *Journal of the British Society for Phenomenology* 39, no. 2 (2008): 167–85.

Meister Eckhart, *The Essential Sermons, Commentaries, Treatises and Defense*. Translated by E. Colledge and B. McGinn. Mahwah, NJ: Paulist Press, 1982.

Mendell, Henry. "The Only Good Philosopher Is a Dead Philosopher." Unpublished paper, 2002.

Merleau-Ponty, Maurice. *The Phenomenology of Perception*. Translated by D. A. Landes. New York: Routledge, 2014.

Mills, Charles W. *The Racial Contract*. Ithaca, NY: Cornell University Press, 1997.

Mill, John Stewart. *The Basic Writings*. New York: Random House, 2002.

Mokray, W. G., L. W. Donald, et al. "Basketball." In *Encyclopaedia Britannica.* Accessed January 22, 2020. https://www.britannica.com/sports.basketball, accessed Mar. 2, 2020.

Moore, Ian Alexander. *Eckhart, Heidegger, and the Imperative of Releasement*. Albany: State University of New York Press, 2019.

Moran, Dermot. *Introduction to Phenomenology*. London: Routledge, 2000.

Moran, Dermot, and Joseph Cohen. *The Husserl Dictionary*. London: Continuum, 2012.

Nagel, Thomas. *The View from Nowhere*. Edited and revised. Oxford: Oxford University Press, 1989.

Nails, Debra. *The People of Plato: A Prosopography of Plato and Other Socratics*. Indianapolis: Hackett, 2002.

Naismith, James. *Basketball: Its Origin and Development.* Lincoln: University of Nebraska Press, 1996.

Nietzsche, Friedrich, *Beyond Good and Evil.* Translated by Walter Kaufman. New York: Vintage, 1989.

———. *Twilight of the Idols*. Translated by Richard Polt. Indianapolis: Hackett, 1997.

———. *The Will to Power*. Translated by Walter Kaufmann and R. J. Hollingdale. New York: Vintage, 1968.

Nightingale, Andrea. *Spectacles of Truth in Classical Greek Philosophy: Theoria in Its Cultural Context*. Cambridge: Cambridge University Press, 2004.

Ovid, *Metamorphoses*. Translated by A. D. Melville. Oxford: Oxford University Press, 1986.

Partenie, Catalin, and Tom Rockmore, editors. *Heidegger and Plato: Toward Dialogue*. Evanston, IL: Northwestern University Press, 2005.

Patočka, Jan. *Heretical Essays in the Philosophy of History*. Translated by Erazim Kohák. Chicago: Open Court, 1996.

———. "Negative Platonism." In *Philosophy and Selected Writings*. Translated by Erazim Kohák. Chicago: University of Chicago Press, 1989.

Pfeifer, Geoff, and S. West Gurley, editors. *Phenomenology and the Political.* Rowman and Littlefield International, 2016.

Plato, *Complete Works.* Edited by John M. Cooper. Translated by C. D. C. Reeve, G. Grube, et al. Indianapolis: Hackett, 1997.

———. *Great Dialogues of Plato.* Translated by W. H. D. Rouse. New York: Signet Classic, 1999.

———. *Platonis Opera*, vol. 1. Edited by E. A. Duke et al. Oxford: Oxford University Press, 1995.

———. *Platonis Opera*, vol. 2. Edited by J. Burnet et al. Oxford: Oxford University Press, 1901.

———. *Platonis Opera*, vol. 3. Edited by J. Burnet et al. Oxford: Oxford University Press, 1903.

———. *Platonis Opera*, vol. 4. Edited by J. Burnet, et al. Oxford: Oxford University Press, 1978).

———. *Platonis Opera*, vol. 5. Edited by J. Burnet, et al. Oxford: Oxford University Press, 1907).

———. *The Republic of Plato.* 2nd ed. Translated, with introduction, notes, and interpretive essay, by Allan Bloom. New York: Basic Books, 1991.

Plutarch, *Lives.* Translated by John Dryden. New York: Modern Library, 2001.

Pokorny, Julius. *Indogermanisches Etymologisches Wörterbuch.* Vol. 1. Bern: Franke Verlag, 1959.

Polt, Richard, *Heidegger: An Introduction.* Ithaca, NY: Cornell University Press, 1999.

———. "Alain Badiou: Plato's Republic: A Dialogue in 16 Chapters." *Teaching Philosophy* 37, no. 1 (2014): 122–26.

———. *Time and Trauma: Thinking through Heidegger in the Thirties.* Lanham, MD: Rowman & Littlefield, 2019.

Proclus. *Proclus' Commentary on Plato's* Parmenides. Translated by G. R. Murrow and J. M. Dillon. Princeton, NJ: Princeton University Press, 1992.

Ralkowski, Mark A. *Heidegger's Platonism.* London: Continuum, 2009.

Rawls, John. *A Theory of Justice.* 2nd ed. Cambridge, MA: Harvard University Press, 1999.

———. *Justice as Fairness.* 2nd ed. Cambridge, MA: Harvard University Press, 2001.

Reid, James D. *Heidegger's Moral Ontology.* Cambridge: Cambridge University Press, 2019.

Rilke, Rainer Maria. *Turning-Point: Miscellaneous Poems 1912–1926.* Translated by Michael Hamburger. London: Anvil Press Poetry, 2003.

Rogers, Katie. "White House Hosts Conservative Internet Activists at a 'Social Media Summit.'" *New York Times.* July 11, 2019. Accessed January 1, 2020. https://www.nytimes.com/2019/07/11/us/politics/white-house-social-media-summit.html.

Roochnik, David. *Beautiful City: The Dialectical Character of Plato's Republic.* Ithaca, NY: Cornell University Press, 2003.

———. *Retrieving Aristotle in an Age of Crisis.* Albany: State University of New York Press, 2013.

———. "Socratic Ignorance as Complex Irony: A Critique of Gregory Vlastos." *Arethusa* 28, no. 1. (1995): 39–52.

Rosen, Stanley. *Nihilism: A Philosophical Essay.* New Haven, CT: Yale University Press, 1969.

———. "Leo Strauss and the Quarrel between the Ancients and the Moderns." In *Leo Strauss's Thought: Towards a Critical Engagement,* edited by Alan Udoff. Boulder: Lynne Rienner Publishers, 1991.

Rubenstein, Mary-Jane. *Strange Wonder: The Closure of Metaphysics and the Opening of Awe.* New York: Columbia University Press, 2011.

Russell, Bertrand. *A History of Philosophy.* New York: Simon and Schuster, 1945.

Sallis, John. *Being and Logos.* 3rd ed. Bloomington: Indiana University Press, 1996,

———. *Chorology: On Beginning in Plato's Timaeus.* Bloomington: Indiana University Press, 2019.

———. *The Verge of Philosophy.* Chicago: University of Chicago Press, 2007.

Santas, Gerasimos. *Understanding Plato's* Republic. Oxford: Wiley-Blackwell, 2010.

Schmidt, Dennis. "Heidegger and the Call for an Original Ethics." *Kronos* 6 (2017): 112–19.

Schmitt, Carl. *The Concept of the Political.* Translated by G. Schwab. New Brunswick, NJ: Rutgers University Press, 1976.

Schürmann, Reiner. *Heidegger on Being and Acting: From Principles to Anarchy.* Translated by Christine-Marie Gros. Bloomington: Indiana University Press, 1987.

Shakespeare, William. *Macbeth.* Washington, DC: The Folger Shakespeare Library, 2018. Accessed June 20, 2020. https://shakespeare.folger.edu/shakespeares-works/macbeth.

Shaw, Steven D., and Richard P. Bagozzi. "The Neuropsychology of Consumer Behavior and Marketing." *Society for Consumer Psychology* 1 (2018): 22–40.

Sheehan, Thomas. "A Paradigm Shift in Heidegger Research." *Continental Philosophy Review* 34, no. 2 (2001): 183–202.

———. *Making Sense of Heidegger: A Paradigm Shift.* London: Rowman & Littlefield International, 2014.

Simpson, William K. editor. *The Literature of Ancient Egypt: An Anthology of Stories, Instructions, and Poetry.* New Haven, CT: Yale University Press, 2003.

Stone, Allison. "Essentialism and Anti-Essentialism in Feminist Philosophy." *Journal of Moral Philosophy* 1, no. 2 (2004): 135–53.

Strauss, Leo. *The City and Man.* Chicago: University of Chicago Press, 1978.

———. "How to Study Spinoza's 'Theological-Political Treatise.'" *Persecution and the Art of Writing.* Chicago: University of Chicago Press, 1988.

———. *On Tyranny.* rev. ed. Ithaca, NY: Cornell University Press, 1968.

Suhay, Elizabeth, Bernard Grofman, and Alexander H. Trechsel, editors. *The Oxford Handbook of Electoral Persuasion.* Oxford: Oxford University Press, 2020.

Szymborska, Wisława. *Poems New and Collected 1957–1977.* Translated by Stanisław Barańczak and Clare Cavanagh. New York: Harcourt, 1998.

Tomasello, Michael. *A Natural History of Human Morality.* Cambridge, MA: Harvard University Press, 2016.

Townsend, Mary. *The Woman Question in Plato's* Republic. Lanham, MD: Lexington Books, 2017.

Trott, Adriel M. "Saving the Appearances of Plato's Cave." *Proceedings of the Boston Area Colloquium of Ancient Philosophy* 36, forthcoming 2021.

Watkins, Calvert. *Dictionary of Indo-European Roots*. 3rd ed. New York: Houghton Mifflin Harcourt, 2011.

Weil, Simone. *The Need for Roots*. Translated by A. F. Wills. London: Ark Paperbacks, 1987.

West, Thomas G., and Grace Starry West, *Four Texts on Socrates*. Translated by T. G. West and G. S. West. Rev. ed. Ithaca, NY: Cornell University Press, 1998.

Whitehead, Alfred North. *Process and Reality*. New York: The Free Press, 1985.

Williams, William Carlos. *Selected Poems*. New York: New Directions, 1985.

Wittgenstein, Ludwig. *Culture and Value*. Translated by Peter Winch. Rev. ed. Oxford: Blackwell, 1998.

Wordsworth, William. *The Collected Poetry of William Wordsworth*. Ware, UK: Wordsworth Editions, 2006.

Young, Iris Marion. *Justice and the Politics of Difference*. Princeton, NJ: Princeton University Press, 1990.

Zuckert, Catherine. *Postmodern Platos*. Chicago: University of Chicago Press, 1996.

Index